ALSO BY DAVID O. STEWART

*Impeached: The Trial of President Andrew Johnson
and the Fight for Lincoln's Legacy*

The Summer of 1787: The Men Who Invented the Constitution

Aaron Burr's Challenge to Jefferson's America

AMERICAN EMPEROR

DAVID O. STEWART

SIMON & SCHUSTER

NEW YORK   LONDON   TORONTO   SYDNEY

Simon & Schuster
1230 Avenue of the Americas
New York, NY 10020

First Simon & Schuster hardcover edition October 2011

SIMON & SCHUSTER and colophon are registered trademarks
of Simon & Schuster, Inc.

For information about special discounts for bulk purchases,
please contact Simon & Schuster Special Sales at
1-866-506-1949 or business@simonandschuster.com.

The Simon & Schuster Speakers Bureau can bring authors
to your live event. For more information or to book an event,
contact the Simon & Schuster Speakers Bureau at
1-866-248-3049 or visit our website at www.simonspeakers.com.

Designed by Ruth Lee-Mui
Maps by Paul J. Pugliese

Manufactured in the United States of America

10   9   8   7   6   5   4   3   2   1

Library of Congress Cataloging-in-Publication Data
Stewart, David O.
    American emperor : Aaron Burr's challenge to Jefferson's America / by David O. Stewart.
        p.   cm.
    1. Presidents—United States—Election—1800.   2. United States—Politics and
government—1797-1801.
    3. Jefferson, Thomas, 1743-1826.   4. Burr, Aaron, 1756-1836.   I. Title.
    E330.S84 2011
    973.4'6092—dc22   2011002647
ISBN 978-1-4391-5718-3
ISBN 978-1-4391-6032-9 (ebook)

Illustration credits will be found on page 389.

For Nancy

CONTENTS

AMERICAN EMPEROR

LEADING CHARACTERS

Burr's Family

AARON BURR ALSTON: The only child of Theodosia and Joseph Alston, he died of a fever when eleven years old.

JOSEPH ALSTON: Born into a prominent South Carolina family, Alston was twenty-two when he married the seventeen-year-old Theodosia Burr. He served in the South Carolina legislature from 1802 until 1812, when he was elected governor. He died in 1816.

THEODOSIA BURR ALSTON: Burr's only child from his marriage with Theodosia Bartow Prevost. The younger Theodosia was born in 1783 and married Joseph Alston of South Carolina at the age of seventeen. Burr exactingly supervised Theodosia's education, even after her marriage, and she has been called the best-educated American woman of her generation. She boarded a ship in late 1812 to see her father in New York City, but the ship never returned to any port.

DR. JOSEPH BROWNE: Husband to the sister of Theodosia Bartow Prevost Burr, and secretary to James Wilkinson when he was governor of Louisiana Territory in 1806–07.

THEODOSIA BARTOW PREVOST BURR: The widow of a British army officer when she married Burr in 1782, who was ten years her junior. They had one child, Theodosia. The elder Theodosia died in 1793.

JOHN BARTOW PREVOST: Son of Theodosia Bartow Prevost Burr by her first marriage, and a judge in Orleans Territory at the time of Burr's expedition in 1806–07.

Burr's "Little Band" in New York City

MATTHEW DAVIS: Burr loyalist who, as Burr's "literary executor," destroyed much of Burr's correspondence.

JOHN SWARTWOUT: A blond giant and completely loyal to Burr, he served as U.S. marshal in New York City and dueled with Senator DeWitt Clinton of New York in 1802.

SAM SWARTWOUT: John's younger brother and companion to Burr during his travels in the South immediately after the Hamilton duel. Sam carried one of the two copies of the "cipher letter" to General James Wilkinson in the fall of 1806. He was arrested by Wilkinson and shipped to Washington City for trial for treason, but he was released by the United States Supreme Court.

WILLIAM VAN NESS: A young lawyer in New York City, he wrote a powerful pamphlet in defense of Burr in 1802 and served as Burr's second for the duel with Alexander Hamilton.

Burr's Inner Circle for the 1806–07 Expedition

GENERAL JOHN ADAIR: A former Continental Army soldier, veteran of Indian wars in the West, and general of the Kentucky militia, Adair served in the U.S. Senate in 1805–06. He was arrested by Wilkinson when he arrived in New Orleans in January 1807 and was shipped east for trial, but he was released by a federal judge in Baltimore.

HARMAN BLENNERHASSETT: Heir to an estate in Ireland, Blennerhassett married his niece and moved to America in the late 1790s, settling on an island in the Ohio River below Marietta. Bewitched by Burr in 1805 and 1806, Blennerhassett recruited heavily for Burr's expedition and went deeply into debt to support it. Though he was indicted for treason and violation of the Neutrality Act, he never stood trial.

ERICH BOLLMAN: A mercurial German émigré who had attempted to free the Marquis de Lafayette from an Austrian prison in 1793. Burr designated Bollman to represent him in negotiations with the United States government during the expedition. Bollman carried the second copy of the cipher letter to James Wilkinson in the autumn of 1806. Wilkinson had him arrested and sent to Washington City with Sam Swartwout, where Bollman also was charged with treason and then released by the U.S. Supreme Court.

JONATHAN DAYTON: Boyhood friend of Burr's in Elizabethtown, New Jersey, a captain in the Continental Army, the youngest delegate to the Constitutional Convention, the Speaker of the U.S. House of Representatives from 1795–99, and senator from New Jersey. Dayton engaged in extensive land speculation in Ohio and the West; the city of Dayton, Ohio, is named for him. As Burr's closest confidant, Dayton conducted overtures to the British and Spanish governments on Burr's behalf. He was indicted for treason and violation of the Neutrality Act but was never tried.

DAVIS FLOYD: A river pilot and militia officer in Indiana Territory, Floyd recruited adventurers for Burr and served as an officer during the expedition. He was the only participant to be convicted of any offense connected to the expedition, though his sentence was three hours of confinement in an Indiana jail. Immediately upon his release, he was chosen clerk of the Indiana territorial assembly.

ANDREW JACKSON: A general of the Tennessee militia and former congressman, the combative Jackson agreed to bring his militia into Burr's expedition, but he backed out when he learned that the government did not support Burr. Jackson led an invasion of Florida and seized that territory for the United States in 1818. He became the seventh president of the United States.

PETER OGDEN: Son of the sister of Jonathan Dayton and Matthias Ogden, another of Burr's boyhood friends, Peter Ogden served as a courier for Burr for the expedition. Arrested by Wilkinson and sent east, Ogden was freed by a federal judge.

SENATOR JOHN SMITH OF OHIO: A merchant in Cincinnati and principal supplier to the U.S. army in the West, Smith also owned a boatyard that built ships for the navy and owned land in Mississippi Territory. Smith was charged with treason for his involvement with Burr but was never tried. A U.S. Senate committee recommended his expulsion from that body, but the motion to expel him failed by a single vote. He resigned from the Senate the next day.

COMFORT TYLER AND ISRAEL SMITH: Frontiersmen from western New York State who enlisted a band of adventurers for Burr's expedition and served as officers during it. Both were charged with treason and violating the Neutrality Act, but never tried.

JAMES WILKINSON: Reared in Maryland, a brigadier general in the Continental Army at age twenty-one, and general in chief of the army and governor of Louisiana Territory during Burr's expedition. For twenty years, during most of which time he was a high officer in the U.S. army, Wilkinson also was a secret agent of the Spanish king. Deeply involved in the planning for Burr's expedition, Wilkinson turned on Burr, arrested many of his confederates, and served as his chief accuser, while never admitting his own role.

Burr's Pursuers

JOSEPH HAMILTON DAVEISS: A flamboyant Kentucky lawyer and United States attorney, Daveiss married the youngest sister of Chief Justice John Marshall. He twice attempted to prosecute Burr in November and December 1806.

JOHN GRAHAM: A Virginian, Graham was secretary of Orleans Territory in autumn 1806 when Jefferson's Cabinet dispatched him to trail Burr through the West and to prompt state authorities to oppose Burr's expedition.

GEORGE HAY: The United States attorney for Virginia and devoted Jeffersonian, Hay led the unsuccessful prosecution of Burr in Richmond from August through October 1807. Though Hay's ability to gather evidence was severely limited by the distances involved and by balky witnesses, his flawed indictment and theory of prosecution also contributed to Burr's acquittals.

THOMAS JEFFERSON: Author of the Declaration of Independence, former American minister to France and Secretary of State, and third President of the United States. Jefferson and Burr were never friendly, particularly after the disputed election of 1800. Though Burr was chosen as Jefferson's running mate that year, a flaw in the constitutional voting procedure resulted in a tie in the electoral vote totals of the two men. The tie was resolved in Jefferson's favor after thirty-six ballots in the House of Representatives. Jefferson never forgave Burr for not stepping aside more emphatically and dropped him from the Republican ticket in 1804. Jefferson ignored many reports of Burr's plans in the West but finally took action in late 1806. He closely managed the prosecution of Burr for treason and violation of the Neutrality Act.

ALEXANDER MACRAE: The third member of the prosecution team and lieutenant governor of Virginia, MacRae became a diplomatic official in France, where he helped to obstruct Burr's return from exile to the United States.

COWLES MEAD: Acting governor of Mississippi Territory when Burr's expedition reached it in January 1807, Mead negotiated Burr's initial surrender to civil authorities and prompted a grand jury inquiry into the expedition.

JUDGE THOMAS RODNEY: A Delaware politician who was appointed judge in Mississippi Territory, Rodney presided over a grand jury that inquired into Burr's conduct. By refusing to release Burr from his recognizance bond, Rodney provoked Burr to jump bail and flee to the east.

WILLIAM WIRT: Recruited to assist the unsuccessful prosecution of Burr in Richmond, Wirt won plaudits for his stirring orations, notably his classic "Who is Blennerhassett?" speech. Wirt became a leading Supreme Court advocate and served as Attorney General of the United States for twelve years.

Burr's Defenders

HENRY CLAY: The future Speaker of the House of Representatives, senator, and "Great Compromiser," the twenty-nine-year-old Clay was Burr's defense lawyer in two grand jury inquiries in Frankfort, Kentucky.

LUTHER MARTIN: Longtime attorney general of Maryland and delegate to the Constitutional Convention of 1787, Martin defended Supreme Court Justice Samuel Chase in his 1805 impeachment trial in the United States Senate and was one of Burr's defense counsel in Richmond. Martin was so loyal to his client that he posted part of Burr's bail. Martin's courtroom style mixed prolixity, bombast, brandy, and shrewdness.

EDMUND RANDOLPH: Formerly governor of Virginia, Attorney General and Secretary of State of the United States, and delegate to the 1787 Constitutional Convention, Randolph served as one of Burr's defense counsel in Richmond but was largely eclipsed by the other lawyers.

JOHN WICKHAM: A native New Yorker and the foremost lawyer in Richmond, Wickham took the leading role in Burr's defense during the three legal proceedings against him in 1807.

Others

WILLIAM C.C. CLAIBORNE: A native Virginian and congressman from Tennessee at the age of twenty-five, the youthful Claiborne was appointed interim governor of newly formed Orleans Territory in 1803. He never opposed General Wilkinson's repressive measures in New Orleans during the winter of 1806–07. Claiborne became the first elected governor of the state of Louisiana in 1812.

DANIEL CLARK: Merchant-politician in New Orleans, who invested with General Wilkinson in frontier lands and was an early ally of Burr's. In 1806, Clark was chosen to be the Orleans Territory delegate to the United States Congress.

WILLIAM EATON: American soldier and consul in North Africa, Eaton led a motley group of mercenaries and marines against Tripoli in 1803. Burr attempted to recruit him for his expedition, but Eaton became a prominent witness against him.

WILLIAM HENRY HARRISON: Governor of Indiana Territory and future president, Harrison also was a confidant of Jonathan Dayton and James Wilkinson. Burr visited Harrison while he was recruiting adherents for his western expedition.

BENJAMIN HENRY LATROBE: Architect and designer of the Capitol in Washington, D.C., and friend to both Burr and Jefferson. Burr consulted with Latrobe on the design of riverboats and the construction of canals in the West.

JAMES MADISON: Secretary of State for all eight years of the Jefferson administration and close friend of the president. At Madison's request in 1794, Burr had introduced him to the widow Dolley Payne Todd, who became Madison's wife. Madison succeeded Jefferson in the presidency and led the nation through the War of 1812.

HUMPHREY MARSHALL: Cousin to Chief Justice John Marshall, U.S. senator, and Federalist leader of the Marshall clan in Kentucky, Humphrey sponsored the *Western World,* a Frankfort newspaper that ran a multi-part exposé of Kentuckians who collaborated with the Spanish government to support secession. The articles aroused public skepticism toward the activities of Burr and General Wilkinson.

JOHN MARSHALL: A Virginia Federalist, Marshall was an army officer during the Revolutionary War and then a lawyer in Richmond. He served as congressman, diplomat, and Secretary of State before being appointed the third chief justice of the United States in 1801. Marshall presided in Richmond over the Burr treason trial, a second trial for violation of the Neutrality Act, and a preliminary hearing on additional treason charges. His landmark decisions during the Burr case, including *Ex Parte Bollman,* established the availability of habeas corpus relief in national security cases, the narrow definition of treason in American law, and the qualified "executive privilege" for papers of the president.

THOMAS TRUXTUN: A successful commander in the United States navy during the undeclared war with France in the late 1790s, Truxtun then resigned from the service. Burr attempted to recruit him for his western expedition.

PART I

"It's this Bonaparte who's turned all their heads; They all wonder how it is that from the lieutenants he landed among the emperors."

Leo Tolstoy, *War and Peace*[1]

1

The Dark Star of the Founding

I n early 1800, at the dawn of a new century, Aaron Burr was on every short list of men who could become president of the United States. He was the most prominent Northern leader of the Republican party, which was poised to win the national elections that fall. As an emerging political star, he seemed fated to shape the infant republic as it struggled for its place in a world of warring monarchies and despotisms.

Burr had reached this extraordinarily favorable position by measured steps. From an early age, Burr preferred to advance on his own careful terms, beholden to no one. He had been just old enough to join the fight for independence from Britain. In 1776, when the Continental Congress issued the Declaration of Independence, the twenty-year-old Burr served as a lieutenant colonel in the Continental Army. When General George Washington picked him as a personal aide, Burr swiftly lateraled into another assignment, out from under the great man's shadow. When the Constitutional Convention met in 1787 to create a new government, Burr avoided the highly charged debates, building his New York law practice and local political standing. When the new Congress convened in 1789 and George Washington assembled the first government under the Constitution, Burr served in the New York State government. Yet by 1800, Burr was a leading contender for the highest national offices.

Writing some years later, former president John Adams struggled to explain Burr's rise. "There is in some souls a principle of absolute levity that buoys them irresistibly into the clouds," he wrote grumpily. "This I take to be precisely the genius of Burr."[1]

There were better explanations for Burr's success. His family was distinguished. A grandfather, Jonathan Edwards, had been America's leading divine, famously warning that we are all sinners in the hands of an angry God. Burr's father was president of the College of New Jersey, the future Princeton University. Orphaned at an early age and raised in an uncle's family, Burr was kin to prominent Americans from New Jersey through Boston. But his advancement grew from achievement as much as from fortunate birth.

Burr won distinction as a soldier and cut a military figure all his life, though he did not serve in uniform after the age of twenty-five. His intelligence and persuasive powers brought success as a lawyer and a politician: attorney general of New York State, then United States senator, then candidate for vice president in 1800. Burr's adroit campaign management in the 1800 election marked him as a master of the new art of electioneering. The nation's first two vice presidents, Adams and Jefferson, used the office as a stepping-stone to the highest office. Burr, whose talents and charisma were acknowledged even by his adversaries, intended to do the same.

Yet Burr never rose beyond vice president. Rather, he became the greatest problem of America's founding years, a bright promise tarnished by treason, a traitor never punished, a terror never quite exorcised. Leading historians wring their hands in dismay over Aaron Burr. For Gordon Wood in *Revolutionary Characters*, Burr "violated the fundamental values of [the] experiment in republicanism" and "ultimately threatened the meaning of the Revolution." For Joseph Ellis in *Founding Brothers*, Burr's enemies correctly accused him of being an "unprincipled American Catiline," the malcontent whose conspiracy against the Roman Republic was thwarted by the great orator Cicero.[2]

In the popular rendering of America's early years, Burr's principal sins were three.

First, the indictment goes, he schemed to cheat Jefferson in the tumultuous deadlocked election of 1800, failing to step aside decisively in favor of
his own running mate as an honorable man would have done.

Second, the indictment continues, Burr ruthlessly killed the genius
Alexander Hamilton in a duel in 1804, even though Hamilton had nobly
resolved not to fire at Burr.

Finally, there is the most fantastic charge: that from 1804 to 1807, Burr
conspired to lead a secessionist rebellion of western states and territories,
or maybe he sought to conduct a coup d'état against the American government, or perhaps he planned to invade Mexico and South America, install-
ing himself as Emperor Aaron I, the Napoleon of the New World. Whatever
he was up to—opinions differed then and differ now—he has been routinely
condemned. Yet Burr, this avatar of evil, was never punished. His trial for
treason in 1807 before Chief Justice John Marshall ended in his acquittal,
an outcome some attribute to Burr's legal skill, others to his subversion of
the legal system, and still others to Marshall's desire to defy Jefferson, his
bitter political opponent and distant cousin. Equally galling, Burr survived
to an amiable and unrepentant old age, dying quietly on Staten Island in
1836, on the eve of the presidency of Martin Van Buren.

This orthodox version of Burr is deeply rooted. It has fascinated nov-
elists and playwrights for two centuries, more than seventy of whom have
produced works that try to make sense of the man and his actions. In *The
Man without a Country* in 1863, Edward Everett Hale portrayed Burr's
treason as a self-betrayal, ultimately a self-negation. For James Thurber in
the 1930s, Burr's malice was raw and magical, capable of killing a man a
hundred years after Burr's own death. Eudora Welty favored the romance of
Burr's story, depicting him as a hero to a young boy on the American frontier. A generation ago, Gore Vidal gave us Burr as a rollicking nihilist whose
only flaw was an inability to ignore the failings of his more pompous peers,
the ones we revere (and capitalize) as the Founders.[3]

Burr's story also has spawned historical analogies and extravagant
comparisons, most often to Catiline, the notorious Roman conspirator, and
sometimes to Shakespeare's Earl of Warwick, as a man who made a king
(Jefferson), then strove to unseat him.[4]

How did this one man, who never actually gained power, provoke generations of speculation and wonder? His audacity is surely part of the answer. To contemporaries, Burr radiated danger and daring, a willingness to attempt deeds from which others shrank. His posture was martial, his attitudes were military, and he did not shy from conflict.

Some of his adventurism was undeniably sexual. A widower at age thirty-seven when his wife died of cancer, Burr avidly pursued romantic liaisons. One longtime confidant marveled at Burr's fascination with women:

> It is truly surprising how any individual could have become so eminent as a soldier, as a statesman, and as a professional man, who devoted so much time to the other sex. . . . For more than half a century of his life they seemed to absorb his whole thoughts. His intrigues were without number.

His romantic advances often met success: With unmistakable rue, this same friend confessed that Burr, "by a fascinating power almost peculiar to himself . . . retain[ed] the affection, in some instances, the devotion, of his deluded victims."[5]

Another part of the answer can be found in Burr's mysteries, which have long survived him. His published papers fill a scant two volumes. In contrast, the writings of Hamilton—produced in a life thirty years shorter than Burr's—fill twenty-seven. Jefferson's papers have mounted to forty-one volumes, while scholars still labor to produce the ones that will cover six years of his presidency. Burr's skimpy documentary record is no accident. He was wary of political theorizing, even of the written word. As a lawyer, he recited the maxim "Things written remain," and he lived by it.[6] He often kept his own counsel on controversial issues, preserving his ability to adjust his position as needed. He preferred to influence men face-to-face, where his compelling gaze, graceful manners, and incisive intelligence were most effective. In addition, in a time of fierce party loyalties, he maintained cordial relations with Federalists and Republicans alike, which meant that few completely trusted him. When his own Republican party failed to support him in an election, an old friend observed that "they respect Burr's talents, but they dread his independence. They know, in short, he is not one of them."[7]

Burr's mystique also grew from his iconoclastic views. Male superiority was assumed in Burr's time, yet he believed that women's talents equaled those of men and that women should have equal rights. He hung above his hearth a portrait of Mary Wollstonecraft, the English advocate of women's rights. Burr pressed his daughter to intellectual accomplishments as a sort of demonstration project for his beliefs. An Englishman found that young Theodosia Burr had been educated "with uncommon care":

> She is elegant without ostentation, and learned without pedantry
> . . . speaks French and Italian with facility, is perfectly conversant
> with the writers of the Augustan age, and not unacquainted with the
> language of the Father of Poetry [Greek].[8]

Burr also held advanced views on slavery. Though he periodically owned slaves himself, Burr belonged to an antislavery society and sponsored legislation to abolish human bondage in New York State.

This bust of Burr stands in the chamber of the United States Senate, where he served for six years as a senator from New York and presided for four years as vice president.

Burr's political iconoclasm extended to America's ruling elite. Washington, the father of his country? For Burr, the man was a poorly educated farmer unfit to command the Continental Army, much less serve as political leader of the nation. Jefferson, the apostle of liberty? Burr found him an intellectual hypocrite whose physical cowardice produced a languid, ineffective style of governing. Hamilton, the architect of the nation's economy? In Burr's view he was temperamentally unsuited to public responsibility.[9]

Indeed, much of the power of Aaron Burr's story lies in his daring to be dissatisfied with early America, his refusal to see it as a constitutional Eden from which democracy and all good things would flow. It is no great stretch to conceive of Burr as America's Satan: not the biblical Satan but the tragic, too-human hero of Milton's *Paradise Lost*. If the early republic was the earthly paradise of later imagining, then Burr was the fallen angel who denied the greatness of the immense leader (Washington), who struck down the leader's favorite (Hamilton), and himself was felled by an archangel (Jefferson). Satan's lament in Milton's epic resonates when applied to Burr:

> *O Sun, to tell thee how I hate thy beams,*
> *That Bring to my remembrance from what state*
> *I fell, how glorious once above thy sphere;*
> *Till pride and worse ambition threw me down*

This book begins at the moment when Burr's hopes flared most brightly, with the election of 1800. Burr finished that election in a surprising tie with Jefferson, who was the Republican candidate for president, with Burr slotted for second position. By not sufficiently deferring to Jefferson in that constitutional standoff, Burr allowed—even encouraged—the opposing Federalists to use his candidacy to tie up Jefferson's selection for months. By the time the contest was decided, Burr had tarnished his image as a practical man of affairs with a gift for leading men. Most important, Burr had irretrievably ruined his relationship with Jefferson, the dominating political figure of the time. Never close to Burr, Jefferson froze out his vice president, then dropped him from the Republican ticket in 1804. As a politician, Burr became badly damaged goods, which led to his greatest and most baffling alleged sin: his treason, or conspiracy, or planned invasion of Mexico and beyond. But Jefferson, having blocked Burr's advancement in electoral politics, also stood between Burr and his extravagant project for redrawing the map of North America.

That project played out in 1805 and 1806, when Burr made two long trips through what was then the American West, down the Ohio and Mississippi Rivers. Before and during those trips, he made urgent, secret plans with the general in chief of the American army, James Wilkinson, a thoroughgoing scoundrel and paid agent of the Spanish king. Burr drew support from two men who later became president (Andrew Jackson and William Henry Harrison), and from three U.S. senators, a former Speaker of the House of Representatives, and an implausible Irish émigré. He even intrigued for alliances with foreign kings.

When Burr assembled his adventurers in late 1806, the expedition swiftly floundered. Grand juries in Kentucky and Mississippi investigated him but then set him free. Finally arrested and taken as a prisoner to face treason charges in Virginia, Burr's life became the prize in a desperate legal war mounted by Jefferson. In the courtroom, Burr escaped Jefferson's vengeance thanks to his own legal talents and the exertions of Chief Justice John Marshall. While presiding over Burr's case, Marshall issued rulings that defined America's law of treason, constrained the powers of the president, and vindicated the constitutional right of habeas corpus. Marshall also gave the former vice president his freedom, whereupon Burr set sail for Europe to seek foreign backing for an expedition to liberate the American colonies of Spain.

From start to finish, Burr's western expedition was a protean undertaking. His plans matured and foundered, reformed and were overturned again. They played out on a continent of possibilities, not certainties. Much about the United States was in flux in 1805. Even its physical boundaries were changing. North American borders had shifted repeatedly for as long as anyone could remember. European wars had often ended with the combatants trading North American land, and then the new republic arose, full of energy and ambition. In 1805, the United States was still digesting the massive Louisiana Territory, acquired from France two years before, which offered a narrow outlet to the Gulf of Mexico through New Orleans. But the country did not yet reach to the Pacific, and Spanish lands blocked it from much of the Gulf Coast.

Nor had an American identity fully formed by 1805. Americans older than thirty had been British subjects at birth. The United States government under the Constitution was only a sapling, not yet twenty years old, mistrusted by many of its citizens. Secession movements simmered in the West and in New England. Twice in the previous decade substantial groups of Pennsylvanians had refused to pay federal taxes. A restlessness pulsed through the country. Hungry for new land and new opportunity, Americans pressed across the continent while powerful gusts buffeted the nation from the Napoleonic wars in Europe.

As he strode westward through this volatile land, Burr imagined different roles for himself in the American future. If the United States were to grab for Spanish lands, Burr could lead the conquering armies. But private forces might also liberate those Spanish lands, which then could form a new empire on the shores of the Gulf of Mexico; Burr could lead that effort too. If the western portions of the United States wished to join that new empire, so much the better.

While pursuing these western dreams, Burr made conflicting statements about his intentions. A few times he said he wished to unseat Jefferson at the head of the government. At other times, he encouraged the separation of the western states from the rest of the country. More often, he said he intended to take control of New Orleans and "revolutionize" Mexico and Spanish America. And when he faced the gallows in a Richmond courtroom, he insisted he was a simple settler of the American frontier.

The search for Burr's single plan is a pursuit of a mirage. Burr made conflicting statements of his purpose because that purpose changed as he careened from setback to new hope to hairsbreadth escape to disaster. His most ambitious plans involved the creation of a new nation that would rival or even dwarf the United States. But Burr also made contingency arrangements with less ambitious goals, in case events turned against him. He had plans to be broadcast in public squares, others to be discussed candidly in small gatherings, and yet others to be confided quietly to a few intimates and foreign ambassadors. In truth, he intended all of the purposes that were attributed to him, but he also intended to abandon any that he could not achieve. The fluid, opportunistic quality of his plans and hopes caused confusion about them at the time and have continued to do so.

All of Burr's feverish efforts, however, flowed from the same pride and ambition. He strained to break out of the political corner into which Jefferson had painted him, to win the glory he craved. For Aaron Burr, who always presented himself as a hardheaded politician, it was the heady dream of glory, driven by "pride and worse ambition," that ultimately earned him the obloquy of history.

By pursuing his dream of glory, Burr mounted a profound test of the emerging republic. He sought out the country's most unstable elements: discontented military officers, alienated and land-hungry frontiersmen, French-speaking residents in the lands of the Louisiana Purchase. With these combustible materials, Burr proposed to transform the continent. Burr forced many Americans, after fewer than twenty years of national existence, to consider whether their republic was worth continuing, or whether the disparate parts of the country should go their separate ways, with Burr leading those who wished to build something even newer in frontier lands. His challenge to Jefferson's leadership roused the Virginian, whose lax governing style allowed Burr the freedom to organize his expedition for more than a year. Through a combination of luck and timely intervention by others, Jefferson had the satisfaction of seeing Burr's bright ambitions turn to ashes. Indeed, Burr's challenge strengthened the union and sharpened Jefferson's own commitment to it.

Burr's expedition also tested the dedication of Americans to the revolutionary principles proclaimed a generation before, which were embedded in the Constitution and the Bill of Rights. That challenge crystallized during the extraordinary spectacle of Burr's trial for treason in the summer of 1807. President Jefferson, fed up with his former vice president, was willing to sacrifice constitutional liberties—even the rule of law—to preserve the union and punish this infuriating miscreant. In contrast, Chief Justice Marshall enforced every constitutional and statutory protection in Burr's favor, insisting on the preservation of personal rights and the independence of the judiciary.

The largest significance of Burr's audacious expedition involved consequences he did not intend. By demonstrating that few Americans would abandon their infant republic to join his pursuit of glory, he reinforced the bonds that held the nation together. When Burr's trial strained the nation's commitment to individual rights when national security is at stake, John Marshall vindicated the vision of a republic rooted in the rule of law. That Burr did not intend those consequences did not make them less central to the building of the nation.

Burr's western expedition expressed the boldness and the complexity of Burr's singular personality. The daring side of his character was visible in an incident from his old age, when he and a companion faced a stormy night crossing of the Hudson River. Burr's companion recoiled from the river's dangers. " 'Why,' exclaimed the old gentleman [Burr] as he sprang lightly into the boat, 'this makes an adventure of it. . . . This is the fun of the thing. The adventure is the best of all.' " [10]

Blending the promise of the West with dreams of empire and freedom, no American adventure has been like Aaron Burr's.

2

Do Not Play the Fool with His Name

New York and Washington, D.C.
May 1800–February 1801

In early May 1800, James Nicholson left his house on William Street in Manhattan to call at the nearby home of Aaron Burr. Almost by accident, Nicholson held Burr's future in his hands. Both men, active in New York Republican politics, had served bravely during the Revolution. Nicholson, now in his early sixties, had been the senior captain of the new nation's navy. Burr, forty-four, had been a young army officer. If this meeting went well, Nicholson could propel Burr to the highest level of the nation's political life.

Burr's prospects shone brightly in that heady springtime. He had already performed a signal service for the Republican party. In the presidential election that fall, Thomas Jefferson would be the Republican candidate against Federalist incumbent John Adams. The Republicans, strongest in the South and in rural areas, had to carry New York to win. Because the state assembly would cast New York's electoral votes, the spring contests for assembly seats was pivotal. Burr had masterminded a brilliant campaign that brought home a Republican majority in that body. That majority could give Jefferson the presidency.

To lock in New York support for Jefferson, the Republican congressional caucus in Philadelphia meant to choose a New Yorker as the party's candidate for vice president. They asked one of their own, Albert Gallatin of Pennsylvania, to sound out the two principal contenders: Burr and New York governor George Clinton. Unable to get to New York himself, Gallatin delegated the task to Nicholson, his father-in-law.

Nicholson visited George Clinton first. At sixty-one, Clinton was godfather to New York's Republicans, having served as governor for eighteen years. But the governor's wife had died recently and he talked wistfully of retirement. Clinton responded tepidly to Nicholson's approach, explaining that he was "averse to engage in public life yet." Grudgingly, he said his name could be submitted for the vice presidency so long as he retained the right to resign from the job whenever he wished.

Burr, in contrast, hungered for advancement. His recent election triumph had made him the favorite for the nomination. In a letter to Gallatin, Nicholson celebrated Burr's efforts: "His generalship, perseverance, industry and execution exceeds all description, so that I think I can say he deserves anything and everything of his country."[1]

Something about Burr seemed to mark him as blessed. Though charisma is an evanescent quality that is difficult to describe or appreciate two centuries later. Burr's contemporaries uniformly acknowledged his personal appeal. Small, trim, and handsome, he had the gift of transfixing both sexes. Perhaps Burr's magnetism can best be gauged from contemporary efforts to describe his unforgettable eyes.

A British diplomat wrote of Burr's "dark eyes glancing perpetually and rapidly from right and left." The gaze of those "deep hazel" eyes, another writer recalled, made a companion feel "that they pierced his innermost thoughts." A bitter opponent awarded him the "eyes of the lynx," then decided they were "basilisk eyes." A young woman in Kentucky settled for "bright and piercing"; a Mississippian said Burr's "glance was most penetrating and fascinating"; a German woman found his eyes "sparkling." The description in a Kentucky newspaper was near ecstatic:

His eyes are . . . of a dark hazel; and from the shade of his project-
ing eye bones and brows, appear black, they glow with all the ardor
of venereal fire, and scintillate with the most tremulous and fearful
sensibility—they roll with the celerity of phrensy of poetic fervor,
and beam with the most vivid and piercing rays of genius.

Almost seven years after Burr's meeting with Nicholson, a stranger recognized him in the forests of southern Alabama solely because Burr's eyes
were reputed to be "remarkably keen," and so they were.

Burr dominated social occasions but not with glittering conversation.
He listened courteously, commented insightfully, and maintained a gracious
reserve. That same Kentucky newspaper called him "rather taciturn." His
charisma, though, had a universal impact. When Burr spoke, according to
one observer, he did so "with such animation, with such apparent frankness
and negligence, as would induce a person to believe he was a man of guilt-
less and ingenuous heart." Much of his allure came from the impression that
he was holding something back. Burr implied secrets, thrilling and even
risky ones. "In my opinion," the observer continued, "there is no human
more reserved, mysterious and inscrutable." [2]

The meeting between Nicholson and Burr turned out to be a rocky
one. The older gentleman showed Burr a letter he had drafted to report
Clinton's ambivalence about the vice presidency. Clinton's lack of interest
seemed to clear the way for Burr to be the party's nominee. Nicholson asked
for Burr's reaction to the draft letter.

Burr seemed annoyed, then grew agitated. Nomination by the Republican caucus, he observed, was not worth a great deal to him, since he could
not trust southern Republicans to honor any promise to support him. He
was certain, he added, he would win New York's governorship at the next
election; he could not imagine relinquishing that certainty for a doubtful
chance at the vice presidency. Then he stalked from the room. Nicholson,
left alone in Burr's parlor, had to wonder at the divalike temperaments of
these New York politicians: Clinton had sniffed diffidently at the offer of the
vice presidency, while the same proposal threw Burr into a snit.

Two of Burr's friends entered the parlor and sat with Nicholson. They explained that Burr would accept the designation as Republican candidate after all; indeed, they said, he "was obliged to do so on principle," since he had recently lectured Republicans that "all personal considerations should be given up for the good of the public." A subdued Burr, with a restored sense of decorum, then joined his guests. Burr agreed to be the Republican nominee for vice president, but Nicholson thought he did so with reluctance.

Nicholson reported to Philadelphia that Governor Clinton had declined the nomination. Burr, he wrote, was "the most suitable person and perhaps the only man" for the job. He added that every Republican he met in New York agreed with that judgment; they had expressed to him "universal and unbounded" confidence in Burr.

Nicholson then addressed a critical point, the one that accounted for Burr's fit of temper, real or feigned. Based on his experience in the presidential election in 1796, Nicholson wrote, Burr did not trust the Republicans of the South. He particularly did not trust those from Virginia. "I believe he may be induced to stand [for the office]," Nicholson concluded, "if assurances can be given that the Southern states will act fairly . . . but his name must not be played the fool with." [3]

Burr would never abide anyone playing the fool with his name.

Burr's complaint grew from a flaw in the constitutional process for selecting the president. Nine months later, that flaw nearly made him president.

Under the Constitution, each state selects electors who then choose the president. Each state has the same number of presidential electors as its total of congressmen plus senators. Until the Twelfth Amendment was ratified in 1803, the Constitution gave each elector *two* votes for president. If a candidate won the votes of a majority of the electors, he became president; the runner-up became vice president. If no candidate commanded a majority, the House of Representatives chose the president. The potential mischief in the system involved the second vote that each elector held, which made the process unpredictable, even unreliable.

The flaw lay largely dormant during the first two presidential elections, when George Washington was unopposed, but it emerged clearly in the 1796 contest.

In that election, John Adams of Massachusetts led the commercially minded Federalists, who supported a stronger national government and predominated in New England. Adams's opponents, Jefferson's Republicans, championed state powers. Adams won the contest, but Jefferson mustered the second-highest total and became vice president. Having Adams's opponent serve as his vice president was, at best, awkward.

Jefferson slipped into the nation's second highest office because Federalist electors were careless with their *second* votes for president. All seventy-one of them voted for Adams, but fewer than fifty cast their second vote for the party's indicated candidate for vice president, Thomas Pinckney of South Carolina. Because Federalist electors sprinkled their second vote among five other individuals, Jefferson finished second.

Burr's outburst with Nicholson was the result of the even less disciplined voting by the Republican electors in 1796. Though there had been no official Republican candidate for vice president that year, Burr was the leading contender for the slot at the party's caucus. Yet not even half the Republican electors cast their second ballot for Burr. The New Yorker bitterly resented the slight and its distinctly regional pattern. Twenty-eight Republican electors from southern states failed to vote for Burr; eight voted for the Federalist Pinckney. "Burr says he has no confidence in the Virginians," wrote one observer. "They once deceived him and are not to be trusted."[4]

The problem was that the Constitution presumed that disinterested electors would choose the best candidate for president and the second-best candidate for vice president. Once political parties became the order of the day, that presumption became unrealistic. Partisans were not interested in selecting the "best" and "second-best" candidates; they wanted their party's candidates for president and vice president to be elected together. The 1796 contest was a transitional election: Electors followed party discipline on the choice for president, but many followed more personal feelings with their second vote. By 1800 the party system was firmly rooted, and the lesson from the previous election was plain: To win both the presidency and vice presidency, all of a party's electors should vote for the presidential candidate; then all of its electors *except one* should cast their second vote for the vice presidential candidate. Burr's tirade with Nicholson was, in effect, a demand that the Republicans follow that course.

On May 11, 1800, the Republican congressional caucus met in

Philadelphia and unanimously resolved to support Burr for vice president. In view of Burr's demands, that also meant that Republican electors should not abandon him in the final voting.[5]

When the electors met in their respective states seven months later, in early December, the Federalists observed perfect discipline: Adams tallied sixty-five votes and his vice presidential running mate had sixty-four. On the Republican side, however, there was a shocking bungle. The Republican electors slavishly respected Burr's demand that none should forsake him. Seventy-three voted for Jefferson. Seventy-three voted for Burr.[6]

Burr and Jefferson were tied.

With no single candidate holding an electoral majority, the House of Representatives would choose the president. Each state delegation in the House would have a single vote. The candidate supported by a majority of state delegations would be president.

Republican congressmen were going to support Jefferson. He was their party's choice for president. Federalists, however, felt no such limitation. Because Adams had finished third in the balloting, most acknowledged that he was no longer a viable candidate. Some began to consider supporting Burr. For Federalists, a Burr presidency seemed the lesser of two evils. As a New Yorker, Burr was more sympathetic to commercial interests than was the plantation-owning Jefferson. Burr was friendly with many Federalists. He seemed less doctrinaire and more pragmatic than the Virginian. By temperament, Burr would be a more vigorous chief executive. The speculation caught fire. Perhaps a coalition of Federalists and centrist Republicans could place Burr in the executive mansion.

In December, when unofficial reports circulated of the electors' tallies in each state, a tie between Jefferson and Burr seemed distinctly possible. Burr promptly wrote a letter, intended for public release, in which he modestly deferred to his party's leader. "It is highly improbable that I shall have an equal number of votes with Mr. Jefferson," he wrote, "but if such should be the result every man who knows me ought to know that I should utterly disclaim all competition" with Jefferson. He acknowledged that the "wishes and expectations of the U.S." were that Jefferson would become president. It seemed that Republicans could relax. Burr would not support a Federalist scheme to give him the presidency.[7]

Not even two weeks later, though, Burr sent a second letter, also intended for public consumption, with a markedly different tone. He had received many letters about the election, he wrote, which expressed "a degree of jealousy and distrust and irritation by no means pleasing or flattering." Indeed, one correspondent demanded a pledge from Burr that if the House chose him to be president, he would resign. This was more than Burr could stomach. He would defer to Jefferson, as he had pledged in his earlier letter, but he would not declare himself unworthy of the presidency. He wrote indignantly:

> The question was unnecessary, unreasonable, and impertinent, and I have therefore made no reply. If I had made any I should have told that as at present advised, I should not [resign if chosen president]. . . . I was made a candidate against my advice and against my will . . . and now I am insulted by those who used my name for having suffered it to be used.

This second letter, evidently written in anger, revived the risk that the Federalists could use Burr to block Jefferson. Federalist schemers took heart. Although Burr had said he would not seek the presidency over Jefferson, he now said he would accept the office if it were thrust upon him. Burr had to know that his second letter would encourage Federalist maneuvering. Even if he was surprised by the Federalists' response, he could certainly have issued a third statement to dampen their ardor for a Burr presidency. But Burr made no further public utterance on the subject. In a private letter, he offered the practical assessment that the Federalists had it "in their power to make their election and to coerce the [Republicans] to abandon J[efferson]." If they succeeded, Aaron Burr would be president. And he would do nothing more to stop them.[8]

Vote-counters quickly determined that the House of Representatives might replicate the tied electoral vote. Of the sixteen state delegations in the House, Republicans controlled eight, all of whom would support Jefferson. If he could win the support of only one more state delegation, the Virginian would be president. Federalists controlled six state delegations, while two others were split evenly between the two parties. If the Federalists uniformly supported Burr, they could deny Jefferson the ninth vote he needed. The count would be eight states for Jefferson, six for Burr, two states abstaining. Deadlock again. In that deadlock, Federalists thought they might find opportunity: Enough Republicans might switch to Burr to give him the election. Jefferson was dismayed. "We remain," he fumed in a letter, "in the hands of our enemies."[9]

While Burr remained in Albany in February 1801, and while the House of Representatives chose the next president of the United States, Vice President Thomas Jefferson hovered near the Capitol.

Not every Federalist supported Burr, however. Alexander Hamilton of New York was appalled at the thought of his fellow New Yorker at the head of the American government.

For almost a decade, Hamilton had been saying and writing terrible things about Burr. A single year apart in age, both had been dashing young heroes of the Continental Army, then successful lawyers in New York City. They shared so many qualities. Both were small, slight, and handsome.

Both were ambitious, charming, womanizing, and smarter than their contemporaries. In public, they seemed to get on. On occasion, they had jointly represented legal clients.[10]

Hamilton, with the sponsorship of George Washington, rocketed to power as a Federalist. As the first Secretary of the Treasury, he restored the nation's credit and its prosperity. Burr rose to prominence in ways bound to irritate Hamilton: When he won his Senate seat in 1791, Burr replaced Hamilton's father-in-law, Philip Schuyler. Hamilton never forgave Burr. In 1792, he wrote that Burr "is unprincipled both as a public and private man," adding that it was "a religious duty" to oppose him. Burr was, Hamilton continued, an "embryo-Caesar."

Through the winter of 1800–01, with Burr at the threshold of the highest office in the land, Hamilton unleashed more private broadsides against his fellow New Yorker:

> As to Mr. Burr, there is nothing in his favor. . . . He is bankrupt beyond redemption, except by the plunder of his country. His public principles have no other spring or aim than his own aggrandizement. . . . If he can, he will certainly disturb our institutions to secure to himself permanent power, and with it wealth. He is truly the Catiline of America.[11]

When writing to Federalists who liked Burr, Hamilton abandoned this apocalyptic tone. In those letters, he tried to explain more thoughtfully why Burr was so dangerous. "Jefferson, I suspect, will not dare much," he wrote to one. "Burr will dare everything." Developing this theme, Hamilton despaired that Burr "is sanguine enough to hope everything—daring enough to attempt everything—wicked enough to scruple nothing." In Burr, Hamilton saw a uniquely optimistic brand of opportunism and self-interest. Also, in Hamilton's view Burr simply could not be trusted: "No engagement that can be made with him can be depended upon. While making it he will laugh in his sleeve at the credulity of those with whom he makes it." Hamilton had only to point to the current tumult to illustrate his view of Burr's perfidy. By not unequivocally deferring to Jefferson, the ambitious Burr was fomenting Federalist schemes to give him the presidency.[12]

After weeks of penning jeremiads against Burr, Hamilton settled upon his real objection: The man had no definite political principles. "As to his theory," Hamilton wrote, "no mortal can tell what it is." Hamilton admitted that the pragmatic, capable Burr would likely conduct the nation's economic and foreign policies sensibly, but that was not enough reason to support him. "He holds to no pernicious theories," Hamilton acknowledged, but he should be rejected precisely because he was "a mere matter-of-fact man." [13]

Alexander Hamilton, the first Secretary of the Treasury, urged his fellow Federalists to support Jefferson over Burr for the presidency.

Hamilton returned to these themes in a letter to a key Delaware Federalist. Again admitting that Burr's policy views caused him no concern, Hamilton insisted that the danger was the man himself. Burr "is a man of very subtle imagination," he wrote, but he lacked "theory." He asked, "Is it a recommendation to have no theory? Can that man be a systematic or able statesman who has none? I believe not." Calling Burr "far more cunning than wise, far more dexterous than able," Hamilton, with some prescience, distilled his core objection: "The truth is . . . [Burr] is the most sanguine man in the world. *He thinks everything possible to adventure and perseverance.*"[14]

Hamilton's assessment of Burr was penetrating. Burr was impatient with the constitutional theorizing that was the basic vocabulary of politics for America's founding generation. His bent was toward action not words, toward the particular not the general. His talent was for practical politics and the effective exercise of power. Perhaps only during the intellectual ferment of the nation's founding would such an orientation be called dangerous.

Although Hamilton's was the most prominent voice opposing Burr, others shared his doubts. After initially favoring Burr, one Federalist changed his mind for reasons that closely tracked Hamilton's: "Burr's unbounded ambition, courage, and perseverance would prompt him to be a Bonaparte, a King, and an Emperor, or anything else which might place him at the head of the nation." Yet most Federalists disliked Jefferson far more. John Marshall, a Virginia Federalist about to become chief justice of the Supreme Court, wrote that he had "almost insuperable objections" to Jefferson.[15]

As the political jockeying intensified that winter, Burr withdrew to Albany, where he was finishing a term in the state assembly. On February 2 in that frigid upstate town, his daughter, Theodosia, not yet eighteen years old, married Joseph Alston of South Carolina. Because the twenty-two-year-old groom was a wealthy rice planter and aspiring politician, some gossips saw the match as a coldly strategic one, designed to replenish Burr's empty bank account with his son-in-law's riches while strengthening Burr's political network in the South.[16]

Barely a week after the wedding, Congress assembled at the Capitol in Washington City to receive the official electoral votes from each state. Burr was almost four hundred miles away in Albany, but Jefferson stood at the center of the action. Because the vice president presided over the Senate, Jefferson opened the electoral votes from each state on Wednesday, February 11. There were no surprises. He and Burr were tied.

At one o'clock that same afternoon, the House began to choose the next president. As Republicans had dreaded, eight states voted for Jefferson, six for Burr, and two abstained. No new president. Without taking a break, the congressmen voted again. The outcome was the same. Five more times that afternoon they voted. Five more times Jefferson fell one vote short. The House took a break for dinner.

The congressmen voted on the presidency twenty-one more times through that night and into the next day. Each ballot produced the identical outcome: Jefferson 8, Burr 6, abstentions 2. No congressman changed his vote. After twenty-eight ballots, the House recessed until the next day, Friday, February 13. The nation had been attempting to choose its new president for more than four months, but the process was not yet over.[17]

No votes changed on the ballot taken on February 13, nor during four more ballots the next day. The thirty-fourth ballot, held on Monday, February 16, produced the same result. The constitutional process had become a political siege.

That night, letters arrived from Burr in Albany. According to the Federalist Speaker of the House, the New Yorker had "explicitly resign[ed] his pretensions to be president." Burr's concession disgusted another Federalist. "Burr has acted a miserable paltry part," he wrote later. "The election was in his power."[18]

On the first ballot of Tuesday, February 17, the Federalists repeated the deadlock, but the logjam broke on the next vote. Federalists from Maryland and Vermont, the two states that had been abstaining because they were equally divided, now abstained from voting altogether; that allowed their Republican colleagues to cast the votes of those states for Jefferson. The final total on the thirty-sixth ballot was ten states for Jefferson, four for Burr, and two Federalist-controlled delegations choosing to abstain. The siege was over. In three weeks, Thomas Jefferson would take the oath of office as the third president of the United States. Aaron Burr would be his vice president.

Many Federalists groused that Burr had let the presidency slip through his fingers. If only he had made a few simple deals, they insisted, he could have won. "Had Burr done anything for himself," wrote a New York congressman, "he would long ere have been president." A key Federalist congressman from Delaware agreed. "The means existed of electing Burr," he wrote after Jefferson's inauguration, "but they required his cooperation."[19]

Many Republicans were even more unhappy with Burr, complaining that he had schemed to cheat Jefferson of victory. They believed Burr's public statements were carefully calibrated to maintain his Republican credentials while providing *sotto voce* encouragement for Federalists to leapfrog into the presidency—in short, they thought he had played both ends against the middle. If that was his strategy, it had misfired completely. Burr had said just enough to encourage Federalists and anger Republicans, but he did not conclude the deals needed to secure the executive mansion.

Yet Burr's course was consistent with both his ambition and his exacting sense of personal honor. By his own standards, he acted correctly at every stage of the election. His first letter, which disclaimed competition with Jefferson, honored the Virginian's role as the Republican party's choice for president. Indeed, Burr, to the Federalists' disappointment, never negotiated directly with anyone to take the presidency from Jefferson. Burr's honor also, however, required his fateful second letter, in which he said he would accept the presidency if that was the will of the House of Representatives. For Burr, that was what any political leader with an ounce of self-respect had to say. Any other response would have denied his own honor. Yet that statement irretrievably alienated Jefferson.

For the next four years, Jefferson kept Burr at arm's length, never viewing him as either an adviser or an ally. As vice president, Burr lived in the nation's capital for only a few months every winter, presiding over debate in the Senate. He lived in New York for the rest of the year, with minimal involvement in the nation's government. The president cut Burr off from patronage appointments, strangling him politically. When it came time for Republicans to choose a vice presidential candidate for the 1804 election, they dropped Burr.

No matter the interpretation of Burr's conduct during the election of 1800, its result was undeniable. Unlike his two predecessors as vice president, Burr would not use that office as a stepping-stone to the presidency. His path would lead through very different country.

3

The Duel

New York/New Jersey
Summer 1804

T hree young men found Vice President Burr on the couch in his New York mansion, sleeping deeply in the muggy air of midsummer 1804. Dawn was still two hours away. The intruders roused Burr and hurried him into black pantaloons, a dark silk coat, and half-boots.[1]

The three were members of the vice president's inner circle, what his opponents sneeringly called his "little band." William Van Ness, a lawyer of talent, was there to serve as Burr's second in a duel that morning. John Swartwout, the federal marshal for New York City, always stood with Burr. The third man was a printer and another Burr protégé.

At five o'clock a boat would meet Burr and Van Ness at the nearby Hudson River shore. It would carry them across the river to New Jersey and three miles north, to the dueling grounds at Weehawken. Burr was scheduled to fight a duel with pistols that morning, July 11, 1804, against Alexander Hamilton.

The dawn journey to Weehawken was a rite of passage for New York's political leaders. There they engaged in a savage ritual. Six years before,

Burr faced off on that ground against Hamilton's brother-in-law. Burr's shot missed that day, while his adversary's bullet passed through Burr's coat. Burr's opponent then apologized for the remarks that prompted the encounter, ending it without injury. Other journeys to Weehawken, however, brought bloodshed.

In 1802, John Swartwout fought an epic duel against New York senator DeWitt Clinton, nephew and political heir to George Clinton and a bitter rival to Burr. Standing ten paces apart, the two combatants exchanged five rounds of fire. After three rounds, Clinton began to find the range, wounding Swartwout in the left leg on each of his next two shots. Swartwout, described as a blond giant, demanded a sixth round. Declining to blaze away again at a man whose aim had been none too good before being wounded twice, Clinton muttered that he only wished he had been shooting at Burr, adding, "I will meet him when he pleases."[2]

The specter of Weehawken was never far from New York politics. In 1803, Swartwout's brother squared off there against the man who had been Clinton's second in the earlier duel. A few months later Senator Jonathan Dayton of New Jersey, Burr's friend since boyhood, brought Clinton to the brink of a duel. Tacitly acknowledging Dayton's reputation as a marksman, Clinton ducked that encounter.[3]

Alexander Hamilton was no stranger to "affairs of honor" under the *code duello*. Eleven times he had participated in the challenges and byplay that often led to duels, yet all of Hamilton's affairs had ended before the antagonists took up pistols. Less than three years before, his eldest son was not so fortunate. The nineteen-year-old Philip Hamilton received a mortal wound in a Weehawken duel caused by his own political remarks.[4]

Despite the prospect of wounding or death, Burr was calm that morning. A duelist had to be fatalistic. Some died. More survived. Fate would decide that. What mattered was not the outcome but how he conducted himself. As one historian has explained, "duels were demonstrations of manner, not marksmanship; they were intricate games of dare and counter-dare, ritualized displays of bravery, military prowess, and, above all, willingness to sacrifice one's life for one's honor. Each man's response to the threat of gunplay bore far more meaning than the exchange of fire itself." At his earlier duel, Burr's self-possession had amazed his second, who forgot to bring the grease needed to load Burr's pistol. As the second struggled to load the ball, which stuck partway down the gun barrel, Burr called out not to worry: If he missed his opponent "then he would hit him the next shot."[5]

Burr spent the night before the Hamilton duel alone but for his three black slaves. He wrote out his will, along with farewell letters to his daughter, Theodosia, then only twenty-one, and to her husband. His letters addressed awkward matters. He asked Theodosia to burn correspondence he had tied with a red string, along with any others that "if by accident made public, would injure any person." He directed a few specific gifts, including a city lot and fifty dollars for his slave Peggy. Theodosia should dispose of the other slaves as she saw fit. Burr wrote that his assets would cover his debts, a wishful assertion from a man whose rich tastes left him chronically, sometimes desperately, in debt. Then there was nothing left but the emotion of leave-taking from those he cared for most.

"I am indebted to you," he wrote to Theodosia, "for a very great portion of the happiness which I have enjoyed in this life. You have completely satisfied all that my heart and affections had hoped or even wished." Yet Burr could not resist a last bit of parental exhortation:

> With a little more perseverance, determination, and industry, you will obtain all that my ambition or vanity had fondly imagined. Let your son [Aaron Burr Alston] have occasion to be proud that he had a mother.

His message to his son-in-law, Joseph Alston, was similar: "I commit to you all that is most dear to me—my reputation and my daughter." He urged Alston to "stimulate and aid Theodosia in the cultivation of her mind. It is indispensable to her happiness and essential to yours . . . [and] of the utmost importance to your son." He recommended that she study Latin, English composition, and natural philosophy.[6]

For his deadly appointment with Hamilton, Burr followed the duelist's practice of wearing loose clothes; perhaps an opponent would shoot at fabric rather than flesh and bone. He avoided breakfast, fearing infection in the event of a belly wound. Van Ness, the second, had hired the boat to pick them up near Burr's mansion.[7] The four men strode to the river in the dark, but only Burr and Van Ness climbed in. Because dueling was illegal, prudence required that the smallest possible number of people view the contest. Burr and Van Ness carried no weapons; Hamilton was bringing the pistols.

The long ride across the river was punctuated by the rhythmic creaks of oarlocks and the lapping of water. Conversation was at a minimum. Though the boatmen surely knew the purpose of the journey, they would never acknowledge it. As the boat breasted the waters, the New Jersey forests took shape in the slow morning light. Burr had time to reflect on the path that had led him to this boat ride. The nation's second highest official and a prominent leader of the opposition were about to try to kill each other. The reasons were convoluted.

By 1804, the careers of both Hamilton and Burr were wilting. Jefferson's Republicans were routing the Federalists in most elections, and Hamilton was losing influence even within his own weakened party. Burr was faring little better. Jefferson had arranged for New York governor George Clinton to take Burr's place on the Republican ticket for the fall election. To avoid the political obscurity to which Jefferson was driving him, Burr ran in the spring of 1804 for Clinton's job as governor. Once more Hamilton mounted the ramparts against Burr. He denounced Burr for having no principles and insisted that no party could trust him.[8]

At the end of April 1804, New York voters delivered a crushing blow. Burr did not merely lose the election; he lost by the widest margin in New York's brief history, and he lost to a mediocrity, Morgan Lewis. The defeat hit hard. Jefferson had blocked Burr at the national level. Now Burr was stymied in New York politics. Burr's thinking took a grim and resentful turn. Shortly after the defeat, he told a friend that "he was determined to call out the first man of any respectability [who was] concerned in the infamous publications concerning him."[9]

"Infamous publications" had been a staple of Burr's public life. He attracted political billingsgate from many directions, not only from Hamilton. Many of these slurs were tinged with sexual and racial innuendo. Publications accused him of consorting with "nigger wenches" and hosting a "nigger ball" in his New York mansion. One Jefferson-supported slanderer, James Cheetham, attacked Burr violently in the columns of his *New York American Citizen*, supplementing those salvos with long pamphlets that called Burr a liar, a cheat, a usurper, and a danger to the nation. Cheetham compared Burr's mind to "Pandora's box, from whence proceed jealousy, hatred, revenge, desperation, and all the wicked passions that torment and perplex mankind."[10]

Burr mostly avoided political mudslinging. As one friend wrote, "I never knew Colonel Burr to speak ill of any man, and he had a right to expect a different treatment from what he experienced." Yet Burr was not above responding indirectly. William Van Ness, his second for that morning's duel, wrote a powerful rejoinder to Cheetham that achieved wide circulation. Van Ness's tract sold more copies than any pamphlet since Tom Paine's *Common Sense* almost thirty years earlier.[11]

Burr learned of a letter published in an Albany newspaper just before the voting for governor had started that April. According to the letter, Hamilton had told a political meeting that Burr was a dangerous man who should not be trusted with the governor's office. It was hardly the worst thing Hamilton ever said about Burr. But the letter continued: Hamilton also claimed he could offer a "still more despicable" opinion of Burr. Those three words—"still more despicable"—represented a personal attack, implying perversity or worse. They denigrated Burr's personal honor. He would not let them pass.[12]

In a curt note to Hamilton, Burr demanded "a prompt and unqualified acknowledgment or denial" of the Albany newspaper report. Burr had little reason to expect that his note would lead to a duel. On two previous occasions he had objected to statements by Hamilton; each time the other man had withdrawn the challenged remark. Van Ness delivered Burr's demand on June 18.

Hamilton's reply, provided two days later, was a nitpicking stall. Did the Albany report, Hamilton asked, state that he held a "despicable" opinion or a "still more despicable" one? And to whom did the report say Hamilton delivered this opinion, whatever it was? With more flourish than Burr's mood could endure, Hamilton added, " 'Tis evident, that the phrase 'still more despicable' admits of infinite shades, from very light to very dark. How am I to judge of the degree intended?" Hamilton protested that he could not answer for the "inferences, which may be drawn by others, from whatever I may have said of a political opponent in the course of a fifteen years competition."[13] In short, after a decade and a half of slandering Burr, how could Hamilton be expected to recall what he had said on a particular occasion, or what others might think he said?

Hamilton's note fed Burr's anger. In a concise response, Burr wrote that "the common sense of mankind affixes to the epithet ['despicable'] . . . the idea of dishonor: it has been publicly applied to me under the sanction of your name." Anyone so aggrieved, he continued, cared not whether the phrase was used "according to syntax and with grammatical accuracy." He concluded ominously: "Your letter has furnished me with new reasons for requiring a definite reply."[14]

The rituals of the *code duello* consumed twenty more days. To serve as his second, Hamilton recruited Nathaniel Pendleton, a fellow army veteran and lawyer. Pendleton and Van Ness, as seconds, labored manfully to bridge the chasm between their principals. They met several times. They drafted possible clarifying statements by Hamilton. They exchanged seven more writings. Nothing worked. The die had been cast after the first three notes. Burr was implacable; Hamilton would not apologize.

In several notes prepared before the duel, Hamilton expressed a haunted sense that he was responsible for the impending combat. After all, he had denounced Burr's character for many years. Writing on the eve of the encounter, he admitted his role in blackening Burr's reputation:

> My animadversions on the political principles, character, and views of Colonel Burr have been extremely severe; and, on different occasions, I, in common with many others, have made very unfavorable criticisms on particular instances of the private conduct of this gentleman.[15]

Because Burr had no doubt heard of Hamilton's statements "which bore very hard upon him . . . he may have supposed himself under a necessity of acting as he has done." In addition to his confession that "I may have injured Col. Burr, however convinced myself that my opinions and declarations have been well founded," Hamilton wrote words that have spawned two centuries of controversy: "I have resolved . . . to reserve and throw away my first fire, and I have thoughts even of reserving my second fire—and thus giving a double opportunity to Col. Burr to pause and to reflect."[16]

Burr left no comparable confessional. He felt entirely justified in demanding Hamilton's apology or his presence on the field of honor. Indeed, no record has emerged that Burr ever passed a harsh remark about Hamilton before their duel.

Burr and Van Ness arrived at Weehawken first, as the seconds had agreed. The morning was growing bright. Yellow sunlight streamed across the water and lit up the New Jersey shore. The two men climbed a steep slope to the dueling ground, a narrow shelf of land halfway up the bluff. Because the site could not be reached from the top of the bluff, it was an ideal spot for warring gentlemen to settle their differences without disturbance from peace officers. The boatmen remained at the river's edge, looking out over the river lest they become witnesses to a crime.

Burr and Van Ness cleared debris from the site while waiting for Hamilton and his second, Pendleton, who arrived with a portmanteau containing two pistols. A doctor remained with Hamilton's boat. He would treat any wounded duelist.

With their principals standing silently to the side, Pendleton and Van Ness implemented the arrangements they had worked out. They walked off ten paces between the shooters, then cast lots to decide which man would have first choice of position. Pendleton, on behalf of Hamilton, won. Then they cast lots to see which of the seconds would call out the instructions for the duel. Pendleton won again.

The mood was both sober and tense. The encounter involved no burst of homicidal rage, no drunken eruption. Rather, it was a long-considered opportunity for each man to kill the other and to face his own death. Powerful feelings had to surge through each of them, beginning with the prospect of leaving behind the sweetness of life. Both were vital, healthy men. Burr was forty-eight, Hamilton forty-nine. Hamilton had a wife and seven children between the ages of two and twenty. Burr had his cherished Theodosia. Each had served at the highest levels of the government and had won many honors. Despite low political fortunes at the moment, the future could hold further distinctions and opportunities. Moreover, this was no face-off between strangers. They had known each other through most of their adulthood. Hamilton had been a guest in Burr's home.

Each had sound reason to fear the other that morning. During the Revolution, both showed bravery bordering on recklessness. Each thought of himself as a soldier and was ordinarily addressed by a military title: "General Hamilton" and "Colonel Burr." Both had handled firearms all their lives. Burr had stood his ground in his earlier duel with Hamilton's brother-in-law, while only a fool would doubt Hamilton's fortitude.

Yet neither man flinched. On that morning, honor was more than a word or an idea. Each viewed the duel as a chance to demonstrate his worth as a leader by showing courage in the face of death. He had to be steadfast, calm, and determined. By the accounts of the three men who survived, both met that test.

Each second began to load a pistol with powder and a one-ounce lead ball, doing so in view of the other. These same pistols had been used in the duel between Burr and Hamilton's brother-in-law, then again in the fatal duel fought by Hamilton's eldest son, Philip. The pistols had smoothbore barrels, reducing their accuracy. They were heavy, weighing several pounds apiece, so were not easy to handle. They also had a "hair trigger" feature to facilitate quick firing, though there is no evidence that either duelist activated it.

Exercising his choice of position, Pendleton placed Hamilton at a spot that looked toward the rising sun, presumably hoping that the light would outline Burr's body and improve Hamilton's aim. Hamilton complained. Hefting his pistol and aiming it this way and that, he fumbled for his spectacles in his coat pocket, asking the pardon of the other gentlemen. The light, he explained as he put on his glasses, made them necessary. While Hamilton pursued these preparations, evidently designed to assure a deadly outcome for the vice president, Burr did not speak.

Both men struck the duelist's stance. To present the smallest possible target, each turned sideways, right foot toward his opponent. Though both were slim, they pulled in their stomachs to reduce their profiles. Each used his right leg to shield the left, raised his right shoulder to shelter his face.

Even the pistols were used for defense, raised to a position where wood and metal partially shielded vital organs.

Pendleton asked if they were ready. Both said they were. Pendleton called out the signal to begin: "Present!"

This nineteenth-century drawing of the Burr-Hamilton duel, which gained great popularity, implausibly portrays Hamilton clutching his head after being shot in the side.

Both guns fired, seconds apart. Hamilton fell. Burr swayed slightly. As the noise subsided and the gunsmoke began to dissipate, Burr took a step toward his fallen adversary. Both seconds thought Burr's movement was "expressive of regret," but Van Ness intercepted him. No duelist could linger on the field. The risk of arrest was too great. Van Ness led him down to the waiting boat, using an umbrella to cover Burr's face. At the boat, Burr tried to return to the dueling ground, saying, "I must go and speak with him." Van Ness insisted that they depart before the doctor and Hamilton's boatmen could see him. They shoved off.[17]

When the doctor arrived on the ledge, Hamilton told him that the wound was a mortal one, then passed out. The heavy pistol ball had entered his torso above his right hip, tearing through soft and vital tissues, fracturing a rib and lodging in his spine. It would likely be a fatal wound today; with the rudimentary medical tools of 1804, there was no hope. Pendleton, the doctor, and the boatmen returned Hamilton to New York. Unwilling to carry him far, they brought the dying man to the riverside home of a friend. For more than a day, Hamilton endured agonizing pain, his wife by his side. Because he had been shot in a duel, two ministers refused to give him Holy Communion. To overcome the objection, Hamilton insisted that he opposed the practice of dueling and had met Burr "with a fixed resolution to do him no harm." The second minister then agreed to apply the rites. Surrounded by friends and family members, Hamilton died at two o'clock on the afternoon of July 12, thirty-one hours after the duel.

Back in his Richmond Hill home, near the current intersection of Charlton and Varick Streets in Greenwich Village, Burr fretted. He wrote to the doctor, asking "of the present state of Gen. H. and of the hopes which are entertained of his recovery." Shortly thereafter Burr learned of Hamilton's death. Public sentiment instantly sided with the man who fell. Next day Burr grumbled to his son-in-law about the "malignant federalists or tories, and the imbittered Clintonians," who had joined "in endeavouring to excite public sympathy in [Hamilton's] favor and indignation against his antagonist [Burr]." To Van Ness, Burr complained that "the most abominable falsehoods are current and have issued from the house in which [Hamilton] now lies." [18]

To Burr's dismay, the duel began Hamilton's swift apotheosis. The *New York Evening Post*, which Hamilton had sponsored, despaired of the "gloom that overspreads every countenance" due to his death. To mourn his passing, it carried heavy black borders between its columns for days. Newspapers compared Hamilton to Demosthenes, Alexander the Great, Cicero, Pericles, Aristides, Achilles, and Cato, as well as Kings Francis I and Henry IV of France. [19]

Following a city council directive, all New York halted for Hamilton's funeral on July 15. The procession included a military escort and band, the city's physicians and lawyers, representatives of foreign governments, the chamber of commerce and bankers, the faculty and students of Columbia College, and many others. Hamilton's hat and sword rested on the coffin.

His horse followed with Hamilton's boots reversed in the stirrups, led by two black servants with white turbans. New Yorkers watched from doorways, windows, and rooftops, with a preponderance (according to the *Post*) of "weeping females."[20]

Burr found himself portrayed as a murderer, not as the victor in a contest of honor. Cheetham of the *New York American Citizen,* having assaulted Hamilton viciously while alive, now painted him as a "victim to a wicked system of deadly hostility, planned by Mr. Burr and his friends and rigidly carried into execution." Cheetham's theme was that Burr had laid a trap for Hamilton and then shot him down in cold blood. In the columns of Cheetham's newspaper, Hamilton was not a lifelong slanderer who stood at ten paces' length with a loaded pistol and the apparent intent to kill his rival. Rather, Hamilton was a pacific Christian gentleman, lured to his doom like a lamb to the slaughter.

This version of the event received apparent support when the seconds (Van Ness and Pendleton) released the preduel correspondence between Hamilton and Burr, along with their own joint narrative. Because Burr was the duel's instigator, he seemed the more murderous of the two.[21]

Most damaging, though, was the revelation that Hamilton had pledged not to shoot at Burr. He had stated that intention to Pendleton (his second), to another friend, and in a memorandum prepared in the days before the duel. In his farewell letter to his wife, Hamilton repeated the sentiment:

> The scruples of a Christian have determined me to expose my own life to any extent rather than subject myself to the guilt of taking the life of another. This must increase my hazards and redoubles my pangs for you. But you had rather I should die innocent than live guilty. Heaven can preserve me and I humbly hope will.[22]

Hamilton's motives for this course were tangled. His desire to avoid taking Burr's life may have been genuine, but that outcome could easily have been achieved by not accepting Burr's challenge. Many prominent Americans of the era—including George Washington, Benjamin Franklin, and Thomas Jefferson—condemned duels and refused to participate in them.[23] Anticipating the objection that he could have declined to duel, Hamilton protested that he could not do so without losing the "ability to be in future useful." He feared that "public prejudice" would view him as dishonorable if he did not face Burr.

Only speculation, most of it frankly psychological, can begin to explain Hamilton's fear of the consequences of refusing a duel, a fear not shared by Washington, Franklin, or Jefferson. Hamilton's prideful personality seems central, along with his never-quelled ambition for military honor. Declining a duel might carry a taint of cowardice that could cripple his hope to lead an American army. Another factor may have been his humble beginnings as a child of unmarried parents on the island of St. Kitts in the Caribbean, which made him highly sensitive about his honor. Or Hamilton could have chosen the dueling ground to expiate his sense of guilt for maligning Burr, a man who never returned Hamilton's rhetorical fire.[24]

A more cynical interpretation would portray Hamilton as setting—at tremendous risk to himself—a clever trap. If Burr missed his first shot while Hamilton threw his away, then Burr would lose inestimable face. He would be revealed as venal enough to fire at a defenseless man, yet so inept as to miss him. If Burr then abandoned the duel, his quarrel with Hamilton would seem not all that consequential. Should Burr insist on a second round of fire, Hamilton had not ruled out using his second shot. Finally, if Burr should succeed in hitting Hamilton with his first shot, his achievement would only be that of shooting an innocent.

With the disclosure of Hamilton's stated intention not to shoot at Burr, public opinion, already strongly favoring the loser, turned viciously against Burr. More details emerged when the seconds publicly disagreed on key points surrounding the duel. None seemed to help Burr's reputation.

In their initial, joint statement, the seconds attempted to finesse their disagreements. "[B]oth of the parties took aim and fired in succession," they wrote. "The intervening time is not expressed as the seconds do not precisely agree on that point." They agreed that both duelists "took aim," so Hamilton definitely raised his pistol into position to fire. They also agreed that two shots were fired "within a few seconds of each other," which was later confirmed by the boatmen and the doctor.[25] But the joint statement did not say who fired first, or at what.

A week later, Pendleton issued a statement exploring their disagreements.

He wrote that he held "the confident opinion that General Hamilton did not fire first—and that he did not fire at all at Col. Burr." By Pendleton's account, Hamilton must have pulled his trigger in some involuntary muscle response to the bullet crashing into his body. Van Ness, he admitted, "seemed equally confident in the opinion that Gen. H did fire first—and of course that it must have been at his antagonist."

In addition, Pendleton had done some investigative work. On the day after the shooting, he and a friend crossed the river to search for evidence of the ball fired by Hamilton. According to Pendleton, they found a hole in a tree limb that hung about twelve feet off the ground, at a point four feet wide of the line between the duelists. Showing no regard for preserving the integrity of a crime scene, Pendleton brought the tree limb back to New York. If Hamilton's shot truly hit that limb in that position—and if the hole had not been left by some earlier duelist's errant shot—Burr had been in no danger.

Van Ness, Burr's second, issued his own statement, describing in detail Hamilton's actions: sighting down his pistol, examining the daylight, and fishing out his spectacles. Those actions were contrary to Hamilton's professed desire to throw away his shot—and they surely concealed from Burr any such intent. Indeed, they were calculated to place Burr in imminent dread. Van Ness also insisted that both parties "took aim" and that Hamilton fired first. Van Ness thought Burr had been struck because of "a slight motion in his person." Burr later explained that he had lost his balance when a stone slid under his foot. Another interpretation would be that the legendarily cool Burr had flinched. Burr then waited "five or six seconds," according to Van Ness, for the smoke to clear. Then he fired.[26]

In a private letter, Burr agreed with Van Ness's account, including Hamilton's elaborate testing of the light, aiming of his pistol, and donning of his spectacles. Hamilton, he insisted, "took aim at his adversary and fired very promptly." As for Hamilton's preduel pledges that he would throw away his shot, Burr dismissed them as "contemptible, if true."[27]

The accounts by the seconds provided fodder for those who wished to paint Burr as a pitiless executioner. Pendleton's version portrayed Burr as rushing to get the first shot in and annihilate his opponent. Ironically, Van Ness's version placed Burr in a worse light. After Hamilton fired, according to Van Ness, Burr waited for the smoke to clear, sighted down his barrel at a man who could only stand and face his doom, and pulled the trigger. That Burr thought Hamilton had just tried to kill him does little to alter the bloodthirsty texture of that moment.

The chronic debate over the duel often neglects the key point of agreement in the accounts of both seconds and Burr: that the vice president had no reason to think Hamilton either was intending to, or did, throw away his shot. Hamilton said nothing to that effect on the dueling ground. He tested his pistol as they took their places, complained about the light, and employed spectacles to sharpen his vision. Then, on command, he aimed his pistol. According to Hamilton's second, Burr shot first. If true, that means that Burr fired without seeing any indication that Hamilton had fired off to the side. According to Burr's second, Hamilton shot first but betrayed no evidence of having thrown the shot away. So according to both seconds, Burr fired at Hamilton in the belief that his adversary had walked out on the dueling ground in order to exercise the homicidal opportunities of the *code duello*.

Under that code, what else was Burr supposed to do?

Hamilton was dead, and the vice president was a prisoner in his own home. Public feeling against him ran high. The *Charleston Courier* wrote that where his heart should be, Burr had only "cinders raked from the fires of hell." John Quincy Adams, then a senator from Massachusetts, wrote his wife from Washington that social conversation focused only on the duel. Adams found Burr's conduct reprehensible, concluding prissily that "his principal aim appears to have been to make a display of indifference and unconcern."[28]

Two days after the duel, and one day after Hamilton died, the New York coroner's jury began a formal inquiry. Burr, taking a cold view of his prospects, made plans to leave town. He wrote his son-in-law that the reaction to the duel "has driven me into a sort of exile, and may terminate in an actual and permanent ostracism." Burr expected the worst from his New York enemies, principally the Clintons, even though they had despised Hamilton. The coroner's jury would succumb to the Clintons' pressure, Burr predicted, and seek a murder inquest: "Upon this a warrant will issue to apprehend me, and, if I should be taken, no bail would probably be allowed." He fumed to a friend that New York courts had no jurisdiction over the duel, which took place in New Jersey.[29]

Burr defended his actions in another letter. "It is too well known," he wrote, that Hamilton "had long indulged himself in illiberal freedom with my character." Burr had never publicly disclosed the earlier occasions when Hamilton withdrew remarks to which Burr had objected, "always hoping that the generosity of my conduct would have had some influence on his." But Hamilton had continued to malign Burr, which left the vice president feeling "constantly deceived." According to Burr: "It is the opinion of all considerate men here that my only fault has been in bearing so much and so long."[30] Nevertheless, Burr decided to flee New York.

With his slave Peter and the steadfast federal marshal, John Swartwout, Burr again took to the Hudson River on the evening of Saturday, July 21. A boat carried the trio across New York's upper bay, all the way around Staten Island. They brought little luggage.[31]

By morning they landed at Perth Amboy on the Jersey shore. Burr's immediate destination was the Pleasant View estate of Commodore Thomas Truxtun, which overlooked Raritan Bay. Burr's decision to head for Truxtun's home was a considered one. The vice president could have landed near dozens of friendly homes in New Jersey. He had grown up in nearby Elizabethtown (now Elizabeth) and remained close to a variety of Ogdens and Daytons and Burr relations throughout the area. Yet Burr chose to travel up the poplar-lined drive of an American naval hero, one who admired Burr and bore a grudge against the government. Just ten days after the duel, Burr's thoughts already were turning to military operations; indeed, six months hence he would seek out Truxtun with proposals for an astonishing expedition.

As commander of a frigate in the American navy, Truxtun had won bloody victories over French warships during John Adams's undeclared war with France in 1798 and 1799. With a prickly self-regard common to winning captains, Truxtun had argued with his superiors and colleagues, then sought political aid from his friend, Vice President Burr, writing that he looked forward to seeing Burr succeed Jefferson as president. But Burr, having little influence in the Jefferson administration, had not been able to help his friend. By 1802, Truxtun was out of the navy.[32]

News of the duel shocked Truxtun, who also had been friendly with Hamilton. Nevertheless, he welcomed the fugitive, giving him breakfast on July 22. Burr said nothing about any plan or scheme he might be nursing. It was too early for that. Also, Burr could not linger in New Jersey, since that state also might bring murder charges against him. By the next morning Burr was on his way.[33]

In two days he reached Philadelphia, where he was relatively safe from arrest. Matters continued to boil back in New York. A Burr loyalist and one of the boatmen from the morning of the duel refused to testify before the coroner's jury; both were jailed. John Swartwout and Van Ness went into hiding. The editor of the Burr-sponsored *New York Morning Chronicle* left the city.[34] On August 2, the coroner's jury found that Burr had murdered Hamilton "with malice aforethought," and that Van Ness and Pendleton aided and abetted him.[35] Twelve days later Burr also was charged with violating New York's statute against dueling.

The moment was a singular one. The vice president of the United States, charged with murder, was on the run. His closest associates were concealed, in flight, or imprisoned. Burr's concern for his daughter in South Carolina shines through a string of notes dashed off during tense days and nights. He tried to reassure Theodosia that the worst was over. "The ferment has subsided," Burr wrote, "and public opinion begins to take its proper course." When New York lodged its criminal charges, he wrote, "Have no anxiety about the issue of this business." He assured her he was safe. After the duel, he wrote with a small swagger, "Those who wish me dead prefer to keep at a very respectful distance."[36]

Some of Burr's true feelings leaked out in his letters. While still in New York, he had continued a flirtation with a woman he referred to as "La G." He expressed gratitude that she still extended her sympathy to him. That Burr's cares weighed on him emerges in a request for consideration he made to Theodosia: "You must not complain or find fault if I omit to answer [your letters], or even to write. Don't let me have the idea that you are dissatisfied with me a moment. I can't just now endure it."[37]

Burr even attempted a few jaunty poses, confiding to Theodosia about another *amour* ("Celeste seems more pliant") and advising, "If any male friend of yours should be dying of ennui, recommend to him to engage in a duel and courtship at the same time." His jests, though, had a hollow quality.[38]

Not even to Theodosia did Burr reveal his inner thoughts. During quiet moments while trapped in his New York mansion, or crossing the bay to New Jersey, or on the road to Philadelphia, he worked feverishly on the challenges before him. He had to avoid the legal processes of New York and New Jersey (where murder charges would be lodged against him in October).[39] He also would continue to defend his personal honor. That was why he had fought the duel with Hamilton.

But there was more on Burr's mind. What was he to do now? Should he abandon all hope of public distinction, of glory and power? With public feeling so strongly against him, what sort of future could he expect?

Burr did not grow gloomy or sink into self-criticism. Rather, this "matter-of-fact" man resolutely dreamt of still doing great things. This was not to be the end of Aaron Burr's story. As a young man, Burr wrote to a friend that for him, "the moment of indecision [is] the moment of completest anguish," adding, "when our resolutions are taken with determined firmness, they engross the mind and close the void of misery." He advised Theodosia that "occupation will infallibly expel the fiend ennui."[40] In those days after the Hamilton duel, Burr experienced moments of great anguish, but he also resolved on his future course.

He would not be brought low by Jefferson or Hamilton or the Clintons. He would survive this hurricane of political disappointments and public opprobrium. He was a man of stature and accomplishment. He had won the vice presidency and barely missed becoming president. Burr believed in his core that he had not deserved ill treatment at the hands of Jefferson and the Clintons, and that his challenge to Hamilton had been justified. Indeed, he thought he had been wronged by Jefferson, wronged by the Clintons, wronged by Hamilton, and now was wronged by the jackals who pursued him.

Burr resolved to rise again. He knew the great men of America and had taken their measure. Never humble, he could see no reason why he should not reach again for the highest distinctions. He had suffered setbacks, to be sure, but they were the work of enemies, not the result of his own failings. Those setbacks meant that the more conventional routes to power and honor might be barred to him. Something unconventional, something daring, might be necessary. But convention was not such a powerful force in a new nation like the United States; it was even weaker in frontier areas, especially on the western side of the Appalachian Mountains. Burr's talents were great and his daring—that part of his character that had frightened Hamilton the most—was undiminished.

4

On the Frontier

Philadelphia to Spanish Florida and Back
August–October, 1804

I
n early August, with the Hamilton duel only three weeks behind him, the vice president sent an emissary to the British minister in Philadelphia. Burr's message was both astonishing and traitorous.

Burr's representative was Colonel Charles Williamson, a Scot who served in the British army in the final days of the Revolutionary War. Williamson later took an American wife and became an American citizen but retained connections to powerful Britons. He traveled through the Balkans, Russia, and Turkey on errands for the crown.

Williamson met Burr while serving as agent for English owners of a million acres of land in upstate New York. Their friendship warmed when they served together in the New York assembly. Burr later would say his intimacy with Williamson was "such as had I with no other man living, and such as it is utterly improbable I should ever have with any one again." For two years, Williamson was Burr's tenant in New York City, and he sought Burr's advice when he wished to divorce his wife.[1]

Like Burr, Williamson had a taste for schemes of conquest. In 1803, the Scot proposed an invasion of Spain's American colonies with a force of British expatriates. He even recruited officers and volunteers for the venture.[2] Appreciating Williamson's boldness and his access to high British officials, Burr shared with him secret designs and ambitions.

In August of 1804, Williamson presented some of those secret designs to the British minister to the United States, Anthony Merry. According to Merry, Williamson began with a startling opening sally: that Burr might resign as vice president and was willing to assist the British government in any enterprise it might contemplate in North America. The second-ranking official in the American government was offering his services to a foreign power. Yet Burr and Williamson went farther, specifying that Burr's services might be "particularly" useful "in endeavoring to effect a separation of the Western part of the United States from that which lies between the Atlantic and the mountains." In other words, Burr proposed to assist in the dismemberment of his own country. The outrageous nature of the proposal reflected Burr's desperate situation, on the run from the law, his political career in tatters. With Hamilton barely three weeks in the ground, Burr seemed to be fulfilling his rival's most dire warnings about him.

In reporting to his masters in London, Merry took a judicious tone. He struck a note of caution about "the profligacy of Mr. Burr's character" and explained that Williamson was coming to England to present the project directly to the government. Yet Merry added that because of the "talents and activity he still possesses," the vice president might provide good service. Burr, he wrote, "still preserves connections with some people of influence, added to his great ambition and spirit of revenge against the present administration."[3]

Dividing the United States was not an outlandish notion in the summer of 1804. Only a few months before, leading New England Federalists had tried to enlist Burr's support for the secession of New England, New York, and New Jersey. Many New Englanders were bitter about the "Virginia Dynasty" that seemed to hold the government in thrall. First Washington was president. Now Jefferson. Secretary of State James Madison was visibly awaiting his turn. Even the nation's capital had been moved south to the banks of the Potomac River. New England merchants yearned for strong ties to Britain, with its vibrant economy and powerful navy, but the Virginia aristocrats favored France and its terrifying revolution. And the Republican party was growing stronger, even making inroads in New England. "If Federalism is crumbling away in New England," a Massachusetts senator wrote, "there is no time to be lost"; New England should secede. If New York and New Jersey also seceded, so much the better. One Federalist leader foresaw Burr, as governor of New York, leading a northern confederacy. Another hoped that with Burr's election as governor, New York "may be united with the northern states in the project of separation."[4]

In a meeting with two leading Federalists in early April 1804, a few weeks before New Yorkers voted on their next governor, Burr had poured kerosene on the flames of disunion. "The northern states must be governed by Virginia," he pronounced, "or govern Virginia." But Burr did not squarely endorse secession, exercising his politician's knack for being agreeable without quite agreeing. On a similar occasion, a New Hampshire senator told Burr that he expected the nation to break in two and carefully recorded the vice president's response:

> On this subject, Mr. Burr conversed very freely; and the impression made on my mind was, that he not only thought such an event should take place, but that it was necessary that it should. To that opinion I was myself then a convert. Yet, on returning to my lodgings, after critically analyzing his words, there was nothing in them that necessarily implied his approbation of [our] observations. Perhaps no man's language was ever so apparently explicit, and, at the same time, so covert and indefinite.[5]

Burr's artful conversation mattered little after New York's voters rejected him in late April. The New England separatist movement fizzled, but the idea of secession lingered through the nation, and in Burr's mind.[6]

In early August, though, what he most needed was to retire from the public eye. Being vice president imposed few limits on his freedom of movement; he had no official duties until the Senate convened in November, when he would preside over its sessions. In time, the passions unleashed by Hamilton's death should ebb. A sympathetic message arrived from Senator Pierce Butler of South Carolina, inviting Burr to Butler's plantation on

Georgia's Atlantic coast. There, thirty miles north of Spanish Florida, Burr would be far from the arrest warrants of New York.[7] He could stop at his daughter's home in South Carolina, nurse his wounds in her loving company, and dote on his grandson, Aaron Burr Alston, then two years old. He might travel to the border with Spanish Florida, or into Florida itself. That might be a worthy adventure.

In mid-August, as New York was indicting him for murdering Hamilton, Burr boarded a southbound ship on the Delaware River.[8] Before embarking, he spoke confidentially with Charles Williamson, who was leaving for London to present Burr's proposals to divide the United States. Williamson planned to begin with his friend the First Lord of the Admiralty. He hoped also to speak with Prime Minister William Pitt. Burr and Williamson spoke of further ventures on the country's southern frontier.[9]

Arriving at Butler's estate on the Georgia coast by the end of August, Burr reveled in his wealthy host's generosity. Six slaves looked after the vice president and his traveling companion, twenty-one-year-old Sam Swartwout, younger brother of New York's federal marshal. Butler's domain offered fine wines along with ample game, fish, and fruits. Burr toured the countryside. He examined the ruins of Georgia's first settlement, built by British convicts who received a second chance in the wilderness, the sort of second chance that Burr needed. Dryly, he described the landscape as presenting "no scenes for a painter." When his hunting expeditions produced no crocodile meat, he offered a reward for it. A famously light eater, Burr nonetheless promised to eat crocodile "dressed in soup, fricasees, and steaks." [10]

Burr kept his gaze fixed on sparsely populated Florida, which Spain had claimed in the sixteenth century but then neglected for two centuries. Great Britain acquired the province in 1763 at the end of the French and Indian War, only to return it to Spain twenty years later. East Florida, which included most of the current state of Florida, had only about five thousand non-Indian residents, mostly Spanish.[11] West Florida stretched along the Gulf Coast from the Perdido River to Baton Rouge on the Mississippi, covering what is now coastal Alabama and Mississippi, plus southeastern Louisiana. Filled with British loyalists who fled the American Revolution, West Florida had an Anglo-American feel. Many Americans coveted "the Floridas" in 1804.[12]

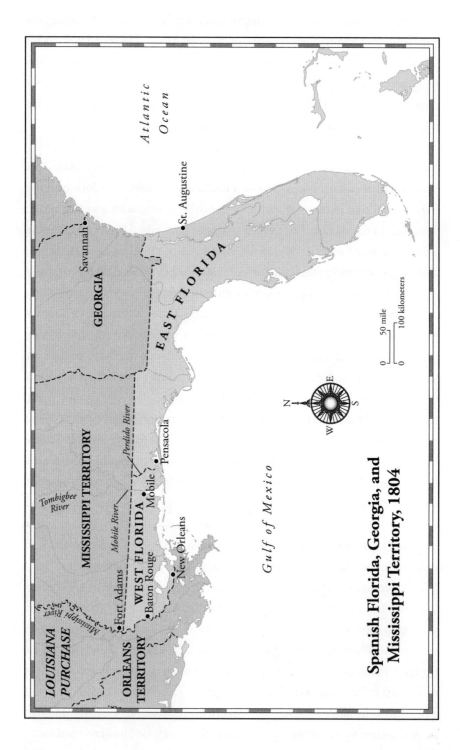

Spanish Florida, Georgia, and
Mississippi Territory, 1804

Burr's political adversaries assumed that his journey involved a scheme for his own advancement. When word reached New York that the vice president was in Georgia, a local newspaper speculated that he intended to become "lieutenant general" of Florida. Another wondered whether Burr meant to "raise rebellion in this quarter." [13]

After Burr had spent ten days in Butler's baronial isolation, a mighty hurricane howled into the coast, flooding the house where Burr was staying, tearing off its porch and toppling a chimney. During the worst of it, Burr huddled in a nearby storehouse with the other plantation residents. Surging tides drowned nineteen of Butler's slaves and washed out his rice crop. [14]

Despite the devastation, Burr wanted a closer look at Florida. The roads, however, were a nightmare. "Every bridge and causeway is destroyed," Burr wrote, "and the road so filled with fallen trees as to be utterly impassable." Somehow Burr acquired a boat and set off for Florida in a journey he called "very rapid: a mere flight." But when his progress was barred by "the effects of the late tempest," Burr turned back near what is currently Jacksonville. His only surviving description of Spanish territory was that "It is a fact that the Spanish ladies smoke segars," which lovers shared "as a mark of great kindness." [15]

Burr returned to Butler's estate, but did not linger, pressing north in his boat. He met another storm in Savannah in early October, reporting that the hurricane "drowned a few negroes, unroofed a few houses, and forced in a few windows." There the vice president chanced his first public appearance since the Hamilton duel in July. The reception was all he could have hoped for. A band played below his window while a group of citizens demanded his appearance. He basked in "invitations which it would require weeks to satisfy." Perhaps his fears of political extinction were exaggerated. [16]

The vice president hurried on to Theodosia's family in South Carolina, keen to see his grandson. In a letter, Burr crowed that the boy would find that his grandfather was now a "black man . . . from the effects of climate, or travelling four hundred miles in a canoe." The vice president happily referred to himself as "gamp," adopting the boy's mispronunciation of "grandfather." He called his grandson "gampy." [17]

Burr was bursting with plans when he arrived at Theodosia's home. He wrote urgently to Philadelphia, sent Sam Swartwout to deliver messages in

New York, and planned another message for Commodore Truxtun in New Jersey. Burr hastened on toward Washington City, where Congress would convene in the first week of November. Though Burr had often skipped the dull early weeks of congressional sessions, this year would be different. He would not hide from those who denounced him for killing Hamilton. When the Senate began its work, Vice President Burr would be in the presiding chair.[18]

Burr's journey took an almost triumphant turn in Virginia, the home of his rival Jefferson. The Republicans of Petersburg staged a party and a dinner in his honor. Richmond offered similar social opportunities, but he could not stay. "Virginia is the last state," he wrote to Theodosia, "in which I should have expected any open marks of hospitality and respect"; he added with satisfaction, "how illy I have judged."[19] If Virginia could welcome Burr, his prospects might be improving. Surely most Americans would understand that the Hamilton duel had been entirely proper, an affair of honor.

A harsher reality struck while Burr was still on the road. He learned that a grand jury in New Jersey had also indicted him for murder. Now the vice president was a fugitive from two of the nation's seventeen states. His home and his furniture in New York had been sold to pay debts, but he still owed much.[20]

Nonetheless, Burr called the Senate to order on November 4. Many were offended by the sight of Burr in the Senate chamber rather than facing murder charges in a court of law. The *New York Evening Post* was "astonished" to find the "second magistrate presiding in the first branch of the Legislature, while he stands indicted for murder." "I have avoided him," wrote a New England senator. "His presence to me is odious." Burr's refusal to respond to the murder indictments seemed particularly offensive because of the impending impeachment trial of Supreme Court Justice Samuel Chase. The vice president, who was ducking murder charges in two states, would preside over that trial in the Senate. A Philadelphia newspaper recoiled at the prospect "that hands stained with the best blood of our nation should be sacrilegiously laid upon the judges of the land."[21]

The contrast was vivid. In the cities of the north and east, Burr was a scapegrace accused of murder, subject to disapproving murmurs and frowns. He could expect no office of public trust there. But the frontier was free of such self-righteous prating. There Burr could meet hearts as daring and souls as restless as his. There a victorious duelist was admired, not reviled. There would be his future.

Turning to frontier lands, which included most areas not on the Atlantic coast, was a natural step for Burr. The Edwards (maternal) side of his family had turned again and again to the nation's periphery. The uncle who raised Burr had explored western New York while helping to settle a boundary quarrel between New York and Massachusetts. Another Edwards uncle lived with the Iroquois and wrote a treatise on the Mohican language. A third speculated heavily in western lands, while several cousins settled on the western New York frontier.[22]

Burr had tried to make his fortune by trading in frontier lands. Such schemes afflicted early Americans like epidemics. "Were I to characterize the United States," wrote one British visitor, "it should be by the appellation of the land of speculation." The Edwards uncles repeatedly drew Burr into land schemes, including one for over 200,000 acres between the Oswego and Chenango Rivers in western New York. From a spot on the Mohawk River in 1788, Burr wrote rhapsodically to his wife, "I could fill sheets in description of the beauties of this romantic place." He exulted in the "sympathizing willows," the "lofty oaks and locusts," and the view of the "stately Mohawk roll[ing] his majestic wave along the lofty Appalachians." Burr concluded, with a pulsing regret, that he could not afford to buy that sliver of paradise.[23]

In his public duties, Burr took special interest in the West. When five hundred French emigrants were stranded in "Gallipolis" in the Ohio Valley in the 1790s, tricked by developers who failed to provide title to their lands, Senator Burr of New York took up their cause. He sponsored legislation granting 24,000 acres to the deceived Frenchmen. Such scandalous episodes were common. A British traveler denounced the land swindles that greeted immigrants to America: "False titles, forged grants, fictitious patents, and . . . sale of land in the clouds were daily imposed on the unwary."[24]

Senator Burr also championed Tennessee's bid for statehood in 1796.

The state's governor lauded Burr's efforts: "I pronounce positively that that Mr. Burr . . . may be ranked among [Tennessee's] very warmest friends."[25]

After declining to seek a second Senate term, Burr returned to the New York State assembly in 1799. With his friend Charles Williamson, he sponsored legislation for a new bridge and a turnpike for the western frontier. After 1801, presiding over the U.S. Senate as vice president, Burr cultivated western senators.[26] When the Louisiana Purchase doubled the size of the nation in 1803, Burr promptly set to learning about the new lands and wrote to prominent men in Louisiana. Through New Jersey senator Jonathan Dayton, a boyhood friend, Burr sought maps of the new territory.[27]

Burr's interest in the frontier reached a new level in late May 1804, after he lost the New York governor's race and a month before he had any notion of dueling with Hamilton. The vice president met secretly for several days with the American who loomed largest on the far side of the Appalachians: General James Wilkinson, the top officer of the U.S. army. Wilkinson, who had made his home in Kentucky for twenty years, knew every person of importance in the West. Though his army was small, it was the only professional military force in the region. In the West, Wilkinson could be a powerful friend or foe.

Specifying that he wished to enter Burr's mansion "without observation," Wilkinson arrived under cover of darkness. The two men were old colleagues from Continental Army days. A mutual friend wrote to Burr that "no friend feels a warmer attachment to you than James [Wilkinson]."[28]

The general was fresh from New Orleans, where he had been one of two American commissioners who accepted the Louisiana Territory from the French. He had the most recent news and the best maps of the West, of Louisiana, and of Spanish lands. Together, Burr and Wilkinson studied those maps, examining the best routes for moving bodies of men and material.

They were opposites in many ways. Burr, cultured and well-spoken, avoided ostentation and maintained a reserve. According to a British visitor, Burr received guests with "that urbanity which, while it precludes familiarity, banishes restraint." In conversation, Burr "was not less skilled in elegant literature, than the sciences of graciousness and attraction." Wilkinson, of medium height and generous build, was a rougher, noisier type. A Frenchman described him as "heavy, squat, good-natured, talkative, and open-faced." The general gloried in splendid uniforms. He ordinarily favored "a gold-buttoned uniform, his spurs and stirrups made of gold, and with a leopard hide, complete with gold claws, for a saddle cloth."[29] Wilkinson's conversation verged on bombast, frequently fueled by alcohol. Yet strong forces brought these disparate men together, then linked them in a bold plan.

Both disdained the Jefferson administration, viewing its policies as insipid. Each resented reverses suffered at Jefferson's hands. The president had deftly pushed Burr to the edges of American politics. For Wilkinson, the picture was only slightly better. Jefferson's Republicans shrank the army by one-third, to 3,300 men, and even considered eliminating Wilkinson's rank as brigadier general. His position survived, but his pride was deeply wounded. The experience, he wrote to Burr, "has awakened me as from a dream." With his customary florid prose, Wilkinson called his critics "a set of prating puppies and coxcombs, who have learned how to mangle truth and to garnish falsehood." Those were skills that Wilkinson himself possessed to a high degree.[30]

The two men shared outsized dreams. Both longed to conquer Spain's colonial lands. Both wondered if a new nation could be forged in the West.

And they shared one more quality: a shallow loyalty to their own government. Just a few weeks after their conference, Burr would send Charles Williamson to offer Britain his aid in dismembering the United States. Fifteen years before, Wilkinson had made a similar offer to Spanish officials. He had benefitted richly from it. In fact, the American general in chief was still in the pay of the Spanish secret service, where he was inscribed as Secret Agent No. 13.

During that New York springtime of 1804, they met fitfully for several days. They reviewed maps, talked of Louisiana, and—recalling that expressions of affection between men were routine—enjoyed a jocular intimacy. In a message sent after they parted, Wilkinson wrote to the vice president about the standard size of barrels in Louisiana, closing with his affectionate wishes, "with or without observation." Two days later, Wilkinson wrote in French to invite Burr to see his maps, striking a flirtatious note: "I think of you always my handsome and dear devil." Next day Wilkinson reminded Burr to send him certain "commandments and calculations."[31]

Wilkinson's reports about Louisiana were consistent with information Burr had gathered elsewhere. Many of the French-speaking residents resented American rule.[32] Such discontent might be put to many uses. As soon would become clear, Burr and Wilkinson had some ideas about that. Though neither ever explicitly described the understanding they reached in May 1804, later events showed that they began to explore a daring joint expedition in the West.

Burr surely expected to be the senior partner in any alliance with this blustery, hard-drinking soldier. Burr was better born, better educated, more polished. He had risen farther in life, almost snaring the highest office in the land. Indeed, Wilkinson led the army largely by default: Few men of talent wished to serve in that ragtag organization. With his exuberant uniforms and operatic personality, Wilkinson could seem clownish.

Underneath Wilkinson's bravado, though, was a hard-eyed realist with a genius for self-preservation. Fifteen years earlier, the general had shared with a Spanish diplomat his theory of politics. In a passage that would make Machiavelli proud, the general wrote, "Some men are sordid, some vain, some ambitious. To detect the predominant passion, to lay hold of it, is the profound part of political science."[33]

Wilkinson was an easy man to underestimate, but underestimating him could be dangerous.

5

The Restless West

The West
To November 1804

When Burr and Wilkinson met in May 1804, the constitutional government of the United States was a wobbly affair. As illustrated by New England's secession flutter earlier that year, Burr had a natural affinity with the wobbly parts. New England was not the only region alienated from the national government. Beyond the high Appalachians, which decisively divided the West from the Atlantic coast, the ties to the union were even weaker. In the West, the idea of secession was older and more deeply entrenched, involving prominent citizens like James Wilkinson. It sometimes merged with the lust for Spanish lands and sometimes competed with it.

Geography shaped western politics. According to one traveler, a day on horseback over those mountain ridges covered only thirty miles and wore out both man and beast. Once past the mountains, travelers confronted deep forests and seemingly endless rivers and streams. A journey to Mississippi Territory crossed hundreds of waterways with neither bridges nor ferries. When a westerner acquired a horse, he always asked whether the animal was a good swimmer.[1]

News took weeks or months to pass over the mountains. A letter could travel from New York to London more quickly than from Boston to Natchez in Mississippi Territory. The journey from New York to Nashville consumed twenty-two days or more. In 1803 the government initiated an "express mail" to Natchez, an early version of the fabled Pony Express. Stations at thirty-mile intervals provided fresh horses to the riders, who were relieved every hundred miles. Under the best of circumstances, mail from Washington City reached Natchez in fifteen days. Accidents, weather, and human failings could double or treble that time.[2]

The distance between the West and the rest of the nation was psychic as well as physical. The coastal states looked over the Atlantic toward Europe. Westerners looked downriver to New Orleans and Florida, and west across the Mississippi.

Daily life in the West involved hardship and risk, and the people who lived there posed some of the risks. Though European arms and diseases had greatly reduced the native population, the remaining Indians could be hostile. The whites were just as scary. Cutthroats lurked on trails and in settlements, ready to separate the weak and careless from their valuables, or their lives.

A traveler in 1804 found the residents of Mississippi Territory "illiterate, wild and savage, of depraved morals." Recent arrivals, he continued, "are almost universally fugitives from justice, and many of them felons of the first order" or bankrupts hiding from their creditors. A Virginia politician referred to Kentucky as "Virginia's Botany Bay." (Botany Bay in Australia was settled by British convicts.) A visitor to Kentucky found that wealthier citizens were "immersed in infidelity and dissipation," gathering in crowds for horse races. The lower classes, he reported, "were downright fanatics and zealots in religion." Kentucky's settlers, according to one of them, "were illiterate . . . and all were poor or in moderate circumstances."[3]

Hard drink suffused the new lands. It assuaged loneliness and boredom, provided comfort after backbreaking labor, and often was the only medicine available. It took a heavy toll. Drinking could begin at noon and continue for the balance of the day. A young law graduate found nine other

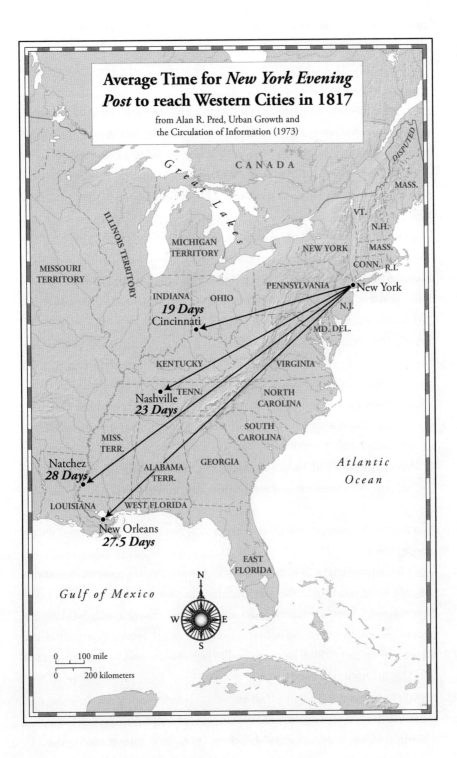

Average Time for *New York Evening Post* to reach Western Cities in 1817

from Alan R. Pred, Urban Growth and
the Circulation of Information (1973)

lawyers living in Cincinnati at the turn of the century; all but one "became confirmed sots and descended to premature graves." A Kentuckian described Saturdays as devoted to "public business, social pleasure, dissipation, and beastly drunkenness."

Fights between westerners had no rules and included "scratching, pulling hair, choking, gouging out each other's eyes, and biting off each other's noses, in the manner of bull-dogs." After one such fight in Kentucky, three witnesses swore that James Meek "bit off a piece of Benj. Vinzant's Left ear." Another tactic, according to a horrified Englishman, was to "tear out each other's testicles."[4]

The frontier amplified American ideas about equality. The West attracted men and women who believed in that principle, while class distinctions eroded in rugged living conditions. A Briton complained that he could find no "idea of subordination" on the frontier, an absence that led to "insolence, impertinence, and rudeness." Yet he offered grudging praise for the vulgar roughnecks he met:

> Although the inhabitants are in reality a rude, barbarous and unpolished set of men, yet you will frequently find pleasure in their conversation; their ideas are bold and spirited, but their sentiments are not liberal. However, they are certainly a sensible, enterprising, hardy, unpolished race, yet open, free and hospitable. Pusillanimousness, cowardice and mean spirit appear not there.

Another visitor summarized the western character as "a restless and enterprising spirit."[5]

The separateness of the West made a powerful impression. A traveler described the lands over the Appalachians as "formed by nature for a distinct empire." Even President Jefferson, the man charged with holding the United States together, recognized the centrifugal forces that pulled the West away. In early 1804, he professed to be unperturbed by the prospect of dividing the nation in two:

> Whether we remain in one confederacy, or form into Atlantic and Mississippi confederacies, I believe not very important to the

happiness of either part. Those of the western confederacy will be as much our children and descendants as those of the eastern, and I feel myself as much identified with that country, in future time, as with this.[6]

Five months earlier, he shrugged away concerns that the nation might divide along the Appalachians. "Why should we dread it?" he asked. "The future inhabitants of the Atlantic and Mississippi states will be our sons. We think we see their happiness in union, and we wish it. . . . but, if they see their interest in separation, why should we take side with our Atlantic rather than our Mississippi descendants?" He concluded with a benediction: "Keep them in union, if it be for their good, but separate them, if it be better."[7]

For westerners, control of New Orleans was the central economic and political issue. Rich western soils yielded abundant crops and fat livestock, but crops and meat had to be sold somewhere else. Riverboats were the best way to move heavy cargoes. They could reach speeds of five miles per hour floating down rivers like the Ohio, the Cumberland, and the Kentucky. Those rivers flowed to the broad Mississippi, which reached New Orleans and the world beyond. New Orleans was the best trade outlet for almost half of the nation. "There is on the globe one single spot," Jefferson observed, "the possessor of which is our natural and habitual enemy. It is New Orleans."[8] To gain control of New Orleans, the United States would have to navigate the perilous byways of European diplomacy.

Founded by France, New Orleans passed to Spanish control in the 1763 treaty that ended the French and Indian War. After the American Revolution, Spanish officials deployed multiple strategies to halt the spread of the new republic and its dangerous ideas. By regaining control of the Floridas in 1783, Spain blocked Americans from the Gulf of Mexico. By recruiting Americans to settle in border regions, Spain tried to form a barrier against the United States.[9] By forging ties with Kentucky leaders and placing some on the king's payroll, Spain secured advocates of an independent western nation allied with Spain, as well as information about American politics. Most important, though, Spain closed New Orleans to American shipping. If no goods could pass downriver to market, perhaps the Americans would stay on the Atlantic side of the mountains. For a dozen years after the Revolution, opening the port of New Orleans was a central problem for the American government. Until that bottleneck was removed, western communities would struggle.

James Wilkinson was part of the secession movement in Kentucky. Born into a prosperous Maryland family in 1757, the youthful Wilkinson joined the disastrous American invasion of Canada at the beginning of the Revolutionary War, during which the equally youthful Aaron Burr won distinction. Wilkinson rose even more rapidly than Burr, becoming chief of staff to General Horatio Gates before the Battle of Saratoga in 1777, then winning a field promotion to brigadier general at the age of twenty-one.

It was too much success, too soon. Wilkinson carelessly disclosed correspondence addressed to Gates that criticized Washington's leadership. The disclosure allowed Washington to move decisively against his army rivals. Wilkinson, caught on the losing side of the bureaucratic battle, withdrew from active duty. He later returned to the army as clothier general, responsible for the mundane but critical task of securing uniforms and bedding for soldiers. Bored by his duties, Wilkinson neglected them, then resigned before he could be cashiered.[10]

General James Wilkinson, the senior officer of the United States Army and also a secret agent for the King of Spain, met secretly with Burr in the spring of 1804 to talk of the West.

In 1783, out of uniform and out of money, Wilkinson sought his fortune in Kentucky. He made a good first impression. One contemporary remembered him as "not quite tall enough to be perfectly elegant," but he "compensated by symmetry and appearance of health and strength; a countenance open, mild, capacious, and beaming with intelligence; a gait firm, manly, and facile; manners bland, accommodating, and popular; and address easy, polite, and gracious." Wilkinson, in short, "captivated." [11]

By 1787 Kentuckians were angry. New Orleans was still closed to their trade. Kentucky was not yet a state. Most settlers felt ignored by the national government. The territory's attorney general predicted that it would "in a few years revolt from the Union and endeavor to erect an independent government." Wilkinson took decisive action. Loading a boat with tobacco, hams, and butter, he set off for New Orleans. [12]

When he reached his destination, Wilkinson found he could do business with the Spaniards. The local Spanish governor allowed the avuncular American to ship goods through the port, then joined Wilkinson in a tobacco venture. In return, Wilkinson swore an oath of allegiance to the Spanish king and composed a report for him on the American West. He enclosed a list of Kentuckians who might also trade their loyalty for Spanish silver. Ignoring the line between solicitude and sycophancy, Wilkinson wrote to the governor that their parting had caused "anguish inexpressible" that "almost unmanned me." [13]

Wilkinson's report advised that in order to make Kentuckians "vassals" to King Carlos, Spain should not allow American goods to pass through New Orleans. Wilkinson pledged to devote "all my faculties to compass this desirable event." In 1792, Wilkinson assured the Spaniards that the American Secretary of War was incompetent and President Washington ignorant. To protect his own reputation, he urged the Spaniards to "bury these communications in eternal oblivion." Wilkinson, now agent "No. 13" of the Spanish secret service, addressed his letters to "Numero Primo," the governor of Spanish Louisiana. Letters to Wilkinson were directed to false names—Abraham Abrams, Isaac Isaacs, Lewis Legendre—in Philadelphia, Washington City, and Baltimore. [14]

Over time, Wilkinson grew comfortable with his Spanish masters, even after his debts forced him back into the American army. At a statewide convention in 1788, he argued that Kentucky should leave the union. Four years later, the Spaniards granted him an annual pension of $2,000 (roughly $80,000 in current value), retroactive for three years. Spain had paid him at least $26,000 by 1795, or over a million dollars in current value, at the same time that he was commanding an American infantry regiment.[15] By any measure, Wilkinson was a traitor in high military office.

And there he stayed. Wilkinson rose to overall command of the army in February 1797, even though prominent Americans had long suspected he was a Spanish agent.[16] In 1797, an unequivocal accusation came from the surveyor who was charting the boundary between Mississippi Territory and Spanish West Florida. The surveyor reported to the Secretary of State that Wilkinson aimed to "detach the states of Kentucky and Tennessee from the union and place them under the protection of Spain." He recorded Spanish payments to Wilkinson and provided one of the ciphers (or codes) Wilkinson used to correspond with Spanish officials. President Adams dismissed the accusation. He had heard that Wilkinson owed loyalties to Spain, Adams wrote to the general, but "scarcely any man arrives from [the West] who does not bring the [same] report along with him."[17]

As Wilkinson cozied up to the Spaniards, other western schemes challenged Spain. In 1793 the French ambassador, Edmond Genêt ("Citizen Genet"), commissioned a military expedition to open the Mississippi. George Rogers Clark, the hero of frontier campaigns during the Revolutionary War, gathered two hundred men for the mission, but they dispersed when the French and American governments repudiated the project.[18] A few years later, Tennessee senator William Blount planned to use Indian tribes to attack New Orleans, Pensacola, and New Madrid (now in Missouri). In the summer of 1797, while Blount's confederates parleyed with the British for naval support, the scheme came to light. The U.S. Senate expelled Blount and the venture died.[19]

The solution to the problem of New Orleans came unexpectedly from the other side of the Atlantic, when Spain decided it needed friendlier relations with the United States. A 1795 treaty between the two nations opened New Orleans to American goods. The impact was immediate. In 1792 only a dozen flatboats made the journey downriver to New Orleans; ten years later more than five hundred did. By 1807, the number was close to two thousand per year, an average of six boats every day carrying tobacco, corn, grain, and hides.[20]

Western population mushroomed. Cheap land drew those who tilled rocky farms in New England or tired tobacco lands in Virginia. In 1800, the federal land office sold 67,000 acres of land to settlers; five years later, it sold almost ten times that amount, 581,000 acres.[21]

From Natchez, Mississippi, a new arrival wrote: "There is daily a great increase of population in this territory." Settlers feverishly cleared the forests. A traveler in western New York reported that "axes were resounding and the trees literally were falling about us as we passed." In the 1800 census, the West held almost 10 percent of the 5.3 million people of the United States. Kentucky, initially part of Virginia, had 220,000 residents, though 40,000 were slaves. Tennessee was home to 105,000 people. Forty-five thousand lived in Ohio. Mississippi Territory numbered only 8,000 non-Indians; almost twice that many lived in New Orleans, the region's metropolis.[22]

The opening of New Orleans shriveled secessionist sympathies in the West. Wilkinson advised the Spaniards to abandon any effort to sever the region, adding that Spain still owed him $10,000 for his services.[23]

But the situation in New Orleans was unstable. Spain decided that Louisiana, which extended up the west bank of the Mississippi to Canada and westward into the Rocky Mountains, was more trouble than it was worth, so it traded the province to Napoleon for Italian kingdoms. This "retrocession" of Louisiana to France was delayed, prolonging Spanish control of the territory, but by the middle of 1801 President Jefferson knew the French were returning to North America.

Compared to decrepit Spain, Napoleonic France would be a far more aggressive neighbor. The *New York Morning Chronicle*, sponsored by Burr, denounced the retrocession and demanded an American attack on New Orleans. Jefferson, despite his sympathies for France and its revolution, sent a message to Napoleon that if France controlled Louisiana, America would ally itself with Britain.[24]

The French plan to return to North America foundered in San Domingo, the Caribbean island that is now divided between Haiti and the

Dominican Republic. The island's slaves had rebelled and claimed their independence. Napoleon sent two armies to recover the island, but disease and black resistance consumed his armies. By late 1802, Napoleon needed a new plan.

At that moment, Spanish officials in New Orleans suddenly revoked the Americans' right to "deposit" goods in that port, arguing that the 1795 treaty had granted that right for only three years. Americans responded vehemently. Spain again was bottling up the West. Newspapers thundered that American troops should take New Orleans and the Floridas. Jefferson, who wanted no war, worried that "the fever into which the western mind is thrown by the affair at N[ew] Orleans threatens to overbear our peace."[25]

To control the crisis, the president asked Congress for two measures. The first appointed James Monroe to negotiate with France and Spain to protect America's rights in the Mississippi River and "the territories *eastward* thereof" (the Floridas). The second approved $2 million to cover expenses in dealing with foreign nations—in reality, as Jefferson wrote to Monroe, the money was for "purchasing N[ew] Orleans and the Floridas."[26]

When Monroe reached Paris in April 1803, he and the American minister, Robert Livingston, walked into a stunning opportunity. Napoleon wished to sell all of Louisiana, which would double the size of the United States. Recognizing that the parcel offered was "infinitely larger" than they were authorized to buy, the Americans did not wait for new instructions from across the Atlantic. After a few days of haggling over the price, they struck a deal.[27]

For $15 million, or about $600 million in current value, the United States bought 828,000 square miles of North America, which ultimately became fourteen states. Concluded in haste, the treaty did not describe the borders of this massive tract. Instead, it stated that France conveyed all of the lands it received in the retrocession from Spain. This shortcut was a practical approach, since there were no reliable maps defining Louisiana's western borders, but it left an ambiguity that would bedevil Americans for years to come.

When news of the great purchase arrived in the United States in early

July 1803, it triggered widespread jubilation. In Washington, a celebration dinner lasted until dawn. Without bloodshed, the nation had gained control of the Mississippi River, New Orleans, and untold miles beyond. Some Federalists questioned whether the Constitution allowed the government to accept territory beyond the borders that existed in 1787. Jefferson thought that question far from clear, but he was willing to relax his legal concerns to achieve this extraordinary boon. Congress ratified the purchase in October.[28]

The massive acquisition was one more demonstration that the American future lay to the west.

Jefferson appointed Wilkinson one of the two American commissioners to accept the new lands from the French. The other, twenty-nine-year-old William C.C. Claiborne, was a native Virginian who had been a congressman from Tennessee.[29] The departing French governor detested both Americans, neither of whom could speak French or Spanish. Both had, he wrote, "on all occasions, and without delicacy, shocked the habits, the prejudices, the character of the population." The Frenchman found in Claiborne "little capacity and much awkwardness." General Wilkinson, he added, was a "flighty, rattle-headed fellow, often drunk, who has committed a hundred impertinent follies."[30]

One of Wilkinson's more conspicuous follies occurred at a formal dance, where events bore an uncanny resemblance to a scene in the movie classic *Casablanca*. To keep the peace, the band alternated between French and American tunes. When the Americans demanded a song out of turn, Wilkinson led a rousing chorus of "Hail, Columbia," followed by "God Save the King" (presumably selected for its capacity to annoy Frenchmen rather than for any American quality). The French responded with "La Marseillaise," concluding with shouts of "Vive la Republique!" After a bracing round of fisticuffs between the factions, Wilkinson led the Americans out of the hall.[31] All that was missing were Humphrey Bogart and Ingrid Bergman.

Wilkinson also kept busy in New Orleans's private rooms. On the day of the transfer, he buttonholed two Spaniards to demand another $20,000 in payoffs. Breathlessly, he later assured the Spanish commander of West

Florida that he had "much to communicate of deep import to the interests of his Majesty." The general soon had a new agreement with Spain, for $12,000 in bribes and a permit to export flour to Cuba. In return, he wrote a lengthy analysis of American policy. With bags of Mexican silver dollars, he purchased sugar for resale in New York.[32]

Wilkinson's new advice to King Carlos IV was straightforward. Only strong measures would block the Americans from sweeping down on Mexico with "an army of adventurers similar to the ancient Goths and Vandals." Spain must fortify its Texas and Florida borders, "drive back every illegal usurpation," and block American expeditions on the Red and Arkansas Rivers. Otherwise, he warned, the Americans "will very quickly explore the right path which will lead them to the capital of Santa Fe." Wilkinson, the double agent, knew well of what he wrote: He was then trying to acquire maps of the route from the Mississippi to Santa Fe.[33]

Wilkinson revealed to the Spaniards that President Jefferson was sending an expedition to explore Louisiana, led by Meriwether Lewis and William Clark. He recommended that Spain arrest Lewis and Clark, and also break up Daniel Boone's settlement on the Missouri River. Guided by his unique moral compass, Wilkinson simultaneously prepared a report for President Jefferson about the land between the Mississippi and Rio Grande, along with twenty-eight precious maps. If Spain and the United States were to clash over Texas, then both sides would value the general more highly: Spain would pay more for his information, and Jefferson might finally appreciate his army.[34]

America's gigantic acquisition presented two major challenges. One was external and the other internal.

The external problem was the uncertainty over Louisiana's borders. Within ten days of learning of the purchase, Jefferson sent letters throughout the West, asking poignantly, "What are the boundaries of Louisiana?" He also asked who were the leading citizens of the territory, how many people lived there, who owned what lands, and what laws applied there.[35]

Congress divided the new lands into two territories. Below the 33rd Parallel (the current northern border of the state of Louisiana) was Orleans Territory. Above that line was Louisiana Territory. Though the northern territory was many times larger, most of the people were in Orleans, where Claiborne became the acting governor.

But the eastern and western boundaries were disputed. To the east, Jefferson and his diplomats concocted a theory that the Louisiana Purchase included West Florida. The theory was weak: The purchase treaty stated that France was conveying those lands acquired by retrocession from Spain, and the retrocession had not included the Floridas.[36]

Nevertheless, Americans in Mississippi Territory itched to acquire West Florida and the port of Mobile. The Spaniards taxed American goods coming down the Mobile River, occasionally shutting them out altogether.[37] In August 1804, some thirty Americans led by three high-spirited brothers—Reuben, Samuel, and Nathan Kemper—crossed the Mississippi border, seized Baton Rouge, and proclaimed the new nation of West Florida. They hoisted a flag with seven blue-and-white stripes and two stars on a field of red. Few locals rallied to their banner. Facing the Florida militia and Spanish troops from Pensacola, the Kempers scampered back to American territory.[38]

The United States claim to Texas was stronger. The French thought the Rio Grande was the western boundary of Louisiana. Spain insisted that it still owned Texas all the way east to the Arroyo Hondo, now called the Calcasieu River, which runs roughly parallel to the current border between Louisiana and Texas but twenty to forty miles east of it. The United States did not press its Texas claim, however, probably because few Americans coveted that land. To secure the Floridas, Jefferson was willing to drop the claim to Texas altogether, plus pay $2 million.[39]

The U.S. minister to France, Robert Livingston, soon reported that neither West Florida nor Texas could be gained by negotiation. He recommended force. "You will have your own boundary to make," he wrote to Secretary of State Madison. "Your military post should as soon as possible be extended as far west as possible." Jefferson would not take such aggressive action, but the boundary dispute could flare into war at any time.[40]

The internal challenge posed by Louisiana was even greater: How would the United States assimilate the predominantly French population? Governor Claiborne feared the task was impossible. In the summer of 1804, he warned Madison that "many years will elapse before the strong partiality of the

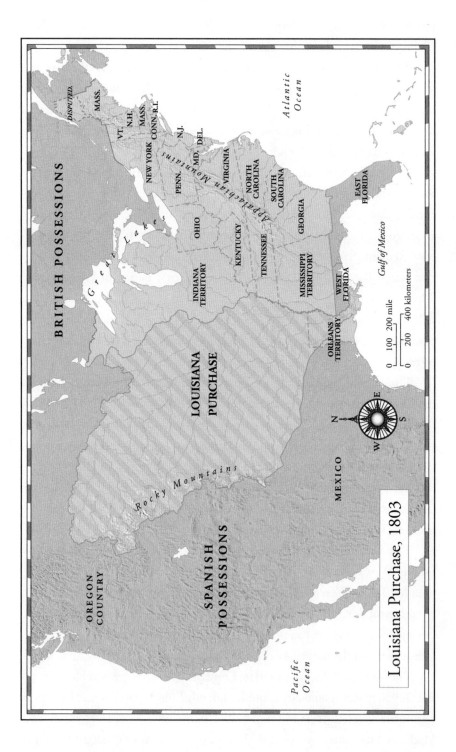

Louisiana Purchase, 1803

Louisianans for their Mother country will be effaced; this partiality is not confined to the emigrants from France; it seems infused more or less into all the descendants of Frenchmen." [41]

For the Creoles, as the French-speaking residents were called, American control was obnoxious, imposing the English language, American law, and American taxes. Louisianans had to prove to their new government that they held title to their land, even though the Spaniards took away most land records when they left. [42]

The Creoles resented another change: Congress banned the importation of foreign slaves to Orleans Territory, even though the Constitution guaranteed such imports in the rest of the country until 1807. Because disease and brutal conditions produced a high mortality rate among local slaves, the planters demanded additional imports. "There seemed to be but one sentiment throughout the province," Governor Claiborne wrote to the president. "They must import more slaves, or the country was ruined forever." [43]

But the Creoles did not want slaves from San Domingo and Jamaica, who were full of revolutionary ideas. Indeed, Americans arriving in New Orleans feared the racial situation there. Under Spanish rule, the militia included men of mixed-race backgrounds. "The people of color are all armed," General Wilkinson warned, "and it is my opinion that a single envious artful bold incendiary, by rousing their fears and exciting their hopes, might produce those horrible scenes of bloodshed and rapine" of San Domingo. Claiborne worried constantly about slave revolts, reporting that his government foiled two such plots in the fall of 1804. [44]

On July 8, 1804, after barely six months of American rule, two hundred leading citizens gathered in New Orleans to approve a petition detailing their complaints. They chose three delegates to present it to Congress in Washington City. [45] Though the meeting's leaders were overwhelmingly Creole, the petition was written by a recent arrival from New York, Edward Livingston, the much younger brother of the American minister to France. Edward had been a congressman from New York and an ally of Burr. In the pivotal election of 1800, however, he sided with Jefferson and was rewarded with appointment as United States attorney in New York. There, matters went awry. Forty thousand dollars of federal tax receipts disappeared from

Livingston's office; an employee was charged with the theft, but Livingston's reputation suffered and he faced huge personal debts. He moved to New Orleans for a fresh start.[46]

An experienced lawyer, Livingston quickly gained stature in his new city. His petition to Congress complained that the territorial government was despotic. Jefferson appointed all local officials, denying the American promise of self-government, while all government business was conducted in English. The petition also complained about the absence of slave imports and demanded that Louisiana be admitted as a state.[47]

Before the three delegates left for Washington City, a prominent New Orleans merchant carried Livingston's petition through the territory, gathering signatures and spreading discontent. "I have encouraged, and will continue to encourage, the outcry and opposition," wrote Daniel Clark, boasting that he "everywhere pointed out to the people . . . the disregard and violation of their rights." When he read Livingston's petition at public meetings, "it was universally approved of." Governor Claiborne became so frustrated with Clark that he denounced the merchant as an enemy of the United States.[48]

By the time Burr arrived in Washington City in November 1804, he was thinking about undertaking a great expedition, a great adventure, in the West. That would require political support, military force, and money. Burr had none of them, so he would have to contrive all three.

For political support, he had to reach beyond his longtime friends in New York and New Jersey. He needed allies in the West, with its secessionist past and its longing for Spanish lands. He knew leading figures in Ohio, Tennessee, and Kentucky, and he could meet more. In New Orleans, discontent seethed among the unhappy Creoles, and Burr knew some of the new American officials there. His stepson—his wife's son by her first marriage—was a judge in Orleans Territory, and a friend was Governor Claiborne's secretary.[49]

For military force, the vice president thought first of the Royal Navy. His confidential friend Charles Williamson was buttonholing top officials of the British empire on his behalf. Some of those officials had a keen interest in an American initiative. In mid-October 1804, a senior British admiral endorsed an expedition to free Spanish America and pave the way for Britain to take over trade with that continent.[50]

For military power on land, Burr could look to General Wilkinson, the disloyal head of the American army. Direct army support would be a great advantage, but it might be enough if Wilkinson merely failed to oppose a Burr expedition. After all, the West was full of men ready to take up arms for glory and profit. If George Rogers Clark, worn out and alcoholic, could recruit two hundred men to fight for France, how many thousands would respond to an appeal from the charismatic Burr, a national leader, the man who had slain Hamilton?

Finally, there was money. Money was always a problem for Burr. It bored him, except for the spending of it. His son-in-law, Joseph Alston, was a rich man. Burr knew lots of rich men. If they invested in his expedition, he could promise them conquered lands, trade rights, and Mexican silver in return. If the adventure's prospects were bright enough, the money should come.

The next four months would be Burr's last as vice president. With Jefferson's reelection a certainty, George Clinton would become vice president on March 4, 1805. Rather than approach his final months in office with bitterness, Burr resolved to use them to advance his dreams. Still vice president, he would be a prominent figure in America's rustic capital city. With broad access to the nation's political and military leaders, he could remind them of his abilities while recruiting sponsors, allies, and followers.

With his trademark self-assurance, Burr saw no reason why the next four months had to mark his political farewell. They could begin a glorious new chapter of his life.

6

Vice President Burr

Washington City
November 1804–March 1805

A merica's early vice presidents were usually bored. The Constitution spelled out a single, rather dull, duty of the office: presiding over the Senate, ruling on procedural matters, unable even to join in the debates. "I go to the Senate every day," wrote John Adams when he was vice president, "read the newspapers before I go and the public papers afterward, see a few friends once a week, go to church on Sundays." Jefferson, his successor, kept busy compiling rules of Senate procedure. And the Senate met only four or five months a year. Excluded from the president's Cabinet and generally ignored, the early vice presidents often felt, as Adams put it, that they occupied "the most insignificant office that ever the invention of man contrived."[1]

From his first days as vice president, Burr won praise as an effective presiding officer. During his second year, he wrote: "The Senate and the vice-president are content with each other, and move on with courtesy." He insisted, according to a New Hampshire senator, on "good order, silence—and decorum in debate" and "confined the speaker to the point."

He allowed only senators and congressmen on the Senate floor, "a measure which contributes much to good order."[2]

Though the vice presidency placed Burr at the center of affairs, it also made him largely a spectator. When not in the Senate, he wrote to his son-in-law in 1802, "I dine with the president about once a fortnight, and now and then meet the ministers in the street. They are all very busy; quite men of business." Vice President Burr, alas, was not.[3]

In November 1804, as Burr settled in at Joseph Wharton's boardinghouse near the Capitol, the congressional session promised welcome activity. At the instigation of President Jefferson, Republican congressmen planned to impeach a Supreme Court justice for the first time. Their target was Samuel Chase of Maryland, an able Federalist judge with a hot temper and a partisan bent. As vice president, Burr would preside over Chase's trial in the Senate.

General Wilkinson took a house not far from Burr's lodging. Through the congressional session, according to Burr's landlord, the general's visits to the vice president "were more frequent and at different hours than those of any other gentleman." The landlord added that Wilkinson's visits were "more private." The landlord also explained that Burr kept "a number of maps and charts, of East and West Florida, of Orleans, of Louisiana, and of adjoining country." An army officer who frequented Wilkinson's rooms reported that the vice president was often there. Tracing over maps with Wilkinson, Burr learned about roads and rivers of the frontier, mountains and valleys, people and towns, who was influential and who possessed energy and vision. The vice president absorbed all he could. And he made plans.[4]

Washington City in 1804 reflected the bantling nation around it, suspended between a rude frontier reality and bright future hopes. Northern congressmen, who had to cross Maryland's slave country to reach the capital, complained that the city illustrated how Virginia and the South had captured the national government. What other reason could explain placing the capital in such a godforsaken spot?

The city was designed to afford commanding public spaces, boasting

seventeen wide boulevards and thirty-seven public squares. But in 1804
it was an American land bubble that had burst. Several companies had
bought large parcels, cleared them, and begun construction, only to run out
of money. Building slowed, then stopped. Land values plunged. "Immense
sums have been squandered," wrote a Cabinet officer, "in buildings which are
but partly finished, in situations which are not, and never will be, the scenes
of business."[5] A Cabinet member complained that the residents were so poor
they survived "like fishes, by eating each other." The British minister sent to
Baltimore for groceries, to Philadelphia for butter. Water came from private
wells or those drilled in public squares. Petty thieves beset residents.[6]

By late 1804, the area held four or five thousand souls, living in perhaps
seven hundred buildings. In the four years that the federal government had
been housed there, the encampment had improved, but it was by no means
a city. As a British traveler commented sarcastically, "It only wants 40,000
elegant buildings, and a corresponding population, to constitute . . . one
of the handsomest cities in the world!" A New England senator called it an
"abomination of desolation." A traveler arriving from the east reported that
Washington was more a "thickly-settled country than a city":

> Being told that we were entering Washington city, I continued look-
> ing for the houses for some little time; but seeing none, I thought I
> had misunderstood the gentleman who made the remark, and turn-
> ing round for an explanation, he told me, laughing, that we were
> almost in the very middle of it, and asked if I did not see the Capitol
> a little before us. I did, indeed, see a stately edifice, but no other ap-
> pearance of a city.

Even the Capitol, for all its architectural pretension, was unfinished. It had a
north wing for the Senate, but its south wing was still under construction. A
walkway connected the two.[7]

Residents clustered in three settlements, each focused on a major public
structure. The Capitol, flanked by businesses that served the congressmen, stood on a hill to the east that afforded fine views of the countryside.
The core of congressional life was the boardinghouse, where meals were
consumed at common tables. Inns took on the identity of partisan retreats,

A view of Washington City from Capitol Hill, looking west to the Executive Mansion, in 1800.

with Southern Republicans sharing one while New England Federalists lodged at another. Other shops included a grocery store, an ironmonger, a saddlemaker, a liquor store, bookstores, stables, a bakery, and taverns. To spruce up congressional appearances, there were tailor shops, bootmakers, an itinerant barber, and a bathhouse. Visiting preachers led Sunday services in the House of Representatives.[8]

The settlement provided excellent hunting. "Quails and other birds are constantly shot within a hundred yards of the Capitol," reported one visitor, "even during the sitting of the houses of congress." The British minister praised the snipe and partridge that could be bagged there, as well as the perch found in nearby Tiber Creek.[9]

A mile of meadow—some called it a swamp—divided the Capitol from the presidential mansion (not yet called the White House), which anchored another settlement. A brick building near the mansion held the government's administrative offices. Towering tulip poplars lined Tiber Creek and dotted the meadow. In cold weather the residents hacked down the trees for fuel. To President Jefferson, the felling of the trees was "a crime little short of murder."[10]

Pennsylvania Avenue barely linked the president's home to the Capitol. From the east, it was a footpath covered with the stone chips left over from construction of the Capitol, while the portion from the executive mansion was a flagstone walk. The two halves did not actually meet up and could be submerged by flash floods or spring tides. When the tides were full, fishermen might hook a sixty-pound rockfish only steps from the nation's main street.[11]

The town's third settlement surrounded the navy yard on the east branch of the Potomac, which was home to America's fleet of frigates. The work force there alternated between times of idleness and periods of frenetic activity outfitting warships.[12]

Social diversions were few. Public performances featured rope dancers (tightrope walkers who balanced hoops and swords), traveling musicians, and dramatic readings. "One must love the drama very much," one woman complained, "to pass three hours amidst tobacco smoke, whiskey breaths, and other stenches, mixed up with the effluvia of stables, and miasmas of the canal." Annual horse races in November were popular, as were public dinners to honor visiting celebrities. Only two buildings—the president's mansion and the British minister's residence—could house large social gatherings. Most times, as a British diplomat put it, the congressmen "lived like bears, brutalized and stupefied." They played cards and talked politics, then played cards some more and talked more politics.[13]

With legislators crammed into such close quarters, far from their families, the congressional session resembled a governmental boot camp, offering full immersion in the problems of the republic. A political rumor could reach every senator and congressman within twenty-four hours, quickly crossing with its counterrumor and doubling back on itself in a new form. Many grew heartily sick of the scene. A decade later, a congressman referred to Washington as "This city which so many are willing to come to and all so anxious to leave."[14]

With but four months left to his term in office, Vice President Burr plunged into this unique community of politicians.

The Republicans greeted Burr warmly. The Jefferson administration extended some superficial signs of favor. Burr was a guest at the president's mansion. Albert Gallatin, now Secretary of the Treasury, called frequently at Wharton's boardinghouse on the north side of Pennsylvania Avenue. Burr was seen riding in a carriage with another old friend, Secretary of State Madison. Ten years earlier, Burr had arranged the formal introduction between Madison and his future wife, the then–Dolley Payne Todd.[15]

One Federalist, viewing this favorable treatment as evidence that Burr "is an exception to all rules," scorned the Republicans for "caressing [Hamilton's] murderer." The vice president's murder indictments remained high on his list of problems. He could not return to New York or New Jersey without facing arrest, and either state could seek his extradition for trial. Here, too, the president's men tried to help. A Virginia senator, close to Jefferson, circulated a petition urging the governor of New Jersey to halt the prosecution of Burr. Eleven Republican senators signed the appeal, which pointed out that New Jersey never prosecuted many other Weehawken duelists. The New Jersey governor, another boyhood friend of Burr's, took no action on the petition, but he also did not attempt to extradite Burr for trial.[16]

The Jefferson administration's solicitude for the vice president grew from its urgent wish that Justice Chase be impeached and removed from office. The Chase trial marked the third and most important step in a campaign to purge Federalists from the courts. After his election as president, Jefferson groused that his opponents "have retired into the judiciary as a stronghold." From that position, he continued, "all the works of republicanism are to be beaten down and erased." With his party winning more and more elections, President Jefferson bridled at the power of Federalist judges, immune from voters.[17]

The Republican attack on the judges began with the 1803 removal of a Pennsylvania state court judge. Then the first federal impeachment targeted District Judge John Pickering of New Hampshire. An alcoholic or mentally ill, or both, Pickering was charged with drunkenness on the bench and erring in an admiralty case. He attempted to resign, but the Senate insisted on removing him formally.[18]

The sixty-four-year-old Chase was next. Sometimes called "Old Bacon Face" for his ruddy complexion and blunt features, Chase was a signer of the Declaration of Independence. As a judge, he freely obtruded his political opinions into his judicial performance. Five of the impeachment charges concerned his conduct of the trial of the notorious Republican editor James Callender, while two more concerned the treason trial in 1798 of John Fries of Pennsylvania, who led a local rebellion against federal taxes. A final accusation targeted a speech Chase made to a Baltimore grand jury in which he criticized Congress.

Burr prepared carefully. He consulted with architects on how to arrange the Senate chamber. The vice president knew the building's idiosyncrasies, since a chunk of its ceiling had crashed down the year before, barely missing the chair in which he sat. For the Chase trial, he did not disturb the portrait of George Washington above his chair, nor those of French King Louis XVI and Queen Marie Antoinette on either side. The monarchs' support for the American Revolution continued to command respect despite their grisly deaths by guillotine.[19]

On January 2, 1805, thirty-four senators made their way through snowdrifts to the trial's opening day. They found a chamber transformed with colors. Burr's chair remained at the center. Before him were two boxes covered with green cloth—one for the prosecutors from the House of Representatives and one for Justice Chase and his lawyers. The senators' morocco leather seats were gone, replaced by red-draped benches that flanked Burr's chair. Other seating was assigned for visiting dignitaries, along with a ladies' gallery.[20]

The witness testimony began a month later. Burr quickly took command of the trial, interrogating witnesses and often cutting to the core of the case.[21] Burr was a stickler for decorum. He chastised lawyers who wore heavy coats in the chamber, demanding they appear in appropriate attire (heat was indifferently provided by two large fireplaces). Burr pressed the Senate, unsuccessfully, to sit for more than four hours a day. When three Federalist senators, including his friend Dayton, left the chamber before the end of the testimony one day, Burr demanded that they apologize. He chided another for eating cake during the trial. The vice president, according to one senator, was "remarkably testy—he acts more of the tyrant—is impatient and passionate—scolds."[22]

Burr's exacting conduct won grudging respect. "I could almost forgive Burr for any less crime than the blood of Hamilton," wrote a Massachusetts

Only the Senate wing of the Capitol was completed in 1805, so it housed the Senate, the House of Representatives, and the Supreme Court.

congressman, "for the decision, dignity, firmness and impartiality with which he presides in this trial. He is undoubtedly one of the best presiding officers I ever witnessed." Chase's lawyer thanked Burr for his "impartiality, politeness, and dignity." He might well thank Burr: By insisting on regular and sober proceedings, Burr created an environment in which the politically motivated charges against Chase seemed small, even frivolous. The Senate acquitted Chase by comfortable margins.

Burr's performance reminded everyone in Washington City that he was a serious man and one of talent while also displaying his disdain for reflexive partisanship. He demonstrated that he cared more about a just outcome than about his party's agenda. "He despises the meanness and littleness of the [Jefferson] Administration," wrote a Federalist. According to Senator John Quincy Adams, the Republicans' impeachment drive was intended to show that a judge could be removed for making unpopular decisions. Burr stood apart from his own party's efforts. Though Jefferson did not complain openly about Burr's performance, he could not have been pleased with it.[23]

In the midst of the trial, one event underscored Burr's slim political prospects. On February 13, the vice president received the electoral votes of the 1804 election. Burr calmly recorded the thumping win by Jefferson and George Clinton under the procedures of the new Twelfth Amendment, which directed the electors to vote separately for president and vice president. A New York senator admired Burr's poise. Though Burr "feels that the most outrageous wrongs have been done him," the senator wrote, "he really acted his part with so much regularity and composure that you would not have seen the least deviation from his common manner, or heard the smallest departure from his usual tone." The senator concluded that Burr, "some years disciplined in the school of adversity," had learned "to behave like a stoic." [24]

With his return to the national stage, the vice president also resumed favored pastimes. His letters to Theodosia were again playful and instructive. From Washington, he moaned, "What a dull thing is sense. How it mars half the pleasure of life, and yet how contemptible is all that has it not." He warmed to his subject:

> Too much sense, by which I mean only a great deal, is very trouble-some to the possessor and to the world. It is like one carrying a huge pack through a crowd. He is constantly hitting and annoying somebody, and is, in turn, annoyed and jostled by everyone.

Burr implored his daughter to tell him if ancient mythology included "a goddess of nonsense. A god won't serve my purpose." New Year's Eve found him reflective. "Now, how much wiser or better are we than this time last year?" he asked. "Have our enjoyments for that period been worth the trouble of living?" Such questions were unavoidable after the Hamilton duel and his disastrous race for governor of New York. With a shrug, he resolved to avoid them: "These are inquiries not wholly congenial with the compliments of the new year, so we will drop them." [25]

He ever acted as Theodosia's schoolmaster, urging her to read the Roman writer Quintillian—in Latin, "not in translation; and let me entreat you not to pass a word or sentence without understanding it." Upon finishing a play or book, he advised her, she should write a summary of the work and her own critical views of it.

Though Burr was directing efforts to torpedo the murder prosecutions against him, to his daughter he affected a bemused contempt for the cases. New York and New Jersey, he wrote, were contending for "the honor of hanging the vice president." Should there be a trial, he assured her, "you may rely on a great concourse of company, much gayety, and many rare sights: such as the lion, the elephant, etc." He insisted Theodosia was taking the matter too seriously. "It should be considered as a farce," he wrote, that would bring "only ridicule and contempt to its abettors." [26]

The legal proceedings were not, however, wholly toothless. In early February, New York convicted the seconds from the duel, William Van Ness and Nathaniel Pendleton, of violating the state's antidueling law. Both men were stripped of their voting rights for twenty years. Burr wrote warmly to Van Ness: "I sincerely wish that all the personal inconveniences which flow from this transaction could fall on me alone—Those which are suffered by my friends are a source of most mortifying regret." [27]

And, because he was Burr, the vice president returned to affairs of the heart, specifically the mysterious "Celeste," her identity still cloaked in Burr's code name for her. For close to two years, Burr had intermittently courted this lady of Philadelphia, at one point describing their encounters to Theodosia in a fanciful allusion to "The Loves of Reubon and Celeste." He proposed marriage to Celeste in 1803, but she rejected him. They continued to see each other, though Burr also wrote happily to his daughter about his amorous pursuit of another woman, whom he called "La G." In mid-January 1805, the vice president confided that he was traveling to Philadelphia to see Celeste, though many people were "ascribing to the [trip] motives of profound political importance." He sought, he wrote to Theodosia, a final decision from the lady. Two weeks later he reported that the "affair of Celeste is forever closed, so there is one trouble off hand." [28]

Burr's investigation of western opportunities, pursued avidly with the nearby General Wilkinson, began to include Jonathan Dayton, whose Senate term would end in early March, as did the vice president's.

Burr had known Dayton all his life. In the Elizabethtown of his youth, the prominent families included the Daytons, the Ogdens, and the

Edwardses (the aunt and uncle who took in Burr and his sister after their parents died). Burr, whose aunt was an Ogden, sported with young Jonathan Dayton and the brothers Matthias and Aaron Ogden. That circle of friends tumbled toward manhood on New Jersey fields and over the waters of the Kill Van Kull. They all attended the College of New Jersey (later renamed Princeton). Burr and Matthias Ogden together joined the Continental Army in 1775. Their circle grew tighter when Matthias married Dayton's sister, Hannah. Connected to Dayton and the Ogdens by blood, class, marriage, and experience, Burr relied on them for support and friendship throughout his life.

Jonathan Dayton, Burr's boyhood friend, became a Federalist senator from New Jersey and Burr's closest confidant.

Around Dayton the whiff of greed, even scandal, sometimes lingered. His character, one Virginia lady asserted, was "that of an unprincipled speculator and crafty politician, who never appeals to his reason, but to deceive, and never departs from it, but to be sensual." Like Burr a romantic enthusiast, Dayton maintained a cool reserve in society. A British diplomat recalled the New Jersey politician as "a great rake" with a blasé manner who had once confided that "he thought a reward should be offered for the discovery of a new pleasure."

During the Revolutionary War, Dayton served as a captain in his father's regiment and was suspected of profiting from illicit trade with the British. Afterward, he speculated heavily in frontier lands, frequently relying on Burr's legal advice when dealing with the uncertain ownership rights that were routinely bought and sold in the West. Dayton acquired a huge expanse of southwestern Ohio, bequeathing his name to the largest city in the region. His reputation for probity was not improved by his friendship with the dubious General Wilkinson, who joined Dayton in some of his land schemes.[29]

Yet Dayton thrived as a Federalist politician. At twenty-six he was the youngest delegate to the Constitutional Convention of 1787. After two terms in the House of Representatives, he became Speaker of that body, holding the position from 1795 to 1799. Despite grumbling that he used that office to advance his land interests in the West, Dayton moved on to a seat in the U.S. Senate.

The bond between Burr and Dayton ran deep. Though one was a Republican and the other a Federalist, both were independent of party and were mistrusted for it. In the 1796 election for president, the Federalist Dayton hatched a scheme to vault the Republican Burr into the presidency. It was only natural for Burr to turn to Dayton, his oldest and closest friend, with his audacious new plan for the West, particularly in view of Dayton's extensive contacts through the region.[30]

Indeed, Dayton's enterprising eye fell early on Louisiana. In 1803, before the purchase negotiations had begun, Dayton journeyed to New Orleans, talking politics with French and Spanish officials and looking over real estate. He was sensitive to the shaky grip the United States held on its western territories. He feared French control of Louisiana, he said, because the French "might want to foment divisive wars between [the] western and eastern states, arouse separatist ideas among the states."[31]

Gathered round the maps at Wharton's boardinghouse that winter, Burr and Wilkinson and Dayton spun out their western schemes. They explored a proposal to build a canal around the Falls of the Ohio, a major obstacle to navigation of the Ohio River. To reduce risk of mishap, most cargo was unloaded at Louisville, on the Kentucky side, and hauled overland while local pilots steered the boats through dangerous channels. A canal would save time and money. Kentucky already had chartered a company to build one on its side of the river.[32]

In January 1805, Congress received a petition for 25,000 acres of public land to build a canal on the Indiana side. Burr and Dayton were behind it. The request was referred to a committee of three senators—Dayton himself, John Smith of Ohio, and John Brown of Kentucky—though the Senate took no action on it. Months later, a company won a charter from the Indiana legislature to build a canal and promptly named Burr, Dayton, and Brown as directors. Though the canal project was never seriously pursued, it provided a reason for Burr to travel to the West.[33]

Unhappy Orleans Territory was also on Burr's agenda. The Creole delegates had arrived in Washington City with their petition of grievances. General Wilkinson urged them to cultivate Burr, describing him as "the first gentleman of America" and "a man of the most eminent talents, both as a politician and as a military character." As soon as Burr's term ended, the general said, he would travel to the new Louisiana lands, "where he had certain projects," adding that Burr "was such a man as to succeed in anything he would undertake." Wilkinson encouraged one Creole delegate to give Burr all the information he had about the territory."[34]

Those delegates from Orleans Territory achieved a measure of success. Just before Burr left office in March 1805, Congress approved legislation allowing the territory to elect its own assembly and send a delegate to Congress. Examining affairs in Orleans could be another reason for Burr to travel westward.[35]

With Burr's term ending, Jefferson gave him a farewell gift. The president named Wilkinson to be governor of Louisiana Territory, which lay above the current state of Louisiana. Dr. Joseph Browne, Burr's brother-in-law, would be territorial secretary. In a letter to Theodosia, Burr exulted: "Wilkinson and Browne will suit most admirably as eaters and laughers, and, I believe, in all other particulars."[36]

Burr's triumvirate was also beguiled by Mexico, which most Americans then imagined as an El Dorado of riches groaning under the lash of Spanish oppression. According to a friend, Burr ardently advocated bringing freedom to Mexico and its silver mines, which were producing two-thirds of the world's silver output. Dayton later admitted that he often advocated a

Mexican expedition. In March of 1805, Wilkinson announced that he soon would "be on the high road to Mexico." A few months earlier, a Kentucky militia general captured that enthusiasm in a letter to Wilkinson. Kentuckians, he wrote, "are greedy after plunder as ever the old Romans were[.] Mexico glitters in our eyes—the word is all we wait for." [37]

In the winter of 1805 a visitor to Washington City brought firsthand knowledge of the secrets of Mexico. Alexander von Humboldt, a Prussian geographer of global reputation, had just completed an extended tour of the Spanish province. Both Burr and Wilkinson sought him out. When Wilkinson could not attend a dinner for the scientist at the president's mansion, he wrote out a series of questions, including one about routes to Santa Fe, and he asked Jefferson to pose them in his stead. [38]

Soon, Burr had reached the end of his term as vice president. It was time to take leave of Washington City. In early March, he bade a moving farewell to the Senate in which he had served for a full decade—as senator for six years, and as presiding officer for four.

Burr carried no prepared speech when he arrived in the Senate on March 2, 1805. It was the day after the verdict in the Chase impeachment trial, two days before the new vice president would be sworn in. For the first time in the nation's short history, a vice president was leaving office for private life, not to become president. For several days, Burr thought about how to mark the occasion. He chose a moment during executive session, with only senators and clerks present. His words, he told Theodosia, were inspired by "the solemnity, the anxiety, the expectation, and the interest which I saw strongly painted in the countenances" of the senators.

In public speech, Burr was plain and direct. He avoided flowery metaphors and appeals to emotion. He was, as one admirer put it, "calm and persuasive," his addresses "short, and pithy." He spoke deliberately but fluently, without groping for words. On this day, below average in height, slight of build but ramrod straight, with a high forehead, he was the center of rapt attention. "Every gentleman was silent," one senator wrote that evening, "not a whisper was heard, and the deepest concern was manifested." [39]

After suggesting several changes to the Senate's rules, Burr turned to more personal matters. He knew, he said, his procedural rulings had "wounded the feelings" of some senators. He acknowledged that he ruled quickly and ordinarily did not explain himself, in order to avoid derailing debate. But, he urged, "to be prompt was not therefore to be precipitate, and to act without delay was not always to act without reflection." Indeed, "error was often to be preferred to indecision."

Turning to his most heartfelt principle, Burr said he hoped the senators would agree that as presiding officer he "had known no party—no cause—no friend," but was scrupulously impartial. Burr insisted that adherence to the Senate's rules was essential to its dignity, as well as to "preservation of the law, of liberty, and the Constitution." The Senate, he continued:

> Is a sanctuary and a citadel of law, of order, of liberty—and it is here—it is here—in this exalted refuge—here, if anywhere[,] will resistance be made to the storms of popular frenzy and the silent arts of corruption; and if the Constitution be destined ever to perish by the sacrilegious hands of the demagogue or the usurper, which God avert, its expiring agonies will be witnessed on this floor.

Burr said he "consoled himself," one senator recorded, "with the reflections that, though separated, he and the senators would be engaged in the common cause of disseminating principles of freedom and social order."[40]

Though Burr's sentiments today seem prosaic, even hackneyed, his magnetic presence and precise delivery, combined with the occasion and the youthfulness of the nation, gave a powerful resonance to his twenty-minute talk. He spoke to the senators of their shared service and experiences, and their mutual hopes for the future. Burr spoke to their hearts, apparently from his own, without concern for ideology or party affiliation.

The vice president's sense of his audience was near perfect. A New York senator described the scene:

> When Mr. Burr had concluded he descended from the chair, and in a dignified manner walked to the door, which resounded as he with some force shut it after him. On this the firmness and resolution of many of the Senators gave way, and they burst in to tears. There was a solemn and silent weeping for perhaps five minutes.

The flinty John Quincy Adams recorded approvingly that Burr spoke "with great dignity and firmness of manner, but without any apparent emotion of sensibility." Adams thought many senators "appeared deeply affected" but recorded that only two wept.[41]

Burr's cloudy future heightened the senators' emotional response. "He is a most uncommon man," one wrote that evening, "and I regret more deeply than ever the sad series of events which removed him from public usefulness and confidence." That senator posed precisely the puzzle before Burr. He was under indictment for murder in New Jersey and New York, where his life and career had been centered, and he was a political pariah to many: "Where he is going or how he is to get through with his difficulties, I know not."[42]

7

"I . . . Shall Seek Another Country"

Philadelphia and Washington City
Spring 1805

A few days before Burr's farewell speech, Congressman Matthew Lyon of Kentucky passed Wilkinson's house near the Capitol. The general hailed the Irish-born Lyon, a fierce Republican who first won a congressional seat from Vermont in 1796. Lyon crashed onto the national scene when he wielded fireplace tongs against a Federalist adversary in a brawl on the House floor. Later, Lyon was jailed for criticizing President Adams in his Vermont newspaper. The Irishman moved to Kentucky in 1803 and won a House seat there.

Lyon and Wilkinson shared a mutual regret that Burr was leaving public office. Might the vice president, Wilkinson asked, be appointed ambassador to a foreign nation? Lyon answered that Jefferson would never do it. What else, the general pressed, could be done for Burr? Lyon said that if the vice president rode to Tennessee on March 4 and hung out his shingle as a lawyer, he could be elected to Congress within a year. The Hamilton duel would not injure him with western voters.

Pronouncing Lyon's idea "heavenly," Wilkinson pulled on his boots and rushed to arrange a meeting between Burr and Lyon. At the appointed hour, the congressman presented himself at Wharton's boardinghouse. He met a chilly reception. A servant told him Burr was engaged. Lyon persisted. Burr came to the door and directed him to a waiting area. While Lyon cooled his heels, he could hear Wilkinson and Senator Dayton in the next room. After almost an hour, Burr returned. As Lyon described their conversation:

> Colonel Burr said the meeting [with Wilkinson and Dayton] was about some land concern in the western country . . . and [we] soon commenced on the subject of the coming election in Tennessee. . . . Burr admitted the probability of the course I pointed out; but did not seem to be so enamoured of the project.[1]

Politely, and without exactly saying so, Burr made it clear that his interest in the West did not include winning a seat in Congress. His interest was far more ambitious than that, as he told the British minister, Anthony Merry, shortly after leaving the vice presidency in early March. Burr was following up on Charles Williamson's overture during the previous summer, when he conveyed Burr's offer to assist projects of the British government. Only days after leaving the second highest office in the republic, Burr plunged into talk of insurrection and secession.

He told Merry that the people in the Louisiana lands "seem determined to render themselves independent of the United States," if only they could secure "an assurance of protection and assistance from some foreign power." Merry accepted the statement, knowing that Burr had befriended the Orleans delegates to Congress. Burr added that the Louisianans planned to act jointly with "the inhabitants of the western parts of the United States." The former vice president, Merry wrote later, intended "to be the instrument of effecting such a connection," though Burr said "it would be too dangerous and even premature to disclose to me the full extent and detail of the plan he had formed." That plan, Burr explained, would be described to British officials by a "confidential person." Indeed, just a few weeks earlier Williamson had pressed Burr's case before a former Admiralty official in England, apologizing that his supporting papers were so bulky.[2]

In asking Britain to support the secession of Louisiana and the West, Burr stressed the trade opportunities with "the inhabitants of so extensive a territory, where the population is increased with astonishing rapidity." With only one seaport in New Orleans, Burr assured Merry, an independent nation in the Mississippi Valley would never be a naval power to rival Britain.

Burr's plea for support, which was admirably specific, reflected a bold and comprehensive plan. First, King George should send to the mouth of the Mississippi "two or three frigates, and the same number of smaller vessels." That would prevent the U.S. navy from blockading New Orleans. Also, Burr needed a loan; one hundred thousand pounds (about $10 million today) would suffice, although he might need more later. Burr even proposed a scheme for laundering the funds. The United States had a treaty obligation to pay much more than that amount to cover American debts to British merchants; Merry could redirect part of that repayment to Burr "without its destination being either known or suspected." Burr added that although he would prefer to ally with Britain, he was certain that France would eagerly support a western independence movement. His message was clear: If Britain did not support him, Burr would turn to Britain's mortal enemy.

The British minister was impressed with both Burr and his scheme. If Burr would divide the United States, he concluded, the British government should aid him. Merry endorsed Burr's plan in a report to his superiors in London, enthusing that Burr "certainly possesses perhaps in a much greater degree than any other individual in this country, all the talents, energy, intrepidity and firmness which are requisite for such an enterprise." Merry included one qualification: "If a strict confidence could be placed in him."[3]

Not suspecting that the ship carrying Merry's report to London would be delayed for more than six months, Burr turned to the mundane preparations for his western trip. He wrote Theodosia that he remained in Washington to address "trifling, important concerns of business, for trifles are important in matters of finance." He proposed to travel first to Philadelphia, then to Pittsburgh and down the Ohio and Mississippi Rivers to New Orleans. With an epistolary wink, he hinted that the journey could be significant: "This tour has other objects than mere curiosity. An operation of business, which promises to render the tour both useful and agreeable."[4]

Burr's optimism barely cloaked his desperate situation. He had neither a job nor income. He could not practice law while under indictment for murder. He could not return to his New York home or to New Jersey. When he reached Philadelphia after the first leg of his journey, he admitted his limited options in a letter to his son-in-law: "In New York I am to be disfranchised, and in New-Jersey hanged. Having substantial objections to both, I shall not, for the present, hazard either, but shall seek another country." Joseph Alston probably did not realize that Burr's statement was literally true: that his father-in-law was thinking of creating an entirely new country.[5]

When in higher spirits, Burr often fired off advice to Theodosia. Scolding her for laziness, he instructed: "People who are occupied are never dull, never melancholy." He counseled her on diet (chamomile tea without sugar or milk, and ginseng) and hygiene (salt water baths). "It is high evidence of the barbarism of our Southern states," he added, "that, in an extent of three hundred miles, filled with wealthy people, and in a hot climate, there should not be, in any one private family, a convenient bathing-room."

Then he offered another wink: "As the objects of the journey, not mere curiosity . . . may lead me to [New] Orleans, *and perhaps further*[,] I contemplate the tour with gayety and cheerfulness." Nothing lifted Burr's spirits like the prospect of adventure.[6]

He planned to meet with influential westerners, including Senator John Smith in Cincinnati, Senator John Brown in Frankfort, and Andrew Jackson, a Tennessee militia general and former congressman. He could visit Wilkinson at his new posting in St. Louis, while the Creole delegates to Congress promised him a warm welcome in New Orleans.

Throughout the West, Burr would be both a novelty and a celebrity. No president or vice president had yet crossed the Appalachians. The people of the West would want to see the man who held such high office. Thanks to the Hamilton duel, Burr commanded an even greater measure of fame and notoriety. Every frontier village knew that he had shot down his rival while defending his honor.

Before Burr left Pennsylvania, a Kentucky newspaper advertised a traveling exhibition of wax figures, "as large as life," portraying famous scenes in history. The display included images of George Washington, Thomas Jefferson, and John Adams, as well as the bathtub assassination of Jean-Paul

Marat during the French Revolution. But the first display listed was "A striking representation of the LATE UNFORTUNATE DUEL between Col. Burr, vice-president of the U. States, and Gen. Alexander Hamilton." Such an exhibition could smooth Burr's way through the West, and beyond.[7]

Departing Washington City, Burr left behind a national administration that aimed to do little. Jefferson's plan for the government, in his own words, was to follow a "noiseless course, not meddling with the affairs of others, unattractive of notice." Through his first term, Jefferson shrank the nation's military and concentrated on paying off the public debt. In the winter of 1805, Jefferson's quiet governing style became even more remote. His inaugural address on March 4, 1805, promised a foreign policy of wishful lassitude. "With nations, as with individuals," he said, "our interests, soundly calculated, will ever be found inseparable from our moral duties." He assured Americans that "a just nation is taken on its word," while lesser nations have to resort to "armaments and wars."[8]

Vigorous at sixty-two, Jefferson's unassuming personality was surprising in a national leader. He detested giving speeches and was a poor orator. He avoided arguments, or personal conflict of any sort. A woman meeting him in 1800 wondered whether a man could be president who was "so meek and mild, yet dignified in his manners, with a voice so soft and low, with a countenance so benignant and intelligent." His demeanor, she thought, was "almost femininely soft and gentle." A diplomat described him as "a tall man with a very red freckled face and grey neglected hair, his manners goodnatured, frank and rather friendly though he had somewhat of a cynical expression of countenance." With a fondness for comfortable clothes and "slippers down at the heel," Jefferson reminded the diplomat of "a tall large-boned farmer." Another visitor found him "without pomp."[9]

Jefferson's interests ranged far beyond government. He was a tinkerer, inventor, and architect, with a lively curiosity about every part of life. Early in his presidency, he convened a dinner of scientists. The discussion ranged from the construction of arches to the properties of limestone, to new experiments with light, to emigration, manners in Paris, and distinguishing features of the English and French languages.[10]

Despite his genial manner and preference for minimal government, Jefferson in 1805 dominated political life in America. His reelection over his Federalist opponent, Charles Cotesworth Pinckney, had been a cakewalk. Jefferson's margin in the electoral vote was 164–12. Although only eleven states allowed their citizens to vote directly for president that year, Jefferson was the choice of 73 percent of those who voted.

Those numbers do not fully capture Jefferson's preeminence. His Republicans held overpowering margins in the House of Representatives, 114–28, and in the Senate, 26–8. Indeed, Jefferson's party had started the Federalists spiraling into oblivion. For the next two decades, substantial parts of the United States had only one viable political party.

How did this contemplative man, who disliked public events, so command a democratic political system? He certainly had stature as the author of the Declaration of Independence, a former minister to France and the first Secretary of State. And his unassuming demeanor was a small liability at a time when presidential candidates did not stump for votes. Indeed, Jefferson's modest manners appealed to Americans who spurned royalty and aristocracy. The president's skill with the written word, beginning with the Declaration, certainly helped. On paper, Jefferson could explain and inspire better than any contemporary, even Hamilton.

But Jefferson's political ascendancy principally flowed from a remarkable congruence between his ideas and those of his countrymen. Many of America's early leaders were elitists, mistrusting common people as ill-informed and easily swayed by demagogues. Jefferson embraced the most revolutionary elements of the American experiment. "The tree of liberty must be refreshed from time to time," he wrote in 1787, "with the blood of patriots and tyrants. It is its natural manure." Of the leading figures in the early Republic, he had the fewest reservations about popular government. "The republican is the only form of government," he insisted, "which is not eternally at open or secret war with the rights of mankind."[11]

Because he distrusted any government action, Jefferson always wished to avoid war. "Our constitution is a peace establishment," Jefferson insisted, "it is not calculated for war. War would endanger its existence."[12] On this point, he and Aaron Burr profoundly disagreed. Burr, whose youthful military success helped form his personality, insisted that government must defend the nation's interests with energy and purpose.

Yet Jefferson embodied a mass of contradictions, beginning with his personal life. A widower from the age of thirty-nine, Jefferson rarely sought the company of women of his class. He preferred time with his family to any social event. When his younger daughter died in the summer of 1804, he wrote of his "inexpressible grief." The loss, he added, "has increased my anxiety to retire, while it has dreadfully lessened the comfort of doing it." In 1806, a visitor to the home of his surviving daughter found the president on the sofa, chatting about gardening as one grandchild hung from his neck and two more played on his knees.[13]

Yet Jefferson had a second family, one he never acknowledged. He owned them. His sexual involvement with a female slave, Sally Hemings, was rumored at the time, fueled by the striking resemblance between Sally's children and the president. Though controversy still flares over the question, the evidence of a relationship between Jefferson and his slave, and his paternity of her children, is powerful. The situation carries a peculiar resonance because Sally Hemings was the half-sister of Jefferson's long-dead wife: Sally was the daughter of a liaison between Jefferson's father-in-law and one of *his* slaves.[14]

There were other, more public contradictions. The devotee of the common man was a cultured aristocrat who spent himself deep into debt by splurging on fine objects and excellent wines. The champion of liberty owned hundreds of slaves. Though he fervently defended the principle of free speech, his administration jailed Federalist newspapermen who dared to criticize him. Indeed, the Jefferson-inspired impeachment of Justice Chase was political payback for the judge's outspoken opinions. Jefferson always urged the virtues of the government that intruded least on its citizens, yet at the end of his presidency he enforced an embargo against foreign trade that restricted American liberties more tightly than any measure adopted by the Federalists.

About Aaron Burr, though, Jefferson's views were consistent, and involved a visceral dislike. When he first met Burr in the 1790s, he later wrote, the New Yorker "inspired me with distrust. I habitually cautioned Mr. Madison against trusting him too much." To the Virginia planter, Burr seemed "always at market," too openly ambitious. Despite his apparently mild disposition, Jefferson was a shrewd political operator who could injure his adversaries without getting caught at it. As Secretary of State in the Washington administration, he placed on his payroll a printer who produced punishing attacks on the Federalist party, on Hamilton, and even on President Washington. As president, Jefferson resolutely turned his face from Burr, his vice president. He appointed few Burr allies to patronage jobs, favoring the Clintons in New York's fratricidal politics. The absence of presidential favor smothered Burr's prospects.[15]

Jefferson and Burr had very different ideas about the West. When Spain would not agree to the boundaries of Louisiana that Jefferson wanted, he told his diplomats to keep negotiating. When those talks proved fruitless, he sent them back for more. His governor in Louisiana, William C.C. Claiborne, urged that the president take decisive action. Claiborne insisted that marching "a few thousand troops to the Western Frontier of Louisiana would make Spain tremble for her Mexican possessions, and promptly yield to our just claims." But that was not the president's way.[16]

Burr preferred action. "The bent of his genius," wrote one follower, "was military."[17] When events justified force, as the standoff with Spain seemed to, Burr reached for his sword. If Jefferson would not use American power to resolve this unsettled situation, Burr would travel west and see what he might be able to do.

That Burr intended to fish in troubled western waters was no secret to Louis Turreau, the French minister to the United States, a famously bloody leader during his country's revolution. The Frenchman's cruel abuse of his wife, while an aide played music to drown out her screams, made him an object of horrified fascination in Washington City.[18] Outside his tumultuous home, the French minister kept an eye on Burr and Wilkinson. He took a jaundiced view of Wilkinson, describing him as "the most devoted creature, of Colonel Burr." His "military capacity is small," Turreau wrote, while he was "ambitious and easily dazzled, fond of show and appearances." Turreau also noted that Wilkinson "complains rather indiscreetly, and especially after dinner, for the form of his government, which leaves officers few chances of fortune."

In contrast, the French minister found Burr was yet a man of consequence.

"Mr. Burr's career is generally looked upon as finished," Turreau wrote, "but he is far from sharing that opinion, and I believe he would rather sacrifice the interests of his country than renounce celebrity and fortune." Louisiana, Turreau predicted, would be "the theatre of Mr. Burr's new intrigues; he is going there under the aegis of General Wilkinson." The minister prophesied: "I am not the only person who thinks that the assemblage of such men in a country already discontented is enough to give rise to serious troubles there." [19]

For all of his air of mystery and discretion, Burr had not kept his plans very secret. Perhaps such secrets could not be preserved in the close quarters of Washington City. Or perhaps scheming openly with Wilkinson was Burr's way of thumbing his nose at the president he did not respect.

The whisperings about Burr's intentions must have reached the president's ear. Jefferson's friends could hardly have resisted sharing such a delectable morsel of political intelligence. Yet the Virginian gave no notice of it. Aaron Burr was no longer a major concern for him. After all, Jefferson was beginning his second term as president. Aaron Burr, under indictment for murder in two states, was leaving for the West and whatever destiny he might cobble together out there. Jefferson did not anticipate that Burr would be a far greater problem in the future than he had ever been in the past.

8

The Adventure Begins

Pittsburgh to New Orleans
May–July 1805

After a vain attempt to coordinate his travel with Wilkinson, who was taking his family to St. Louis, Burr set out for the West.[1] Once under way, the former vice president sent a cheery note to the British minister, describing his prospects as "in the most prosperous train." Burr vowed to send a confidential person to divulge his plans more fully. The minister dispatched another positive report to London. "Mr. Burr," he wrote, "seems to regain his influence with great rapidity."[2]

A Philadelphia newspaper reported that Burr was going west to view "the natural history and beauties of the country . . . and perhaps to communicate them to the public." The newspaper discounted rumors that he would be Louisiana's governor or a candidate for office in that territory. Such a course, the newspaper commented insightfully, would not suit Burr's "cool impatience." Another newspaper speculated that Burr's trip concerned a canal on the Ohio River.[3]

When he arrived in Pittsburgh, Burr was delighted with the riverboat he had ordered. It was "a floating house," he wrote to Theodosia, "sixty feet by fourteen, containing dining-room, kitchen with fireplace, and two bed-rooms." With a walking area on the roof and glass windows, the craft cost $133 (about $5,000 in today's money). "How it can be made for that sum," Burr marveled, "passes my comprehension."[4]

On the river, he overtook a boat carrying Congressman Matthew Lyon to Kentucky. After lashing the two craft together, Burr and Lyon companion-ably floated past settlements on either shore. Man's hand still rested lightly on the Ohio Valley. When the morning fog burned off, they could admire flocks of waterfowl and watch schools of pike darting through river grass.

They paused to tour Indian burial mounds in Marietta, which also was home to several boatyards. The yards produced simple craft like Burr's but also oceangoing brigs and schooners of 100 to 150 tons. Though Marietta was four hundred miles from the nearest seacoast, its ships were floated downriver to the Gulf of Mexico, a challenging journey for a large sailing ship. One Marietta shipyard had just won a navy contract to build two gunboats.[5]

The Marietta shipyards made a lasting impression on Burr, who had just asked the British minister to send warships to the mouth of the Missis-sippi. Burr's plans required naval power. Only warships could hold New Orleans, the mouth of the Mississippi, or Mobile Bay, or launch an amphibi-ous assault on Mexico through Vera Cruz. But warships were the techno-logical marvels of the day, taking years to build and outfit at a cost that an out-of-work politician could hardly meet. Even merchant ships, which often carried cannon to protect against pirates or to operate as privateers, were expensive. Perhaps Burr's seapower could come from the nation's interior. In coming months, Burr would cultivate several inland boatbuilders.[6]

On an evening in early May, after Lyon had floated ahead, Burr's boat swung around the Belpre bend of the Ohio. A white mansion rose from an island in the river. Guarded by a heavy stone gate and featuring a two-acre flower garden, the home cast a spell of enchantment. Spring blooms blanketed dogwood trees and crowned a peach and apple orchard. This unexpected paradise, twelve miles below Marietta, was hailed in an 1808 guidebook as a "situation perhaps not exceeded for beauty in the world." Burr had landed at Blennerhassett Island, its incongruously elegant home occupied by an equally incongruous family. The island would haunt Burr for the next two years.[7]

The gracious mansion on Blennerhassett Island in the Ohio River, which burned down in 1811, has been rebuilt to the rough proportions of the original.

That evening, he dined with Harman and Margaret Blennerhassett, the Irish expatriates who had created the island Eden. Having inherited a comfortable estate in Ireland, Blennerhassett married his own niece, sold out, and left for America in 1796. They settled first in Marietta, home to many Continental Army veterans who received land grants for their military service. The Blennerhassetts selected their island for practical as well as esthetic reasons. Because the island was part of Virginia (now West Virginia), the Irish couple could use slave labor to build their mansion and farm the land.

At forty years old, Harman Blennerhassett cut an Ichabod Crane figure: six feet tall, slender, with gray hair, a large nose, and weak eyes. When reading, he held books so close that his nose brushed the page. His mansion included a library and a scientific laboratory. His favorite pursuits were music and chemistry. In contrast, Margaret Blennerhassett was a skilled horsewoman, tall and athletic, able to vault the five-foot fence that surrounded their property. Educated far beyond the norm for the Ohio Valley, the Blennerhassetts liked to display their learning. Harman spouted passages from the *Iliad* in Greek. Margaret favored Shakespeare, though she also read to guests in French, following with her own translations.[8]

Burr delivered a microscope sent to Blennerhassett by a friend in

Marietta. The couple, who had three young children, entertained Burr until eleven o'clock. Burr declined the offer to spend the night in the mansion, insisting that "there is no society in sleep." As the Blennerhassetts walked him to the riverboat, he slipped and fell, calling it "an ill omen." Brushing off the spill, he soon continued down the river.[9]

For the next six weeks, Burr crisscrossed the West. His boat stopped in Cincinnati and Louisville. He rode on horseback through Kentucky and down to Nashville in Tennessee, then returned to the water to descend the Cumberland, lower Ohio, and Mississippi Rivers. The journey took on an improvisational character. Though Burr always visited a region's prominent men and assiduously tracked down old army colleagues, he also pursued relationships from chance encounters, examining the countryside along the way. He pursued anyone who could help him with the three essentials for his plans: money, political influence, and military force.[10]

With those he met, Burr spoke of the West and its future. Many of his conversations followed a rough template that appealed to his listeners' self-interest and also to their sense of adventure. He usually insisted that the rest of the nation was plundering the West, that "it was not right that the Eastern states should draw so much money from the West for land." The nation, he argued, should take West Florida and Texas by force. He sometimes mentioned building a canal at Louisville but often steered the talk to Spain. He was eager, he said repeatedly, to lead troops against the Spaniards.[11]

Westerners were gratified that this eminent man understood their problems and saw their situation so clearly. Burr's criticism of Jefferson's government had to be sharp enough to attract and inspire those who shared his dissatisfaction, yet not so bitter that he was deemed seditious. By measuring his listeners' responses to his carefully calibrated remarks, Burr could identify men of spirit who might join his expedition. It was delicate work, requiring smooth talking and sharp judgments of character. How well he judged the men he recruited might well determine his success.

When he left a town, rumors swirled in his wake. After meeting with Burr in Cincinnati, the county sheriff began predicting the nation would divide along the line of the Appalachian Mountains. With its capital in Cincinnati, he said, a new western empire would send five hundred men to conquer Mexico.[12]

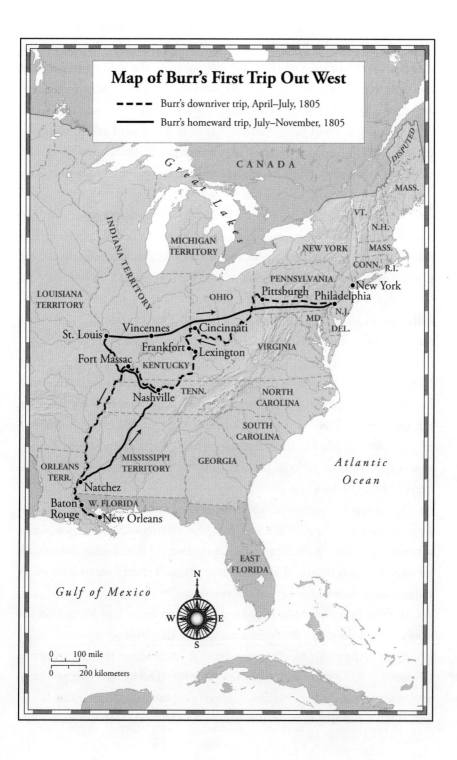

Map of Burr's First Trip Out West

- - - - Burr's downriver trip, April–July, 1805
———— Burr's homeward trip, July–November, 1805

A few westerners received extra attention from Burr. In Cincinnati, Burr lingered with his friend from the Senate, John Smith, a large man with dark features. A leading merchant, Smith supplied the military throughout the West, which gave him invaluable knowledge of army posts on the Ohio and Mississippi Rivers. A few months earlier, Smith had contracted with the U.S. navy to build two gunboats. Smith also had land and business interests in Mississippi Territory, where his agents had been none other than the three Kemper brothers, leaders of the abortive invasion of Spanish West Florida the year before.[13]

In Indiana, Burr hit it off with a local militia officer and river pilot.[14] In Kentucky, he visited more shipyards and a powerful former senator. Burr stayed a week in Lexington with the director of the Kentucky Insurance Company, from whom he hoped to secure financing.[15]

A warm welcome in Nashville delighted Burr. "I have been received with much kindness and hospitality," he wrote to Theodosia, "and could stay a month with pleasure." He especially valued the company of General Jackson, describing him as "one of those frank, ardent souls whom I love to meet." As men of action, both Burr and Jackson were frustrated by Jefferson's cautious policy toward Spain. Both hankered for invasion, not negotiation. Jackson commanded more than two thousand Tennessee militiamen, a sturdy force in the thinly settled West. The two men formed a strong attachment. Jackson provided a boat to carry Burr down the Cumberland River to the Ohio.

To no one in Tennessee, however, did Burr speak about Matthew Lyon's proposal that he run for Congress. After talking with Burr again, Lyon washed his hands of the former vice president. "There seemed too much mystery in his conduct," Lyon said later. "I suspected him to have other objects in view, to which I could not penetrate."[16]

In early June, Burr met with General Wilkinson at Fort Massac on the north side of the Ohio River, in what is now Illinois, and reported on his progress.[17] After their meetings the general wrote effusively about Burr to a Spanish official then posted in New Orleans. The former vice president was, the general gushed, "brave, learned, eloquent, gallant, honorable . . . and rich in the affections of the human heart." Wilkinson promised that

Burr would shake up affairs in New Orleans, and would send that "black-guard," Governor Claiborne, "to the devil." [18]

Wilkinson also sent a note introducing Burr to Daniel Clark, the merchant-politician in New Orleans who helped lead the challenge to American rule. Burr, Wilkinson wrote, "has claims to all your civilities, and your services." The general added a conspiratorial aside: "To him I refer you, for many things improper to letter, and which he will not say to any other." [19]

Though Wilkinson missed the opportunity to introduce Burr to General John Adair of the Kentucky militia, he knew the two men should talk. Six months earlier, it was Adair who wrote to the general that "Mexico glitters in our eyes—the word is all we wait for." After Burr left Fort Massac, Wilkinson assured Adair that the former vice president "understands your merits, and *reckons* on you. Prepare to visit me, and I will tell you all." Wilkinson added in a written whisper, "We must have a peep at the unknown world beyond me." [20]

Burr left Fort Massac in an army barge and soon reached the Mississippi River, where the water changed from sparkling clear to thick with sediment. The current strengthened and the boat sped up. Farmsteads became rare, poor and bedraggled.[21] With few places to stop, Burr raced down the continent to Natchez.

To men who had spent weeks cooped up on a riverboat, Natchez "Under the Hill" offered liquor, gambling, and female companionship. Burr avoided those haunts, concentrating on the genteel folk who lived on the bluffs above the river and on the plantations around the town. Their wooden homes, built for the heat with wraparound galleries and ample windows and doors, reflected a French sensibility. The Natchez planters were prosperous; the 1808 guidebook reported that in Natchez "the accumulation of wealth [is] the grand polar star to which all pursuits of the inhabitants are directed." Burr found educated and refined men there; those men found Burr charming and compelling. Here was fertile ground on which to prospect for supporters.[22]

Burr slowed his pace. He adopted an early version of a politician's door-knocking campaign, moving downriver plantation by plantation, trading on his fame: "Whenever I hear of any gentleman whose acquaintance or hospitalities I should desire," he wrote to Theodosia, "I send word that

I am coming to see him, and have always met a most cordial reception."[23]
Each day Burr breakfasted with a new planter, dined with another, then continued on his way. On June 25, he reached New Orleans.

"We are happy," exclaimed the *Orleans Gazette* three days later, "to announce the arrival in this city, on Wednesday last, of Col. Burr." The newspaper praised him as "from the first dawn of the revolution a republican" and "a man of splendid talents, and pleasing manners, a profound lawyer, and an elegant scholar."

Burr, fluent in French and a lifelong Francophile who had never visited Europe, reveled in New Orleans. The city offered a form of European culture in the heavy heat of the Gulf Coast summer, its exotic qualities sharpened by the thousand miles that separated it from the Atlantic coast.[24]

The city was larger than Burr anticipated, with greater wealth. Sugar and cotton production boomed in the countryside. Behind levees that strained to channel the Mississippi, the main streets were the equal of any in the country. Some brick houses rose to two or three stories along a regular grid. "I hear so many pleasant things of Orleans," he wrote to his daughter, "that I should certainly (if one half of them are verified on inspection) settle down there were it not for Theodosia and her boy." To Burr, the people seemed "cheerful, gay, and easy." Another visitor portrayed Louisianans as "having a drinking glass in hand, harmonizing in song, and spending whole nights at frenzied card games."[25]

His stepson, a local judge, greeted Burr, who relished the company he found in the city, particularly the women. He wrote admiringly of one with "sparkling black eyes, which seem to be made for far other purposes than those of mere vision." He promised to return the following autumn.[26]

Burr's success in New Orleans extended beyond the social. Day after day, he forged ties with the city's powerful, beginning with the three-hundred-member Mexican Association. That group, which included Daniel Clark and Edward Livingston, aimed to liberate Mexico, a dream that meshed neatly with Burr's. They imagined an invasion force of eight thousand militia from Louisiana, ten thousand from Kentucky, three thousand regular troops, and five thousand slaves who would be promised their freedom. Burr learned that the French had left fifty-five cannon in New Orleans, which the thrifty Jefferson had declined to purchase. With so much artillery there for the taking, Burr would be spared the expense and trouble of acquiring it elsewhere.[27]

Burr quickly won the loyalty of Daniel Clark, who knew Mexico from business dealings there. The merchant-politician introduced Burr to the city's elite, who showered attention on the former vice president. Clark hosted a dinner in Burr's honor, then advanced him $300 and loaned him horses for the first leg of his return to the Atlantic coast. Clark also pledged $50,000 for a Mexican expedition.[28]

Burr took special pride in winning favor with the hierarchy of the Catholic Church, an important force in New Orleans and in Mexico. The local bishop and the mother superior of the Ursuline sisters supported the Mexican Association. The bishop smiled on Burr, taking him to the Ursuline cloister, an outing that Burr bragged about to Theodosia. At first, the sisters warily conversed with him in their specially built greeting room, where metal grates separated the nuns from visitors. But Burr's charm won out. The sisters showed him around their establishment, then laid out wine, fruit, and cakes. "I asked them to remember me in their prayers," he wrote, "which they all promised with great promptness and courtesy."[29]

Government officials in New Orleans were less smitten with Burr. His dalliance with the Mexican Association alienated both Governor Claiborne and the Spanish officials still in the city. Burr was, Claiborne complained, too friendly with Livingston, Clark, and others who opposed the government. Burr also ignored the senior Spaniard on site and paymaster for General Wilkinson; Wilkinson was forced to apologize for the snub.[30]

After almost three weeks, Burr had built many bridges in that bewitching city. The farther he traveled from the Atlantic coast, the warmer was the reception. Men in Mississippi and Orleans shared his hunger for Spanish land and silver, as well as his disdain for the American government. He was making important alliances, recruiting supporters and fitting his own plans together with the dreams of the people of New Orleans. But it was time to go.

Many visitors to New Orleans sailed home to Charleston or Baltimore or New York, avoiding the grueling trek upriver. Burr, however, wanted to see more of the country and meet more westerners. He set off in mid-July to return the difficult, overland way.[31]

9

Early Doubts

Natchez to Philadelphia
July–November 1805

The dirty part of the return trip began in Natchez. Jefferson's government had pledged to convert the Natchez Trace into a true road all the way to Nashville. "This is imaginary," Burr huffed to Theodosia. "There is no such road." Water was scarce at first. "Think of drinking the nasty puddle-water," he wrote, "covered with green scum, and full of animalculae—Bah!" [1]

For close to four weeks, Burr plowed four hundred miles through dense woods, much of it still occupied by Choctaws and Chickasaws. He slept rough, ate what his party could kill, and exhibited a hardiness that westerners would respect. An earlier traveler described the country as "an impenetrable forest condensed by cane and cemented by grape vines, so that a dozen trees must be cut before one can fall, and this on the most irregular hilly broken and unfinished part of the globe's surface." The West judged a man by his strength, stamina, and gun skills. With his backwoods trek and dueling exploit, Burr could claim western credibility. [2]

While Burr forded streams in Mississippi Territory, Philadelphia's

United States Gazette reminded the nation where he was and what he might be up to. "How long will it be," the newspaper asked in its August 2 edition, "before we hear of Colonel Burr being at the head of a revolution party on the western waters?" When, it inquired further, would "all the military posts at New Orleans and the Mississippi be in the hands of Colonel Burr's revolution party? How soon will Colonel Burr engage in the reduction of Mexico?"

Other newspapers—there were more than two hundred throughout the country—raced to reprint the electrifying speculation. Not even five months after leaving the vice president's chair, was Burr plotting revolution and foreign invasion?

In 1805, American journalism occupied a gray area between news, gossip, and commentary. The item about Burr may have sprung from an editor's suspicions, married to a prescient analysis of Burr's character and the state of the West. Or it may have been planted by an enemy, or even by Burr's inner circle. The British minister, Anthony Merry, inclined to the latter explanations. Burr and his allies had been indiscreet, he wrote to London, "or have been betrayed . . . for the object of his journey has now begun to be noticed in the public prints." The diplomat suggested that Burr's scheme "may be so far advanced, as from the nature of it, to render any further secrecy impossible." Others thought, as Burr did when he learned of the newspaper item, that the Spanish minister had written it in order to block Burr's designs on Spanish lands.[3]

Jefferson's government did not respond to the story. No letters went out to western governors to ask what was going on. Nor did the War Department ask western commanders to report on Burr's travels. No reinforcements went to western outposts. No navy ships were moved. Possibly Jefferson, familiar with the whimsies of the press, thought the item untrustworthy. Possibly he preferred to await better evidence. Jefferson's inaction in the face of this report only confirmed Burr's low opinion of the president as a man incapable of decisive action.

Unaware of the stir back east, Burr continued to nurture the relationships he needed. He stayed for a week with General Jackson. To Theodosia, he portrayed himself lounging with the general's two young nieces, who "have cured me of all the evils of my wilderness jaunt." Tennessee hospitality included a public dinner that was given, he wrote with pride, "not to the vice-president, but to A.B." A press account depicted Burr "in his usual ease and elegance of address appear[ing] quite happy, and indeed all the company were much delighted with his presence." A formal toast honored Burr, urging "may all honest Americans never forget such merit." [4]

Andrew Jackson, a young militia general in Tennessee, formed a strong personal bond with Burr and enthusiastically supported Burr's goal of taking territory from Spain.

In Kentucky, Burr finally met John Adair, the militia general he missed on his outbound trip. Adair brought several friends to a morning meal at Captain Weisiger's tavern in Frankfort and swiftly joined Burr's inner circle. The *Frankfort Palladium* published a vivid portrait of Burr at a public dinner:

To the ladies he is all attention—all devotion—in conversation he gazes on them with complacency and rapture, and when he addresses them, it is with that smiling affability, those captivating gestures, that *je ne sai quoi*, those dissolving looks, that soft, sweet, and insinuating eloquence, which takes the soul captive, before it can prepare for defense.[5]

Burr left Lexington just before the echo of the Philadelphia newspaper item unsettled the town. The *Kentucky Gazette* indignantly rejected the suggestion that Burr would lead the West into rebellion. Noting Burr's "talent for intrigue," the newspaper warned that "if he calculated on withdrawing the affections of the people of the Western States from their government, he will find himself deceived."[6]

Although Burr had been traveling for four months, he had many miles still to go. He turned west to St. Louis, where General Wilkinson now was governor of Louisiana Territory. Based on what he had learned during his journey, Burr wanted to revisit their plans.[7]

Wilkinson's time in St. Louis had begun cheerily enough. On the Fourth of July, residents staged an outdoor banquet on the Mississippi to mark both the nation's independence and his arrival. A cannon fusillade called the guests to riverside tables. "As if by magic," according to one account, a gilded pyramid appeared on the central table, adorned on three sides with slogans honoring the nation. Wilkinson's initials shone on the fourth side. Seventeen smaller pyramids, representing the seventeen states, circled the central structure. After dinner, the dancing lasted late into the night.[8]

In his early days as governor, the stocky, florid Wilkinson acted as if he knew a great secret. When alone with a senior officer, he locked the door and paced silently. He asked what form of government would suit Louisiana. The officer replied that representative government was best. The general frowned in disagreement. Frenchmen in the territory would not understand such a government, he said, adding:

> A military government was best for those people, and no other was contemplated for them. That indeed politics had undergone a great change in the U.S., and the honest and wise had united to save the federal constitution, and prevent a division of property which the democrats aimed at.

Over the next day, Wilkinson talked to the officer twice more, always behind locked doors. The general insisted that public opinion favored "energetic measures." Wilkinson said he had "a GRAND SCHEME in contemplation, that will not only make mine, but the fortunes of all concerned." Throughout the next weeks and months, Wilkinson returned to these themes in conversation and predicted war with Spain.[9]

The general shared similar sentiments with a local militia leader. Wilkinson insisted that most Louisiana residents would prefer to separate from the United States. He then urged the man to befriend Burr, "one of the most enterprising men in the United States." Finally, the general said that within eighteen months he would lead an attack on Mexico and Peru; Wilkinson asked how many men the local militia could raise for the invasion.[10]

To a third man, Wilkinson confided that a new situation was developing, "a distant one, full of danger, requiring enterprise, but if successful, full of fortune and glory."[11]

In a letter to Secretary of War Henry Dearborn, Wilkinson argued that the United States should invade West Florida through Baton Rouge, and Mexico through Santa Fe. Spanish troops were unpaid and poorly provisioned, he wrote, while American forces could move far up the Arkansas River toward Santa Fe. He needed only fifteen hundred men and ten cannon; because of the Mexicans' Catholic faith, he proposed to carry before him a banner with a cross on it and to bring a dozen Irish priests.[12]

At the same time, the duplicitous Wilkinson offered soothing words of peace to his Spanish spymaster in New Orleans: "I flatter myself that by reciprocal concessions and des[ire] of conciliation, we shall be able to dispel the clouds which have hung over our political horizon and perpetuate the peace of the two nations."[13]

Burr reached St. Louis in the second week of September, choosing to stay with his brother-in-law, the territorial secretary. His conferences with the general, however, were not entirely harmonious. One of Wilkinson's officers reported tension between the two men: "Burr, I believe, does not entirely approve the governor's notions."[14]

Several factors might have caused the tension. Most obviously, Burr surely confirmed in New Orleans, from Daniel Clark and others, that the worst rumors about Wilkinson were true: that he had taken Spanish bribes for nearly twenty years.

The confirmation of Wilkinson's treason had to be disturbing. How could Burr trust this chameleonlike fellow, so superficially guileless yet so deeply corrupt? Burr's plans centered on war with Spain and the liberation of its American colonies. Could Wilkinson bite the Spanish hand that had fed him for so long? Perhaps Burr decided to use Wilkinson's double-agent status to his own benefit. By threatening Wilkinson with exposure, he might tie the slippery general more closely to himself. Or perhaps Burr resolved to imitate Wilkinson and extort Spanish silver for himself.

However Burr deployed the confirmation of Wilkinson's treachery, the friction between them in St. Louis suggests he did use it. Other factors may have chilled their relationship. They disagreed on the best invasion route into Mexico. Burr favored an amphibious assault on Vera Cruz, then a march inland to Mexico City. Hernan Cortes followed that route in 1519, and Winfield Scott would use it in 1847. Wilkinson, though, preferred a roundabout assault through lightly defended Santa Fe, which he could launch from St. Louis. The press innuendos about Burr's plans, which did not mention Wilkinson, were another problem. Also, Burr had resolved to launch their expedition in the spring of 1806, just seven months away. Wilkinson had a long track record of scheming, but he had always avoided actual insurrection. Burr was pushing him into very deep waters. It seemed the general was growing anxious.

A note from Washington City heightened Wilkinson's anxiety. "There is a rumor," wrote Secretary of War Dearborn, "that you, Burr, etc., are too intimate." There, on the page before Wilkinson, was proof that his plotting with Burr was too widely known. "Keep every suspicious person at arm's length," the Secretary counseled, "and be as wise as a serpent and as harmless as a dove." Another warning came from Daniel Clark in New Orleans. "Many absurd and wild reports are circulated here," Clark wrote, about Burr and western secession. The general, added Clark, was "spoken of as his right-hand man." [15] Now Wilkinson had even more reason to be wary of Burr, whose ability to keep a secret was proving overstated.

Yet Wilkinson, due to his special relationship with the Spaniards, was uniquely well-positioned to reduce his own anxiety by hedging his bets.

Through this period, Spanish officials received warnings of an impending American war from an unidentified informant who was deeply involved with Burr, as well as regular deliveries of American newspaper clippings about the prospects for war. Those messages came from the double-agent general. No matter how events unfolded, Wilkinson intended to have friends on the winning side.[16]

Slowly that autumn, Burr made his way east. In Indiana Territory he enjoyed the company of the governor, William Henry Harrison, a soldier who was, in Burr's special lexicon, "fit for other things."[17] The scion of a distinguished but impoverished Virginia family, Harrison was connected to Burr's inner circle at several points. He called General Wilkinson "my most intimate friend." He had bought land from Dayton, was married to the daughter of an associate of Dayton's, and offered to sponsor Dayton's nephew in Indiana Territory.[18]

Burr kept traveling east, through Kentucky and Cincinnati, where he found Dayton recuperating from a long fever, "much the worse for his late illness." In Ohio he dined with Edward Tupper, a leading militia officer who was building navy ships in Marietta. Burr chatted suggestively about the West and Mexico. He watched and he listened. In late November, after seven months of travel, he started the last leg of his journey.[19]

But Burr could not return home. Since the Hamilton duel, he had moved from inns to friends' homes to frontier forts to houseboats to campsites. As long as the murder indictments loomed in New York and New Jersey, he could not come to rest. How he paid his bills was mysterious at the time, and remains so. He had neither occupation nor assets, yet traveled widely, entertained, dressed well, and leased lodgings as needed. The best evidence suggests that his wealthy son-in-law, Joseph Alston, supported him; he also may have borrowed money from friends.

As Burr looked back on his journey, he could feel some cause for optimism. He had seen the land. Now he knew where hills rose forbiddingly, which forests were impenetrable, and what streams lacked fords. He knew how long it took to get from St. Louis to New Orleans, from Nashville to Fort Massac, from Lexington to Natchez. He understood the patterns of settlement: where French traditions persisted, what lands the Indians still held, how Ohio teemed with small farmers while slave-owning planters prevailed in Mississippi and Orleans.

He also saw opportunity wherever he went. New Orleans, an enchanting powder keg, seemed poised to throw off American rule. Spain was too weak to defend the Floridas or Mexico. High-spirited westerners should embrace the chance to forge a new destiny, to write their names large in the book of history, just below Aaron Burr's. There were so many opportunities. Burr would keep them all open, preserving his ability to shift from one to another as circumstances changed.

When he had started his journey, he knew his dreams required money, political support, and military force. He had made progress on all three fronts.

For money, he now had Daniel Clark's pledge of $50,000 ($2 million in today's value). Burr had met other wealthy men, like Harman Blennerhassett, who could provide more. One Mississippi planter would claim to have supplied another $65,000.[20] Burr could borrow from the Kentucky Insurance Company or raise money through the Indiana canal company. Wealthy John Smith of Cincinnati could help. Burr also could call on his son-in-law's fortune and his rich friends in New York, men with the practical vision to see an invasion of Mexico as an investment opportunity.

Burr found political support, too, especially in Natchez and New Orleans. From the Mexican Association to the Catholic Church to the Mississippi planters, Burr's standing was high and the appetite was strong for adventure and change. In Kentucky, Ohio, and Tennessee, however, Burr had to be more cautious. Those communities were tied more closely to the Atlantic coast. They liked having free trade rights through New Orleans. Nevertheless, his ambitions were supported by leading men from John Smith to Andrew Jackson of Tennessee.

Burr had made only slight progress in his quest for seapower. There was no word from Charles Williamson about British naval support, while Dayton's illness had prevented him from meeting with Merry, the British minister; Burr would have to see Merry as soon as he reached Washington City. A navy could not be assembled on short notice with funds coaxed from a few rich men. Perhaps Burr's western friends would sell him those gunboats whose keels were being laid in riverside boatyards. Indeed, Senator

John Smith of Cincinnati was considering doing just that.[21] Burr still might recruit Commodore Truxtun or another sea captain to command his ships.

Matters on land were more straightforward. New Orleans offered the enthusiasm of the Mexican Association, plus those fifty-five cannon orphaned by the French. Burr also reported finding a stand of ten thousand muskets, probably Spanish arms in Florida.[22] General Wilkinson remained central to any military move, and Burr's friction with the general in St. Louis warranted attention. Still, the venture had started with conversations between Burr and Wilkinson eighteen months before. The general could hardly back out now.

Nevertheless, Burr would not have been human if he did not entertain doubts and questions. Was it really Wilkinson's army to order about as he wished, or as Burr wished? Might interference from Washington City disrupt their plans? Or might Wilkinson's obligations to Spain override Burr's claims on the general? Perhaps Burr should rely on state militias rather than the federal army. Jackson and Adair and Tupper and Claiborne might call out their militias to realize Burr's dreams. What cause would bring militiamen from their homes, or soldiers from their billets?

After seven months in the West, Burr could answer that last question. Although many westerners still had a yen for independence, that urge was not strong enough to trigger insurrection in Kentucky and Tennessee and Ohio. The acquisition of New Orleans and control of the Mississippi had allayed much of the westerners' discontent. And Burr offered no new ideology, no higher goal of liberty or freedom, to call westerners to arms against their own government.

For Burr's purposes, the best development would be a Spanish war. That would stir the blood, rouse the land-lust, hone the greed. Florida. Texas. New Mexico. Mexico. Peru. So much to take. And for those who wanted a veneer of idealism, war could be justified as a way to liberate the millions of souls writhing under the heel of the Spanish king. Here was a chance to export liberty, a call with a resonance that has persisted through American history.

In late 1805, war with Spain was no sure thing. Jefferson did not want one.[23] Even if there were a war, the president would not hurry to give Burr a military command. But if war broke out, the West could respond on its own.

State militias would need leaders, and Burr could step forward. In wartime, separatist feelings in Orleans and Mississippi could spread, especially if General Wilkinson looked the other way or sent his troops to attack far-away Santa Fe. Once Burr was at the head of an army, who knew what he might achieve?

Burr was resolved. He would make his move in the spring, just six months away, when the western rivers were high and travel was easier. He needed to coordinate many elements, to raise men and arms, acquire supplies, dispatch agents throughout the West and Spanish lands. The challenges were daunting: raising an insurrection, mounting an invasion, conquering vast lands, establishing a new government. A more modest man might have been intimidated by the tasks and the risks.

10

On the World Stage

Washington City/Philadelphia
November 1805–February 1806

U pon reaching Washington City in late November 1805, Burr
pursued a daring diplomatic initiative. His plans for transforming
America's frontier and Spain's colonies would play out on the
world stage. He still hoped for British support, but he also hoped to reduce
Spain's vigilance by allaying its fears of a border conflict. With impressive
pretension, Burr opened talks with both countries on behalf of a new nation
that existed only in his mind. For such sensitive conversations, he turned to
Jonathan Dayton, his lifelong friend.

They began with the British minister, Anthony Merry. Charles Williamson was still urging Burr's case on the other side of the Atlantic. He
soon would write to a British official that with only a modest investment,
King George would see "50,000 North Americans, with Colonel Burr at
their head, far on their march to the City of Mexico," striking a heavy blow
against Napoleon's ally, Spain.[1] Williamson's entreaties, however, went un-
answered.

So Dayton called on Merry when Burr arrived from the West. Soon

Burr was meeting directly with Merry. He explained that his expedition would launch in March, less than four months away, on a breathtaking scale. Presented in Burr's composed, confident manner, his plan captivated the Englishman.

The enterprise would begin in New Orleans. People there, Burr assured Merry, were "so firmly resolved upon separating themselves from their Union . . . that he [Burr] was sure the revolution there would be accompanied without a drop of blood being shed." That revolution would begin by late May of 1806. The American army was no obstacle: American soldiers, Burr predicted, would join him.

The Floridas would next declare themselves independent and the western states would follow. The result, Burr emphasized, would be the end of the United States. "Once Louisiana and the western country become independent," he told Merry, "the Eastern States [New England] will separate themselves immediately from the Southern." Burr did not weep for the demise of his country. Instead, he warned that if Britain did not aid him, France would. The people in Louisiana, he said, would soon invite the French to deliver them from the unwelcome clutches of the United States. Napoleon could again plant the tricolor in North America.

Once more, Burr pulled out his shopping list. He needed the same aid he had requested nine months before: a Royal Navy squadron at the mouth of the Mississippi and 110,000 pounds sterling. The warships, Burr pressed, should include "two or three ships of the line [battleships]—the same number of frigates and a proportionable number of smaller vessels."

And Burr wanted them fast. He needed a response in three months. At all events, he continued, the British ships must reach the Gulf of Mexico by April 10; Burr or Daniel Clark would send word to the ships when Orleans declared its independence. Then Burr and the Royal Navy squadron could coordinate operations against the Floridas and Mexico.[2]

Impressed, Merry fired off a new report to London, painting another encouraging picture of Burr's prospects.

With the Spanish minister, the Marquis de Casa Yrujo, Burr and Dayton could not tell the truth. After all, Burr ached to liberate Spain's American possessions. Burr wanted to shower Casa Yrujo with false reassurances, encouraging Spain not to fear his western plans. To that end, Burr played on Spain's dread of the United States, presenting himself as potentially a much better neighbor of Mexico and the Floridas.

The border dispute between Spain and the United States still smoldered. A few months earlier, the Spaniards had mounted an eccentric raid into Mississippi. A dozen whites in blackface, plus seven actual blacks, crossed the border and kidnapped the three disruptive Kemper brothers, dragging them from their beds in the night. While the kidnappers were transporting their captives by canoe, American troops intervened, freed the Kempers, and imprisoned the kidnappers. Westerners raged over the insult to American sovereignty.[3]

In Natchez, the *Mississippi Messenger* called for an immediate rupture with Spain. "We cannot see how peace is to be preserved," intoned the *Orleans Gazette*. In November, the *Kentucky Gazette* demanded the seizure of Baton Rouge from Spain for "safekeeping." For several reasons, Secretary of State Madison asked that Spain recall Casa Yrujo as its minister.[4]

In this highly charged situation, Burr and Dayton chose to play Wilkinson's old game, teasing the Spaniards with the prospect of western secession. Why should Wilkinson be the only one to pocket Spanish silver? Spain, fearing American expansion, might underwrite an effort to break off the western part of the nation. Burr set out to persuade the Spanish diplomat that he, the enemy of Spain's enemy, was a friend.

In early December, Dayton met Casa Yrujo in Philadelphia. The Spaniard, red-haired and fastidious about his dress, was well versed in American politics. Not only had he held his post for almost ten years, but also his father-in-law was the Republican governor of Pennsylvania.[5]

The tall, aristocratic Dayton began with a startling claim about Burr's travels in the West. He said that Burr "has found the most favorable disposition, not only for this emancipation [of the West] . . . but also for making an expedition against the kingdom of Mexico." Louisiana, he added, "would be quick to take arms in order to seize the Floridas and add it to the new republic." The British, Dayton lied, were supporting Burr. The arrival of British warships off the Gulf Coast would trigger an uprising in New Orleans in

February or March. After the Floridas fell, an invasion force would sail for Mexico.[6]

At this point, Casa Yrujo might well have wondered if Dayton had taken leave of his senses. Why would this American tell him about a plan to invade the lands of King Carlos? Was Dayton betraying Burr? Or was Dayton asking Casa Yrujo to betray his sovereign and join this mad venture? Somehow, Dayton managed to assuage some of the Spaniard's doubts.

In his report to Madrid, Casa Yrujo endorsed Dayton's basic propositions. Louisiana and the West would soon separate from the United States, the Spaniard predicted, and the Floridas would join them. But he did not swallow the lie that Burr had British support; if that were true, Burr would not waste his time talking to Spain. The diplomat also thought Jefferson would not be deceived about Burr's intentions, but that Burr, "his expansive ambitions destroyed in the Atlantic states, perhaps can capture the goodwill of those of the west and be declared president of this new republic."[7]

Days later, Dayton was back to confer again with the Spaniard. In two further meetings, he admitted he had lied about British support for Burr. There was none. Dayton unveiled a new plan, which Casa Yrujo described as "almost insane," yet "easy to execute." The first characterization was certainly true.

According to Dayton, Burr intended to infiltrate armed men in ordinary dress into Washington City. Upon a signal, they would seize the president, the vice president, and the president pro tempore of the Senate. Burr's forces would empty the local banks, then sail away on the best ships in Washington's navy yard, burning the others so they could not follow. Once Burr's desperadoes arrived in New Orleans, they would proclaim the independent nation of Louisiana and the western states. For all of its extravagance, the scheme would meet Burr's most acute needs. If Britain would not supply money and ships, Burr could steal them.

Casa Yrujo accepted Dayton's assertion that Burr had support from "an infinite number of adventurers, without property, full of ambition, ready to unite at once under the standard of a revolution which promises to better their situation." Dayton insisted that Burr's plan posed no threat to Spain; it would reduce the power of the United States, leave the Floridas intact, and produce permanent borders for Louisiana that Spain would find acceptable. Casa Yrujo reported that Spanish agents confirmed Dayton's story, so "there hardly remains any doubt of some plot against the existing government."

Incredibly, Casa Yrujo, a seasoned diplomat, recommended that Spain help pay for the plan Dayton had unveiled. "Spain would view with extreme satisfaction," he wrote to Madrid, "the dismemberment of the colossal power [the United States] . . . growing up at the very gates of her most precious and important colonies." The "men of talent and study" in Jefferson's government, he added, did not appreciate the danger that Burr posed.[8]

Casa Yrujo produced only a pittance in material support; the diplomat gave Dayton $3,000. It is a wonder he paid anything.

There was, of course, a third government with an even more vital interest in Burr's plans: the United States. Burr had little leverage with Jefferson's administration, though the president could give Burr the war with Spain that he craved. Men on the march and inflamed passions would create the perfect environment for Burr's plans. He needed tumult, even anarchy, to create opportunity.

But Jefferson had no appetite for military action, even though his envoy to Madrid, James Monroe, recommended it,[9] and even though Spain's strength seemed to ebb daily. In late 1805, only 141 soldiers defended Spain's Texas border. In October, Lord Nelson annihilated the Spanish and French fleets at the Battle of Trafalgar. After that debacle, only rarely could a Spanish ship elude the Royal Navy in the Atlantic and reach Spain's American colonies.[10]

In a letter to a friend, the president admitted that his preference for peace "has begun to produce an opinion in Europe that our government is entirely in Quaker principles." Jefferson recognized that "this opinion must be corrected . . . or we shall become the plunder of all nations."[11] His Cabinet resolved in November 1805 to offer a new proposal to Spain, but it looked a lot like Jefferson's old proposals: The United States would cede Texas beyond the Rio Grande and would buy the Floridas. In a secret message, Jefferson asked Congress to authorize the payment of $2 million for West Florida. Congress secretly approved the "Two Million Dollar Bill" in February, though the nation did not learn of the legislation for more than a month.[12]

Once more, Jefferson would seek a peaceful solution. As a French diplomat commented about Americans, "To conquer without war is the first fact in their politics."[13]

Frustrated by the absence of war preparations, Burr approached the president directly. During the same week that he predicted to the British minister the imminent dissolution of the United States, Burr sat down for a private two hours with Jefferson. He certainly described his travels out west. Tales of natural phenomena—plants, crops, animals—always interested the scientist-president. In the course of their session, Burr probed on the matter he cared most about, the prospects for a Spanish war. He left the executive mansion a disappointed man.

"There will be no war with Spain," he harrumphed in a letter to his son-in-law, "unless we shall declare it, which is not expected." He sent the same message to General Wilkinson.[14]

In the winter of 1805–06, Burr was not the only man who wanted to liberate Spain's American possessions. Francisco Miranda of Venezuela was pursuing the same dream in New York City. Unlike Burr, Miranda was ready to strike.

A soldier for Spain as a young man, Miranda joined the French revolutionary forces in 1791, then two years later was imprisoned by those same revolutionaries. He barely escaped with his life. For close to a decade, Miranda sought European aid for a South American revolution. Finished with waiting, he had resolved to make revolution himself.

Burr bristled at the appearance in America of this rival insurrectionist. When the two met, they did not get along. Asked what he would do about the South American revolutionary, Burr muttered, "Hang him." To a friend, Burr seethed that Miranda was a fool, "totally unqualified for such an expedition." Yet the South American was raising money from the same New York merchants whose wallets Burr needed to empty for his own expedition. Miranda was backed by Samuel G. Ogden, a member of the sprawling Ogden clan of New York and New Jersey; two of the merchant's relations, George and Peter Ogden, would play key roles in Burr's expedition.[15] Also behind Miranda was William Smith, son-in-law to former president John Adams. "I fancy Miranda has taken the bread from your mouth," General

Wilkinson chided Burr in a letter.[16] Burr could only gnash his teeth and wish Miranda ill luck.

Miranda bundled men, weapons, and ammunition into Ogden's ship, *Leander*, in New York harbor. The effort was far from secret. Dozens of suppliers delivered military goods to *Leander* while Miranda's agents recruited fighters. Miranda offered the same blend of plunder and idealism that Burr used. One officer explained his motives for joining Miranda:

> Appearing for the relief of the oppressed, under the banners of a celebrated chief . . . of lending our assistance to found an independent state . . . presents itself to our imaginations and hearts in the most attractive light. . . . If we succeed, our fame will take care of itself.

The recruits also believed that the U.S. government gave Miranda, in the words of that officer, "its implied sanction," since "the official language of the President, and the known sentiments of some of the political party that now prevails, leads us to suppose that our government expects or intends, very soon explicitly to authorize the use of force against Spain." [17]

Jefferson and Secretary of State Madison did meet with Miranda. Though they later denied supporting him, neither did they interfere with his preparations. Before *Leander* departed, Miranda wrote to Madison that he had "conform[ed] myself in everything to the intentions of the [United States] Government." As expressed by a leading New York Federalist, the universal understanding of Miranda's venture was that Jefferson "would wink at the things being done by individuals." [18]

Leander sailed in February 1806 with 180 men, 30 cannon, and a printing press to produce Miranda's proclamations. The force was laughably small for conquering a continent, but Miranda expected the people of Spanish America to rise and sweep their masters into the sea.[19]

Miranda left behind him a political mess for the president. The *Philadelphia Gazette* shouted that the nation's honor was ruined "in the most scandalous manner by a hostile armament fitted out in our ports under the eyes of public officers." [20] How could the nation remain at peace when its shores spawned foreign invasions? In response to the outcry, the Jefferson administration indicted William Smith and Samuel Ogden for violating the Neutrality Act, which barred hostile actions against countries with which the nation was at peace.

The separate trials of Smith and Ogden, held in New York in July 1806, were a humiliation for the president. The defendants conceded that they had shredded the Neutrality Act. They nonetheless demanded acquittal, as one lawyer put it, because "this military enterprise was begun, prepared, and set on foot with the knowledge and approbation of the executive department of our government." To support that claim, the defense subpoenaed records from Madison and the State Department. The government stonewalled the subpoenas, but both juries returned verdicts of not guilty.[21]

For Burr, the Miranda episode was an agony, threatening to spoil nearly two years of scheming. Newspapers lavished adulation on Miranda, published transcripts of the Smith and Ogden trials, and splashed the electrifying report that John Adams's grandson (Smith's son) had joined the expedition. Most grating, the Royal Navy escorted *Leander* through part of the Caribbean, but the British still showed no interest in Burr, passing over him like a wallflower at a dance.[22]

Not until the fall of 1806, after months of rumors, did the happy news arrive that Miranda had failed. His August landing in Venezuela met only indifference from the people. Spanish forces drove him back onto his ship.[23]

In a letter to Andrew Jackson in March 1806, Burr clutched at the sole feature of Miranda's expedition that might help his own plans. Foreign nations, he wrote, would hold the United States to account "for the conduct of an armament composed of American citizens and openly fitted out in an American port." In retaliation, Spain and its ally France would seize American ships. And then there should be, Burr earnestly wished, war.[24]

11

Burr's Threats

Philadelphia/Washington City
March–April 1806

B urr's diplomatic offensive included two remarkable threats. The first threat—that he would attack the American government in Washington City—emerged in Dayton's conversation with Casa Yrujo in December 1805. Remarkably, the Spaniard was not the only one to hear it. A few weeks after Dayton had unfolded that bold scheme, Burr repeated it to William Eaton, one of those disaffected military men Burr found so appealing. As spring began to warm Washington City, Burr delivered a second threat—that he would cripple Jefferson's presidency—directly to the president.

William Eaton was an excitable New Englander with a taste for derring-do and a poor reputation for sobriety. A former army captain, he became the American consul to Tunis in North Africa in the late 1790s. When the American navy arrived in the Mediterranean in 1803 to punish the piracy of the Barbary States, Eaton leapt into an epic adventure. In Egypt, he formed a partnership with a rival pasha of Tripoli. They assembled a polyglot force of mercenaries, plus a handful of U.S. marines, and crossed five hundred miles of desert to capture Derna, forcing Tripoli to sue for peace.[1]

Lauded as a hero, Eaton grew resentful when Congress dragged its feet in reimbursing his considerable expenses. In Philadelphia shortly before Christmas 1805, Dayton brought Eaton and Burr together. The former vice president sympathized with the mistreatment Eaton was suffering at Jefferson's hands. Burr certainly knew what that felt like. Slowly, Burr revealed his plans, drawing Eaton into his confidence in conversations that extended through the end of March.

The discontented soldier did not flinch when Burr disclosed that a revolution in New Orleans would establish him as sovereign of a new western nation. Nor did Eaton shrink when Burr spoke of conquering Mexico. Then Burr went too far.

"He said," Eaton later explained, "if he could gain over the Marine Corps, and secure the naval commanders . . . he would turn 'Congress neck and heels out of doors,' assassinate the president; seize on the treasury and navy; and declare himself the protector of an energetic government." Burr asked Eaton to recruit naval officers for the enterprise. Eaton refused.[2]

Though there is no evidence that Burr took any steps to mount such a coup, the idea evidently was preying on his mind. That Burr would even speak of it, while allowing Dayton to describe it to Casa Yrujo, is a measure of his rage at Jefferson.

Eaton related Burr's threat to two congressmen. They replied that he should never repeat such outrageous statements again. Eaton, still troubled, visited the president to deliver a similar warning, but he did so in a peculiar fashion. After telling Jefferson that Burr might foment insurrection in the West, Eaton recommended getting Burr out of the country by appointing him to an important diplomatic post. Jefferson brushed aside such contradictory advice—that he should reward supposed treachery with high office. Eaton claimed later that he also tried to sound the alarm against Burr through a toast delivered at a public dinner: "To the United States: Palsy to the brain that should plot to dismember, and leprosy to the hand that will not draw to defend our union." Whatever those in attendance thought of this gruesome sentiment, no one recognized it as a warning to beware of Aaron Burr.[3]

Burr cultivated other military figures that winter, including Navy Captain Stephen Decatur, recently lionized for a daring raid in Tripoli harbor. Assuring Decatur that war with Spain was certain, Burr announced that he would invade Mexico with seven thousand men and invited Decatur to be part of it. Burr also tried to recruit Commodore Truxtun, still languishing in Perth Amboy, no prospect of a naval command. Neither sailor signed up.

Burr had better luck with westerners. General Adair of Kentucky was in Washington City as a brand-new senator. Showing the effects of his alliance with Burr, Adair openly advocated western independence. Edward Tupper, general of the Ohio militia, asked Burr for a command in the coming war with Spain.[4] From his island in the Ohio River, wealthy Harman Blennerhassett volunteered for "an engagement against, or subjugation of, any of the Spanish territories," and offered to enlist his friends in the effort.[5]

Burr's most important ally, of course, was James Wilkinson. The general's stay in St. Louis grew bleak that winter. His wife of many years was dying from tuberculosis. The army's officer corps had been roiled by Wilkinson's rancorous dispute with his second-in-command over the length of the man's hair, a conflict that produced two courts-martial.[6] As territorial governor, the blustery Wilkinson was proving clumsy. Louisiana Territory was riven with conflict over land rights. The traditional French community, with Wilkinson's support, challenged land claims purchased by late-arriving "Americans." The Americans were bitter. "We go constantly armed," one complained in a newspaper diatribe, "and expect an enemy in every political opponent we meet in the streets."[7]

In letters to the general, Burr tried to reinforce the reasons for Wilkinson to continue with their western venture. If there were war with Spain, Burr warned, Jefferson would not be loyal to Wilkinson, but would replace him with a Virginian.

Burr also offered encouraging, though veiled, words about their plans. Referring to "the subject of certain speculation," Burr said he would write about it when "the whole can be communicated," insisting that "the auspices, however, are favorable." Burr did not, however, sugarcoat Jefferson's aversion to war with Spain. "The utmost intended," he wrote in December, "is [a] sort of marine piracy." A second letter advised that "we are to have no Spanish war except in ink and words."[8]

Throughout that winter, Burr had taken the most imprudent risks. Supposedly secretive and mysterious, he had made explosive comments to far too many people. Merry or Casa Yrujo might reveal Burr's plan, including Dayton's description of a coup in Washington City. Stephen Decatur could describe the army Burr intended to muster in the West. William Eaton had already disclosed part of Burr's shocking proposal to take over the United States government, but his disclosures were so odd that they drew no response. Still, someone was bound to talk to someone, who would pass the word on. It all had to come to light.[9]

In early December, President Jefferson received two anonymous letters warning him against Burr. The writer, or writers, knew exactly what Burr was saying behind closed doors. "You held a long and private conference with him [Burr] a few days ago," the first letter observed, "at the very moment he is meditating the overthrow of your administration and what is more conspiring against the state." The writer emphasized Burr's conversations with the British minister. A second letter cautioned that though Burr spoke of invading Mexico, "the destruction of our government, your ruin, and the material injury of the Atlantic States are their true object."[10]

Jefferson ignored those warnings, but a third message stirred him. The United States attorney in Kentucky, Joseph Hamilton Daveiss, wrote him on January 10, 1806. "We have traitors among us," Daveiss declared, adding that conspirators intended "the separation of the Union in favor of Spain." He reported that General Wilkinson was in the pay of Spain. After showing Daveiss's letter to his Cabinet, Jefferson asked Daveiss to send "everything known or heard by you relating to [the conspiracy], and particularly the names of all persons" in it.[11]

Through the beginning of 1806, the brightest prospects for Burr's plan were in New Orleans, where the Creoles continued to chafe under American rule. Governor Claiborne feuded with the new legislative council over land laws and public education. Claiborne complained that the "ancient Louisianians" had "a jealousy of the executive, and the base intriguers will spare no pains to widen the breach." In a speech, he said he looked down on his critics "with contempt, from that eminence on which conscious rectitude has placed me." Small wonder they disliked him.[12]

William C.C. Claiborne, governor of Orleans Territory, quarreled with the Creoles of New Orleans while worrying about slave revolts and war with Spain.

Claiborne's opponents were led by Burr's friends, men like Edward Livingston, Burr's old New York ally. Daniel Clark, who had served as Burr's escort and would become the territorial delegate to Congress, spread unflattering stories about Claiborne.[13] On two ostensibly commercial trips to Mexico, Clark accumulated information about Spanish military and naval defenses. Clark opposed an attack on Mexico by the American army but longed for a private invasion, hoping to become a duke in conquered lands.[14]

The specter of racial conflict also haunted Orleans Territory. When a free black man reported a revolutionary plot in January 1806, Claiborne wrote that he had "no doubt, but that the free people of color have been tamper'd with, and that some of them are devoted to the Spanish interest." To meet the threat, the governor ordered nightly militia patrols.[15]

Claiborne's greatest problem, however, was Spain. Spanish officials still lingered in New Orleans for desultory negotiations over the Florida and Texas borders. The Spaniards boasted that they would soon recover the west bank of the Mississippi. Customs officers in Mobile, which was part of West Florida, exacted duties on American goods; in response, Americans in the Tombigbee region above Mobile vowed to sell no goods to the

Spaniards. Claiborne anxiously reported a Spanish military buildup. The repaired fort at Baton Rouge now held 142 Spanish soldiers. Four hundred more arrived in Pensacola from Havana. To the west, eight hundred Spanish soldiers now camped on the Texas border.[16]

The governor begged for American troops. He doubted the reliability of the Orleans militia, which Daniel Clark had organized. Regular army troops, he argued, could deter a Spanish attack and also ensure the loyalty of the Creoles. It was essential, he urged Madison, to "give our new fellow citizens a confidence in the American government—which, I am sorry to say, many of them at this time do not possess."[17]

But Claiborne also itched to fight Spain. He could capture Baton Rouge in fifty hours, he wrote Jefferson. With artillery, he would take Mobile too. Burr's friends in the Mexican Association had the same idea. Proposing toasts to Aaron Burr, they recruited American army officers and the notorious Kemper brothers to lead an assault on Baton Rouge and Mobile, and simultaneously packed thousands of cartridges for muskets. They also laid plans to seize the banks and ships in New Orleans to support an invasion of Mexico, a variant of Burr's plan to loot banks and capture ships in Washington.[18]

A February news dispatch from New Orleans described the atmosphere simply: "We are in considerable expectation of a war with Spain."[19]

Small units of Spanish and American soldiers were playing cat-and-mouse on the Louisiana-Texas border. The Americans were willing to respect an unofficial boundary along the Sabine River, now the western edge of the state of Louisiana. Spanish officials, however, feared the reports of American expeditions against Texas, especially when they found an American army party exploring the disputed lands in the valley of the Red River. The Spaniards pushed their soldiers east and promised freedom to American slaves who escaped to the lands of King Carlos. In February, the governor of Texas ordered Spanish forces to attack all American soldiers who crossed the Arroyo Hondo. War could have erupted then, but local Spanish commanders ignored the order, fearing the American forces were too strong for them.[20]

Jefferson finally responded to the heightening tension, but only barely. In a message to Congress, the president reported the Sabine maneuvering and invited Congress to "make such provision for its security as in their

wisdom they shall deem sufficient." The Secretary of War ordered Wilkinson to send three companies of troops to Fort Adams on the West Florida
border, then directed that Wilkinson follow them down the Mississippi.[21]

Although the situation was not quite war fever, Burr strained to capitalize on it. In late March, he wrote to Andrew Jackson that although the government preferred peace, "there is great reason to expect hostility." In that
event, Burr went on, "a military force on our part would be requisite and
that force must come from your side of the mountains." Flattering Jackson
that a Tennessee brigade "would drive double their number of Frenchmen
off the earth," Burr asked for a list of officers "composed of fellows fit for
business and with whom you would trust your life and your honor." Burr
promised to have the War Department make the appointments. He sent the
same request, with the same promise, to General Tupper in Ohio.[22]

But Burr doubted there would be war. He had observed Jefferson for
many years. The man was no warrior.[23] Without a Spanish war, Burr's plans
could founder. The prudent lawyer inside him raised a question: Before
gambling everything on insurrection and invasion, why not explore less
risky paths to success?

In late March, Burr called on Jefferson again. In a long, weird meeting,
Burr sequentially assumed the poses of supplicant, of public-minded citizen, and of potential deposer. Throughout, his words and attitude conveyed
contempt for the president whose favor he sought. Burr only alienated further a man who had never liked him.

Burr began by repeating a remark the president had made after the
election of 1800: that if Burr were not vice president, Jefferson would have
placed him in a high office. Now, Burr pointed out, he would welcome such
an office. Insisting that he had never asked a favor before, the former vice
president complained that Jefferson "had always used him with politeness,
but nothing more," despite Burr's support for the administration. (Jefferson
might have silently disagreed with that last assertion.)

Also, Burr added, he could do Jefferson much harm.

The threat was unmistakable. Burr had the president's full attention. He
would rather, Burr continued, not cause harm. He currently had no employment, so he could take on any position that Jefferson might offer. He would
be in Washington City for a few more days to await Jefferson's answer.

The president was not amused by Burr's request, more like an extortion demand. Stiffly, he replied that the public had lost confidence in Burr. Before the election of 1804, "not a single voice" had urged that Burr continue as vice president. (This might have been Burr's moment to register silent dissent: Jefferson, not the public, had dropped Burr from the Republican ticket.) Then Jefferson addressed Burr's threat.

"I fear no injury," Jefferson said, "which any man could do me." Gathering his self-righteousness about him, he added, "No threat or fear on that head would ever be a motive of action with me." Burr left empty-handed.

When President Jefferson recorded Burr's threat in March 1806 to harm him, he misleadingly attributed the threat to a pending lawsuit over the election of 1800.

In notes composed weeks later, Jefferson speculated that Burr's threat related to a lawsuit over the disputed election of 1800. In that lawsuit, Burr's friends hoped to prove that Jefferson cut political deals to win the runoff vote in the House of Representatives. Jefferson's notes include no suspicion that the threat grew from Burr's journey out west, or that it concerned insurrection, secession, or a Mexican invasion. Despite Jefferson's silence on the subject, no other explanation makes sense. The lawsuit over the 1800 election was barely an annoyance to a president who had won so resoundingly in 1804, especially since there was no evidence that Jefferson had made a political deal to win the earlier election. But the rumors about

Burr's nefarious western activities were numerous: press reports, anonymous letters, the January letter from Daveiss in Kentucky, the warning from William Eaton. Indeed, Daveiss had written a second letter, describing Burr's western travels and conferences with Wilkinson, and listing Burr among those likely engaged in a western conspiracy. "Show this letter to nobody," the Kentuckian implored the president. "Mr. Burr's connections are more extensive than any man supposes." [24]

Only a naive or fatuous man could have failed to connect Burr's threat to his western activities. Jefferson was neither naive nor fatuous. Perhaps he was honoring Daveiss's entreaty that he not reveal his knowledge of Burr's scheming. Perhaps he could not admit even in private notes that his former vice president was threatening to undermine the government if he did not receive a high appointment. That Jefferson recorded a wholly unpersuasive interpretation of Burr's threat is remarkable enough. Yet more remarkable, though, was Burr's willingness to threaten Jefferson face-to-face. He truly thought the Virginian was a weakling. [25]

By mid-April, with no presidential appointment forthcoming, Burr had a new timetable for his expedition. "The execution of our project," he wrote to Wilkinson, "is postponed until December." Burr attributed the delay to "want of water in Ohio [which] rendered movement that way impracticable." By "want of water," Burr likely meant that he was still gathering funds.

Referring to himself and Wilkinson in the third person, Burr was upbeat. "The association is enlarged," he assured the general, "and comprises all that Wilkinson could wish." Addressing the problem of secrecy, Burr wrote: "Confidence limited to a few." The delay, Burr insisted, "will enable us to move with more certainty and dignity." He promised to press their plan energetically: "Burr will be throughout the United States this summer."

Then Burr revealed his own anxiety about Wilkinson. "Nothing has been heard from [the] brigadier since October," he complained, adding a question about the American officers who faced the Spaniards across the Sabine River. Did they, he inquired, understand the importance of fomenting a war. [26]

The dance between Burr and Wilkinson was becoming intricate. Not quite sure of the general, Burr had been willing to abandon their venture in favor of a high place in government. With the failure of that maneuver, Burr needed Wilkinson more than ever. But Burr was not discouraged. In fact, he was contriving new ways to pursue his dream of glory.

12

The Baron of the Ouachita Valley

Philadelphia/Washington City
Summer 1806

The Dutchman was entirely charming, comfortable with lords and frontier brawlers alike. Physical beauty, abetted by gracious manners, eased his way. His conversation was described as "agreeable without being brilliant." He claimed to be a noble who fled the French republican hordes, yet his lack of pretension disarmed Americans. Above all else, Felipe Neri, the Baron de Bastrop, was a thorough reprobate. As one French traveler wrote, "He deceived people everywhere, regardless of their station in life or education. In the United States, and in Kentucky particularly, he ruined all who became interested in his projects, which were all marked by disaster." For this elegant confidence man, every person he met was just another mark.[1]

In 1795, Bastrop and an aristocratic partner—bemusingly titled the Marquis de Maison Rouge—arrived at the Spanish outpost of Fort Miro, now the site of Monroe, Louisiana. Bastrop secured a contract from King Carlos to settle five hundred families on more than one million acres that included the current Morehouse Parish of Louisiana. The king needed settlers to pay taxes and to block American expansion. Bastrop promised to produce them.

The Bastrop Tract was largely virgin meadow and forest between the current cities of El Dorado, Arkansas, and Bastrop, Louisiana, drained by the Ouachita River ("WAH-shita"), which flows into the Red River, and then into the Mississippi and Atchafalaya. The spot was remote, a 250-mile trek from New Orleans. Boats had to be poled upriver to get there.

The baron did not own a square inch of it. All he had was a concession to recruit settlers on 400-acre farm sites and to provide services to them. If he brought in five hundred families, then he would acquire title to the remaining land. Three times Bastrop searched in Louisville for enterprising souls willing to become subjects of King Carlos. He induced dozens to make the move, giving them Spanish land titles and building a flour mill for them.

In 1799, Spain cut off its subsidies for new settlers. The baron was stuck, well short of the goal of five hundred new families and with no prospect of reaching it. Rather than despair, the smooth-talking Bastrop began a series of transactions that illuminate the slack ethical standards of frontier land deals. Speculators often swapped rights to far-off lands that neither party had seen. The winners were usually those who found a greater fool on whom to foist off a bad title before the music stopped and values plunged.

First, the baron sold his Ouachita land interests—whatever they were— to Abraham Morhouse of Kentucky, a former New Yorker and current bigamist. Not only did the Spanish government refuse to approve that sale, but in 1802 it voided Bastrop's concession.

The baron barely blinked. He reacquired his now-canceled land interests from Morhouse in return for $85,000 in bonds and mortgages, paper likely as worthless as the land interests, which then ended up in the hands of another Kentuckian, Charles Lynch. By 1804, Bastrop, Lynch, and Morhouse had several times bought and sold various papers purporting to convey interests in the tract, at steadily escalating prices. Predictably, the dizzying transactions produced lawsuits in Kentucky and Orleans.

In May 1805, the baron withdrew to Texas, where he assisted Spanish preparations for war with the United States, and the two Kentuckians split the land interests between them. That summer, as Burr frisked in the

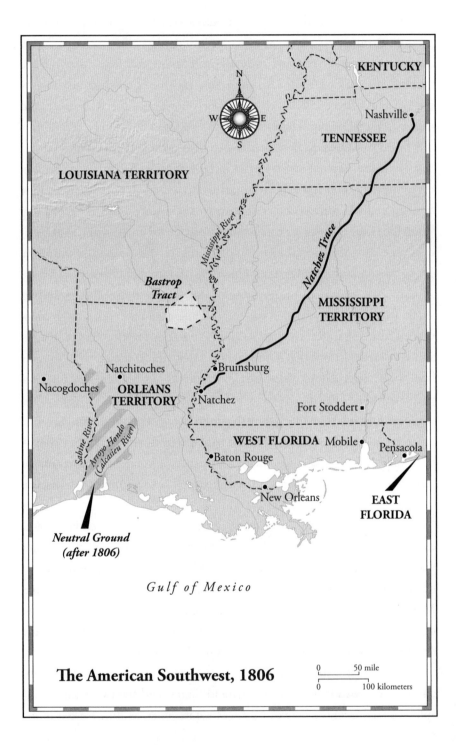

The American Southwest, 1806

parlors of New Orleans, the local talk buzzed about Bastrop's tract. Daniel Clark bought part of the neighboring Maison Rouge tract. Burr's friend Edward Livingston was pressing a claim he had acquired from the charming Bastrop. In March 1806, Judge John Prevost of Orleans Territory, Burr's stepson, delivered a ruling that further undermined Lynch's questionable share of Baron Bastrop's shaky interest in some 700,000 acres.[2]

As Burr prepared for his second western journey, he waded into the Bastrop snarl. An astute lawyer with experience in western land deals, Burr had to know it was a poor investment. The flaws in the Bastrop claim included: (i) the baron never met the contractual requirement of settling five hundred families; (ii) he never held title to any lands under Spanish law; (iii) the United States did not recognize Spanish land titles anyway; and (iv) no title to the land was ever registered in the United States. Moreover, recent explorers described the land as having "thin, poor soils," and they thought that periodic flooding explained its lack of fish and water fowl.[3]

But Burr was not looking for a financial opportunity, even less an agricultural one. Though he coveted land, he had always lived in cities and had no interest in tilling the soil. Of America's founding generation, he was among the most urban in outlook and experience.

Burr saw the Bastrop Tract in political and strategic terms. Situated near the Spanish border, it was an ideal location for inciting war. A company of high-spirited Americans in those empty spaces could provoke the Spaniards and then retaliate, lighting the fuse for war and changing history. It would no longer matter that Jefferson wanted peace. Burr, with his boots on the border, could start the war he needed. Defects in the Bastrop land title would matter little to a man leading an army into Mexico City or Baton Rouge.

In addition, the Bastrop Tract would provide the perfect cover for Burr's other plans. The descent of a large body of men down the western waters, led by Burr, could hardly be concealed. Questions would be asked. Was this a revolution? Western secession? The prelude to a foreign invasion? Local and national officials might try to obstruct Burr and his men. But if Burr could say he intended to settle the Ouachita Valley, there could be no objection. Nothing could be more patriotic than filling up western land.[4]

Burr now had five alternative goals for his expedition. Depending on the circumstances of the moment, he could claim the intention of joining a war against Spain, or of mounting a private expedition against the Spanish lands, or of raising revolution in Orleans, or of detaching the western states and territories, or simply of settling the Ouachita Valley. More realistically, the expedition might aim at two or more of these goals—say, combining a rising in Orleans with a private invasion of Spanish lands. From Burr's perspective, this complex matrix of possible goals was a key strategic advantage. The political and diplomatic situation was fluid. He could not be sure exactly what would be possible once his men were on the rivers, armed and provisioned. Moreover, having multiple and alternative goals allowed Burr to tailor his recruiting pitch to each audience. Some, like Daniel Clark and the Mexican Association of New Orleans, responded best to the private invasion option. Others, like Andrew Jackson, wanted to join an American war with Spain. Still others might prefer a rising in Orleans or western independence. So long as he recruited the right type of "ardent spirits," Burr would rely on his own leadership to direct his men to the best opportunity available.

Yet the complexity of his planning, festooned with alternatives and contingency options, also could become a liability, confusing his recruits and muddying his message to westerners generally (not to mention future historians). By expecting that men would follow in any direction he might lead them, Burr was placing an extraordinary value on his own charisma. It was a huge gamble.

Through the spring and early summer of 1806, Burr mostly stayed in a quiet part of Philadelphia, occasionally traveling to Washington City.[5] In his small rented house, he laid his plans with a colorful cast of characters.

The most restless of Burr's companions was the German-born Erich Bollman, a physician with little interest in medicine. Fifteen years before, Bollman had assisted the escape from the Paris mobs by Madame de Staël, famed author and salon hostess; then he failed gallantly in two plots to free the Marquis de Lafayette from an Austrian prison. After his own arrest and imprisonment by French officials, Bollman made his way to New York, then Philadelphia, trying his hand at a steam engine enterprise, a trading business, a metal-rolling plant, and a waterworks.[6] Burr welcomed the kinetic Bollman to his inner circle, where he joined Julien De Pestre, a former officer in both the French and British armies who was advising on military matters. Rounding out this international staff was a German secretary and, of course, Jonathan Dayton.

Burr again turned his persuasive powers on the Spanish minister, Casa Yrujo. The diplomat joined Burr, Bollman, and Dayton in sessions to plan the western expedition. By including the Spaniard in his inner circle, Burr hoped to lull him and the Spanish government. In May, Casa Yrujo wrote that he believed "not only of the probability, but even of the facility, of [Burr's] success, under certain circumstances." According to Casa Yrujo, Burr had information that Spanish officials in Mexico would abandon Vera Cruz to an invading force.[7]

When the Spaniard balked at bankrolling the expedition, Burr tried intimidation, threatening to invade West Florida and Mexico. Dayton played the peacemaker, explaining that he was urging Burr to postpone a decision on whether to invade Spanish territory until the expedition "chiefs" seized New Orleans in December, six months away.[8]

Burr also paid a call on Anthony Merry, the British minister, eager for encouraging news from London. There was none, which Burr, according to Merry, "lamented exceedingly." Burr insisted that in the West and Orleans the yearning for independence was so high that rebellion would occur "without any foreign assistance whatever; and his last words . . . were that, with or without such support, it certainly would be made very shortly."[9]

In June, Burr withdrew to a rural retreat near the Delaware River. To his joy, Theodosia joined him. She had been ill in South Carolina, and Burr insisted that she spend the summer in more healthful northern climes. Theodosia brought her son, who also was recovering from a serious illness.

Family setbacks, though, did not slow Burr's planning, though that planning sometimes lacked focus. Burr sought military advice from an exiled French general. He conferred with Davis Floyd of Indiana, a militia officer and river pilot who was entering the inner circle. Charles Williamson, Burr's confidential emissary to Britain, was in New York and doubtless was in touch with Burr.[10]

In July, Burr again tried to bring Commodore Truxtun into his plan. Spreading out drawings for a gunboat being built in a western boatyard, Burr asked whether it might operate both on the Mississippi and on the ocean. Truxtun studied the plans and heard Burr out. "[He] intended to provide a formidable navy," Truxtun said later, "at the head of which he intended to place me; [and] he intended to establish an independent government [in Mexico], and give liberty to the enslaved world." Burr predicted war with Spain; if there was no war, he added, he would start a settlement on the Ouachita.

Truxtun asked whether the government had approved Burr's plan. Burr said no. Truxtun declined to join the effort, dashing Burr's last hope of enlisting an experienced naval leader.[11]

In early summer, Burr renewed his friendship with the architect Benjamin Latrobe. The year before, Burr had invited Latrobe to review the potential site of a canal at the Falls of the Ohio; the architect did not go because Burr never paid him. In June 1806, Burr again spoke of the canal. He asked Latrobe to hire five hundred Irish laborers and transport them to Louisville. Latrobe arranged to send the laborers, but Burr again failed to conclude the deal, leaving Latrobe and his Irishmen in the lurch. Fortunately, none of the workers actually departed for Kentucky.[12]

Burr's thinking in this episode is elusive, at best. No riverside land had been acquired for a canal. No engineering plans were drawn. No funds had been raised. How could Burr propose to bundle five hundred laborers to Louisville for a nonexistent project? He may have hoped that laborers stranded in Kentucky would sign up for his expedition downriver, although workers deceived into traveling hundreds of miles to work on a nonexistent project might have been extremely reluctant to follow Burr anywhere else.

Burr's doubts about the expedition surfaced again, this time in a request to a friend, Charles Biddle of Philadelphia. Burr insisted to Biddle that gentlemen "of the first respectability" wanted him to revolutionize Mexico, but he asked his friend to explore whether Burr might be appointed to a vacancy on Pennsylvania's highest court. Biddle quickly determined that Burr had no chance for the position. Those who had signed up for Burr's expedition would have been startled to learn that he was scrambling for a last-minute exit from it.

During this period, Burr's efforts more resembled the path of a pinball through an arcade machine than the tightly focused advance that marks successful revolutionaries and military leaders. The common thread in his actions was a desperate quest to redeem his reputation. Some months later, when much of the nation was wondering what Burr was really up to, the architect Latrobe made this point:

> The truth is, that Burr, ruined in fortune and influence since his duel with Hamilton, is determined on a new establishment of some kind, at the head of which he can place himself, either a separate republic, West of Alleghany, or a province near Mexico should we have war with Spain, or a little government *under* the U. States on the Washita. He is ready for any of these schemes.[13]

As July ended, Burr put aside his doubts. He wrote to Harman Blennerhassett that before August 20 he would be on the Irishman's enchanted island in the Ohio River. He issued orders implementing his long-nurtured, ever-shifting plans.[14]

Dayton, not fully recovered from the illness he contracted in Ohio the year before, would remain in the East, where he could assist with finances and supplies.

Bollman and two others sailed to New Orleans, where they would coordinate with the insurrectionary leadership in that unstable city. Burr was depending upon a rising in Orleans Territory. His reputation there remained strong.[15]

Wilkinson had been ordered south from St. Louis, so Bollman might meet that other linchpin of Burr's plans in New Orleans. On that chance, Burr confided to Bollman a letter for the general. Because letters could fall into hostile hands, much of the message was rendered in several ciphers that Burr and Wilkinson had used for almost ten years. Such ciphers were common in an era when mail often went astray and messages might be read by strangers or adversaries.

Burr sent a duplicate of the cipher letter by another route, in the hands of two young men who were almost part of his family: Sam Swartwout, his former traveling companion in Georgia and Florida; and Peter Ogden,

Dayton's nephew, whose older brother, George, was Burr's banker.[16] Peter Ogden and Swartwout left to search for Wilkinson down the Ohio and Mississippi Valleys. They also carried a letter for Kentucky's General Adair.

Burr and Julien De Pestre, his military adviser, would travel on horseback. They would assemble his corps of adventurers from men identified on his first trip, and would recruit more. From western New York to St. Louis, his lieutenants already were gathering men. Boats had to be built, supplies purchased.

In the first week of August, Burr, De Pestre, and Burr's German secretary saddled up and headed west.

13

The *Western World* Ignites

Kentucky
Summer 1806

A few days before Burr's departure for the West, the *Philadelphia Aurora* reprinted an article from the first issue of the *Western World,* a newspaper in Frankfort, Kentucky. Titled "The Kentucky Spanish Association, Blount's Conspiracy, & General Miranda's Expedition," it was a sensation. Through more than a dozen more installments, the *Western World* dredged up decades-old evidence of General Wilkinson's involvement with agents of the Spanish king, along with similar information about other Kentuckians.

The series also claimed that advocates of western secession still clung to the cause. "Another scheme is in agitation," the newspaper asserted, naming conspirators like Edward Livingston of New Orleans and Jonathan Dayton. Burr's name did not appear until the fourth article, but the reports came frighteningly close to describing the plans he had been nursing for two years.[1]

Latrobe, the architect, showed Burr the *Aurora*'s reprint of the first article, joking that it might be an election ploy. After scanning the piece, Burr betrayed no alarm. He laughed gently, then insisted the article had no electioneering purpose. Rather, he attributed it to "the family of the Marshalls," which included Chief Justice John Marshall. Burr predicted that the article would "occasion great uneasiness to the Westward." Politely, Burr asked if he might keep the piece. Latrobe sent him the later numbers in the series.[2]

Most Kentuckians agreed with Burr that the *Western World* was a front for the sprawling Marshall clan, which formed the core of the Federalist party in Kentucky.[3] Ironically, President Jefferson had helped make the fortune of this family of his political rivals. While governor of Virginia during the Revolutionary War, Jefferson had sent Colonel Thomas Marshall—a cousin of Jefferson's father and father of the great chief justice—to survey lands in frontier Kentucky. With the benefit of that advance look at the wilderness, Colonel Marshall and several of his fifteen children amassed more than half a million of Kentucky's best acres.

Humphrey Marshall, the colonel's nephew, led the Kentucky clan, having settled on the frontier after marrying one of the colonel's daughters. Staunch Federalists, the Marshalls thrived during the Washington and Adams administrations. The colonel was Kentucky's chief tax collector. Humphrey became a United States senator. John Marshall, staying behind in Virginia, served as congressman from Richmond, diplomat, Secretary of State, and finally chief justice.[4] When Kentucky shifted to support Jefferson's Republicans at the polls, the Marshalls did not trim their Federalist views.

Neither of the editors of the *Western World*, John Wood and Joseph Street, had any previous connection to Kentucky. They left jobs with the *Virginia Gazette* in Richmond and walked to Frankfort on the Wilderness Road, carrying only knapsacks and a Godfrey's quadrant (a tool for calculating latitude). Someone had recruited them and staked their venture. Wood described himself as romantically involved with Street. They shared an "ardent friendship," he wrote, which made them "slaves of such a strong passion" that it was the principal reason they left Virginia. Once they started publication, no one in Kentucky cared about their private passions. For a season, Wood and Street turned the state's power structure upside down.[5]

Wood, the older of the pair, was described by a contemporary as "a singular looking man, with a countenance expressive of great oddity."

Tongue-tied in public but a fluid writer, Wood was one of several British newspapermen who packaged scandal and innuendo for the early American republic.[6] Burr knew Wood well, rather too well. Four years before, Wood had written a stridently critical history of the Adams administration, hoping to win favor with Republicans. Finding that Wood's error-filled work was so libelous that it could boomerang against Republicans, then–Vice President Burr bought the entire print run to keep it from circulating.[7] In contrast, Street was a good-looking young man with a feisty disposition. The *Western World*'s policy was that "Wood writes" and "Street fights."

At its peak, the newspaper printed only 1,200 copies of each issue, but its accusations resounded through the West, then through the nation. Other newspapers, from the *Richmond Enquirer* to the *Philadelphia Aurora*, reprinted its articles. During that era, a single copy of a newspaper might be read by dozens of people. Coffee rooms, hotels, and other businesses used newspaper subscriptions to attract trade. Individual subscribers, especially in remote areas, were expected to share each issue, which passed from hand to hand until it was tattered and worn. An English traveler reported that when a coach arrived in town, the residents surrounded those lucky few receiving newspapers and "stood, with open mouth, swallowing 'the lies of the day,' which would be as readily contradicted on the morrow."[8]

The *Western World*'s attacks mixed fact and fantasy. One far-fetched thrust imagined that Burr, Dayton, and Wilkinson joined in a land venture in the 1790s with the then-exiled French diplomat Talleyrand, which featured a side bargain to abandon America's interests when Talleyrand returned to power in Paris. Yet many of Wood and Street's charges were backed by evidence, especially the claim that Spanish bribes were paid for years to Wilkinson and other Kentuckians, including a prominent judge. By September, Humphrey Marshall had openly entered the fray, publishing essays supporting the *Western World*'s accusations. Years later, Humphrey wrote with pride that the newspaper had caused "very great astonishment of the innocent part of its readers; and the no less great consternation of some of the guilty."[9]

Rage was the principal response from local Republican leaders. One threatened to send a Negro to thrash Wood and Street, the task being beneath him to perform personally. Challenges to duels flowed into the

Western World office. Street disdainfully printed the challenges in the newspaper, adding unflattering commentary about their authors.[10]

Twelve days after the newspaper's first issue, one Republican ran out of patience. He walked up to Street, pulled out a pistol, and shot him. The bullet grazed the fiery young editor in the side. More angry than injured, Street pulled a dagger and chased his assailant through Frankfort, but could not catch him. When both men were later arrested and charged with assault, Humphrey Marshall posted bail for Street. A jury accepted Street's claim of self-defense and convicted his assailant, but the man went free because the prosecutor had botched the charging document. The controversy only increased the newspaper's popularity. Its accusations reached all the way to President Jefferson's desk.[11]

From New Orleans to Washington City, treason and western secession were suddenly at the center of the nation's politics. Those named in the articles instantly became objects of public mistrust. A judge in Mississippi Territory reported that though many of his neighbors knew of the Spanish conspiracy of the 1780s, "the new one seems to be a secret yet." The newspaper's accusations, he added, prompted many to wonder why General Wilkinson still commanded the army.[12]

While the *Western World* stirred up public passions, Kentucky's United States attorney again bombarded the president with accusations. Jefferson had reason to be skeptical of Joseph Hamilton Daveiss, who was a passionate Federalist. According to Henry Clay, a Kentucky contemporary, Daveiss so admired Alexander Hamilton that as an adult he adopted "Hamilton" as his middle name and always used it. Daveiss also was a member of the Marshall clan, having married the youngest sister of Chief Justice John Marshall.[13]

Though Daveiss was a rock-ribbed Federalist, he also was very much a young man of the West. Tall and athletic, he rode from country court to country court with a rifle on his arm, wearing denim trousers and a trademark blue hunting shirt, trimmed with yellow fringe. So attired, he dominated court proceedings with his imposing physical presence and hard-charging determination. A few years earlier, Daveiss had served as second for a duelist who killed his adversary. The lawyer then defended the duelist against murder charges and won an acquittal.[14]

In late March 1806, Daveiss received the president's request for more details about the supposed western conspiracy. His reply the next day corrected the list of conspirators he had sent the month before, adding Dayton's name, and provided a detailed description of Wilkinson's dalliance with the Spaniards in the 1780s. Much of this information also would be published in the *Western World*, reinforcing the suspicion that the Marshalls were behind both the newspaper and Daveiss's accusations. Daveiss, however, had little more to report about the conspiracy beyond Burr's meeting with General Adair in Kentucky. Aware that he was short on facts, Daveiss promised Jefferson, "I'll soon *know* all about it without *suspecting*."[15]

Daveiss made elaborate preparations to take his one-man investigation on the road. He arranged for a newspaper to report that Jefferson had fired him from his government job; the report, Daveiss explained to the president, was to "render unsuspicious the dissatisfaction I may occasionally betray towards the government." Then Daveiss traveled to St. Louis to speak with the treacherous Wilkinson. By posing as a recently fired official, Daveiss hoped to draw out the general's antigovernment feelings. To complete his cover story, Daveiss sent Jefferson a resignation letter in case events should require that the president accept it. Daveiss conveyed to Jefferson another bit of evidence: General Andrew Jackson of Tennessee had sent to a friend an "abstrusely worded" note from Burr that ended with the assertion: "Mr. Burr would eventually prove to be the savior of this Western country."[16]

Reaching St. Louis in early May, Daveiss first consulted the records of the surveyor who ten years earlier had reported to President Adams that Wilkinson was an agent of Spain. As he reviewed the surveyor's file, Daveiss grew increasingly frustrated with Jefferson, who was keeping an obvious traitor at the head of the American army.

When Daveiss met Wilkinson, the general made it clear that he knew about the Kentuckian's investigation, flourishing an anonymous warning he had received about Daveiss. Despite the warning, the gregarious Wilkinson spoke freely about Burr. "I have never observed," Daveiss wrote later, "a greater admiration of one man for another than the general manifested for Mr. Burr." Pointing to a map of the route to Santa Fe, Wilkinson proclaimed that "had Burr been president, we would have had all this country before now." Though Wilkinson scoffed at the suggestion that he had a connection

Joseph Hamilton Daveiss, United States Attorney for Kentucky and brother-in-law to Chief Justice John Marshall, twice tried to prosecute Burr. He is in his Kentucky militia uniform in this portrait.

with Spain, Daveiss claimed he could "clearly discern through the veil of [Wilkinson's] laughter that he was thoroughly alarmed." [17]

Daveiss returned home by early June but did not write to Jefferson until July 14, a week after the issues of the *Western World* began to startle the West. Daveiss was disgusted that while he chased this malign conspiracy, Jefferson neither said nor did anything to halt it. Daveiss's new letter explained that he would report what he knew even though Jefferson was ignoring his warnings. The lawyer then outlined the conspiracy's purposes as a revolt in the Spanish lands and separation of the western states. Jefferson ignored Daveiss's new letter too. [18]

Although the *Western World*'s campaign threatened to upend Burr's plans, events on the Spanish frontier seemed to be bringing war ever closer, just as Burr hoped. When Secretary of War Dearborn ordered Wilkinson to Orleans Territory in May, he stressed "the hostile views of the officers of his Catholic Majesty" and directed the general to "repel any invasion of the United States east of the river Sabine, or north or west of the bounds of what has been called West Florida." Wilkinson should treat any Spanish move across the Sabine as "an actual invasion of our territorial rights."[19]

Here was the opening Burr needed. Spanish officials were edgy. They should be easy to provoke. Surely Wilkinson could ignite a confrontation on the Sabine border, or among the restless men of West Florida. Burr and Wilkinson could meet in Natchez or New Orleans in late summer or early fall, start the war, and crash through to Mexico City.[20]

But rather than seize this shimmering opportunity, Wilkinson sat in St. Louis, conducting powwows with Indian chiefs. He ordered that American troops near the Sabine avoid fighting with Spain except "in the last extremity." In June, he directed Lieutenant Zebulon Pike to take an expedition to the headwaters of the Arkansas and Red Rivers and to the border of Spanish New Mexico. He quarreled with two officers on his staff, court-martialing one for insubordination. And he stayed with his ailing wife. "For more than thirty days," the general wrote, "Mrs. Wilkinson has trembled over the grave, and I have waited in agonizing suspense the moment of her dissolution."

The one thing the general did not do was follow the order that he take command of the explosive situation in Orleans Territory. One explanation for his delay was a message sent by Burr in early May, reporting his own delay in getting under way. By stalling, Wilkinson was giving Burr a chance to produce the volunteer force he had promised.[21]

In early August, as Burr rode west through Pennsylvania and Wilkinson lingered in St. Louis, Spanish troops crossed the Sabine. They stopped an American party exploring the Red River Valley, sending the Americans back to Natchitoches (pronounced, inexplicably, "NAH-guh-dush"). With Wilkinson nowhere in sight, militia from Orleans and Mississippi were dispatched to the Sabine country. Governor Claiborne hurried west from New Orleans to protest the Spanish aggressions. The Spanish commander replied blandly that Spain was merely exercising dominion over its own lands. Tension mounted. When Spanish reinforcements reached the Sabine, the Spaniards began regular patrols close to the American troops in Natchitoches. Claiborne was warned that the Spaniards numbered fifteen hundred. Many predicted war. In late August, Wilkinson finally began to descend the Mississippi.[22]

With Burr, Wilkinson, and the Spaniards converging on Orleans Territory, President Jefferson retired from Washington City to his Monticello estate. The president always fled the capital's heat in August and September. Drought parched the Virginia countryside that summer, and the dry conditions spread across the nation's midsection. The *Kentucky Gazette* reported that rain fell only once that summer. Poor crops, the newspaper worried, would cause "greater scarcity than before known in this state."[23]

Jefferson was grieving over the recent murder by poisoning of his mentor and friend, George Wythe, America's first law professor and a distinguished judge. "I had reserved with fondness for the day of my retirement," Jefferson wrote years later, "the hope of inducing him [Wythe] to pass much of his time with me." At his hilltop plantation, the president undertook a study of landscape gardening.[24] If Jefferson suffered any anxiety over the movements of his renegade former vice president, or the loyalty of his traitorous commanding general, he did not show it.

14

High Water Mark

Pittsburgh to Nashville
August–October 1806

When Burr arrived in Pittsburgh on August 21, 1806, he expected that soon he would lead a thousand or more men downriver. Armed with only his reputation, his personal magnetism, and his dream of glory, Burr was assembling an expedition that outnumbered the residents of Cincinnati; it would be almost one-third the size of the U.S. Army. He would ride at the head of dozens of boats, an inland armada, each crammed to the gunwales with those ardent spirits that he so loved. No comparable private force had ever been assembled in America. Who could resist it, wherever he should lead it? Most important, who could question the quality of the man who conjured it out of nothing?

To launch this expedition, though, would require energy and tight organization. Burr had identified many allies and potential allies. Some had signed up eagerly. Others were less enthusiastic. Now he had to mobilize as many as possible.

In Pittsburgh, Burr met with Comfort Tyler from western New York, who was emerging as a key lieutenant. Known for his rugged constitution and prudent judgment, Tyler had served with Burr in the New York assembly and also as sheriff of Onondaga County. He and Israel Smith led two dozen men to Beaver, Pennsylvania, on the Ohio River. There they built boats and acquired supplies. They sent barrels of flour, pork, and beef, plus whiskey, all the way to a merchant in Natchez, paying with drafts on George Ogden in New York. (Drafts were a cross between a bank check and a promissory note, directing a third party—in this case, George Ogden—to make a specific payment when the draft was presented.)[1]

Asked to explain his activities, Tyler said he was engaged in a secret enterprise but that it was not directed against the American government.[2]

Burr visited local veterans of the Revolutionary War, many of whom had settled in the West. His appeal to the martial traditions of the Continental Army reverberated with the sons of his former military colleagues, who were coming of age with no war to fight and the peace-loving Jefferson as president. Burr miscalculated, however, when he dropped in on Colonel George Morgan near Cannonsburg.

The visit to Morgan carried great promise. Eighteen years before, Morgan had founded New Madrid on the Mississippi, in what was then Spanish territory and is now Missouri. Spain promised 15 million acres for Morgan's settlement, but Morgan left the venture after two years. Here was a man who knew the West, the Spaniards, and the challenge of leading a large group to the frontier. If Burr was serious about a settlement on the Bastrop Tract, he could learn much from Morgan's experience.[3]

Sitting with Morgan and his two sons, Burr waxed expansive, but not about settling the Ouachita Valley. Within five years, he predicted, the overtaxed West would secede from the union, weary of seeing its land squandered to enrich the Atlantic states. He scorned the "imbecility" of Jefferson's government. Burr insisted he could seize New York with five hundred men, or Washington City with two hundred. As recounted by Morgan's son, Burr's message was clear: "He said that great numbers were not necessary to execute great military deeds. All that was wanting was a great leader, in whom they could place great confidence, and who they believed would carry them through." Burr plainly was offering himself as that great leader.

Colonel Morgan was not swept up by the rhetoric. Next day, the old frontiersman resolved to report Burr's remarks to President Jefferson.[4]

Burr made his way to Marietta and its shipyards, where he ordered fifteen large boats, paying with more drafts on George Ogden of New York. Each boat could accommodate fifty men, providing a total capacity of more than seven hundred. But Burr expected many more to join the expedition. Comfort Tyler and his men were building more boats in Beaver, as was Davis Floyd in Louisville and another agent on the Wabash River of Indiana Territory. Burr himself would soon order an additional five boats from Andrew Jackson in Tennessee. Based on the boat construction alone, Burr was expecting to lead a force of well over one thousand.[5]

Still, however, he had no warships. Senator John Smith in Cincinnati made a conditional offer: If the government failed to pay for the gunboats Smith was building near Cincinnati, Burr could have them. Perhaps Burr had similar arrangements with other boatbuilders on the western waters.[6]

Below Marietta, Burr and his European aides paused at Blennerhassett Island. In a single evening's conversation, Burr set Blennerhassett's imagination ablaze, confiding that a majority of the people in Mississippi and Orleans Territories would soon revolt. After seizing the bank in New Orleans, along with the customs house and the leftover French cannon, the rebels would embark on an invasion of Mexico. The western states would have to choose between joining Burr or staying with the Atlantic states.[7]

Harman Blennerhassett (left), who was the uncle of his wife, Margaret (right), left Ireland to settle on an island in the Ohio River.

Burr's vivid, romantic images spoke powerfully to Blennerhassett. An oppressed people revolts. A commanding figure arrives on a riverboat, mounts a charger, and forges a new republic. Wielding the sword of justice, he expels the Spanish despot from Florida and Mexico, bringing freedom to yet more people. Whole vistas open up for settlement while Mexican silver lies in heaps at the feet of the liberators. In a time when Napoleon had risen from corporal to emperor of France, Burr's vision was a potent one. A few days after Burr's visit, Blennerhassett explained to a neighbor that "under the auspices . . . of Colonel Burr a separation of the Union was contemplated." New Orleans, he continued, would be seized, its banks and military stores looted.[8]

Blennerhassett's enthusiasm drove him to his writing table. He swiftly composed a rallying cry for western secession. Printed in the *Ohio Gazette* under the pseudonym "The Querist," Blennerhassett's diatribe circulated through the West. He adopted Burr's rallying cry: the mercantile Atlantic states were plundering the West with heavy taxes and unfair land and trade policies. The only answer, "The Querist" concluded, was independence. "The Querist" also derided criticisms of Burr, comparing them to emanations from swamps that would dissipate upon "a spark from the genius of a Burr."[9]

The articles incited angry responses in the *Scioto Gazette* of Chillicothe, Ohio. "If this secret and mysterious plan is not hostile towards the general government," a writer asked, "why is the veil of mystery thrown over the whole of these transactions?" Soon, the writer promised, westerners would "discover in their lurking holes, the traitors of your country."[10]

Combined with the accusations that the *Western World* was still shouting from its columns, the newspaper exchanges further agitated the West. Secession, revolution, war—the talk swirled and spiraled, reaching the most remote settlements. Some rallied to defend the union. Others were intrigued by Burr's promise of adventure, glory, and liberty. A few, including Colonel Morgan, wrote to warn Jefferson that trouble was brewing on the far side of the Appalachians.[11]

Having set Blennerhassett in motion, Burr next stopped at Cincinnati with Senator John Smith, whose sons enlisted in the expedition. Burr visited the federal arsenal across the river in Newport, Kentucky, which held eight thousand muskets and ample ammunition. He tried to draw the arsenal's keeper into a political conversation, making "numberless inquiries of him respecting the state and number of arms in his charge." Though the officer remained aloof, Burr's overture set more tongues wagging. With the arsenal's muskets, with Comfort Tyler's activity, with the Marietta boats, and with the gunboats being built by John Smith and others, Burr's expedition seemed more and more martial.[12] Burr's provocative talk continued. He compared the oppressed situation of the western states with that of the Atlantic states before the Revolutionary War. Leading men like Dayton and Blennerhassett, he said, were dissatisfied with the government. Senator Smith confided to friends that Burr would revolutionize Mexico with support from the Catholic clergy.[13]

When Burr turned south from the Ohio River, De Pestre split off toward St. Louis and General Wilkinson. Using transparent euphemisms, De Pestre described the expedition's schedule in a letter to New Orleans. He was taking Burr's letters to "the merchants of St. Louis," the Frenchman wrote, "where I shall be charged with all the affairs of the company, while [Burr] will have the management on the Ohio. We will try to have our merchandise ready in October that it may be delivered at New Orleans by the middle or end of December."[14] Burr, De Pestre, and their merchandise were to meet in New Orleans by the end of the year.

Burr's pace accelerated. He hurried to Andrew Jackson in Nashville, arriving on September 24.[15] Since their last meeting, Jackson had fought a bloody duel. Four months before, the Tennessean had killed Charles Dickinson after first taking a pistol ball in the ribs. The ball, too near his heart to be removed, stayed in his chest for the rest of his life. Jackson's legendary toughness was returning after a difficult recuperation. The fellow duelists fell happily into each other's company.

Sandwiching their talks around a public reception at Talbot's Hotel, Burr stressed that war was coming on the Sabine. Burr would be at the center of it. Jackson should join. The Tennessean, who relished a scrap more than most people, did not have to be asked twice. He issued an order for his militia to be ready to march on short notice. He also wrote to Jefferson, offering three Tennessee regiments whenever they were needed.

Jackson and Burr were planning a major undertaking. To pay for five more riverboats, Burr gave Jackson $3,000 of drafts on George Ogden in New York, paying another $700 to a friend of Jackson's to fill the boats with seventy-five fighters. Jackson proposed to put two thousand militia in the field. Combined with Burr's force and the army troops already in Orleans Territory, Jackson thought they could take Santa Fe and Mexico, giving "freedom and commerce to those provinces and establish[ing] peace, and a permanent barrier against the inroads and attacks of foreign powers on our interior."[16]

Burr bustled from Nashville back to Lexington. The dream was drawing closer as his message resounded through the West. The seeds he planted during his travels the year before were bearing fruit. Westerners understood that this charismatic man of distinction had returned to their country because he nurtured outsized ambitions that centered on them. Young men responded to the excitement Burr generated. So did older, influential ones. Shipwrights were shaping his boats. The rich men of Lexington would soon advance him another $25,000. For a ludicrous price, he had acquired the supposed rights to 350,000 acres of the Bastrop Tract—$5,000 in cash, mostly in the form of more drafts on the far-off George Ogden, and the assumption of a $30,000 debt. The price matched the flimsy legal title he acquired. No matter. Burr would not spend much time in the Ouachita Valley.[17]

He eagerly anticipated sharing this heady moment with Theodosia, her husband, and their son. The Alston family had descended the Ohio on a boat that also held their carriage and horses, then stopped at the magical Blennerhassett Island.[18] Now they would meet Burr in Lexington. Everything was looking good, very good.

Through much of September, American and Spanish troops continued to fence at the western edge of Orleans Territory. The Spaniards arrested three Americans suspected of spying. Four hundred Spanish troops, including Baron Bastrop, set up camp on the east (American) side of the Sabine, then welcomed another hundred reinforcements. Facing them, the Americans had three infantry companies and two cannon.[19]

The Spanish provocations stirred more war talk. Governor Claiborne pressed the army to attack the Spaniards, but Wilkinson had ordered his army to avoid combat. The local American commander followed Wilkinson's orders.[20]

By September 7, while Burr was angling for muskets at the Kentucky arsenal, General Wilkinson arrived in Natchez. He promptly wrote to the Secretary of War that he would "drain the cup of conciliation to maintain the peace of our country, and that the sword shall not be drawn but in the last extremity." Wilkinson displayed a peculiar notion of the contents of the cup of conciliation: He also recommended attacking Baton Rouge, reporting that its fort was "tumbling to pieces, and it is surrounded by a disaffected American population, which could overwhelm the feeble garrison." In addition, Wilkinson proposed to take Nacogdoches (pronounced "Nah-go-DOACH-us"), west of the Sabine. The general seemed intent on fulfilling Burr's hopes for war.[21]

Wilkinson pushed across Orleans Territory, arriving at Natchitoches, east of the Sabine, by September 22. The land had more cattle and horses than people, though cotton fields and cotton gins were spreading.[22] The Spanish troops, Wilkinson learned, were dirty, ill equipped, and hungry.

A few days after reaching Natchitoches, Wilkinson wrote to both Senator John Smith in Cincinnati and General John Adair in Kentucky, assuring each that war would come. By writing to both, Wilkinson could be sure that his message reached Burr.[23]

To Smith, Wilkinson wrote, "I shall be obliged to fight and to flog them [the Spaniards]." With five thousand troops, he pledged, he could reach the Rio Grande. Five thousand more would bring him to Monterrey. With even more, he could take Mexico City. Between Burr and Jackson, the first three thousand men could be floating downriver to Wilkinson in a few weeks.

In his letter to Adair, Wilkinson was even more warlike. "The time long looked for by many and wished for by more," he wrote, "has now arrived for subverting the Spanish government in Mexico. Be you ready and join me." He repeated the same predictions of how much land he could conquer, adding: "We cannot fail of success."[24]

Burr had long waited for word that the general was ready to move. Other pieces of the plan were falling into place. The boats were forming on the Ohio, the Cumberland, and the Wabash. Jackson was ready. Erich Bollman, Burr's agent, was in New Orleans organizing Burr's allies in that city. Sam Swartwout was searching for Wilkinson to deliver Burr's letter in cipher. But nothing was more important than Wilkinson.[25]

After all the indignities Burr had suffered at the hands of Jefferson and the Virginians, after all the planning, the careful conversations and the calculations, the great adventure was stirring to life. The boats soon would launch, the men would march, and Aaron Burr would be the man who made it happen. Glory, fame, redemption—all stretched before him on the river route to New Orleans, and then on to Mexico. His plan had been outrageous. A single man would spark a revolution, a secession, and a foreign invasion. Now it was within reach.

Unless something went wrong.

15

Dancing on the Sabine

The Texas/Orleans Border
October 1806

S am Swartwout arrived in Natchitoches on an evening in early October 1806. Alighting from a boat on the nearby Red River, he found
General Wilkinson in rudimentary quarters, sitting with his second
in command, a colonel. With the sun below the horizon, whiskey was no
doubt on the table.

The border confrontation with the Spaniards had slid into stalemate.
When disease swept through the Spanish troops, they pulled back across the
Sabine to its western shore. Wilkinson responded by pushing his men to the
river's edge, assuring a Spanish official that "this movement is made . . . with
no hostile intentions."[1] Wilkinson was waiting for the next Spanish move.

Swartwout, not yet twenty-five, presented a letter of introduction from
Dayton. With the colonel present, Swartwout volunteered his services against
the Spaniards. After the colonel withdrew, Swartwout dropped that pretence.
He dug a sealed envelope from his pack, this one from Burr. Wilkinson expressed no surprise that Swartwout had tracked him down with a message
from Burr. Nor did he give anything away when the colonel returned.[2]

Late that night, alone, Wilkinson tore open Burr's envelope. He confronted a long message that mixed three different codes. Parts were expressed in a "book" code, based on the 1800 edition of *Entick's New Spelling Dictionary*. That code used two numbers to designate the page number and word position of the correct word. A second code used Arabic numbers to represent individuals: 14, 15, and 16 were Burr; Wilkinson was 45. Finally, a series of hieroglyphics stood for either words or letters. A square was England; France was a square with a dot in the middle.[3]

Two versions of the "cipher letter," sent by Burr to Wilkinson in the summer of 1806, are preserved at the Newberry Library in Chicago.

The general deciphered enough of the letter to know that it was Burr's announcement that the expedition was underway.

"I have at length obtained funds," Burr began, "and have actually commenced. The Eastern detachments, from different points and under different pretence, will rendezvous on Ohio [River] on 1 November." The letter burst with optimism, announcing that "everything internal and external favor our view," and trumpeted the gathering of "a host of choice spirits." It included false claims that Commodore Truxtun and the Royal Navy would join the expedition. It stroked Wilkinson's vanity, assuring him that "Wilkinson shall be second to Burr only." It was practical, urging Wilkinson to order six months of provisions. The heart of the letter told Wilkinson where Burr would be:

Burr's plan of operation is to move down rapidly from the falls [Louisville] on Fifteenth November, with the first 500 or 1000 men in light boats now constructing for that purpose; to be at Natchez between 5 and 15 December, there to meet you; then to determine whether it will be expedient in the first instance to seize or to pass by [Baton Rouge].

One passage made it clear that Mexico was part of the plan: "[T]he people of the country to which we are going are prepared to receive us—their agents, now with me, say that if we protect their religion and will not subject them to a foreign power, that in three weeks all will be settled."

In a stirring finale, the letter concluded, "The gods invite us to glory and fortune. It remains to be seen whether we deserve the boons."

The cipher letter enclosed a note from Jonathan Dayton that sounded the same themes in equally ringing tones. "Are you ready?" Dayton asked. "Are your numerous associates ready? Wealth and glory, Louisiana and Mexico."[4]

Staring at the messages from Burr and Dayton, Wilkinson faced a pivotal decision. This was the moment. For Burr, the scheming of the last two years had not been empty talk. The drawing-room dandy was calling the bluff of the boasting soldier. Burr was on the march. He intended to raise an insurrection in New Orleans, to invade Mexico and West Florida, to proclaim a new nation, and to invite the West to join.

The stakes were higher than Wilkinson had ever played for. He had grown comfortable with backroom disloyalty that levered cash from the hapless Spaniards. But this—revolution, war, treason in the light of day—was very different. It would all be so open, so daring. He would be attacking Spain, his longtime sponsor, without the approval of his own government. Most of all, Burr's plan could fail. This would bear some serious thought.

The general later claimed that Burr's message in the cipher letter came as a surprise. He had some suspicions of Burr's intentions, he admitted, but he denied any foreknowledge of this bold plan to redraw the map of North America.

Wilkinson's protestations of surprise rang hollow then, and they still do. The cipher letter is part of a longer correspondence. It begins by saying that Burr had received Wilkinson's letter of May 13. It reflects no sense that the writer was unveiling new information. Rather, it continues a conversation, proclaiming that Burr had "at length" acquired money to go forward. Only a lunatic would send such a letter to an army commander who was not expecting it. Aaron Burr was called many things, but never a lunatic.

James Wilkinson made a cold, rational decision that night in lonesome Natchitoches. He resolved to double-cross Burr. The Spaniards, it had turned out, wanted no war. Without a Spanish war to rally westerners to his side, the former vice president had less chance of success. Those odds would grow steeper still if Wilkinson and his troops stood in Burr's way.

By opposing Burr, the general could pose as the savior of the union, thwarting insurrection and secession. He also could claim to be the savior of Spain's colonies, preserving them from Burr's invasion. Such heroism could win American honors and Spanish silver.[5] And what would Wilkinson gain by backing Burr? The chance to lead the army of a new, vulnerable nation, to play second fiddle to the great Burr. Wilkinson was already the head of an army. And Wilkinson had to ask himself, as every conspirator must, how much he trusted the leader of the scheme. The answer was, for Wilkinson, not enough.

The general's new course would be a delicate one. Peace on the Sabine frontier was the first priority. Now he truly had to drain the cup of conciliation. Then he had to secure New Orleans. An uprising in that turbulent city was central to Burr's plans. To oppose Burr successfully, Wilkinson would have to be vigorous, ruthless.

Wilkinson had great advantages in the coming conflict. He knew Burr's plans. He knew Burr's agents. And he had one of them, Sam Swartwout, within his power. The general would pump the young man for information, then chart his course. He was in a perfect position to send Burr straight to the hangman as a traitor.

•   •   •

Next morning, Wilkinson summoned his colonel and swore him to secrecy. The general explained that individuals of "wealth, popularity and talents" were gathering for purposes hostile to the government. Burr was at their head and Swartwout his agent. To end this plot, Wilkinson announced, he would personally advance to the Sabine River and make peace with Spain, then move on New Orleans to secure the French artillery there.[6]

Once more, though, Wilkinson did not move, dawdling for several days at Natchitoches. He talked earnestly with Swartwout, trying to elicit the last of Burr's secrets. According to the general, he learned that Burr intended to seize the banks and ships of New Orleans, while Swartwout's elder brother John was to lead a second contingent of five hundred adventurers downriver. Swartwout revealed, according to Wilkinson, that seven thousand men were committed to the expedition, including Commodore Truxtun, Captain Stephen Decatur, General Jackson, and General Adair. Sam Swartwout later denied telling Wilkinson any of that. "I first heard of such a project from Wilkinson," Swartwout insisted. "I never heard anything of the kind from Burr." According to the young messenger, Wilkinson said he wished Burr would separate the union and "that he should like to be in his empire."[7]

Whatever passed between Swartwout and the general, for more than a week Wilkinson made no effort to advise President Jefferson of Burr's plans. Instead, he wrote a letter to Burr, of all people, for delivery in Natchez.[8] When Wilkinson finally wrote to the president, he did not mention the cipher letter or Sam Swartwout's arrival in Natchitoches. He did not mention Aaron Burr. Instead, he concocted a blend of half-truths and outright lies.

Wilkinson started by creating a false document, a "communication" that he supposedly received from an unnamed source. This forgery reported that eight thousand to ten thousand men would arrive in New Orleans for an attack on Mexico through the port at Vera Cruz. Wilkinson placed his own cover letter over the forged memorandum, professing to be puzzled by the enclosure. "I am not only uninformed of the prime mover and ultimate objects of this enterprise," he lied, "but am ignorant of the foundation on which it rests." In that cover note, Wilkinson said he would make the best deal he could with Spanish officials and "throw myself with my little band into New Orleans, to be ready to defend that capital against usurpation and violence."[9]

By starting his report to Jefferson with this false "communication" and the equally false cover note, Wilkinson committed to unfolding Burr's crimes gradually, bringing Jefferson along step by step. He also drafted a note to Secretary of War Dearborn. Gone was the warlike Wilkinson of the month before. He would propose, he wrote, that Spanish and American forces withdraw to the positions they held when the United States took possession of Louisiana.[10]

Wilkinson confided his messages to Lieutenant Thomas Smith, insisting that they must reach Washington City "in a shorter time, if possible, than the same route had ever been traveled." Wilkinson instructed Smith to tender his resignation from the army to forestall suspicions about his abrupt departure from camp; the general would restore Smith's rank later. Near sundown on October 22—roughly two weeks after Swartwout delivered the cipher letter—Smith set off. First, though, Wilkinson had the lieutenant sew the messages to Jefferson between the soles of a slipper. Wilkinson also made Smith swear an oath to conceal his mission from all persons, "unless from sickness or some other occurrence, I should be unable to proceed."[11]

Wilkinson then turned to the Spaniards. He sent an aide to their headquarters with a proposal. If Spanish troops stayed west of the Sabine, then American forces would remain on the east side of Arroyo Hondo. The soldiers could remain behind those natural barriers until diplomats could agree on the final border. The land between the two rivers would become "Neutral Ground."[12]

The captain-general of the Interior Provinces of Mexico, who was in Nacogdoches, rejected Wilkinson's proposal. Fortuitously, the returning American messenger paused at the Spanish army camp on the Sabine. The local Spanish commander, showing notable independence, accepted Wilkinson's proposal on the spot. Delighted, Wilkinson drew up an agreement for the stopgap arrangement. It was signed on November 5.[13]

Wilkinson had pulled it off. The Neutral Ground agreement would meet favor with Jefferson, who wanted no war over a scrap of ground at the western edge of Orleans Territory. With the Spanish threat removed, Wilkinson could concentrate on the threat from the north and east—Burr.

After ordering his troops back to Natchitoches, Wilkinson rushed ahead of them, covering sixty miles in a single day. In Natchitoches he met

a messenger from Erich Bollman in New Orleans, who delivered the duplicate of Burr's cipher letter along with a new message from Dayton, also in
cipher. Dayton's incendiary message reflected the central role Wilkinson
was supposed to play in Burr's expedition. "Everything, and even Heaven
itself," Dayton wrote, "appears to have conspired to prepare the train for
a grand explosion, are you also ready?" Dayton exhorted the general to
remain at the head of the U.S. army "until your friends join you in December, somewhere on the river Mississippi. Under the auspices of Burr and
Wilkinson, I shall be happy to engage." Wilkinson also received a letter from
Natchez claiming that the West was about to explode in a secessionist rebellion. That letter reported that Julien De Pestre, sent by Burr to St. Louis,
had persuaded "the most influential characters" to join Burr.[14]

The general could move quickly when he had to. By November 11 he
was in Natchez, preparing to oppose Burr's hordes. The first thing Wilkinson did, though, was to retrieve and destroy the letter he had written to Burr
the month before, shortly after receiving the cipher letter from Sam Swartwout. Wilkinson never disclosed the contents of that letter to Burr.[15]

Another development in October soured Burr's prospects further. The
president, back in Washington City after his two-month hiatus at Monticello, found that the drumbeat of warnings about Burr had grown too insis-
tent. He had to do something.

Alarms about Burr were streaming in. One came from western New
York, another from Colonel Morgan in Pennsylvania. Commodore Truxtun
sent an outline of a military response to Burr's attempt "to dismember the
empire." Latrobe, the architect, reported that Burr had asked him to design
boats to carry men down the Ohio and Mississippi.[16] Two Pennsylvanians
wrote to Madison. While Burr was there, they reported, he said a western
secession plan was afoot and asked about the strength of the local militia.
From Kentucky came a warning about Burr's Marietta boats, that Blennerhassett's "Querist" articles were reviving talk of western secession, and that
"designing bad men may do a great deal of mischief in this country."[17]

The alarm that finally moved the president arrived in a roundabout
fashion. A lawyer in Marietta wrote to a friend in Massachusetts that "Burr
fever" was infecting the West; the people of Wood County, Virginia, which

included Blennerhassett Island, would soon challenge Burr. The letter's recipient showed it to William Eaton, who was dismayed to learn that Burr was on the move. Eaton reported that letter to Madison and to a Massachusetts congressman, who passed it on to the postmaster general, who told Jefferson.

Having not responded to all the earlier warnings—from newspapers, from anonymous letters, from Eaton, from Joseph Hamilton Daveiss, and from the *Western World*—the president finally stirred. He called a Cabinet meeting for October 22 to discuss Burr.[18]

Only four Cabinet officers attended. Reflecting Jefferson's indecision, they struggled to frame a response to this unprecedented yet uncertain risk. Was the evidence strong enough to take action? Should they simply have Burr and his allies watched closely? Or should they dispatch federal agents to swoop in and nip this threat in the bud? Or something in between?

After reviewing the American forces in the Southwest—just more than a thousand soldiers were on duty in Natchitoches, New Orleans, and Fort Adams—the Cabinet approved several measures. Confidential letters should be sent to warn western governors to arrest Burr if he engaged in any overt act against the union. Gunboats from New Orleans should ascend the river to Fort Adams so they could intercept Burr. The Cabinet reached no decision about what to do with General Wilkinson, even though Eaton had included him in his accusation and even though the Cabinet considered him "disobedien[t]" for loitering in St. Louis over the summer.[19]

Two days later, still troubled, Jefferson convened a second Cabinet session on Burr. The group approved more actions. Command of the New Orleans gunboats should be assumed by two navy captains (including Stephen Decatur, who had been solicited by Burr). More gunboats should sail from Atlantic ports to the Mississippi. A single official should be sent from Washington City to shadow Burr through the West; he could alert local and state officials of the danger from Burr.

Next day, the Cabinet reversed itself. The western mails had arrived with no whisper of a concern about Burr. This "total silence" in a single day's mail, Jefferson recorded, "proves he is committing no overt act against the law." Westerners arriving in Washington City for the new session of Congress were expressing no concern about Burr either. Showing the reluctance to take action that Burr so despised, Jefferson's men rescinded most of the measures they had just approved. The only steps they retained were to send a lone official to dog Burr's steps and to send warning letters to Orleans and Mississippi territories.[20]

Though this response was minimal, the man selected to be Jefferson's bloodhound would prove a wise choice. John Graham was a loyal Virginia Republican who understood affairs between the United States and Spain, having been an aide to the American minister in Madrid. As secretary of Orleans Territory since 1805, Graham was familiar with the atmosphere in that tinderbox. He knew members of the Mexican Association, as well as the rumors connecting Burr to it and to insurrection. Graham also knew that time was very short. It was already late October. Burr's cipher letter said that on November 15 the expedition would leave Louisville, which was almost six hundred miles from Washington City.[21]

Graham left Washington City right away.

16

The Daveiss Factor

Kentucky
November–December 1806

Through much of October 1806, Burr had every reason to feel optimistic. Unaware that Wilkinson was turning against him, or that Jefferson was stirring, Burr used Kentucky as his base, organizing the expedition and enticing adventurers. He stressed how close the nation was to war with Spain. "All reflecting men," he wrote to Governor Harrison in Indiana, "consider a war with Spain to be inevitable." Enclosing a copy of Andrew Jackson's order placing the Tennessee militia on alert, he suggested that Harrison issue a similar order to the Indiana militia.[1]

Burr repeatedly implied that the highest American officials supported his private invasion of Mexico, but that they could not say so publicly. With some men, like Davis Floyd, he brandished a letter, supposedly from the Secretary of War, expressing that support. He told Blennerhassett that a Mexican invasion "would be very pleasing" to the government. The plausibility of Burr's claims was reinforced by the widespread belief that Jefferson had extended such tacit support to Francisco Miranda's expedition, which sailed earlier that year.[2]

Juggling many balls at the same time, Burr also touted the Bastrop Tract and solicited funds. He coordinated money and supplies to support an expedition of hundreds of men from all over the West. Though Burr left few tracks during this key period, observing his favorite maxim that "things written remain," Blennerhassett wrote later of the three October weeks he spent with Burr in Lexington. During that time, the Irishman "observed Burr's popularity daily increasing; heard of no jealousy or suspicions of his views or designs on the part of the government or its agents, nor from any other quarter."[3]

Traveling the countryside, Blennerhassett freely offered Bastrop land to potential recruits. If a young man brought a rifle and a blanket, the Irishman promised, he would receive twelve dollars a month plus provisions plus 150 acres of land after six months. Blennerhassett often departed from that message. Once, when challenged about his offer, Blennerhassett confided that "we are going to take Mexico, one of the finest and richest places in the whole world." Burr would be the king, he added, and his daughter the queen. "Colonel Burr had made fortunes for a great many in his lifetime," Blennerhassett said. "But now he was going to make something for himself."[4] To another recruit the Irishman predicted they would establish an independent government in Spanish lands. The people of New Orleans, he added, were dissatisfied with American rule. When another asked about rumors that Burr would sever the union, Blennerhassett confirmed the rumors. With yet another, Blennerhassett spread out a map of Mexico and lauded the country's "wealth, fertility, and healthiness." Sometimes he too was mysterious. On one occasion, he declined to describe the expedition's purpose unless his questioner first committed to join it.[5]

Yet most westerners, including those intending to join Burr, remained uncertain of his intentions. "Public curiosity is still on tiptoe," wrote the *Kentucky Gazette* in late October, "relative to the object of Col. Burr's visits to the Western country." Though Burr's intentions "are enveloped in mystery," the newspaper was confident that "some grand object is in contemplation."[6]

Late in October, a messenger brought an urgent note from Mrs. Blennerhassett. Their neighbors in Wood County, Virginia (now Parkersburg,

West Virginia) were up in arms over the reports that Burr and Blennerhassett were planning to lead a western secession. The men of Wood County threatened to burn Blennerhassett's house and seize his supplies.[7]

Blennerhassett hurried home to defend his family. Burr remained in Kentucky, where the next threat to the expedition arose from the frustrated federal prosecutor, Joseph Hamilton Daveiss.

At noon on Wednesday, November 5, Daveiss rose in the federal court in Frankfort, the state capital. Reading from his sworn affidavit, the lawyer accused Burr of preparing an illegal expedition to make war on Spain. Daveiss added that Burr had bought "large stores of provisions as if for an army," yet he concealed "in great mystery . . . his purposes and projects." Daveiss asked the judge for an unusual order: one barring Burr from preparing an illegal expedition.

Daveiss did not stop there. He was, as he put it, "staggered by the silence of the [Jefferson] administration," which he denounced months later as "this snoring administration." He told the court "that all the western territories are the next object of the scheme—and finally, all the region of the Ohio is calculated as falling into the vortex of the new proposed revolution."[8]

The presiding judge, Harry Innes, could hardly miss the political dynamite that Daveiss had flung into his courtroom. On the heels of the *Western World*'s campaign, this young champion of the Marshalls was accusing Burr of insurrection and treason. The stakes for the judge were almost as high as they were for Burr. Innes had been a member of the "Spanish Conspiracy" in Kentucky in the 1780s, which flirted with secession from the United States and alliance with Spain. As Daveiss pressed his attack on Burr, Judge Innes was defending himself against an inquiry by the Kentucky legislature into bribery by the Spaniards.[9]

Due to the novelty of Daveiss's motion, Innes said, he would consider it overnight. The delay allowed news of the court proceedings to reach Burr, thirty-five miles away in Lexington.

Burr resolved to meet this danger head-on. Daveiss plainly aimed to destroy his plans. Even if denied, Daveiss's motion could blacken Burr's reputation, discouraging both recruits and financial backers. Burr sent word that he would come to Frankfort to defend the case. In a note to Blennerhassett, Burr called Daveiss's action "absurd and ridiculous," but he also recognized that the judge "must expect a tornado of abuse from the *W[estern] World*."[10]

After riding through the rain to Frankfort, Burr retained young Henry Clay as his lawyer. Already prominent at age twenty-nine, the tall, lean Clay was just starting the political career that would earn him the nickname "The Great Compromiser." Burr's arrival in Frankfort caused a sensation. In that small frontier town, the former vice president of the United States would face charges of plotting secession and an illegal invasion of Mexico.[11]

On Saturday, before Burr arrived in court, Judge Innes rejected Daveiss's motion on largely procedural grounds. He explained that he could not order that Burr *not* commit a crime; he could only hear charges that Burr *already* had committed a crime. Observing that "if the facts stated in [Daveiss's] affidavit are true, the project ought to be prevented and the offender punished," Innes invited the prosecutor to bring his evidence to a grand jury.

Daveiss took the bait. He requested a grand jury for the following Wednesday. Innes issued the order. Walking into court just as the judge announced his order, Burr spoke in his usual calm and direct manner. He invited an investigation of his conduct but asked that it be done quickly, as he had pressing affairs. He seemed confident of vindication. Observers were impressed.[12]

Five days later, on Wednesday, November 12, excited spectators jammed into the courtroom. Daveiss had summoned twelve witnesses. "All was eagerness and impatience," according to a local newspaper.[13] But one witness never arrived. Davis Floyd, who had been assembling supplies and boats for Burr in Louisville, did not appear.

The federal attorney announced he could not proceed without Floyd. He asked that the judge dismiss the grand jury. The packed courtroom reacted with hoots and laughter. Burr left in triumph. Public opinion, according to the local newspaper, "has all along been strongly in favor of Col. Burr, [and] now burst forth without disguise."[14]

Burr had faced down Daveiss, but he had lost valuable time. He would not be able to make a last trip to Philadelphia before setting off downriver. "It is impossible for a man to make any calculations of his time," he lamented, "when he is liable to be detained by public prosecutions." He left for Cincinnati, where he could confirm supplies and other arrangements with Senator John Smith.[15]

Daveiss deplored the attitudes of his neighbors in Frankfort. They treated him like a pariah, he complained, while they "vie[d] with each other in . . . zeal to distinguish and caress [Burr]. Balls and parties were held for him." But the prosecutor refused to throw in the towel. On November 25, having located Floyd, Daveiss requested a new grand jury. His motion announced he would present an indictment against Burr. Daveiss had to move fast, a local newspaper wrote, or "Mr. Burr would be afloat with his flotilla."[16]

Once more, the former vice president hurried to Frankfort, this time to face formal criminal charges. Burr issued self-righteous statements that began to stray from the truth. In a letter to William Henry Harrison, he wrote that he had "no wish or design to attempt a separation of the Union, that I have no connection with any foreign power or government, that I never meditated the introduction of any foreign power or influence into the U.S." Both the British and Spanish ministers could have contradicted those assertions. His plans, Burr insisted, were not "hostile to the interest or tranquility or the union of the U.S. or prejudicial to its government." Perhaps half a dozen witnesses could have countered that assertion.[17]

Burr attempted to retain Clay again, but his lawyer had developed a case of cold feet. In the three weeks since the first hearing in Frankfort, General John Adair had resigned his seat in the U.S. Senate; Clay had been selected to serve out Adair's Senate term. Clay worried that a U.S. senator should not defend Burr against such explosive charges. Burr insisted he was blameless. "I have no design," he wrote to Clay, "nor have I taken any measure, to promote a dissolution of the Union or a separation of any one or more States." Burr's desperation was carrying him into ever more doubtful statements. His views, he added, "have been fully explained to and approved by several of the principal officers of government, and, I believe, are well understood by the Administration and seen by it with complacency." The story worked. Clay agreed to remain on Burr's case.[18]

When the grand jury convened on December 3, Daveiss presented an indictment of John Adair, Burr's ally. Contrary to usual practice at the time,

Daveiss asked to question the witnesses summoned to the grand jury. Burr objected. The grand jury was supposed to protect citizens, he protested. Allowing the prosecutor to question witnesses would convert the grand jury into "an engine of oppression." Judge Innes agreed. Daveiss moaned that if he had known he would be excluded from the grand jury, he would not have asked for one. The judge allowed him to submit written questions that the grand jury could choose to ask, or not to ask.[19]

After less than a day of inquiry, which included testimony by Adair, the grand jury refused to indict the militia general, returning a judgment of "no true bill." Undeterred, Daveiss gave the grand jury an indictment of Burr. The grand jurors heard more witnesses, including Street and Wood, editors of the *Western World*. In a distinct anticlimax, both editors denied having any evidence against Burr. They said their articles were based on information supplied by Humphrey Marshall, the Federalist leader and cousin of John Marshall.[20]

The grand jury returned a judgment of "no true bill" against Burr, adding a stout vindication of both Adair and Burr:

> There has been no testimony before us which does in the smallest degree criminate the conduct of either of these persons, nor can we . . . discover that anything improper or injurious to the interest of the government of the United States . . . is designed or contemplated by either of them.[21]

Burr had dodged another bullet; in some respects, the episode increased his stature in the West. Even Humphrey Marshall conceded that Burr's courtroom deportment was "grave, polite, and dignified." The grandees of Frankfort held another ball in his honor, then Kentucky's governor honored him with yet one more. As recorded by a young woman in attendance at the first ball, the former vice president commanded center stage in elegant costume: "Small in stature, dignified in mien, with gold knee buckles and immense rosettes on his pumps; a queue tied with black ribbon, and powdered wig."[22]

Despite the elation, even euphoria, that followed the collapse of the Frankfort legal proceedings, Daveiss's assault inflicted lingering damage on

Burr's enterprise. The case was a terrible distraction. For two critical weeks, Burr was fending off Daveiss, not organizing his expedition. By questioning Burr's true intentions, Daveiss's charges also raised doubts that could deter volunteers. The realities of the Ohio River made every new obstacle a potentially fatal one. At some point in December, the river's water level would drop too low for boats to pass, throttling the expedition before it could begin. Worse, every delay gave Burr's adversaries additional time to mobilize. Time was not on Burr's side.

Other factors were contributing to delay Burr's enterprise. Most worrisome, the Marietta boatyard was struggling to fill his order for fifteen boats, including one specially fitted out for the Blennerhassett family.[23]

If only Burr could get the expedition moving, he still could hope for good results. So far as he knew, Wilkinson was in position to start the Spanish war; the fighting might even have begun. Erich Bollman had reported from New Orleans, where he was intimately engaged with Burr's allies. If all else failed, Burr could travel to the Bastrop Tract and start the war himself.[24]

Burr expected the expedition to gather strength as it moved downriver. Comfort Tyler's men would push off from Beaver, Pennsylvania. When they arrived in Marietta, Blennerhassett and his recruits would join them. In Louisville, the flotilla would meet Davis Floyd and his men. More volunteers would join where the Wabash flowed into the Ohio. Burr would ride overland to Nashville to pick up boats and men from General Jackson, then float down the Cumberland to join the others on the Ohio. John Adair of Kentucky, no longer a senator, would ride through the southwestern forest to New Orleans, prospecting for men in the Mississippi settlements above Spanish West Florida. Senator John Smith of Ohio would take goods downriver to Mississippi, ignoring the new session of Congress that was convening in Washington City.

In Nashville, Burr and Adair lodged at the same inn.[25] This time, however, Andrew Jackson received Burr frostily. A visitor had told Jackson, based on remarks by Burr's friend John Swartwout, that Burr intended a rising in Orleans Territory. Shocked, Jackson had fired off a warning to Governor Claiborne in New Orleans. Without naming Burr as a suspect, he wrote:

Be on the alert—keep a watchful eye on our General [Wilkinson].
. . . I fear there is something rotten in the State of Denmark—you
have enemies within your own city, that may try to subvert your
government, and try to separate it from the Union.

To a Tennessee senator, Jackson cautioned that a plan was under way to
"take possession of New Orleans," cloaked by stories of settling new lands
and invading Mexico.[26]

Burr protested his innocence to Jackson, pointing to his success in the
Kentucky courtroom. The two men reached a rapprochement of sorts. Jackson delivered two of the five boats that Burr had ordered, along with some
supplies. Burr did not need the other three boats, since no recruits had
materialized in Tennessee. By December 22, Burr was on the Cumberland
River with two flatboats, a few hired boatmen, and some horses.[27]

Other events were turning against Burr. When Wilkinson arrived in
Natchez on November 11, he issued emotional alarms about a dangerous
conspiracy. To Claiborne in New Orleans, he wrote ominously:

You are surrounded by dangers of which you dream not and the
destruction of the American Union is seriously menaced. The
storm will probably burst in New Orleans, where I shall meet it and
triumph or perish.[28]

Wilkinson's dramatic mood suffused a new letter he wrote to the president.
They faced "a deep, dark, and wicked conspiracy," the general wrote, "embracing the young and the old, the democrat and the federalist, the native
and the foreigner, the patriot of '76 and the exotic of yesterday, the opulent
and the needy, the ins and the outs." Decrying this "spectacle of human
depravity" but still not naming Burr, Wilkinson wrote that seven thousand
men would fall upon New Orleans and then invade Mexico. He promised
a heroic defense of the city, which would include declaring martial law. "Although I may smile at danger in open conflict," his letter ended, "I dread
the stroke of the assassin, because it cannot confer an honorable death."
He confided his letter to a Quaker merchant to hand directly to Jefferson in
Washington City.[29]

While preparing to save the republic, Wilkinson found time for another shakedown of Spain. The general dispatched an aide to Mexico City. His letter to the viceroy of Mexico explained that he was blocking Burr's attempt to revolutionize Mexico. In return, he demanded that King Carlos reimburse him for "expenses" of 121,000 pesos, roughly translating to $4 million in today's value.[30]

After a week in Natchez, Wilkinson left for New Orleans. At Fort Adams, he found Peter Ogden and Sam Swartwout; biding his time, the general took no action against Burr's confederates. He reached New Orleans on November 25.[31]

For Burr, developments in Washington City were even worse. Lieutenant Smith, Wilkinson's messenger from Natchitoches, had taken little more than a month to reach the capital. Ushered in to see Jefferson on November 25—the same day Daveiss made his second demand for a grand jury, and the day Wilkinson arrived in New Orleans—Smith did an odd thing. He tore the sole off a slipper. Then he extracted papers from it. They were the "communication" Wilkinson had forged as the anonymous report of a mysterious expedition coming downriver, along with Wilkinson's false cover note. Smith handed them over.[32]

Jefferson, the least formal of chief executives, was unfazed by this unique delivery technique. The messages themselves—vague, yet urgent—consumed his attention. No matter how slippery the morals of his army chief might be, Jefferson could not ignore these messages. Two days later, the president issued a proclamation on the subject.

Still short on facts, Jefferson told the nation what he could. Certain persons, he wrote, "are conspiring and confederating together to begin and set on foot . . . a military enterprise against the dominions of Spain." He accused the unnamed plotters of "deceiving and seducing honest and well-meaning citizens, under various pretences, to engage in their criminal enterprise." Jefferson commanded all Americans to withdraw from that enterprise and he authorized officials to stop it.[33]

Ambiguous though it was, Jefferson's proclamation would prove a powerful blow against Burr.

17

Escape from Blennerhassett Island

Blennerhassett Island to Mississippi Territory
November 1806–January 1807

While Burr danced to Daveiss's tune through November and early December, Blennerhassett Island became the visible heart of the expedition. Beginning at the end of the summer, preparations on the island transfixed neighbors on both sides of the river.

Harman Blennerhassett had built a kiln to dry corn at high temperatures; corn meal ground from kiln-dried corn would remain edible far longer. The Irishman produced 130 barrels of corn meal for the expedition. He acquired flour and a hundred barrels of pork. To a workman, Margaret Blennerhassett explained that they were laying in provisions for an army for a year.[1]

Two types of supplies were conspicuous by their absence. Burr's lieutenants gathered no agricultural tools, a striking omission for any settlement of new lands. Also, the island did not contain the weapons necessary for a military invasion. Many of the adventurers brought hunting rifles and shotguns. Visitors saw a few pistols. But there were no muskets with bayonets, the weapons of soldiers. Two boats supposedly passed Cincinnati in late

November with heavy loads of guns, powder, and bayonets, manned by eight men who spoke only French. Perhaps those were for Burr's expedition.[2]

News of the Kentucky court proceedings did not deter Blennerhassett, but matters took a darker turn when John Graham, Jefferson's bloodhound, arrived in Marietta in late November.[3] The Irishman dined in a local tavern with Graham, whom he had met before. Blennerhassett mistakenly thought that Graham was volunteering for the expedition, so he spoke openly. Once the Ouachita lands had an independent government, he said, they would invade Mexico. He was engaging young men for the effort—single, without families—and would arm them. They would join with the Mexican Association in New Orleans, which was dedicated to invading Mexico.

When Graham identified himself as the president's agent, sent to stop the expedition, Blennerhassett recoiled. Graham pressed him, arguing that Burr had no title to the Bastrop lands and that an invasion of Mexico would be illegal. Insisting that the expedition was legal, the Irishman left.[4]

Graham then appealed to the citizens of Wood County, Virginia, who were already inclined to obstruct Burr's expedition. By early December, that county was awash with rumors that vigilantes would descend on Blennerhassett Island, raze the mansion, and lay hands on any adventurers found there.[5]

If the boatyard delays continued, the expedition might be strangled in its crib. Burr, struggling with Daveiss in Kentucky, wrote to Blennerhassett to make haste. He must leave before the water level in the river sank too low. Blennerhassett set a departure date of December 6. The day came, but the boats were not ready. Electrifying news reached Marietta. William Eaton, a national hero due to his North African exploits, had published a statement revealing Burr's proposal to lead a putsch in Washington City. Young men began to abandon the expedition.[6]

Meanwhile, John Graham rode to Chillicothe, Ohio's state capital, where he persuaded the legislature to call out the state militia against Burr. Legislation adopted on December 6 authorized the arrest of everyone associated with the expedition. The governor of Ohio dispatched soldiers and cannon to Cincinnati to intercept boats going downriver.[7]

On December 7, Comfort Tyler's four boats arrived at the island with about twenty-five men aboard. Tyler took charge of the island in the cold air, brushing aside the bookish Blennerhassett. Trampling a recent snowfall into mud, the men conducted target practice and melted lead to form bullets. The Irishman again demanded the boats from the Marietta yard.[8]

On the morning of December 9, a copy of the new Ohio statute arrived in Marietta. Two militia leaders mustered forty volunteers on Front Street and made plans to stop the expedition.[9]

Next day, eleven of Blennerhassett's boats were ready. With so many recruits backing out of the expedition, Blennerhassett decided that eleven would be enough. Under the darkening skies of the late afternoon, the militia seized all but one of the boats as they floated down the Muskingum River laden with cargo. The captured boats held 130 barrels of corn meal and 60 barrels of pork.[10]

The adventurers on the island were in peril. The Ohio militia loomed on one side of the river, having posted an officer to arrest any adventurer who stepped on that shore. From the Virginia side, the Wood County vigilantes were expected at eight o'clock the next morning. It was time to go.[11]

In the midst of "hubbub and confusion" on that cold, anxious night, Blennerhassett's creditors arrived to settle business matters. In each of Tyler's boats, a few men sat in the dim light of a single candle. Several huddled around a fire, sharing rumors. Inside the mansion, weapons lay scattered about. The Irishman thought the Ohio law was unconstitutional, but he did not care to wait around to test it. He considered strategies for evading the Virginia mob and the Ohio militia. Floating slowly downriver, the adventurers would be sitting ducks for riflemen on the shore. Two of Blennerhassett's slaves took advantage of the chaos to run off. A search party quickly recovered them.

Tyler polled his men: Would they accept Blennerhassett in their boats? They agreed. It was close to midnight when slaves loaded his five trunks on the boats. Mrs. Blennerhassett came to the shore to bid her husband farewell. She planned to follow in a couple of days with their children. Close to one o'clock in the morning, the boats shoved off.[12]

The Wood County vigilantes arrived with the sunrise. They found only Mrs. Blennerhassett, the children, and some slaves. After rampaging through the house and liberating its wine cellar, the vigilantes made an ineffectual effort to capture the boats downriver.

Over the next several days, two more boats filled with adventurers floated into the region. One included two young men in splendid blue uniforms trimmed with yellow and gold. Their boat barely escaped angry citizens in Marietta, only to be seized at Blennerhassett Island by fifty Wood County vigilantes who were still loitering in the pillaged mansion. A hastily assembled court acquitted the adventurers of any offense. Mrs. Blennerhassett and the children left in that boat to pursue the main party downriver.[13]

Despite the alarms raised against them, the adventurers drifted uneventfully past Gallipolis, then Cincinnati. On the river, the frigid December air was punishing. After an early stop ashore for warm fires, Tyler's men floated straight through to Louisville, where Davis Floyd was waiting with more boats and more men.[14]

Several figures watched from the Kentucky shore as the adventurers loaded Floyd's supplies. One was Daveiss, the federal attorney, certain that a terrible crime was unfolding before his eyes. The adventurers packed away three large crates, presumably filled with muskets and bayonets, along with several boxes of cartridges. No hand was raised against Burr's men. While Daveiss looked on in impotent rage, the adventurers fired several rifle volleys.

Daveiss reported the scene in a letter to the Kentucky governor. Burr's flotilla now numbered nine boats and between sixty to eighty men. Then Daveiss went home to his farm. In a few months, Jefferson fired him, weary of this Federalist Cassandra who had the ill grace to have been correct about Burr. Two weeks after the expedition had left Louisville, the Kentucky militia—summoned in response to John Graham's warnings—seized three ammunition-filled boats on the river, likely intended for Burr.[15]

Cruising downriver for the next nine days, the adventurers struggled with dirty weather, submerged trees, and hidden rocks. The roofs of the boats leaked. More volunteers joined up, and the boats met no hostile government forces. At Shawneetown on the north side of the river (now part of Illinois), they laid up for repairs. Comfort Tyler presented "articles of agreement" to the men. At least thirty of them signed, committing themselves to any "legal and honorable enterprise" of the Washita Land Speculation Company.[16]

Many of the adventurers had been promised $10 or $12 a month. Some hoped for Baron Bastrop's land. Few were frontiersmen or farmers; many were gentlemen. When the journey ended, they were described as "school-masters, singingmasters, dancingmasters, and doctors in abundance."[17]

Most of them claimed later that they had entertained little idea of the purpose of the expedition. "I felt much disposed to see the country," shrugged one who had recruited men for Tyler. Others evaded the question or said they planned to settle the Ouachita. According to Blennerhassett, many adventurers never asked about the expedition's purpose. Back on Blennerhassett Island, though, Comfort Tyler and his men had asserted, as Blennerhassett said repeatedly, that their goal was Mexico. That was what Davis Floyd told his recruits. On several occasions, the expedition leaders promised that the famous Colonel Burr would reveal their true destination when he joined them.[18]

For two weeks, they heard nothing from Burr, who was in Tennessee. On Christmas Eve, a message arrived: Burr would meet them at the junction of the Cumberland and the Ohio.[19]

While Burr and his men groped their way toward each other, the nation wondered about the former vice president. For almost two years, his movements and statements had made him an object of speculation. What did he really want? Was there anything this bold man would not dare? "At present," commented the *Richmond Enquirer*, "nothing but clouds and darkness rest upon this subject." From Washington City, where speculation was rampant, a congressman wrote: "As to B[urr], out of a thousand stories, 999 ought to be disbelieved." As he traveled through the forests of the western country, silent and out of reach, Burr grew more dangerous and more fascinating in the public mind.[20]

After the Kentucky prosecutions and the articles from the *Western World*, many believed the worst. Newspapers around the country reprinted Eaton's scandalous revelations. Burr aimed to create a new empire in Mexico, the *Richmond Enquirer* announced in December, and would become monarch of the western country. Hungry for facts, newspapers reported every transaction that could be tied to Burr, every draft with which he paid a bill. They hinted about his ties to "two distinguished federalists, one lately a U.S. Senator."[21]

The *Philadelphia Aurora*, a loyal Jeffersonian paper, did not wait for facts. The newspaper reported breathlessly that six thousand muskets had been shipped from Baltimore for Burr. With his "resemblance of Bonaparte," the report continued, Burr intended a "vast and dazzling project" to become despot of the lands washed by the Gulf of Mexico. The *National Intelligencer* in Washington City screamed that "a thousand circumstances" proved that Burr intended to dismember the union and invade Spanish lands. Newspapers printed names of adventurers and declared (incorrectly) that the expedition was coordinated with Miranda's assault on Venezuela.[22]

The classically minded again compared Burr to Catiline, the Roman nobleman who was accused of plotting to overthrow that republic a decade before Julius Caesar did just that. Denounced by Cicero as "daring, insidious, and shifting" and an "expert in feigning what he did not mean," Catiline had captivated the young men of his time. In all these qualities, the newspapers insisted, Burr was identical.[23]

Burr met the adventurers at the mouth of the Cumberland a day or two after Christmas. He contacted the commander at nearby Fort Massac, who only sixteen months earlier had been his traveling companion from Natchez to Nashville. At Burr's request, the commander granted a furlough to Sergeant Jacob Dunbaugh so he could join the expedition, not knowing that Burr had urged the sergeant to incite other soldiers to desert their posts and join the expedition, and to steal weapons from the fort.[24]

On the morning of December 28, Burr called together the adventurers, plus the Blennerhassett family, on the chilly river shore.

The entire company, not quite one hundred men from ten boats, stood before him. They showed the effects of two weeks of river travel. His expectations had been so much higher. Many more had pledged to join the expedition. When a federal agent arrived in Pittsburgh in early December, he had been shocked by the "multitudes" who supported Burr. "Many of our young men have gone down the Ohio to join [Burr]," wrote a Pittsburgh Republican. A Spanish agent found one hundred men drilling in a plaza in Pittsburgh and planning to join Burr's conquest of Mexico; they said they expected another hundred and thirty men from farther east. Blennerhassett had hoped to enlist five hundred men from the Marietta area. More were expected from St. Louis, Tennessee, Indiana, and Kentucky.[25]

But a few adverse developments—Daveiss's prosecution, Graham's agitation, Eaton's statements—dissuaded many. Except for Blennerhassett and his family, no one came from Marietta. From Tennessee, also no one. Burr's recruiter on the Wabash had abandoned the cause altogether.[26]

For most of the adventurers on that freezing riverbank, this was their first opportunity to see the man whose fame had attracted them to the expedition. They drew themselves up as three sides of a square. Working around the formation, Tyler introduced Burr to each. The small, plainly dressed man shook hands, passing with each man a greeting, a look, a nod of acknowledgment. When he was done, the adventurers circled him, awaiting his words.

Here was the moment for a stirring speech, for unfurling the banner, pointing downriver and declaring their glorious purpose.

Burr, however, remained Delphic. Curious local residents hovered nearby, making him reticent. "He said he had something to communicate," one adventurer recalled, "which he would take another time for." Another remembered Burr saying that "he had intended to communicate his designs at that place, but that certain reasons prevented him." According to a third, Burr said that "it was not a proper time to divulge his secrets; there were too many bystanders." They would learn his designs, he assured them, from Tyler and Floyd. Without uttering a word that could be used against him in a court of law, Burr unmistakably implied that the settlement on the

This portrait of Burr, produced from a silhouette of him made in 1807, captures a determined set of his jaw.

Ouachita was a charade, that there was another purpose to their shared venture, as had been rumored for months. If peaceful settlement was their purpose, why not say so? Instead, he said nothing.

Though he remained largely mute, Burr managed to connect with the men, even to inspire confidence. His own resilience was clear. Regardless of the setbacks, Burr now was committed to the venture, whatever it was. It was a measure of Burr's charisma, and of the adventurers' wanderlust, that none of the men left or sought refuge at nearby Fort Massac. They cast their lot with this dignified, impressive man with an air of command and mystery.[27]

Two days later, they launched the boats again. Their pace picked up with the strong current of the Mississippi. Along this stretch, the shore was mostly empty. In the heart of winter, they met no other boats but floated steadily downriver. Burr still could hope for success. Wilkinson would meet them. Adair was traveling through Mississippi to their rendezvous. Bollman was in New Orleans with the Mexican Association.

On board, the adventurers enjoyed some elbow room. Each boat, fifty feet long and built for fifty men, carried only about ten. The men sometimes performed military drill on the roofs. Sometimes they smelted lead and ran musketballs. Most of the time, though, they tried to keep warm and watched for hazards. They did not travel at night for fear of eddies and "sawyers" (submerged trees or logs). It proved difficult to keep the flotilla together. Boats were trapped for hours in powerful eddies—one day all but one boat fell into one—but each time they escaped.

Their diet was dull, the salt pork and corn meal of a military campaign. The two boats that Burr had brought from Nashville held the expedition's scanty livestock: a cow and two saddle horses, which would ensure that the leader would be suitably mounted when they reached land.[28]

During a stop at New Madrid, Burr's men scoured the town for new volunteers. The expedition was seriously shorthanded. Burr left a recruiter there. The flotilla stopped again at the fort at Chickasaw Bluffs, the site of present-day Memphis.[29]

Talking with the fort's commander, Burr tried again to address his manpower shortage. He was more forthcoming with the commander than he had been with his own men. Spanish subjects were in a distressed condition, Burr said, and he proposed to "relieve them from the tyranny of their government." Though the American government did not want an open war, Burr continued, it secretly supported him. Burr offered a captain's commission if the commander would raise a company for the expedition. The officer, already thinking of resigning from the army, promptly agreed. Burr asked for some of the fort's weapons, but the commander declined. He did, however, allow Burr's men to smelt more lead into musketballs.

Burr sought help with two other matters. He wanted to send a letter to the federal agent with the Chickasaw tribe, asking him to recruit Indian fighters for the expedition. He also wrote to Senator John Smith, an early ally but one whose loyalties had become difficult to sort out. When the Ohio militia had been mustered to intercept Burr's men, Smith issued weapons to them. But then the senator followed Burr down the Ohio with boats full of supplies. Smith later claimed the supplies were intended for the U.S. army, but that claim did not explain why Smith chose to deliver them personally rather than attend the session of Congress then meeting in Washington City.[30]

Burr gave the commander at Chickasaw Bluffs enough money to cover his expenses, along with a draft on John Smith. When Burr returned to his boat, he announced that the commander and his eighteen soldiers would follow them downriver.

On Saturday, January 10, almost forty miles above Natchez, Burr's boat ran ahead of the others to land at Bayou Pierre, near the home of Judge Peter Bruin. Burr had visited Bruin, an old Continental Army comrade, on his first trip downriver. Neither Burr nor any of the adventurers was prepared for what he learned there.

18

Wilkinson Unchained

New Orleans
November 1806–January 1807

I
n late November, General Wilkinson quietly entered New Orleans. The
people there were on edge, anxious about reports of a western revolt,
a hostile force floating down the river toward them, and five hundred
Mississippi militiamen coming to defend them. Burr's expedition, according to one resident, was "almost the sole topic of conversation in the city." [1]

Preparing to oppose Burr, Wilkinson moved carefully at first. He knew
he had time to gain physical control of the city and to undermine Burr's
agents. But the general had another goal: not only to thwart Burr's expedition, but also to silence those who could reveal his own ties to Burr.

"I must hold out false colors," Wilkinson wrote to Jefferson before he
reached New Orleans, "conceal my designs, and cheat my adversaries into a
state of security, [so] when I do strike, it may be with more force and effect."
Wilkinson did not add, of course, that he also had held out false colors in
his reports to Jefferson. [2]

Soon enough, the city bristled with military activity. Wilkinson secured
the French artillery. When his soldiers arrived from the Sabine frontier,

eight hundred of them went to work on the city's defenses with the help of militiamen. Edward Livingston, Burr's friend, scorned the city's bulwarks as a "parade of rusty guns on rotten carriages, and of sentinels at hingeless gates." The defensive ditches, he scoffed, "were so narrow that an active stripling could leap the widest of them with ease." Because of the town's recent growth, most lines of fire from the city's fort threatened homes and businesses as much as they menaced attackers.[3]

General Wilkinson declared martial law in New Orleans in anticipation of Burr's arrival and also to silence those who knew of his connections to Burr.

After three days in New Orleans, Wilkinson sent an upbeat message to the president. "My difficulties are stupendous, my means to be provided, my time short, and the occasion urgent and critical," he wrote, "but a good cause, the favor of heaven, willing hands and patriotic hearts may work wonders."[4]

Only after gaining firm control of the army units, the militia, and the city's key points did Wilkinson confide in Governor Claiborne and the local navy commander. Showing them the cipher letter, he insisted on declaring martial law, but Claiborne was reluctant to approve that drastic step. Separately, Wilkinson sought out a federal Indian agent; he offered the man a $5,000 bounty (roughly $200,000 in today's value) for the capture of Burr.[5]

Wilkinson met several times with Burr's agents in New Orleans, Erich Bollman and James Alexander. Leading them to think he was still in league with Burr, the general milked them for specifics about their plans. Bollman disclosed that Burr and two thousand followers should reach Natchez on December 20. Four thousand more would follow. With that news, the general dropped his facade. He would oppose Burr, he told Bollman, in any way he could.[6]

After two weeks in New Orleans, Wilkinson took the offensive. He warned the Spanish commander at Baton Rouge of Burr's designs on West Florida, and he sent an alert to the British admiral in Jamaica about Burr's expedition. "I am at a loss how to answer," the admiral replied, unsure why the affair should concern him. Wilkinson sent a navy officer to Fort Adams, below Natchez, to arrest Sam Swartwout and Peter Ogden, providing an affidavit supporting the arrests. In the affidavit, which also went to the president, Wilkinson finally disclosed an altered version of the cipher letter, nearly two months after he had received it.[7]

For Wilkinson, the cipher letter posed tricky issues. Passages in it reflected his ongoing correspondence with Burr, as well as his engagement in Burr's plans. Releasing a true version of the letter would be risky. Wilkinson sought advice from a lawyer. Would it be appropriate, Wilkinson asked, to alter the document to ensure an effective government response to the current crisis? The lawyer gave the answer his client wanted to hear.

So Wilkinson improved the cipher letter. The opening sentence referred to Wilkinson's earlier letter to Burr. That could be incriminating. Wilkinson erased it. Throughout the letter he wiped out the first-person plural, which implied a joint enterprise between him and Burr. Twice Wilkinson removed "us." He substituted "views" for "our view." He twice replaced "Wilkinson" with "you" and deleted a reference to Burr's grandson. Particularly disturbing for Wilkinson was the statement "Our project my dear friend is brought to the point so long desired." Out went "our" and "my dear friend," leaving the disembodied "The project is brought to the point so long desired."[8]

Thus improved, the cipher letter was fit for a wider audience, though it did not reach the president in Washington City until the third week of January. On December 9, Wilkinson brandished it before the New Orleans chamber of commerce. Thousands of armed men were coming to attack the city, he warned, while a British fleet might arrive any day and pounce on the American navy's six small vessels.

Frustrated that Claiborne still would not agree to the imposition of martial law, the general demanded that the city's merchants halt all waterborne trade. This device, by denying work to the city's sailors, would make them more willing to serve on navy ships. That would spare the navy from the need to resort to impressments—the British practice, detested by Americans, of forcing seamen into service. Cowed by the imperious general and the stress of the moment, the merchants agreed, raising money to provide the seamen with clothing and equipment. Within days, however, local residents were questioning how the general's embargo would defend against Burr's hordes. Wilkinson, however, was just getting started.[9]

On a quiet Sunday, December 14, the general struck. He dispatched soldiers to arrest Erich Bollman, detaining him with Sam Swartwout and Peter Ogden, who had arrived from Fort Adams under military guard. Local judges—including James Workman, a stalwart in the Mexican Association—issued writs of habeas corpus to review the arrests. Dating from Magna Carta in 1215, the writ of habeas corpus is a critical check on the arbitrary power of executive officials, promising that a neutral judge will review an arrest to ensure it is based on sufficient evidence. Wilkinson brushed the writs aside. He bundled Bollman and Swartwout onto a navy ship in the harbor, beyond the reach of the courts. Ogden's lawyer, another pillar of the Mexican Association, sprang his client from jail only to see Wilkinson rearrest the young man.

At high noon on December 18, the general stalked into the territorial courtroom to have it out over those annoying writs of habeas corpus. As described by Edward Livingston, who was acting as Bollman's lawyer, the general arrived with several aides, "all dressed as on a field day; with their side arms, a la mode de Paris, in metal scabbards rattling along the floor, and all the other usual insignia of military pomp. Even the spurs were not forgotten." After delivering a speech about the dangers facing the nation, Wilkinson proclaimed that Bollman was guilty, as were his lawyers. The judges ruled that the evidence did not support Bollman's arrest. The general replied that he would make the arrests on his own responsibility.[10]

Sam Swartwout did not submit meekly. When guards tried to move him to a new location, farther from the prying eyes of lawyers and judges, Swartwout demanded a sword so he could die like a man. Denied a weapon, Swartwout leapt over a railing to make his escape. The arresting officer drew six guards into a firing line and ordered them to shoot. Luckily for Swartwout, dampness caused all six muskets to misfire. The guards ran him down anyway. Soon Swartwout and Bollman were on a ship sailing to Washington City, where they would face treason charges.[11]

The general lashed out at the judicial system, arresting two lawyers, James Alexander and Lewis Kerr, who were representing Burr's friends. Then he arrested Judge Workman.[12] Workman demanded that Governor Claiborne defend the liberties of American citizens, but the governor was no match for the burly general. Wilkinson insisted on his authority to arrest men who are "the known agents, emissaries, or supporters of the dark and destructive combinations" directed by Burr.[13]

Wilkinson targeted the press as well, several times arresting the editor of the *Orleans Gazette*. The arrests muzzled the *Gazette* and other printers in the city, who prudently chose not to report the general's actions.[14]

Gay New Orleans took on the sullen and mistrustful air of an occupied city. The general foraged through the public mails, reading anything that caught his eye. He sent secret investigators to sniff out Burr sympathizers. Citizens doubted each other. Tale-bearing became endemic. "No man in New Orleans felt himself safe," Livingston wrote, "and, in truth, few escaped suspicion." The lawyer continued:

> Even loose, unguarded expressions . . . were instantly carried to headquarters, and there officiously dressed up in the solemn garb of sedition. Neighbors avoided each other reciprocally as spies and traitors, neither could tell why. Private friendship was everywhere poisoned.[15]

When the New Orleans council convened on January 7, it approved Wilkinson's arrests, but nine days later the territorial assembly debated a

statement deploring the general's conduct. A local grand jury denounced
the general's actions, dismissing the "mere specious reasons [that] are urged
in justification of those arrests." [16]

On January 14 General John Adair, the Kentucky militia leader, arrived in Wilkinson's police state, having travelled for a month through the
backwoods of Mississippi Territory. He went directly to Madame Fourage's
boardinghouse. Judge Prevost, Burr's stepson, assured Adair that Burr
would arrive within three days and release the city from Wilkinson's tyranny. By another account, Prevost acclaimed Adair as Burr's second in command. While Adair dined at Madame Fourage's, more than one hundred
soldiers arrived to arrest him. Wilkinson held the former senator in a swamp
near New Orleans for several bitterly cold nights, then sent him to Baltimore
by ship. [17]

General John Adair of the Kentucky militia was arrested as soon as he arrived in New
Orleans in early January.

Wilkinson exulted over Adair's arrest. "If Adair had been permitted
the liberty of the city for twenty-four hours," he wrote to Jefferson, "his
art, address and daring spirit, supported by 500 boatmen and the mass

of disaffection which infests this city, would infallibly have produced an insurrection." Over the preceding month, the general had jailed more than twenty men without any legal process and shipped five of them (Bollman, Swartwout, Adair, Peter Ogden, and James Alexander) to the Atlantic coast.

The president applauded Wilkinson's repressive methods. Approving the arrests of Bollman and Swartwout, Jefferson wrote in early February that the general was "on ground extremely favorable with the public" and concluded with his own pledge of support. No matter how unappealing were General Wilkinson's character and actions, no matter how long Jefferson had drowsed through reports of Burr's plans for secession and foreign invasion, the president backed his traitor general against Burr, the dangerous apostate. The general, his self-regard dangerously inflated, did not reciprocate the president's warm feelings. In a letter in early December, he disparaged Governor Claiborne as a fool and Jefferson as "his contemptible fabricator."[18]

By mid-January, though, Wilkinson learned that Burr had stopped above Natchez, at Judge Bruin's home near Bayou Pierre. The showdown would come in Mississippi, not New Orleans.

19

Burr in Chains

Mississippi Territory to Richmond
January–March 1807

Burr arrived at Judge Bruin's settlement on a Saturday night, January 10, during the coldest winter anyone in Mississippi Territory could remember. One resident said the freeze was so piercing that blood oozed from his fingertips as he pulled on the oars of a skiff. The harsh weather proved an ill omen for Burr.[1]

At Bruin's home, Burr asked to see newspapers, eager for word of a Spanish war or that Wilkinson and Adair were awaiting him in New Orleans. Instead, he read Jefferson's declaration of November 25, warning of a western conspiracy. He also read Wilkinson's version of the cipher letter and a statement by the acting governor of Mississippi Territory, Cowles Mead, that residents should seize all conspirators.

Standing in Bruin's riverside home, Burr knew the game was up, his hopes destroyed. There was no war with Spain. Wilkinson had abandoned him. The government was opposing him. And he had only about one hundred men in his expedition. The Floridas, Mexico, New Orleans—all were receding from his grasp. But there was more than bitter disappointment and rage; now there was the risk of arrest or even attack by other Americans.

Burr was still in a fury when he returned to his boat the next morning. He told his sergeant to carry a rifle and to keep a bayonet under his coat. Wilkinson, he sputtered, had betrayed him and was "the greatest traitor on the face of the earth."[2]

When the other boats arrived at Bayou Pierre, Burr passed the word that the expedition would be opposed. He had the adventurers polled: Should they abandon the journey? Lacking good alternatives—they had been chased out of Ohio and Virginia, and Burr had faced jail in Kentucky—the men voted to press on. Burr sent a boat ahead to Natchez to gauge the situation. That night, with Mississippi militia gathering in the forest near his camp, Burr moved the boats to the west side of the river, in Orleans Territory. They cleared the ground for military drill and waited for the next move by the powers of Mississippi Territory.[3]

By the morning of Tuesday the thirteenth, the militia numbered almost three hundred at the mouth of Cole's Creek on the Mississippi side. Militia officers crossed over several times to talk with Burr. Most were disarmed by the dignified welcome they met and the small size of Burr's group. With so few men, with Wilkinson and the army against him in New Orleans, and with the navy's gunboats now at Natchez, Burr could not fight. He had nowhere to run. He would have to talk his way out. To soften up the territorial authorities, Burr sent provisions to feed the militia. After several days, he agreed to meet with Acting Governor Mead of Mississippi.[4]

Burr blamed Wilkinson for everything. He told the militia officers that the general was a perfidious villain. In a note to Mead, Burr protested his innocence, attributing the accusations against him to "the vile fabrications of a man notoriously the pensioner of a foreign government." Burr's tactic was well chosen: A month before, Mead had warned Claiborne in New Orleans to "be on your guard against the wily general—he is not much better than Catiline—consider him a traitor and act as if certain thereof." Mead instructed a militia officer to assure Burr that he would be protected from injury by "rumor or the Pensioned [Wilkinson]."[5]

While negotiating, Burr clung to the forlorn hope that the expedition might resume. That was the message conveyed by the small group of adventurers he sent ahead to Natchez. They explained to local residents, including the Kemper brothers, that after General Adair and additional men arrived from Kentucky and Tennessee, Burr would take Baton Rouge and prepare for the invasion of Mexico.[6]

Four inches of snow fell on January 17, a week after Burr's arrival. Both militia and adventurers were miserable, weary of shivering on opposite sides of the river. Burr crossed to the Mississippi side to meet with Mead. He was adamant that he would surrender only to civilian authorities, not the military. On the following day he rode to the town of Washington, the territorial capital, six miles inland from Natchez, where he was placed under house arrest. Four days later, two friends posted a $5,000 recognizance bond to secure his release for two weeks, when the territorial court could take up his case.[7]

Burr allowed two searches of his boats for military equipment, but only after his men had hustled off all muskets and bayonets. The searchers found only a few squirrel rifles. A few weeks later, one of the adventurers offered to sell fifty muskets at one-third their price. This black marketeer scorned the idea that Burr ever intended to settle the Ouachita lands. The adventurers, he pointed out, were "too well fixed at home to embark on so dull an enterprise."[8]

Waiting for his day in court, Burr stayed at Windy Hill Manor, the home of Benijah Osmun, a Continental Army veteran who had posted part of the recognizance bond. The former vice president again mixed comfortably with local society. After the alarms that thousands were bringing revolution and mayhem to the frontier, Burr's company—estimated at between 60 and 130 men—seemed inoffensive. Burr renewed warm relationships formed during his earlier stays in Natchez and attended several balls in his honor. The local newspaper defended him, pointing out that Wilkinson reigned despotically in New Orleans while Burr is "always submissive to law, and friendly to our territories." When Governor Robert Williams returned to the territory and resumed his duties in late January, he also seemed friendly to Burr and skeptical of Wilkinson.[9]

While facing investigation in Mississippi, Burr stayed at Windy Hill Manor and supposedly courted a winsome neighbor, Madeline Price.

By the legend of the region, Burr's romantic nature revived in the wintry air. The story holds that when he left Windy Hill Manor for the nearby home of Major Isaac Guion, the path took him past a cottage where a widow dwelled with her winsome daughter, Madeline Price. As one chronicler puts it, Burr exercised on Madeline "his witchery night after night, and [she] loved him with all the fervor of a Southern nature."[10]

The adventurers, however, were freezing on the riverbank. Idleness and liquor eroded their discipline, while arguments flared between militia officers and Burr's lieutenants. After two weeks, some adventurers threatened to leave. Others proposed to seize the expedition's provisions as their payment. Burr returned to the camp to try to maintain order, but he left on January 28 to prepare for his court hearing.[11]

Though he faced a new criminal inquiry, Burr spoke recklessly with several men from the Tombigbee area, upriver from Mobile. The men were complaining that the territorial government ignored the needs of their remote region, adding that their neighbors would support an attack on the Spaniards of West Florida. Burr replied that they had "a natural right . . . either to erect a new government for themselves, or to take protection under such other government as would promise them a happier situation."

Inflammatory words from a man accused of fomenting secession and insurrection.[12]

Burr also talked with John Graham, Jefferson's bloodhound, explaining that he expected the West to separate from the nation due to "moral, not physical causes"—that is, the West would *choose* to secede, without any action by Burr. As for an invasion of Mexico, Burr said that would occur only if the United States were at war with Spain, or if Burr's Ouachita lands had an "independent government." When Graham urged him to make a public declaration of his intentions, Burr demurred, objecting that "he was a party concerned, and that no statement of his could have any effect."[13]

From New Orleans, Wilkinson anxiously watched events in Mississippi. "A moment of awful suspense has arrived," he wrote. He feared that Burr would "baffle inquiry as he did in Kentucky."[14]

In territorial court, Burr's case would be heard by two judges: his old friend Peter Bruin and Thomas Rodney from Delaware. Both men embodied the truism that frontier justice could be rough. Bruin was an alcoholic who often failed to take the bench; when he did manage to show up for court, he sometimes napped during the proceedings. Bruin approached the hearing as Burr's friend, not an impartial arbiter. One observer reported that Bruin "both before, and on the day of Burr's trial, advocated [Burr's] cause."[15]

Thomas Rodney was an underachieving member of a distinguished family: His brother Caesar had signed the Declaration of Independence and his son (also named Caesar) was Jefferson's attorney general. Judge Rodney took credit for one of the turning points of the American Revolution. He claimed that on Christmas Eve, 1776, an archangel inspired him to goad George Washington into leading his troops across the Delaware River to attack Trenton. During a lengthy period of unemployment after the war, Rodney wrote an epic poem commemorating the angelic intercession.[16]

Like Bruin, Rodney had prejudged the case, though from the opposite side. As early as October 1806, Rodney was investigating rumors of a western conspiracy. Ten weeks before he presided over Burr's case, Rodney wrote President Jefferson that "Burr, Wilkinson, and others [plan] to set up an empire in the Southwest in conjunction with Spain and England."[17]

When court convened in early February, most activity in the area ground to a halt. The proceedings proved to be as singular as the judges presiding over them. Judge Rodney read the charge that Burr intended to lead the West into secession and to invade Mexico, but the federal attorney refused to prosecute the case, denying that the court had jurisdiction over Burr. Depositions of adventurers and others, he said, produced no evidence of a crime committed in Mississippi. In truth, Burr had done little in Mississippi except arrive and be arrested. The prosecutor suggested sending Burr to Washington City, where the United States Supreme Court could decide what to do with him.

Judge Rodney insisted that a grand jury review the evidence, much of which he had gathered. For a day, a grand jury heard testimony from Graham and two others. Its report, delivered on February 4, not only declined to charge Burr but also complained about the militia expedition that arrested him, as well as General Wilkinson's high-handed arrests in New Orleans. Burr demanded his immediate release. Judge Bruin supported his demand, but Rodney insisted that Burr's recognizance bond continue in effect.[18]

Vindicated but not free to leave Mississippi, Burr had seen enough of Judge Rodney. That night, he returned to the adventurers' camp on the far side of the river. His men gathered round him at the crest of a slope. The air was icy, the mercury down to 11 degrees. Though he had been acquitted, Burr told the adventurers, he expected the prosecution to be renewed. So long as he remained with the expedition, he would be a thorn in its side. So he would leave. The men could divide his property among them. He encouraged them to settle the Ouachita lands. Then he took refuge with Judge Bruin's son-in-law, a fact the judge kept secret through the next week.

The court, after standing in recess for two days while Judge Rodney presided over and celebrated a wedding, reconvened on February 7. The day was so frigid that the judges and lawyers huddled in a patch of sunlight at the far end of the courtroom. Burr did not appear. Judge Rodney declared him in violation of his recognizance bond and authorized his immediate arrest. Governor Williams offered a $2,000 reward for his capture.[19]

When Burr bade farewell to the adventurers, he did not disclose all of his reasons for flight. Most urgently, he feared that General Wilkinson's agents would kidnap or kill him. His fear was well founded.

In December, Wilkinson had offered a $5,000 reward for Burr's capture. In late January, impatience overtook the general. He gathered five worthies, including four army officers, and ordered them to travel to Mississippi Territory and seize Burr. They should disguise themselves in civilian clothes, he instructed, to deceive Burr's friends. Armed with pistols and daggers, Wilkinson's agents left for the town of Washington. Rumors of a plot to kidnap Burr swept through Mississippi.[20]

Burr had another reason to run. He was working on a new plan, one that did not rely on Wilkinson or Adair. The remote Tombigbee region had begun to fire Burr's imagination, his most capacious and unreliable gift. Perhaps he could retrieve his situation by mounting an expedition from there to liberate West Florida. In the backwoods of Mississippi Territory, he might find the ardent spirits who would undertake the desperate stroke.

From his hiding place, Burr sent letters to Governor Williams demanding that he not be sent from the territory. He had "retired from public view," he explained, because of the "vindictive temper and unprincipled conduct of Judge Rodney." Williams declined to negotiate. By then, a slave owned by Burr's host had been found wearing clothes thought to be Burr's, with a startling message thought to be in Burr's handwriting. The note, addressed to "C.T." [Comfort Tyler] and "D.F." [Davis Floyd], stated: "If you are yet together keep together and I will join you tomorrow night. In the meantime, put all your arms in perfect order."

That night, Governor Williams arrested dozens of adventurers. All but three were released a day later, but the arrests prevented any rendezvous between Burr and his men, who ended up selling off their boats and provisions and dividing the money among them.[21]

For close to two weeks after Burr's disappearance, the authorities could not locate him, and his hiding places have never been discovered. Both Burr and the people of Mississippi kept that secret. Governor Claiborne speculated that Burr was headed for Europe or Washington City, or was waiting in Natchez for more adventurers to arrive, or was with the Spaniards in Baton Rouge. Wilkinson understood Burr better. "It is probable," he wrote to Jefferson, "he will make some desperate attempt against the Spaniards" in order to "gild his crimes by some extraordinary stroke of fortune."[22]

Mississippi legend insists that Burr begged Madeline Price, the local beauty, to accompany him in his flight. Though hopelessly in love, Madeline would not compromise her virtue. After exchanging pledges of marriage, Burr supposedly rode into the night on a fine horse. For several years, the story concludes, Madeline spurned suitors and awaited Burr's return, until he released her from her pledge.[23]

The next sighting of Burr came on a lonely road two hundred miles east of Natchez, at midnight on Wednesday, February 18. On horseback, he and a companion passed through the village of Wakefield, above Mobile. His companion stopped at the local courthouse to ask directions to a homestead some miles away. The county land register, Nicholas Perkins, warned that the bridges were broken on the way and recommended spending the night at the local tavern. The two travelers rode on. Suspicious of anyone who ignored good advice at that late hour, Perkins thought one of the men might be Colonel Burr, since the news of Burr's vanishing had penetrated even to Wakefield. Perkins woke up the county sheriff to join him in pursuit of the travelers.

In the small hours of the morning, they found their quarry at the homestead the riders had been seeking. Perkins maneuvered in the weak light to get a good look at the mysterious stranger. Dressed like a frontiersman, the small, unshaven man wore a broad-brimmed white hat, a checked handkerchief around his neck. A tin cup hung off his belted coat, as did a butcher knife. Though Perkins had never seen Burr, he knew that the man's eyes were supposed to be "remarkably keen." That was enough. "I got a glance at his eye, as he looked aside at me," Perkins recalled, "upon which I became confident this was Colonel Burr." Perkins immediately set off to alert soldiers at nearby Fort Stoddert that they should arrest the renegade Burr.

Though Perkins departed without speaking to Burr, the former vice president knew he had been recognized. He befriended the local sheriff, who stayed behind, and the two men set off to the east in the morning. Burr's traveling companion from the night before left to confer with two militia leaders about Burr's new scheme.

Perkins soon rode up with Lieutenant Edmund Gaines from Fort Stoddert, who placed Burr under arrest. Burr did not resist.[24]

Confined at Fort Stoddert, Burr passed the hours playing chess with Mrs. Gaines while his captors dithered over their next move. There could be no trial in that wilderness, but Lieutenant Gaines could spare few men to escort Burr somewhere else. When a Spanish officer from Mobile arrived to see Burr, Gaines decided he had to get his prisoner away from that volatile borderland. He prevailed upon Nicholas Perkins to deliver Burr to Washington City, promising the $2,000 reward to Perkins and the rest of the eight-man escort.[25]

Burr and his guards left Lake Tensaw on March 5 for the long forest trek to the northeast. The little party had to cross streams and rivers swollen with spring rains, using canoes while their horses swam alongside. Burr slept in the only tent. So long as they stayed in wilderness, Perkins let Burr keep his pistols and knife, but he hobbled and belled the horses at night. After covering three hundred miles to Milledgeville, Georgia, they stopped at the unhappily named Fort Wilkinson for their first night with a roof over their heads.

Entering more settled areas where Burr might find sympathizers, Perkins had the prisoner ride in the center of the escort. Perkins grew more anxious in South Carolina, home to Burr's son-in-law, Joseph Alston. Sure enough, Burr made his move there.

As the party rode through Chester, near the North Carolina border, Burr leapt down from his horse. Running to a group on the street, he cried out, "Is there a magistrate here?" He begged for protection from the escort. They were transporting him illegally, he insisted. Before the men of Chester could respond, Burr's guards grabbed him, sat him forcibly on his horse, and left town at a brisk clip.[26]

Perkins adjusted his procedures again, acquiring a carriage to transport his prisoner. Later, Perkins moved Burr by stagecoach. It was an extraordinary and public humiliation for the former vice president, riding past homes and towns filled with people who knew his name, who gawked at the great man brought low, still wearing the white floppy hat and homespun clothes in which he had been arrested.[27] His failure was there for every citizen to see.

"Burr's enterprise," Jefferson wrote with wonder, "is the most extravagant since the days of Don Quixote." From retirement in Quincy, Massachusetts, former president John Adams compared Burr's expedition to "a kind of waterspout, a terrible whirlpool, threatening to engulf everything."[28]

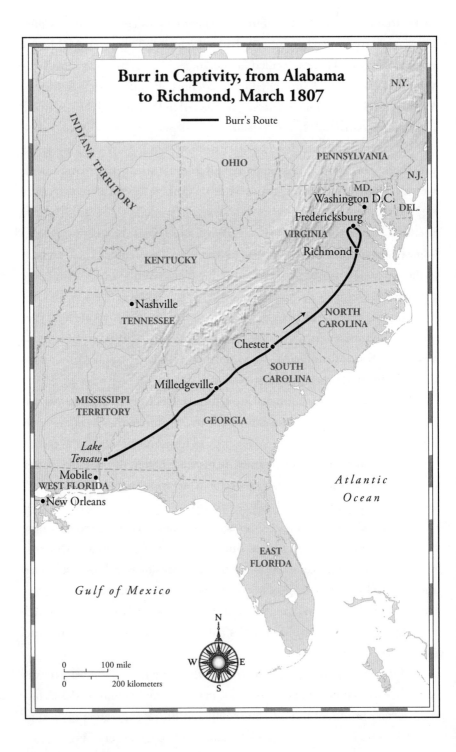

Burr in Captivity, from Alabama
to Richmond, March 1807

——— Burr's Route

A messenger met the Burr party in Fredericksburg, Virginia, some fifty miles from Washington City. They should turn around, the message said, and return to Richmond, Virginia's capital, sixty miles to their rear. They reached Richmond on March 25, the guards on horseback and Burr in a stagecoach. They had covered more than a thousand miles in three weeks.[29]

The escort delivered the prisoner to the Eagle Tavern. Burr, who had not changed his clothes since his arrest, immediately wrote his daughter: "It seems that here the business is to be tried and concluded."[30] Days later, writing to his good friend Charles Biddle, Burr let a sliver of his anger spill on to the page. "It is not easy for one who has been robbed and plundered till he had not a second shirt," he wrote, "to contend with a Gov[ernmen]t having millions at command and active and vindictive agents in every quarter."[31]

All that was left to Burr was to save himself. The government had not dragged him a thousand miles to set him free. He would be prosecuted, presumably for treason. Treason was a capital crime, punished by hanging. His judge would be Chief Justice John Marshall, which seemed cold comfort. Though Marshall was no friend of the president's, his cousin Humphrey Marshall had bankrolled the *Western World,* while his brother-in-law, Joseph Hamilton Daveiss, twice tried to prosecute Burr in Kentucky. Burr's prospects looked grim.

He needed skilled lawyers and a sound strategy. Burr immediately began to gather a formidable legal team, but he intended to direct the effort himself. Whatever his failures as a revolutionary, Aaron Burr's future would depend upon his own ability as a lawyer.

PART II

"I am anxious to see the progress of Burr's trial, not from any love or hatred I bear to the man. . . . But I think something must come out on the trial, which will strengthen or weaken our confidence in the general union."

John Adams, September 1, 1807[1]

With Burr's arrest, the story of his expedition moved from frontiers and forests to the nation's center stage. The crisis on the Texas and Florida borders, which loomed so large through 1806, subsided. Wilkinson's improvised "Neutral Ground" agreement with the Spaniards was holding, and Burr's expedition had collapsed. Most of the adventurers looked for opportunity in Mississippi and Orleans Territories while parrying questions from federal agents.

Under the bright light of public scrutiny, the contest now would be over the consequences of Burr's expedition and how it would be labeled for history. Jefferson and Wilkinson wanted to paint Burr's intentions in lurid and extravagant terms, but Burr would soon be able to explain himself and his remarkable activities. There were many questions for him, but also for the other principal players. When and how did the president learn of this danger to the republic? Why had Jefferson been so slow in responding to it? General Wilkinson's ambiguous role would attract greater attention. Why had he rushed to occupy New Orleans when most military men thought the best place to intercept Burr was near Natchez and Fort Adams in Mississippi? Indeed, that was where Burr's expedition came to grief, with the general and his army almost two hundred miles away. Why had Wilkinson imposed such repressive measures in New Orleans when Burr's expedition never drew anywhere near the city? What was the connection between Wilkinson and Burr, who had long been known to be friends and allies? And what of Wilkinson's connection to Spain?

The largest questions, though, revolved around Burr's trial. What should be done with a man who had earned the highest honors from the nation but then apparently turned on it, scheming to lead a private invasion of foreign lands and to fracture the union? What was the proper punishment for such open defiance of the government Burr had served for so many years? Could the judicial system provide a fair resolution of the fundamentally political crisis presented by insurrection and the mounting of private invasions?

As a search for truth, the trial in Richmond would prove frustrating. Burr and his lawyers ran rings around the government prosecutors, concealing more evidence than was revealed. Indeed, at times Chief Justice Marshall seemed to be Burr's willing tool, positively abetting that concealment. But Marshall was concerned with questions beyond the fate of the slender, well-spoken politician before him. He was considering the balance of powers among the president and the courts, as well as what liberties the Constitution truly guaranteed, even in times when the nation's security might be at risk. Those questions would place Marshall squarely athwart the wishes of the president, his distant cousin.

Jefferson was now convinced that Burr had threatened the nation's existence, seeking to wage war on its neighbors and to dissolve the union. But the issue between Burr and Jefferson also was personal. Burr's actions expressed a profound contempt for the president and his place in history. Had Burr succeeded in invading Mexico, or in fomenting insurrection in New Orleans or the West, he would have indelibly branded Jefferson as a leader who failed to control his own nation, or even as one who presided over its demise. Less than a year before, Burr had warned Jefferson that he could do him harm; it seemed that Burr had done his level best to make good on that threat. For the president, this was no time for legal niceties: Burr should be convicted of treason and punished harshly. In Jefferson's

view, no other outcome would vindicate the government's interest in preserving itself.

Marshall agreed that the case raised core questions about the nature
of the American republic, but different ones. The Constitution and Bill of
Rights guaranteed certain liberties, but those were simply words on paper.
In times of emergency, when the nation's survival seemed to be at stake, it
was easy for presidents and generals to wave mere words aside, to disparage
the rights of those who endangered the public peace. If those rights were
to have substance in notorious cases like Burr's, the courts had to protect
them. Many years later, another Supreme Court justice, Felix Frankfurter,
would write: "It is a fair summary of history to say that the safeguards of
liberty have been forged in controversies involving not very nice people." At
the beginning of the nation's history, Marshall understood that proposition,
and that the rights provided in the Constitution meant nothing if they were
not available to someone as reviled as Aaron Burr was in 1807.

20

When Cousins Collide

Washington City
January–February 1807

E ven Jefferson's friends decried his slow reaction to Burr's expedition. In early January, a Republican senator complained that a proclamation had been the president's only response to the threat from Burr. Noting the irony of depending on General Wilkinson, "a man whose honor and fidelity [are] doubted by all except a very, very few," the senator concluded that if Wilkinson had not exposed Burr, "the President would have folded his arms and let the storm collect its whole strength."[1]

Jefferson's caution grew from several sources. The evidence from the West had trickled in over many months, which may have obscured the risk that Burr posed. After receiving Wilkinson's first report about the threat, which included a few facts and was riddled with falsehoods, Jefferson's limited response might be attributed to the general's irredeemably poor reputation. As late as November 27, the Secretary of War was warning his top general that "your name has been very frequently mentioned with Burr, Dayton and others." Jefferson could not help doubting Wilkinson's loyalty and truthfulness; everyone else did.

Jefferson abandoned that cautious approach when Wilkinson's second messenger arrived at the executive mansion on New Year's Day, 1807. The president's first question to the messenger was, "Is Wilkinson sound in this business?" The messenger's enthusiastic response—"There is not the smallest doubt of it"—greatly eased Jefferson's mind. From that point forward, the president backed his general to the hilt.[2]

Jefferson's slow response also was based on political principle. When westerners fought federal taxes in the Whiskey Rebellion of 1794, President Washington responded with massive force, marching more than ten thousand militia through Pennsylvania to overawe the rebels. Jefferson, in contrast, mistrusted the military and disliked conflict. He sought a different path. Though he had last-ditch plans for aggressive military action, he hoped that Burr's effort would fizzle from lack of support. Thus he wrote to Wilkinson that the western country should deal with Burr in the first instance, and "my confidence in them is entire." That was the proper republican response to the expedition, which should be withered by the disdain of the people, not smashed by the iron fist of government. Jefferson made this point in a triumphant letter to Ohio's governor: "The hand of the people has given the mortal blow to a conspiracy which, in other countries would have called for an appeal to armies, and has proved that government to be the strongest of which every man feels a part."[3]

Many in Congress had neither the president's patience nor his access to information. They clamored to know exactly what was happening and what Jefferson proposed to do about it. They found their voice in the talented and erratic John Randolph of Virginia.

Only thirty-four years old in 1807, Randolph was the leading member of Congress. He already had served as chair of the Ways and Means Committee and as Jefferson's floor leader in the House. Though a Republican and another of Jefferson's distant cousins, Randolph had become a critic of the administration. His prominence was all the more remarkable because his physical qualities were so strange. Whippet thin, with the high voice of a *castrati*, the congressman from Roanoke named his plantation "Bizarre," which captured how most people found him.

"He is rather taller than middle size," wrote one observer, "extremely slender, he never had a razor on his face and has no more appearance of a beard than a boy of 10 years old, and his voice is the same." Yet Randolph excelled in debate, "his voice squeaking, but clear and distinct." His instinct for the jugular was unerring, as one contemporary wrote:

> He used his tongue as a jockey would his whip; he hit the sore place till the blood came, and there was no crack, or flourish, or noise, or bluster in doing it. It was done with a celerity and dexterity which showed the practiced hand, and its unexpectedness as well as its severity often dumbfounded the victim so completely that he had not one word to say, but writhed in silence.[4]

On January 16, Randolph squeaked that Jefferson's failure to take "a manly and decisive attitude towards Spain" had encouraged Burr's venture "at the head of an unprincipled banditti." Randolph presented a resolution demanding that the president disclose all information about any conspiracy against the union or to invade a foreign nation. The House overwhelmingly approved it.[5]

Jefferson responded on January 22 with a special message in which he confessed that his information included "a mixture of rumors, conjectures, and suspicions." With such uncertain evidence in hand, Jefferson declined to name the participants in the conspiracy, "except that of the principal actor, *whose guilt is placed beyond question.*" With that single phrase, Jefferson accused, tried, and convicted Aaron Burr. It would prove a rash claim. John Adams disapproved. Even if Burr's "guilt is as clear as the noonday sun," he wrote to a friend, "the first magistrate ought not to have pronounced it so before a jury had tried him."[6]

The president falsely claimed his first news of Burr's expedition came in late October; in truth, the first accusations had arrived ten months earlier and had trickled in steadily thereafter. Jefferson attributed two purposes to Burr: "the severance of the union of these states by the Allegheny Mountains; the other, an attack on Mexico." Jefferson dismissed the Bastrop settlement as a "merely ostensible" scheme, a cover. He drew a dark portrait of Burr, accusing him of intending to "seize on New Orleans [and] plunder the bank there," with the aid of "all the ardent, restless, desperate, and disaffected persons who were ready for any enterprise analogous to their characters."

Jefferson described Wilkinson as having "the honor of a soldier and the fidelity of a good citizen," and he defended the general's military reign in New Orleans. No other course, the president said, was feasible in that tumultuous city.

Above all, Jefferson praised the westerners who shunned Burr's expedition. He applauded the people of the frontier for their "unequivocal fidelity to the Union," adding that Burr "found at once that the attachment of the western country to the present Union was not to be shaken; that its dissolution could not be effected." The president also released Wilkinson's improved version of the cipher letter.[7]

On the day Jefferson issued his special message, Erich Bollman and Sam Swartwout reached Washington City as prisoners. Wary of Bollman's known predilection for jailbreaks—his long-ago attempts to free the Marquis de Lafayette from an Austrian prison were legendary—the government locked them up at the marine barracks.[8]

Months before, Burr had awarded a difficult assignment to the cosmopolitan Bollman. Once Burr and his adventurers sailed from New Orleans to liberate Mexico, Bollman was supposed to explain the expedition to Jefferson. Though Burr would not be sailing to Mexico any time soon, Bollman resolved to present Burr's case to the president anyway. He asked for an audience with Jefferson, whom he had met before. Indeed, the president had purchased wines from Bollman's importing business and had offered him several government appointments, including the consulate in Rotterdam and the Indian agency in Natchitoches. Bollman had preferred to enlist in Burr's expedition. Jefferson jumped at the opportunity to hear from one of Burr's closest aides.[9]

It was a measure of the small size of the American government, and Jefferson's self-confidence, that the president met informally with a man accused of fomenting secession and revolution. Bollman likely is the only visitor to the executive mansion to arrive directly from jail while under a charge of treason. The president asked James Madison, his Secretary of State, to sit in on the interview and take notes.

The soft-spoken Jefferson began by assuring Bollman that nothing he said would be used against him in court. With that promise, the president began to taint the value of Bollman as a witness in any prosecution, but

Jefferson was not thinking about a court case. He wanted to hear Bollman's story.

When Erich Bollman, facing treason charges, asked to meet the president to explain Burr's plans, he was taken from jail to the Executive Mansion, not yet called the White House.

Bollman spoke expansively. He insisted that Burr's principal purpose was to invade Mexico, a course that would be "happy for Spanish America and beneficial to the United States." Without such an invasion, Bollman continued, Spain's weakness would allow France, "the scourge of Europe," to take over Spain's American colonies. By keeping the wealth of Spanish America away from the French, Burr would protect the United States from hostile French aims. In a phrase that better reflected Burr's motivation, Bollman added that the venture also "promis[ed] a glorious place in the history of events."

Bollman repeated what he had told Wilkinson in New Orleans: that Burr had intended to lead two thousand men to Natchez by December 20, with four thousand more close behind. As Bollman gabbled on, the German expatriate betrayed little sense that the American president might find his tale disturbing.

Burr's forces were to move to New Orleans, Bollman explained, avoiding violence if possible, and grab the French artillery there. Then they would seize ships for the voyage to Vera Cruz and the invasion of Mexico. In a July letter, according to Bollman, General Wilkinson pledged to resign his army commission and, with other soldiers, join the "corps of Burr."

The questions erupted from Jefferson. Did they not expect the American army to be an obstacle? What foreign aid had Burr received? Were the Spanish involved? The British? What government was Mexico to have? Did Burr propose to unite Mexico and Louisiana? Did Burr think the American government would not oppose this astounding enterprise?

According to Bollman, Burr deceived the Spaniards by claiming he would lead a western secession. The prisoner portrayed the Marquis de Casa Yrujo, the Spanish minister, as a dunce. He said the British minister, Anthony Merry, supported Burr's plan in spirit, though not with money. Bollman insisted that Burr intended for Mexico to become an independent monarchy, as its people were not "fit for republican government." Bollman did not say who was to be the monarch, but the point hardly needed to be made.

Bollman stressed Burr's total lack of concern that the American government might obstruct his plans. The American army was small and scattered. Burr's measures, according to Bollman, would be "executed with such rapidity that the enterprise would be beyond the reach of the government." When he had heard enough, the president returned Bollman to jail.[10]

Two days later, Jefferson asked Bollman for a written account of Burr's plan. The president gave Bollman his "word of honor" that the document would not be used against him and that the paper would never leave Jefferson's possession.

Bollman replied with a lengthy essay, stressing again that the Mexican conquest would "provid[e] a glorious place in the history of magnificent events." According to Bollman, Burr intended for seven to ten thousand men to "take temporary possession" of New Orleans. One contingent would then attack Spanish territory by land and two others would attack by sea, through Vera Cruz. Burr had expected to capture Mexico City by May 1807. In the summer of 1806, Burr had received a letter from Wilkinson that "perfectly satisfied [Burr's] mind with regard to the General's intentions, that he was his [Burr's] man." Bollman implored Jefferson to halt the "unexpected hostilities between Wilkinson and Col. Burr" and "to declare war against Spain, to allow Col. Burr to proceed, and to render his success indubitable by the loan of a sum of money."[11]

Jefferson, needless to say, took none of those actions. Months later, the president broke his word of honor and sent Bollman's document to Burr's prosecutors.[12]

Though Bollman had hoped his meeting with Jefferson would help Burr, it only strengthened the president's resolve that Burr should face the ultimate penalty. To get at Burr, it would be best for this arrogant German conspirator to continue in prison. To keep him there, Jefferson would have to deal with his two distant cousins, John Randolph in Congress and John Marshall on the Supreme Court.

On the day that Bollman unburdened himself to Jefferson, the Senate took up legislation to suspend for three months the right to seek a writ of habeas corpus in any case involving charges of treason or violations of the Neutrality Act.[13] Although the Constitution protects the right to habeas corpus, it allows Congress to suspend the procedure during times of "rebellion or invasion." The proposed legislation would have stripped Bollman, Swartwout, Burr, and all of Burr's associates of their habeas corpus rights for three months.

In secret session, the Senate overwhelmingly approved the bill. The administration's allies feared that eastern judges, like their brethren in New Orleans, would find the evidence against the conspirators so weak that they would free them. As a Federalist supporter of the measure explained, "theoretic liberty has often endangered the security of nations."[14]

Three days later, the House of Representatives emphatically disagreed. Goaded by John Randolph, the House debated the measure publicly. The debate proceeded before any congressman knew the ultimate outcome of Burr's expedition; news of its failure and Burr's arrest would not reach Washington City for several more weeks. Nevertheless, Republicans and Federalists alike denounced the attempt to deny habeas corpus rights to Burr and those engaged with him. Even the president's son-in-law opposed the legislation, while Randolph was strident. "The military has not only usurped the civil authority," Randolph complained, but "has usurped nothing short of omnipotent power." Approving the legislation, he warned, would leave Americans at the mercy of every man in uniform. By a crushing vote of 113 to 19, the House rejected the bill.[15]

Bollman and Swartwout promptly exercised the right they nearly had lost, asking the circuit court of the District of Columbia to order their release because the evidence against them was insufficient. Public fascination with the case was growing. Shortly thereafter, a large crowd listened to the court arguments; so many congressmen attended that the House of Representatives could not muster a quorum. By a 2–1 vote, the circuit court ordered the prisoners held without bail.[16]

Bollman and Swartwout appealed to the Supreme Court. Though six justices served on the Court, Chief Justice John Marshall was its dominant voice and the one Jefferson most feared.

In his six years on the Court, Marshall had achieved primacy through both personal and intellectual qualities. The tall, lanky Virginian brought such warm spirits to every social interaction that few spoke ill of him. His sister-in-law remembered meeting him during the Revolutionary War, when he was a young army captain. Having heard Marshall praised, she was shocked by "his awkward figure, unpolished manners, and total negligence of person." Yet she soon determined that his eye "penetrated at one glance the inmost recesses of the human character," while "beneath the slovenly garb there dwelt a heart complete with every virtue." A description thirty years later, written by a lawyer who argued many cases before him, reflects the same man:

> [Marshall is] tall, meager, emaciated; his muscles relaxed and his joints so loosely connected, as not only to disqualify him for any vigorous exertion of body, but to destroy everything like elegance and harmony in his air and movements . . . His countenance has a faithful expression of great good humor and hilarity, while his black eyes, that unerring index—possess an irradiating spirit.[17]

Though Marshall was a Federalist, and thus was denounced by Republicans for aristocratic views and for favoring a strong national government, he was equally at ease with the high and the low. According to a

With intellect and charm, Chief Justice Marshall helped establish the Supreme Court as a powerful force in American government.

longtime colleague, people tended to be disappointed when they met the chief justice: "It seemed hardly credible that such simplicity should be the accompaniment of such acknowledged greatness." He was irresistibly pleasant company. "I love his laugh," one colleague wrote, "it is too hearty for an intriguer."[18]

As a young lawyer in Richmond, Marshall organized a monthly lawyers' dinner at his home. He also formed the Quoits Club, which met on summer Saturdays on a farm outside town. Club members feasted on barbecued pig and strong punch, avoiding talk of business, politics, or religion. When well-lubricated attendees engaged in the contest that gave the club its name (a form of horseshoe-pitching), Marshall often got down on hands and knees to use a straw to measure the distance between a quoit and the target peg, biting off bits of straw until he had achieved an accurate measurement.[19]

Marshall's amiable exterior cloaked a strong intellect and a gift for political strategy that rivaled that of his cousin the president. After hearing him argue a case at the Supreme Court, a senator from New York wrote, "His head is the best organized of anyone I have known." As a congressman in the late 1790s, according to a fellow Federalist, "Marshall was looked up to as the man whose great and commanding genius was to enlighten and direct national councils."[20] President Adams agreed, sending Marshall to France in 1798 as a diplomat, then naming him Secretary of State, and finally appointing him chief justice in 1801.

The Supreme Court was not a major part of the American government when Marshall became chief justice. Its judges had to ride circuit, working much of the time as trial judges through the country. The full court sat for only a portion of the year—indeed, it did not sit at all for fifteen consecutive months in 1802 and 1803. It sometimes lacked a quorum. It had no home, hearing cases in the dank Committee Room 2 on the ground level of the Capitol.

Within a few years, Marshall had elevated the Court's position. He started, as he always did, at the personal level. He arranged for the justices to lodge together at Conrad and McMunn's when the Court was in session, and he presided over convivial meals while they conferred on the cases before them. Marshall, the social hub of every gathering, speedily commanded the loyalty and affection of his colleagues. He persuaded them to join a single opinion for the Court in most cases, rather than having each judge separately state his view. The practice gave greater weight, and often greater clarity, to the Court's rulings.[21]

Marshall's 1803 decision in *Marbury v. Madison* has served as the centerpiece of the American judicial system for more than two centuries. It remains a subtle and thoughtful examination of the powers of courts. In a classic jujitsu move, Marshall ruled in favor of Jefferson's administration, holding that the courts had no power to assist a "midnight judge," who had been appointed just before President Adams left office but never received his commission as a judge. To Jefferson's dismay, Marshall simultaneously asserted the Supreme Court's broad power to construe and apply the Constitution. When he was done, the ambiguous terms of Article III of the Constitution, which establishes the federal courts, had content and bite.[22]

Justice Joseph Story, a brilliant judge himself, was unstinting in his admiration for Marshall. "His genius is vigorous and powerful," Story wrote. "He examines the intricacies of a subject with calm and persevering circumspection, and unravels the mysteries with irresistible acuteness."

Perhaps the most enduring testament to Marshall's analytical gifts came from his cousin and rival, Jefferson. "When conversing with Marshall," Jefferson insisted, "I never admit anything." He explained:

So sure as you admit any position to be good, no matter how remote from the conclusion he [Marshall] seeks to establish, you are
gone. So great is his sophistry you must never give him an affirma-
tive answer or you will be forced to grant his conclusion. Why, if
he were to ask me if it were daylight or not, I'd reply, "Sir, I don't
know. I can't tell."[23]

Some of the bad feeling between the distant cousins had its roots in
family history, but the conflict between the two men involved much more
than old resentments.

Though Jefferson was older by twelve years, the cousins collided repeatedly in Virginia politics. They were mirror-image paradoxes: The aloof
Jefferson made himself the champion of individual rights, while the avuncular Marshall was the last great leader of the Federalists, always classed an
aristocratic party. The personal and political feelings that drove the men
apart can be seen in Jefferson's patronizing remark that Marshall's "lax
lounging manners have made him popular with the bulk of the people of
Richmond, and a profound hypocrisy [has made him popular] with many
thinking men in our country." The dislike was mutual. As an old man, the
chief justice said of Jefferson, "I have never thought him a particularly wise,
sound and practical statesman."[24]

On Monday, February 16, as Marshall's Supreme Court began to hear
arguments on the petition of Bollman and Swartwout, Jefferson had reason
to be concerned. His most effective political adversary would decide the
legal battle over what was to be done with Aaron Burr.

21

What Is Treason?

Washington City
February–March 1807

On Friday, February 20, 1807, a 4–2 majority of the Supreme Court ordered that Bollman and Swartwout be released from jail. Marshall's majority opinion in *Ex Parte Bollman,* which would frame the prosecution of Burr, upheld the right to habeas corpus relief even in cases involving the nation's security.[1]

General Wilkinson had arrested the prisoners for treason, so the Court decided only whether the evidence supported treason charges. The principal evidence consisted of two affidavits by Wilkinson, the cipher letter, and an affidavit by William Eaton.[2] The heart of the decision involved defining the crime of treason and evaluating the evidence.

Called the "king of crimes," treason is the only one defined in the Constitution, and it is defined narrowly. The men who wrote that document feared, based on British history, that those in power could use treason prosecutions to suppress dissent in troubled times. Article III, Section 3 states that treason consists *"only* in levying war against [the United States], or in adhering to their enemies, giving them aid and comfort." A conviction can be based either on a confession or on the testimony of at least two witnesses to an "overt act" of treason.[3]

Since the nation was at peace in 1807, Bollman and Swartwout could not have given aid and comfort to an enemy; the United States had no formal enemy. Consequently, the prisoners were charged with "levying war" against the United States. The term "levy" derives from the French *levee*, which generally means "to raise." Applied to soldiers, it ordinarily means conscription; for example, an innovation of the French Revolution was the *levee en masse*, or broad-based conscription. But the treason clause refers to "levying *war*," not simply the conscription of soldiers. Marshall explained that the act of enlisting men to oppose the government is *not* "levying war"; rather, a defendant levies war only when men actually *assemble* for a treasonable purpose.

Though Marshall announced a limited definition of levying war, he included a broad description of treason that seemed at odds with other statements in his opinion:

> If a body of men be actually assembled . . . [to effect] by force a treasonable purpose, all those who perform any part, however minute, or however remote from the scene of action, and who are actually leagued in the general conspiracy, are to be considered as traitors.

When he turned to the evidence before him, Marshall's careful definition of "levying war" did not control his decision. Instead, the chief justice swiftly concluded that the evidence described an intent to make war on Spain, not on the United States.[4]

Eaton's statement, he noted, mostly described an expedition against Mexico. The cipher letter did not speak of attacking any part of the United States, but only Baton Rouge in Spanish West Florida and the unnamed "country to which we are going." According to Wilkinson's affidavit, Sam Swartwout claimed Burr and seven thousand men were coming downriver "to carry an expedition to the Mexican territories" after seizing ships in New Orleans and looting the banks. But even Swartwout, Marshall pointed out, never described "an actual assemblage of men." If the affidavits were true, he concluded, both defendants were "engaged in a most culpable enterprise" against Spain, but not treason.

In a final jab, the chief justice noted that since the prisoners committed no act in the District of Columbia, they could not be prosecuted in Washington City.

Bollman and Swartwout left their jail cells that day.[5]

Marshall's ruling served notice that the courts would not join any anti-Burr stampede but would apply the law in an evenhanded fashion. In part due to Marshall's decision, the public's view of Burr's expedition began to mature. The specter of Burr and his hordes running amok, initially fostered by General Wilkinson's flamboyant reports from New Orleans and the president's January special message, seemed at odds with the facts. On closer inspection, Burr and his men did not seem like wild-eyed insurrectionists bent on severing the union; rather, they appeared to be adventurers who coveted Spanish land—a thoroughly respectable yen shared by many Americans of the day. Even the pacific Jefferson speculated that American troops could capture Mexico City in a month.[6]

Two more of Wilkinson's prisoners, John Adair and Peter Ogden, arrived in Baltimore while the Supreme Court was considering Bollman's case. A fellow passenger on their ship volunteered to file a habeas corpus petition on their behalf. A federal judge in Maryland released them, writing later that "there was not a shadow of proof against them." General Adair promptly published a long letter in the newspapers denouncing Wilkinson's repressive regime in New Orleans. John Wood, formerly of the *Western World*, showed up in Washington City and started a newspaper titled the *Atlantic World*, devoted to defending Burr. "Indignation seems now to be transferred," wrote one Federalist senator, "from Burr to Wilkinson." The general, he added, "has greatly exaggerated the force and importance of Burr."[7]

By March, the press was mocking Burr. The *Philadelphia Aurora* christened him the "Outlaw Emperor." The implied contrast to the great Napoleon was too delicious to resist. Newspapers in Virginia, Maryland, and Washington City adopted the term. The *Baltimore American* decreed Burr "the would-be Emperor of Mexico and King of the West." Other newspapers later referred to him as "the little Emperor of the Quids." ("Quid" was a pejorative term, derived from the Latin phrase *tertium quid*, or "third thing," for those who found no home in either the Republican or Federalist parties.) In his diary, Harman Blennerhassett began to refer to Burr as "the Little Emperor at Cole's Creek." For a man with Burr's immense pride, such derision was mortifying.[8]

President Jefferson's focus also began to shift. With Burr's plan in tatters, Jefferson now addressed the meting out of punishments. Though he had been slow to mobilize against Burr, he would direct a vigorous prosecution.

In late February, the Cabinet began an investigation into Burr's activities from Philadelphia to New Orleans. The logistics of gathering evidence were daunting; Jefferson complained that it would take at least four months. Government agents traveled to wherever Burr had been: Pittsburgh, Marietta, Wood County in Virginia, Cincinnati, Louisville, Nashville, Vincennes in Indiana, St. Louis, Natchez, Philadelphia, Washington City, and throughout New York State. Each agent carried a list of forty-six questions (plus subparts) to put to witnesses. These ranged from the general ("What were the real objects of the said Aaron Burr and his associates?") to the highly specific ("Have you heard . . . Aaron Burr say, that with five hundred men he either could or would send the President of the United States to Monticello, or assassinate him, intimidate Congress to pass the government of the United States into his hands, and effect by force . . . a complete revolution?").[9]

Jefferson also had to deal with the many army officers implicated in Burr's expedition. Newspapers charged that sympathetic officers in Pittsburgh had turned a blind eye to the activities of Comfort Tyler and his band of adventurers from New York. Wilkinson arrested two army officers in New Orleans, accusing them of being "deeply involved in the military part of the conspiracy." In St. Louis, an army captain and two militia officers were charged with conspiring with Burr. Secretary of War Dearborn interrogated several suspected officers himself.

So many of the army's officers were involved with Burr, Jefferson wrote to Dearborn, that he proposed a test "to separate the more from the less guilty": No punishment would apply to those officers, like the commander at Chickasaw Bluffs, who were deceived into believing that the government secretly supported Burr. Full penalties would fall only on those who "meant to proceed in defiance of the government." Jefferson's test, once it became known, was simple to manipulate. To avoid discipline, a suspected officer need only claim that he thought the government was secretly backing Burr. Dearborn never pressed charges against any of them.[10]

As for Wilkinson, Jefferson was stuck with him, though he did remove the general as governor of Louisiana Territory. He appointed Meriwether Lewis, the explorer, to the position.

For the president, the largest problem would remain the Federalists on the bench. He complained bitterly that "the tricks of the judges" would force a trial before the government was ready. "What loophole they will find in [the government's evidence]," he wrote, "we cannot foresee." The evidence, he insisted, "will satisfy the world, if not the judges."[11]

The government's case against Bollman and Swartwout already had failed to satisfy Chief Justice Marshall, but those defendants were bit players in the great national drama. Burr was the ringleader. If Burr were convicted, few would remember the failure to convict his followers.

The simplest prosecution of Burr would have charged him with misdemeanor violations of the Neutrality Act; ample evidence demonstrated that he aimed to lead an invasion of Spanish territory at a time when the nation was at peace with Spain. Indeed, one of Burr's defenses against treason charges was that he intended to invade Mexico, though he also insisted he would not have done so unless there had been war between Spain and the United States. But a misdemeanor prosecution would not satisfy the president's political and emotional investment in the case. It would seem trivial, a slap on the wrist for the monstrous traitor. In any event, invading Mexico did not strike many Americans as much of a crime in 1807. New York juries had set free both Samuel Ogden and William Smith even though both men admitted that their support of Francisco Miranda violated the statute. The charge against Burr had to be treason.

Jefferson and his lawyers studied Marshall's opinion in *Ex Parte Bollman*. It emphasized that the "assembly" of men to levy war represented treason. Burr's men had assembled on Blennerhassett Island in early December. As luck would have it, the island was then part of Virginia, so a prosecution featuring Blennerhassett Island could be brought in Richmond, before a jury stocked with Virginia Republicans who should support Jefferson over Burr. The president and his men also could take hope from Marshall's broad statement that a man commits treason if he is part of a conspiracy and "perform[s] any part of it, however minute, or however remote from the scene of action." Even though Burr had not been on Blennerhassett Island in early December, they resolved to charge him with supporting that assembly from afar, which they would call an attempt to levy war against the United States.

That was why, when Burr and his guards reached Fredericksburg in late March, they were turned around and sent back to Richmond. The prosecution would take place there.

Jefferson's strategy included one substantial weakness. Riding circuit, Chief Justice Marshall would preside over a federal trial in Richmond with District Judge Cyrus Griffin. Jefferson saw the problem: Marshall, he complained to a senator, "had already, in the case of Bollman and Swartwout, given an unfavorable opinion, [while] Griffin district judge was a poor creature."

One admirer of Marshall wrote that he had an "almost supernatural faculty . . . of developing a subject by a single glance of his mind, and detecting at once, the very point on which every controversy depends." The *Bollman* decision represented the first "glance" of Marshall's mind at Burr's case. In that first glance, the chief justice concluded that the government could not prove treason by Burr's confederates. Now, to convict Burr, Jefferson's lawyers would have to achieve one of the most difficult challenges a trial lawyer can face: persuading the judge that his earlier decision was wrong.[12]

22

Sympathy for Villainy

Richmond
March–June 1807

From the moment he arrived at Richmond's Eagle Tavern in late March of 1807, Burr was resolute. Fighting for his liberty and his life, he would challenge every aspect of the government's case while charming the men and women of Richmond outside the courtroom. And he would always maintain his dignity and composure.

Burr's determination suffused his letters to Theodosia. "I beg and expect it of you that you will conduct yourself as becomes my daughter," he wrote, "and that you manifest no signs of weakness or alarm." Classical history, he insisted, proved that his desperate situation was inevitable in any democratic government. "Was there in Greece or Rome a man of virtue and independence and supposed to possess great talents," he wrote, "who was not the object of vindictive and unrelenting persecution?" He directed her to write an essay describing all such instances, promising "great satisfaction and consolation in the composition."[1]

Richmond was built on several hills that marked the boundary between the Virginia Piedmont to the west and the coastal plain that stretched eastward for eighty miles to the sea. More than five thousand people bustled around the town, enjoying a choice of four newspapers and breathing the coal smoke that hovered for much of the year. The location had rich economic advantages. Power for mills came from nearby coal deposits and the James River's seven miles of rapids. Boats from the seaport at Norfolk crowded the city's piers, carrying away products from metal foundries, flour mills, and distilleries and breweries.[2]

A third of the population was enslaved, while another ten percent of the residents were free blacks who mingled with whites in alleys and grog shops. Richmond was as anxious about its slave population as New Orleans was. Seven years before, hundreds of slaves organized a revolt called Gabriel's Rebellion. Betrayal by an informer triggered a brutal reaction, including twenty-seven hangings. Two years later, a second slave conspiracy also was snuffed out. In 1807, the militia conducted a nightly watch through the city to suppress further unrest.[3]

Burr spent his first four days in Richmond under guard at the tavern, which sprawled across a city block near the state capitol. On March 30, the federal marshal led the prisoner through the hushed tavern lobby, which was filled with curious citizens, to a secluded room. Chief Justice Marshall waited there with the federal prosecutor, two lawyers for Burr, some of Burr's friends, and Nicholas Perkins, Burr's escort from Mississippi. The prosecutor asked that the prisoner be held for treason and for violating the Neutrality Act. Releasing Burr on a $5,000 bond, Marshall scheduled another hearing for the next morning.[4]

When morning brought a massive crowd of spectators, Marshall moved the hearing to the largest public room in town, the Hall of Delegates at the capitol building. The crowd buzzed in the capitol rotunda around the life-size statue of George Washington by Houdon, which stands there still. "You cannot conceive," wrote one resident, "the state of anxiety and agitation which the arrival of Burr excited." That the capitol building was designed by Jefferson was one more reminder that Burr was in his enemy's backyard. Though the structure was grand, with a dome artfully concealed under the roofline of a classical Roman temple, its grounds were largely untended. Goats cropped weeds in gullies on either side of the building.[5]

The treason trial of Aaron Burr was held in the Hall of Delegates in the rear of the Virginia state capitol, which was built on a design by Jefferson.

The lawyers at the hearing were a distinguished group. Attorney General Caesar Rodney (nephew of Judge Thomas Rodney in Mississippi) led the prosecution with the United States attorney for Virginia, George Hay. Burr's lawyers included the nation's first Attorney General, Edmund Randolph, and Richmond's finest lawyer, John Wickham. As would be true throughout the trial, though, the defendant was the most effective lawyer in the building.[6]

After both prosecutors and defense counsel had their say, Burr crisply distilled his position, taking advantage of his twin roles as defendant and lawyer. His narrative presented many of the facts that were in dispute, which he knew firsthand; yet because he spoke as his own lawyer, he was neither under oath nor subject to cross-examination.

The case, Burr insisted, grew from alarms without cause: "Mr. Wilkinson alarmed the President," he said, "and the President alarmed the people." Courts in Kentucky and Mississippi had reviewed his conduct and found him blameless. The only evidence against him, from Wilkinson and Eaton, consisted of "crudities and absurdities."[7]

Next morning, Marshall announced that he would hold Burr only on the misdemeanor charge of preparing a foreign invasion. After all, Marshall's *Bollman* decision held that the government's evidence did not support treason charges. In a tart warning to the prosecutors, Marshall observed that treason—levying war against the government—is an act of public notoriety that "must exist in the view of the world, or it cannot exist at all." Though months had elapsed since Burr launched his expedition, the government still had presented no proof that Burr had levied war against the United States.

Marshall set bail at $10,000, which Burr's friends posted. Attorney General Rodney found the granting of bail an "unpromising" development. The chief justice scheduled the grand jury inquiry to begin in seven weeks, on May 22.[8]

Burr's position was perilous. He was still under indictment for murder in New York and New Jersey. The national government was now charging him with treason. His financial condition was a catastrophe. Having lived for two years as a nomad, generating no income, he had no money and dwindling credit. Many of his friends groaned under debts from his expedition. George Ogden in New York was refusing to honor Burr's drafts. Creditors hurried to Richmond to begin decades of hounding Burr for repayment. Two Federalist friends loaned him money to buy decent clothes for the trial. Only the generosity of his wealthy son-in-law, Joseph Alston, kept Burr in room, board, and lawyers. Even that support was briefly in doubt: When the cipher letter first became public, Alston issued a letter distancing himself from his infamous father-in-law. With time, Theodosia's entreaties, and Burr's explanations, Alston rallied to Burr's aid.[9]

Burr selected his lawyers shrewdly. Having a Randolph on your side could never hurt in a Virginia courtroom; at least one juror was bound to be a relation. In fact, Edmund Randolph's nephew (Congressman John Randolph) became foreman of the grand jury. Edmund Randolph also brought the distinction of long public service. Even better was his connection to the judge: When Edmund Randolph became Attorney General of the United States in 1789, he turned his law practice over to John Marshall. Nevertheless, Randolph's career had slid downhill since President Washington dismissed him as Secretary of State for making irresponsible statements to a French diplomat.

For the heaviest legal work, Burr would look to Wickham, a native New Yorker who sided with the British during the Revolutionary War. When he was seized as a suspected spy in Virginia, Wickham showed the persuasive gifts that would serve him so well as a lawyer, winning a suspension of his own prosecution.

Smart and poised, Wickham was, in the words of one observer, "always ready with learning, eloquence, wit, logic or sarcasm, as the case required. Few men ever entered an arena so well armed." That Wickham was a charter member of Richmond's Quoits Club, organized by the chief justice many years before, was a plus. Two younger lawyers also helped with the defense.[10]

John Wickham of Richmond served as Burr's lead trial counsel, except when Burr performed that role himself.

The wild card on Burr's team was Luther Martin of Baltimore. A dissenting delegate to the Constitutional Convention in the summer of 1787, Martin loved both the courtroom and alcoholic beverages, often consuming the latter while at work in the former. Known as "Lawyer Brandy-Bottle," the long-winded Martin could be an acquired taste. He was, according to a fellow delegate to the Constitutional Convention, "so extremely prolix that he never speaks without tiring the patience of all who hear him." His personal habits could be trying as well. Future Supreme Court justice Roger Taney wrote that Martin was "as coarse and unseemly at dinner, in his manner of eating, as he was in everything." Despite his food-stained clothes and extravagant speechifying, Martin was a tenacious combatant who knew a great deal of law.[11]

For Martin, this trial was much more than a professional engagement. He and Burr were friends, fellow graduates of the College of New Jersey. Martin welcomed the opportunity to defend his friend against a president whom Martin detested. Two years before, Martin had tweaked Jefferson by successfully defending Justice Chase in the Senate impeachment trial. Jefferson reciprocated Martin's hostility, referring to the lawyer as the "impudent federal bull-dog."[12]

Burr, eternally strapped for cash, resented the seemingly limitless resources of the prosecution. A week before the trial began, he shared his bitterness with Theodosia. "The most indefatigable industry is used by the agents of government, and they have money at command without stint." If he had the same resources, he boasted, "I could not only foil the prosecutors, but render them ridiculous and infamous." The government's goal, he was sure, was to bias the public against him so it could win a conviction without evidence.[13]

Jefferson did not blink at the expenditures for Burr's prosecution. He directed the payment of witness expenses from the government's contingency fund. The final tab for the trial exceeded $100,000, the equivalent of more than $4 million today.[14]

Attorney General Rodney directed the gathering of evidence, recruiting agents all over the country to identify witnesses and send them to Richmond. He emphasized the need for testimony from the vigilantes of Wood County, Virginia, since the prosecution would concentrate on Blennerhassett Island as the expedition's assembly point. When Rodney's young son fell ill, however, responsibility for the case fell to George Hay, Virginia's federal prosecutor. Hay could not have had a quiet mind as the date neared for the grand jury to convene; his wife had died only a few weeks before. Nevertheless, he dutifully took up the assignment.[15]

Then forty-one years old, Hay was an ambitious and staunch Jeffersonian. In 1799, when the Republicans attacked the restrictions on speech in the federal Sedition Act, Hay wrote a two-fisted call for unbridled freedom of press and speech. He also defended in court the controversial newspaperman James Callender, who was publishing attacks on President Adams and the Federalists. After Jefferson became president, however, Hay substantially revised his ideas about a free press. When Callender printed that the president had sired mulatto children at Monticello with "dusky Sally," Hay caned his former client into unconsciousness.[16]

The Burr case gave Hay an unparalleled opportunity to win courtroom renown and Jefferson's gratitude, yet he was acutely aware of the problems with his case. The trial "commenced under inauspicious circumstances," he wrote to the president. "I have no doubt that its progress will be as unfavorable as its commencement." Hay expressed surprise and sadness that some citizens showed support for Burr. "There is among mankind," he lamented, "a sympathy for villainy." Worse yet, Hay had to present his case before a strong-minded judge who was already skeptical of it. "I do not say that the chief justice does wrong with his eyes open," he wrote, "but that his eyes are almost closed."[17]

Before the grand jury convened, Marshall committed a serious misstep by attending a dinner at the home of his old friend John Wickham. The defense lawyer also had invited his client, the notorious Burr, and judge and defendant spent the afternoon together at the affair. Newspaper criticism focused on Marshall, charging him with "an unpardonable breach of prudence and decorum." Though accounts differed on whether the judge knew in advance that Burr would attend, all agreed that the judge should have left as soon as he discovered Burr in Wickham's house. By unaccountably remaining in Burr's company through the entire meal, Marshall at a minimum compromised the appearance of justice.[18]

Hay recruited two local lawyers to assist him with the prosecution. Alexander McRae, Virginia's lieutenant governor, was a fighter who would not flinch when challenged by the "impudent federal bull-dog." The courtroom star for the government, though, would be its youngest lawyer. Only thirty-five and relatively new to Richmond, William Wirt had a flair for metaphor and an actor's sense of timing. The large, sandy-haired lawyer was said to wield his snuffbox as an oratorical weapon.[19]

Yet the personality at the heart of the government's case would never appear in the courtroom. At first, President Jefferson professed indifference to Burr's prosecution. Whether Burr was convicted or not, he wrote in late February, "is not the subject of even a wish on my part." He protested to a political ally that he never harbored "one hostile sentiment" toward Burr. Then, however, Jefferson's true feelings seeped into his letter: "I never indeed thought him an honest, frank-dealing man, but considered him as a crooked gun, or other perverted machine, whose aim or stroke you could never be sure of." For the president, convicting Burr became a top priority, which only amplified his chronic dissatisfaction with the federal judiciary.[20]

Jefferson fretted that the government could not gather all of its evidence on the chief justice's schedule. After angrily dissecting Marshall's decision to release Burr on bail, Jefferson added that he would have judged Marshall's opinion more charitably if Federalist judges had ever condemned a Federalist or acquitted a Republican.[21]

Through the first month of hearings in Richmond, Jefferson sent George Hay nine separate letters stuffed with exacting instructions. He briefed Hay on his interview of Erich Bollman and sent Bollman's essay describing Burr's expedition and plans. Jefferson also enclosed several blank pardons for Hay to grant to Bollman and to all but "the grossest offenders." Jefferson then revised his instructions: Hay could grant the pardons even to the grossest offenders if "the principal [Burr] will otherwise escape."[22]

No detail of the case was too small for the president's attention. Jefferson's directives reached to such peripheral witnesses as the man who rode with Burr when he was arrested in the Alabama forest, and a man who was a political adversary of General Wilkinson's in St. Louis. Jefferson urged an interview with a Baltimore resident who claimed he heard Luther Martin express sympathy for Burr's expedition; then the president suggested that Hay arrest Lawyer Brandy-Bottle himself. The president also instructed Hay never to mention *Marbury v. Madison;* Marshall's opinion in that case still rankled.[23]

•   •   •

At noon on May 22, Marshall took the bench in the Hall of Delegates. Presiding with him was District Judge Cyrus Griffin, who would speak rarely during the trial. The north-facing courtroom, 76 feet long by 30 feet wide, was a grand setting. Light poured in through tall windows on three sides. A gallery in the rear accommodated spectators eager to see the most important trial in the republic's short history. "A vast concourse of persons attended," an observer wrote, "from all parts of the union." [24]

Facing the judges sat the three prosecutors and five defense lawyers, plus Burr, both defendant and lawyer. Admission to the courtroom was managed by the doorkeeper, a massive young man who was a future general in chief of the United States army. Then only twenty-four, Winfield Scott marveled at Burr's cool demeanor: "There he stood, in the hands of power, on the brink of danger, as composed, as immovable, as one of Canova's living marbles." [25] Burr soon would be in motion.

Burr's story at trial was straightforward: He had intended no hostility to the United States government but only to join a war against Spain; if there was to be no war, he intended to settle the Bastrop Tract. Though he resented the prosecution's deep resources, Burr had one significant advantage: Most of the incriminating evidence would not be available at trial.

Those men most deeply engaged in his plans would not testify against him. Many retained a strong loyalty to their chief. "Bollman, Swartwout, etc.," prosecutor Hay wrote to Jefferson, "will never utter a word injurious to Burr." [26] Others like Jonathan Dayton and Comfort Tyler and Davis Floyd remained silent because they faced prosecution themselves. Perhaps the most incendiary evidence—Burr's proposals to Britain and Spain to foment western secession—would remain sealed in foreign archives for generations.

Burr and his counsel aimed to sound two broad themes: that the case was a political persecution without real evidence; and that it turned entirely on the credibility of General Wilkinson, who could not be believed about anything.

On the first day in court, Burr quickly sounded the first theme. Marshall called sixteen Virginians who had been summoned to serve on the grand jury that would decide whether to indict anyone. Burr objected to two of the grand jurors. Admitting that he had "little chance, indeed, of an impartial jury," he insisted that those two were far too prejudiced against him to serve. One, former senator Wilson Cary Nicholas, was an avowed political enemy. The other, Senator William Giles, had sponsored the recent federal legislation to suspend habeas corpus. Both men, at Marshall's prodding, withdrew from the case. Burr raised no objection to the grand jury foreman, John Randolph of Roanoke, the president's critic and exotic distant cousin, who was Edmund Randolph's nephew. Nor did he object to the grand juror who was a cousin of Chief Justice Marshall's wife. This, after all, was Virginia.[27]

Burr asked the chief justice to instruct the jury on specific legal issues, triggering a mistake by the prosecutor. He hoped, Hay interjected, that the court would not grant Burr "particular indulgences" but would treat him on "the same footing with every other man charged with a crime."

Burr sprang at the opening. "Would to God that I did stand on the same ground with every other man," he exclaimed. "This is the first time I have been permitted to enjoy the rights of a citizen."[28]

On the following day, Hay reinforced Burr's second trial theme by asking that the grand jury stand down until Wilkinson arrived from New Orleans. For the next three weeks, the grand jury waited while the general tied up his business in New Orleans, where his wife had died in late February. Wilkinson's absence also idled dozens of witnesses summoned to Richmond by the government. One of them was Andrew Jackson, whose contempt for Wilkinson had overcome his earlier disillusionment with Burr. "General Jackson of Tennessee has been here since the twenty-second [of May]," Hay reported to the president, "denouncing Wilkinson in the coarsest terms in every company."[29]

"Still waiting for Wilkinson," Burr wrote to Theodosia after ten days of idleness. "The grand jury, the witnesses, and the country grow impatient." Each day of waiting only underscored just how important Wilkinson was. The lawyers used the time to prepare for the trial. The work, Burr told his daughter, extended "from morning till night—from night till morning," and included "things at which you will laugh, also things at which you will pout and scold."[30]

During this anxious interregnum, the lawyers sparred over procedural motions while the affable chief justice largely looked on. Leery of being drawn into legal errors, Marshall made as few decisions as possible, urging the lawyers to work out disputes among themselves and often leaving issues to be resolved at some future time.

With minimal supervision from the bench, the lawyers put on a show. Accusing each other of misrepresentation, foot-dragging, political posturing, or pandering to public opinion, the adversaries engaged in a bruising free-for-all. In a practice that no modern judge would tolerate, every lawyer on both sides addressed each issue in a tag-team format. For the defense, for example, Burr might begin the discussion of a question, followed by Wickham, then Randolph, then Wickham on new points that had occurred to him overnight, and then one of the junior lawyers. Burr would sum up. The river of words, which Marshall deplored but never controlled, guaranteed the numbing repetition of arguments. Republican newspapers bemoaned "the pliancy of the court," which gave Burr such free run that he seemed to preside over his own trial. One sardonic report acknowledged Burr's dominance of the proceedings:

> With all eyes upon him, more cool, more dignified, more important and impressive than ever, in his new situation of *judge*, [Burr] summed up the evidence in a short but masterly style; in a very few words he proved from the constitution itself the impropriety of proceeding against the supposed criminal; fixed himself the quantum of bail necessary to be taken, and amidst the wonder and applause of an audience, charmed by his eloquence and his decision he dismissed the grand [jury].[31]

Dogged George Hay was ill suited for such a contest. The defense lawyers baited him, insulted him, and kept him off balance. The competition became more even only when William Wirt spoke for the prosecution, spitting back what one admirer called "a lava-like ridicule, which flamed while it burned."[32]

On Monday, May 25, Hay asked that Burr be jailed until the grand jury could act. Rumor insisted that Burr would take to his heels to cheat justice, as he had fled the murder prosecutions in New York and New Jersey. Hay did not intend to see him abscond in a case involving "a crime of such gigantic enormity."[33] For the next three days, the lawyers vied to deliver the most passionate speech on the question, scrambling over each other like puppies in a crate. Despite the passion of the arguments, Marshall settled the dispute quietly, with Burr posting a new bond for $10,000 (about $400,000 in today's money). In an act of loyalty that would appall most lawyers, Luther Martin posted part of his client's bond.[34]

After more days of waiting, Burr took the offensive, demanding the original letter that Wilkinson wrote to Jefferson from Natchitoches on October 21, 1806, along with the orders that were issued to military commanders in response to Wilkinson's letter. Hay agreed to try to acquire the papers and provide them to Burr. The defense lawyers, however, would not accept Hay's "yes" for an answer. In a marathon argument, they insisted that no matter what Hay said, the president would not relinquish the papers. Luther Martin, pointing to Jefferson's statement that Burr was guilty of treason, proclaimed that the president "has assumed to himself the knowledge of the Supreme Being himself." Jefferson, the lawyer roared, "has let slip the dogs of war, the hell-hounds of persecution, to hunt down my friend."[35]

Setting a critical precedent for future White Houses when they assert "executive privilege" to keep papers secret, Marshall allowed Burr to issue the subpoena to Jefferson. Though the president faced many demands on his time, the chief justice wrote, those demands were not so unremitting that he could not answer a subpoena. Marshall ruled that if the responsive documents might disclose confidential matters, the president could object to the subpoena on that ground.

Back in Washington City, Marshall's ruling offended Jefferson, particularly the statement that the demands on his time were not unremitting. Suspecting that Marshall was referring to his annual summer retreat to Monticello, Jefferson instructed Hay to inform the court that "I pass more hours in public business at Monticello than I do here [in Washington City], every day." Jefferson recognized that Burr's maneuver aimed to "divert the public attention from him to this battle of giants" between the chief justice and the president. Some presidential papers, he advised Hay, were purely public, but others were inherently confidential. The president, Jefferson insisted, must be the sole judge of what can be released publicly.[36]

In early June, with still no word on Wilkinson's location, the chief justice adjourned the grand jury for several days. "We are enjoying a sort of suspension of hostilities," wrote the visiting Washington Irving, whose elder brother had edited a Burr-sponsored newspaper in New York. The jurors went home, Irving added, to "see their wives, get their clothes washed, and flog their negroes." The future novelist sympathized with Burr, thinking the government had employed "the most underhand and ungenerous measures," while Burr "retains his serenity and self-possession unshaken, and wears the same aspect in all times and situations."[37]

As the day grew near for the grand jury to begin hearing evidence, the prosecutor asked that Erich Bollman be sworn in so he could testify. Jefferson had instructed Hay on when he might offer Bollman a pardon, on how Hay should question Bollman, and on how he might make use of Bollman's written description of Burr's plans (even though Jefferson had promised Bollman never to disclose that writing to another soul).[38]

Hay told the court that Bollman had key evidence about Burr's plans but "could not possibly criminate himself" because Hay would issue a pardon for any crimes he had committed. In opposition, the defense lawyers argued—evidently with straight faces—that Bollman refused to accept the pardon because he was innocent, but he could not testify without incriminating himself. Declining to be drawn into such illogical arguments, Marshall ordered that Bollman be sworn in and deliver to the grand jury whatever testimony he saw fit to give.[39]

Hay was nonplussed by the vehemence and ingenuity of the defense lawyers. He complained in a letter to Jefferson that Burr

> takes every advantage, denies every position advanced in the prosecution, acquiesces in no decision, however solemnly made or frequently repeated, and while he boldly asserts his innocence, adopts every measure within his power to bar the door to an inquiry.[40]

On June 13, the long-awaited news finally arrived: General Wilkinson had landed in Norfolk that morning, with several other witnesses. He would appear in court on Monday, June 15. The main event could begin.

23

A Mammoth of Iniquity

Richmond
June–August 1807

Shortly before eleven o'clock on the morning of Monday, June 15, Burr stood chatting with one of his lawyers before the bench in the Hall of Delegates. General Wilkinson, resplendent in his gold-trimmed uniform, sword strapped round his ample middle, strode into the chamber with a suite of military aides. He paused in the aisle when he approached the bench. There, according to Washington Irving, the general "stood for a moment swelling like a turkey cock, and bracing himself up for the encounter of Burr's eye."

Burr continued his conversation. Only when the chief justice directed that Wilkinson be sworn as a grand jury witness did Burr take notice. "At the mention of the name," Irving wrote with glee, "Burr turned his head, looked him full in the face with one of his piercing regards, swept his eye over his whole person from head to foot, as if to scan its dimensions, and then coolly resumed his former position, and went on conversing with his counsel as tranquilly as ever." The writer applauded Burr's performance:

There was no appearance of study or constraint in it; no affectation of disdain or defiance; a slight expression of contempt played over his countenance, such as you would show on regarding any person to whom you were indifferent, but whom you considered mean and contemptible.

In a letter to Jefferson, Wilkinson related a far different version of the encounter. "My eyes darted a flash of indignation at the little traitor," the general recounted, while Burr struggled "under the weight of conscious guilt, with haggard eyes in an effort to meet the indignant salutation of outraged honor." The general noted with satisfaction that Burr "averted his face, grew pale, and affected passion to conceal his perturbation."

A less partisan witness reported that Wilkinson's "countenance was calm, dignified, and commanding, while that of Colonel Burr was marked by a haughty contempt."[1]

Having waited three weeks for the general, the grand jury fell upon him hungrily in its secret sessions. First, though, John Randolph insisted that Wilkinson remove his sword. "Take that man out and disarm him," Randolph ordered the marshal. "I will allow no attempt to intimidate the jury." The grand jurors questioned Wilkinson for four days. "[I] did not doubt that General W[ilkinson] was an early associate in the conspiracy," one commented later, "and that he did not decidedly abandon it, till it was found impracticable."[2]

Noting irregularities in the cipher letter, the grand jurors explored Wilkinson's doctoring of it. The general admitted erasing part of the letter and changing other parts, which disgusted the grand jurors. According to John Randolph, one grand juror proposed that they indict Wilkinson as part of Burr's conspiracy. Though every grand juror thought the general morally guilty, the motion failed by a 7–9 vote because the evidence did not tie him to the assembly of men on Blennerhassett Island.[3]

In private correspondence, Randolph excoriated the plumed soldier. "Under examination," he wrote, "all was confusion of language and looks." Randolph lamented that Wilkinson was not indicted: "The mammoth of iniquity escaped—not that any man pretended to think him innocent." He called Wilkinson "the only man that I ever saw who was from the bark to the very core a villain."[4]

While the grand jury challenged the general in secret, Burr did so in public. At noon on the grand jury's third day, Wednesday, June 17, Burr presented his most aggressive motion yet: He asked the chief justice to order the arrest of Wilkinson and two others for illegally taking items from the mails and coercing witnesses. Before the grand jury had even finished its work, Burr was trying to place his chief accuser on trial, demanding that he be arrested forthwith.[5] The ever-tolerant Marshall quietly listened to Burr's motion, which evolved into a request that Wilkinson be held in contempt of court. Edmund Randolph, on behalf of Burr, accused Wilkinson of perverting justice to protect himself, lest "like some mock god, he fall down from his imaginary glory, tumbling among ruins, and into a chaos of rubbish."[6] Marshall took no immediate action on Burr's motion.

The defense team continued to throw sand in the wheels of justice. Confronting a letter in cipher sent by Burr to Bollman, the grand jury asked that Bollman or Burr's secretary decipher it. Burr's lawyers denied that the letter was relevant, or that it had been legally acquired by the prosecutors, then blocked a request that General Wilkinson explain how it had been acquired. Both Bollman and the secretary refused to decipher it for fear of self-incrimination, though Bollman still refused Jefferson's pardon on the contradictory ground that he faced no criminal liability and thus needed no pardon. The grand jurors were left to make whatever sense they could of the enciphered letter.

Once finished with Wilkinson, the grand jury speedily questioned fifty more witnesses. Led by John Randolph, its investigation had a decided edge, as was discovered by William Eaton, the veteran of the North African conflict who had disclosed Burr's overtures to him. When Eaton emerged from one session, Burr wrote cheerfully to his daughter, he was "in such rage and agitation that he shed tears, and complained bitterly that he had been questioned as if he were a villain." Burr could not resist adding, "How else could he have been questioned?"[7]

Yet Burr and Wilkinson found common ground when it came to suppressing their correspondence with each other. Noting that the cipher letter responded to a letter from Wilkinson to Burr dated May 13, 1806, the grand jurors asked Burr for the earlier document, hoping it would illuminate the cipher letter.

Burr would have none of it. "It would be impossible," he declared, "to expose any letter which had been communicated to [me] confidentially." No gentleman could do so. Even prosecutor Hay was impressed by Burr's position, as he related to the president: "The attitude and tone assumed by Burr struck everybody. There was an appearance of honor and magnanimity which brightened the countenances of the phalanx who daily attend for his encouragement."

But then Wilkinson consented that Burr could turn over the letter, shredding Burr's mantle of self-righteousness. Weakly, Burr replied that he gave the letter to an unnamed third party "with the express view that it should not be used improperly against anyone."[8]

Yet the general employed the identical device to suppress letters he had received from Burr. He had delivered them to his lawyer in New Orleans and another person, Wilkinson explained, and could no longer remember their contents. He admitted that he gave the two men the key to the cipher and asked them to determine whether his honor required that the letters be revealed. When they advised him that he might well need to disclose the letters, he ignored their advice.[9]

The prosecutors never demanded the letters so diligently concealed by both Burr and Wilkinson. They have never come to light.[10]

On Wednesday, June 24, after sitting for eight days, the grand jury returned an indictment of Burr and Harman Blennerhassett. On the following day, it handed up five more indictments, charging Jonathan Dayton of New Jersey, Senator John Smith of Ohio, Comfort Tyler and Israel Smith of western New York, and Davis Floyd of Indiana. All seven were charged with treason and violating the Neutrality Act. The grand jury lodged no charges against those Burr confidants who had been arrested in New Orleans but were previously released by the courts: Bollman, Swartwout, Peter Ogden, and General John Adair.[11]

The proceedings in the Hall of Delegates gained urgency. Marshall set a trial date of August 3, then rejected Burr's demand that he find Wilkinson in contempt of court.[12]

Marshall also ordered that Burr be moved from a house rented by Luther Martin, where he had been staying, to the Richmond penitentiary, perched on a hill more than a mile from the capitol building. Burr's new situation was grim. Washington Irving called it "of all holes the most horrible and desolate." When the defense lawyers complained that they could not confer with Burr there, the chief justice relented and agreed that he could move back to the front room of Martin's house, so long as bars were installed in the windows and a seven-man guard maintained a watch from the adjacent property. The Richmond council, stung by criticism of its prison, offered to place Burr in a three-room suite at the top of the penitentiary, which Marshall then ordered.[13]

Burr wrote cheerfully to Theodosia about his new quarters at the prison. He described his jailer as a "polite and civil man," finding humor in the following exchange:

JAILER.   I hope, sir, it would not be disagreeable to you if I should lock this door after dark.

BURR.   By no means, sir; I should prefer it, to keep out intruders.

JAILER.   It is our custom, sir, to extinguish all lights at nine o'clock; I hope, sir, you will have no objection to conform to that.

BURR.   That, sir, I am sorry to say, is impossible, for I never go to bed till twelve, and always burn two candles.

JAILER.   Very well, sir, just as you please. I should have been glad if it had been otherwise, but, as you please, sir.

Though the chamber was damp and the season sultry, it was a pleasant form of incarceration, replete with a personal servant. Burr's guests came and went freely, meeting privately with the prisoner. Ladies of the town vied to provide him with fruit (oranges, lemons, pineapples, raspberries, apricots), along with cream, butter, and ice. "It is as difficult to get an audience," one observer claimed, "as if he were really an Emperor." Burr urged Theodosia to join him, offering her a parlor and bedroom in his suite. She would be less concerned for his welfare, he argued, if she could see how he fared. He added, "Remember, no agitations, no complaints, no fears or anxieties on the road, or I renounce thee."[14]

Civilized accommodations provided no relief from Richmond's summertime heat. Washington Irving complained of "red hot strolls in the middle of the day," with the mercury approaching a hundred degrees, and wilting under the "perspiring horrors" of the town's social scene.[15]

The trial threatened to be a long one. The prosecutors had summoned 140 witnesses; Burr was bringing thirty more. The prosecution also had to scour the country for the other six defendants, who would be tried after Burr.[16]

All of the defendants, led by Burr, professed their innocence. One look at Burr's indictment, drafted to satisfy Marshall's explanation of treason in *Ex Parte Bollman*, reveals why. It was an incoherent mess, more than twelve hundred words shoehorned into two sentences that were as murky as they were gargantuan. The government had little chance of proving Burr guilty of the crimes described.

Under the *Bollman* ruling, the prosecutors had to accuse Burr of assembling men to levy war against the United States. Because Blennerhassett Island was the most obvious assembly point and also was within Virginia, the indictment alleged that it was there, on the preceding December 11, that "Aaron Burr . . . traitorously assembled and armed and arrayed[,] most wickedly, maliciously and traitorously did ordain, prepare and levy war against the said United States." The indictment added that Burr "did compass, imagine and intend to raise and levy war, insurrection, and rebellion against the said United States." But Burr was nowhere near the island on December 11, when Comfort Tyler's boats shoved off with Blennerhassett aboard. Burr was in Kentucky, on his way to Tennessee.[17]

The prosecution's only way around this problem was the controversial doctrine of constructive treason. In *Ex Parte Bollman*, the chief justice cautioned that all who play a role in treason, "however remote from the scene of the action," are guilty so long as there is "an actual assembling of men for the treasonable purpose." That passage suggested that Burr could be guilty even though he was remote from the scene of the action. As soon as the indictment was returned, the chief justice recognized that this legal point would be critical. He promptly wrote to his fellow Supreme Court justices, asking their views of the definition of treason and highlighting constructive treason as the difficult question before him.[18]

Burr also concentrated on that legal issue. The indictment, he told Theodosia, asserted that "a war was levied on Blennerhassett's Island by construction; and that, though Colonel Burr was then at Frankfort . . . yet, having advised the measure, he was, by construction of law, present at the island." Burr dismissed the theory: "Not a man of the jury supposed this to be true."[19]

The other prosecution strategy for circumventing the chief justice's *Bollman* opinion was to redirect attention from events on Blennerhassett Island to the rest of the adventurers' journey downriver.[20] Burr had joined the expedition where the Cumberland met the Ohio, and there was testimony that the adventurers acquired muskets and bayonets while traveling downriver. By placing Burr in the lead vessel from that point on, and pointing to crates of muskets on the boats, the government might hope to prove an overt act by Burr of levying war against the United States.

As the grand jury returned its indictments, the threat of a real war exploded one hundred miles away. Britain's death struggle with Napoleon was entering a critical phase, and the Royal Navy was increasing its efforts to recover British seamen from American ships. For years, British sailors had deserted to American craft, and for years the British had forcibly seized ("pressed") those men from American merchant ships. On June 22, 1807, the British took the practice to a new level, stopping a frigate of the U.S. navy. A British frigate, HMS *Leopard,* stopped the American *Chesapeake,* which was leaving Norfolk for duty in the Mediterranean.

Chesapeake was unprepared for battle. Cables and lumber were stacked around the decks, ammunition was stored below, and most of the thirty-eight cannon were lashed down. The United States was not at war. The long voyage across the Atlantic would allow *Chesapeake*'s crew ample time to organize the ship's supplies and munitions. Within minutes of hailing *Chesapeake*, the 52-gun *Leopard* demanded the right to search for deserters.

The American captain played for time, but *Leopard* would not wait. Three deadly broadsides killed four Americans, wounded more, and forced *Chesapeake* to strike its colors. The British claimed four of its crew as deserters.[21]

When the news reached Richmond, a spasm of patriotic ardor swept the town. The one-sided encounter, with the British warship pummeling the defenseless *Chesapeake*, enraged Virginians. A public meeting convened in the capitol on June 27, after the day's trial proceedings concluded. Prosecutors Hay and Wirt were named to a committee to draft resolutions demanding vengeance. The entire nation shivered with war fever. "Never since the battle of Lexington," wrote Jefferson, "have I seen this country in such a state of exasperation."

Militia units drilled in Richmond's capitol square, then marched off to Norfolk. Residents offered accommodations to the passing soldiers. "We are on tiptoe for war," Wirt wrote, describing emotional Fourth of July festivities, with companies of uniformed men marching to band music, with "every window . . . filled with weeping females." He concluded: "I believe war to be inevitable."[22]

War or no war, Burr's trial would begin on August 3. Perhaps a wave of patriotic enthusiasm would help the prosecution overcome the defects of its case. The *Chesapeake/Leopard* crisis carried special risks for Burr. In the midst of clamor for war with Britain, he was most fortunate that no evidence had yet surfaced of his attempt to win British support for his expedition.

24

Searching for an Overt Act

Richmond
August–September 1807

Wen John Marshall gaveled the Hall of Delegates to order at noon on Monday, August 3, the clerk read the names of 101 government witnesses. Only fifteen answered. The chief justice adjourned the case for two days to await the arrival of more witnesses. Seventeen more were present on Wednesday. Hay thought the trial could begin soon, perhaps in two more days. Most of the nation's newspapers splashed the courtroom drama across their pages, reprinting transcripts of the proceedings from the Richmond newspapers.

For the trial, Burr returned to Luther Martin's house near the capitol. As he explained in a note that reached Theodosia on the road to Richmond, the Alstons could stay in a home on the same street. "Received on our approach to Richmond," Theodosia wrote on his note. "How happy it made me!" For the first time in almost a year, Burr was reunited with Theodosia and Joseph Alston. A few days later, when Harman Blennerhassett was deposited by government agents at the Richmond penitentiary, he received a Burr family welcome: Alston visited him, Theodosia dispatched tea and cakes, and Burr sent a friendly note.[1]

Through the next three months, Richmond housed an unusual community that revolved at varying speeds around the trial: witnesses, newspapermen, spectators, friends of the combatants, and creditors hoping for repayment. In his apartment in the penitentiary, Blennerhassett entertained many members of this community: neighbors from home, most of Burr's lawyers, the editor John Wood, several of the adventurers, and not a few men demanding that he honor Burr's drafts.

The visitors attended court, read newspapers, gambled at cards and cockfights and horse races, and drank and talked. Their talk was endless. They graded the lawyers and their performances. They wondered about war with Britain. But they always, like people around the country, came back to Burr. They argued about what his true intentions had been. Had the little emperor intended to conquer Mexico? Or did he mean to lead a western secession? Had he really trusted Wilkinson, of all men? Had he relied upon the comically nearsighted Blennerhassett, or had he just been fleecing the Irishman?

By Monday, August 10, eight more witnesses had arrived, and Marshall turned the lawyers to the thorny problem of selecting a jury. Members of the jury, the chief justice said, should have "a perfect freedom from previous impressions" about the case. That, however, was impossible. Every man in Virginia had an opinion about Burr's expedition. Despite the growing skepticism of General Wilkinson's role, many thought Burr should be hanged from the nearest tree. That was why Jefferson had wanted the trial in Richmond. From the initial jury pool of forty-eight, the defense accepted only four. The rest were hopelessly biased against Burr. The call went out for more potential jurors, the jury selection process stretching on in the heat with no end in sight.

After five more days, the new jury pool was down to forty men without producing a single impartial juror. Burr offered to end the agonizing effort. He would arbitrarily choose the final eight jurors and be done with it. The prosecution agreed. One of the eight men chosen by Burr protested that he could not be impartial: He had publicly declared that Burr should be hanged. Burr was fatalistic. "I am under the necessity," he said, "of taking men in some degree prejudiced against me." The juror stayed.[2]

George Hay began the government's opening statement on that Saturday afternoon, August 15. Though Hay was not a renowned speaker, the Hall of Delegates was filled to capacity again. The prosecutor struggled to free his case from the twin shadows of the clumsy indictment and Marshall's opinion in *Ex Parte Bollman*. He insisted that the indictment contained two counts, one relating to events on Blennerhassett Island and the second concerning the adventurers' descent of the river. He tried to focus on the second count, because that was when Burr joined the expedition. Burr had aimed to seize New Orleans, Hay argued, and that was treason even if New Orleans was to be Burr's stepping-stone to Mexico.

The lines of the battle were clear. The prosecution would resist the defense effort to crowd the case onto Blennerhassett Island. Hay also proclaimed, as he had to, that Burr was guilty of treason so long as his men assembled on the island, "whether they were armed or not, and whether they used force or not." To win a conviction, Hay would have to carry that point.[3]

The prosecution stumbled out of the gate when Burr objected to its first witness, William Eaton. Under *Ex Parte Bollman*, he insisted, the prosecution first had to prove an overt act of treason; Eaton, however, could describe only "conversations said to have happened in Washington." No mere conversation could be an overt act of treason. When Hay tried to respond, the defense table erupted. A new voice, that of Charles Lee, emerged from the din. Lee, who had lately joined the Burr defense, was another former Attorney General of the United States. He had won *Ex Parte Bollman*, so he knew the chief justice's mind on this subject. "An open deed of war," he argued, "committed in the full view of the world on the 10th day of December on Blennerhassett's Island, was susceptible of clear proof." War, he stressed, is not levied in secret. Before proving anything else, the prosecution must prove *overt* acts of levying war.[4]

The next day Chief Justice Marshall ruled for Burr on this critical point. Proving the overt acts of treason first, he held, "is the most useful and appears to be in the natural order of testimony."

When Eaton resumed on the witness stand, he stated, "Concerning any overt act, which goes to prove Aaron Burr guilty of treason, I know nothing."[5] Under the ruling just announced, Eaton's statement appeared to mean that he possessed no admissible evidence. Nevertheless, the chief justice, perhaps reluctant to muzzle the government's first witness, allowed the colorful Eaton to continue.

Over recent months, Eaton had cut a wide swath through Washington City and Richmond, telling all he met about Burr's incendiary threat to lead a putsch against the government. According to a senator who resided at the same boardinghouse in Washington as Eaton, "so irregular wild and confused is his mind that I think every man that converses with him or in his hearing is in danger of being misrepresented by him." In Richmond, Eaton drank heavily in the local taverns. He drew every eye and ear by regularly denouncing the president while garbed in brightly colored outfits from his Saharan adventures, including a broad sash and what was described as a "tremendous hat."[6]

On the witness stand, however, Eaton deported himself with dignity. Seated a few feet from the former vice president, Eaton coolly spun his story, practiced from many tellings. Burr's goal, he said, was "revolutionizing the territory west of the Allegheny; establishing an independent empire there; New Orleans to be the capital, and he himself to be the chief." Burr was relying on Wilkinson to bring the army to his side, Eaton continued, and he viewed western revolution "as a matter of right, inherent in the people, and constitutional."[7]

Eaton's testimony could not convict Burr on the charges before the court. It did not concern events on Blennerhassett Island, nor did it involve an overt act of treason. But it still made for a stunning moment. After all the rumors, an apparently sane human being was calmly describing Burr's dream in all of its audacity.

On cross-examination, Burr tried to challenge Eaton by emphasizing the witness's odd proposal to Jefferson that he divert Burr from insurrection with an appointment to a high diplomatic post. The witness gave as good as he got:

BURR.　　　　　Was it after all this that you recommended me to
　　　　　　　　the president, for an embassy?

EATON.	Yes; to remove you, as you were a dangerous man, because I thought it the only way to avoid a civil war.
BURR.	Did you communicate this to me, and what did I say?
EATON.	Yes; you seemed to assent to the proposition.
BURR.	What had become of your command [in Burr's expedition]?
EATON.	*That* I had disposed of myself.
BURR.	Did you understand that you had given me a definite answer [to accept the command]?
EATON.	No ... I determined to use you, until I got everything out of you; and on the principle that, "when innocence is in danger, to break faith with a bad man is not fraud, but virtue."[8]

The prosecution had less luck with its next witness, Commodore Truxtun, described by one contemporary as "vanity's eldest legitimate son."[9] After much cajoling and intercession by friends, Burr had managed to restore warm feelings between himself and Truxtun, and the sailor appeared as a prosecution witness in name only.

"I know nothing of overt acts, treasonable designs, or conversations on the part of Colonel Burr," Truxtun began. Hay, one court reporter wrote, seemed "indisposed to examine the witness." According to Truxtun, Burr spoke of leading an expedition to Mexico only if there was war with Spain. When a prosecutor asked whether Burr tried to fill Truxtun's mind with resentment against the government, the witness shrugged. "I was pretty full of it myself, and he joined me in [the] opinion."[10]

Ten more witnesses steadily weakened the prosecution case over the next two days. Marshall held court for seven hours each day, from nine in the morning until four in the afternoon, and the days were long for George Hay. Colonel Thomas Morgan of Pennsylvania and his two sons spoke of Burr's visit in the late summer of 1806 but described only conversations, not actions, and certainly not overt acts of treason. Seven witnesses described the preparations on Blennerhassett Island in December 1806, but all agreed that Burr was not there. Even the preparations sounded inconsequential, particularly the absence of military weapons. One witness reported trying but failing to acquire weapons for Blennerhassett to use in resisting the Wood County vigilantes.

One moment of drama came during the testimony of a laborer for Blennerhassett. The man described a tense confrontation between the adventurers and General Edward Tupper of the Ohio militia on the night of December 10. Tupper, the witness said, put his hand on Harman Blennerhassett and stated he was arresting him under Ohio law. The witness claimed that seven or eight men pointed their guns at Tupper and forced him to relent.

Here, the prosecution hoped, was an act of armed resistance to duly constituted authority, an overt act of treason.

The testimony, however, had a fatal weakness: General Tupper denied it. On cross-examination, Burr deflated the story with two simple questions. First he asked, "Did you know General Tupper?" The witness said he did. Pointing to Tupper, who was seated prominently in the Hall of Delegates, Burr asked, "Is that the gentleman?" The witness said yes again. Burr thus planted in the jurors' mind the inevitable question: If General Tupper sat less than twenty feet away, why did the government not call him as a witness? The answer was obvious, as Tupper later swore in a deposition. He said he never tried to arrest Blennerhassett and that no one on the island acted toward him in a hostile fashion.[11]

On the third day of testimony, Burr asked Marshall to stop the trial because there was no evidence of an overt act of treason. The argument on Burr's motion began while the prosecution waited for two more witnesses to arrive. When those two did testify, they added little: They had been on Blennerhassett Island on December 10 but had seen neither Burr nor military weapons.

To begin argument on this pivotal motion, John Wickham rose from the defense table. He knew how to win a jury's trust. "Upon a first address to a stranger," Blennerhassett wrote, Wickham "possesses a talent of infusing into his manner an air of ease and friendly interest that is truly adapted at once to engage the hearts of his acquaintance[s]."[12] Wickham cemented his high reputation with a full day of argument, squarely though politely challenging Marshall to reconsider his statements in *Ex Parte Bollman* that a defendant can be guilty of treason for actions, "however remote," from the actual levying of war.

The Richmond lawyer relied heavily on common sense. Burr, he repeatedly pointed out, was nowhere near the island on December 10. Wickham disparaged evidence that there were guns on the island. "In the upper country every man has a gun," he said. "A majority of the people have guns everywhere." And as for the laborer's story of the standoff with General Tupper, Wickham emphasized that the prosecutors never called Tupper as a witness.[13]

Wickham's speech began a saturnalia of oratory that resounded over the next eight days. For more than fifty hours, the judges listened to impassioned addresses by six defense lawyers and three prosecutors. The lawyers dissected hoary precedents from Mary Queen of Scots through the Scottish rising for Bonnie Prince Charlie, up to the Whiskey Rebellion and Fries's Rebellion in the United States during the 1790s. At least twice a day, often during a learned exegesis of an obscure issue, the chief justice posed a difficult question to a lawyer, thereby proving—against all odds—that he was still alert and following the argument.

It was the grandest stage for lawyers that the young nation had yet provided. The irrepressible Luther Martin solidified his reputation, for good and ill. In a letter to President Jefferson, Hay marveled at Martin's stamina through a fourteen-hour speech, "which does not appear to have the slightest effect [on Martin], even in his voice." The Maryland lawyer, however, could be a loose cannon; at one point, Burr had to interrupt his own lawyer to correct Martin's statement of the defense position.[14]

Martin's personal habits continued to disgust the sensitive, and his personal warmth to charm others. He sipped brandy from a mug through long hot days in the courtroom. After one trial day, Blennerhassett observed that Martin had been "more in his cups than usual," yet "he was happy in all his hits."[15] Blennerhassett was repulsed by Martin's "preternatural secretion or excretion of saliva which embarrasses his delivery," as well as his rude manners, ungrammatical language, and "the verbosity and repetitions of his style." Blennerhassett declared him the "Thersites of the law," comparing him to the Homeric character who, though vulgar and obscene, spoke truth to King Agamemnon and Achilles.[16]

The bombastic Luther Martin of Maryland delivered immense addresses during the trial in Richmond. One lasted for two days; another for three.

On the morning of his second day, Martin paused in his torrent of words to scorn the prosecution evidence: "I would call it the will o' the wisp treason. For though it is said to be here and there and everywhere, yet it is nowhere. It exists only in the newspapers." He also fervently called for the judges to gird their loins in defense of Aaron Burr's liberty.

> When bleak clouds enshroud the sky with darkness, when the tempest rages, the winds howl and the waves break over us—when the thunders awfully roar over our heads and lightnings of heaven blaze around us—it is *then* that all the energies of the human soul are called into action. It is *then* that the truly brave man stands firm at his post.[17]

On the prosecution side, William Wirt carried off the forensic honors. He mocked the defense, which aimed to reduce "the world of evidence . . . to the speck, the atom which relates to Blennerhassett Island." Clinging with both hands to the chief justice's statement in *Ex Parte Bollman*, Wirt implored the judges to lift their eyes from the island in the Ohio River: "Here the object was not an island," he insisted, but an "empire of the west." [18]

Wirt contrasted Burr with Blennerhassett in a passage that, for generations after, would be assigned to schoolchildren to memorize. Wirt's "Who is Blennerhassett?" speech darkened the memory of Burr through all those generations. Wirt answered the question thus:

> On his arrival in America, [Blennerhassett] retired even from the population of the Atlantic States, and sought quiet and solitude in the bosom of the western forests. . . . Possessing himself of a beautiful island in the Ohio, he rears upon it a palace and decorates it with every romantic embellishment of fancy. A shrubbery that Shenstone might have envied blooms around him. Music that might have charmed Calypso and her nymphs is his. An extensive library spreads its treasures before him. . . . Peace, tranquility and innocence shed their mingled delights around him. And to crown the enchantment of the scene, a wife, who is said to be lovely even beyond her sex and graced with every accomplishment that can render it irresistible. . . .

Into this Eden slithered Burr:

With his "Who is Blennerhassett?" speech, prosecutor William Wirt created a staple for schoolboy oratory throughout the nineteenth century.

The destroyer comes; he comes to change this paradise into a hell. . . . Introduced to their civilities by the high rank which he had lately held in this country, he soon finds his way to their hearts, by the dignity and elegance of his demeanor, the light and beauty of his conversation and the attractive and fascinating power of his address. The conquest was not difficult. Innocence is ever simple and credulous. . . . Such was the state of Eden when the serpent entered its bowers. The prisoner [Burr] . . . winding himself into the open and unpracticed heart of the unfortunate Blennerhassett, found but little difficulty in changing the native character of that heart and the objects of its affection. By degrees he infuses into it the fire of his own courage; a daring and desperate thirst for glory; and ardor panting for great enterprises, for all the storm and bustle and hurricane of life.[19]

While Wirt used rhetoric to try to rise above the government's weak evidence, George Hay could not do the same. He began his speech on the wrong foot, clumsily referring to the impeachment charges brought against Justice Samuel Chase for his conduct of a 1797 treason trial. Hay appeared to be threatening Marshall with impeachment if he ruled for Burr. Even the hint of such a threat was highly improper. Moreover, intimidation would not work with John Marshall.[20]

Hay strained to tie Burr to Blennerhassett Island, insisting that the adventurers "met there by his procurement and direction; they leave it by his direction, and he afterwards joins them and takes command." Hay also argued that even if the evidence did not demonstrate that the adventurers levied war on the United States, he should be permitted to present his proof that Burr intended to do so. The chief justice had long since rejected that contention.[21]

When the lawyers finally fell silent on Saturday, August 29, the entire burden of the case rested on John Marshall. That evening and through the next day, Marshall labored over the longest judicial opinion he ever wrote.

Back in the Hall of Delegates on Monday morning, August 31, the chief justice paid tribute to the lawyers for "eloquence seldom displayed on any occasion." The meaning of the treason clause of the Constitution, he said, was of "infinite moment," and much of his opinion focused on the interpretation of the phrase "levying war." Within a few minutes, Marshall was wrestling with his earlier statements in *Ex Parte Bollman*, explaining that, due to the alignment of the justices in the case, the issue might warrant further review by the Supreme Court. At that point, the lawyers knew: If Marshall would not defend his apparent endorsement of constructive treason in *Ex Parte Bollman*, Burr was going to win.

The chief justice walked a careful line. An assemblage of men dedicated to levying war on the United States was treason; war and bloodshed were not required. But the assemblage had to have the "appearance of war" and involve "actual force."

Then Marshall turned to the indictment. Every accused person is entitled, he observed, to face only those charges stated in an indictment. He rejected the prosecution's claim that the indictment covered the passage of the adventurers down the river, including Burr's rendezvous with them at the mouth of the Cumberland. "The whole treason laid in this indictment," he said, "is the levying of war in Blennerhassett Island." Yet Burr was not there:

> If he was not with the party at any time before they reached the island . . . if his personal cooperation in the general plan was to be afforded elsewhere . . . then he was not of the particular party assembled at Blennerhassett Island and was not constructively present.

Marshall refused to allow further testimony about Burr "elsewhere and subsequent to the transaction on Blennerhassett Island," though he would accept evidence that the meeting on the island "was procured by the prisoner." [22]

After studying Marshall's opinion overnight, Hay admitted defeat. He had no evidence that the chief justice would accept. The witnesses who could connect Burr to Blennerhassett Island—Bollman or Comfort Tyler or Blennerhassett himself—would not testify. Marshall sent the jury to deliberate on the hodgepodge of evidence it had heard from fourteen witnesses. It returned in twenty-five minutes with an extraordinary verdict. The foreman read it: "We of the jury say that Aaron Burr is *not proved to be guilty under this indictment by any evidence submitted to us.* We therefore find him not guilty."

The verdict dripped with disappointment that the chief justice had left the jury no way to convict the defendant. Burr and his lawyers vaulted from their seats. The jury should be directed, Burr insisted, to return a verdict of either "guilty" or "not guilty." The jury should not be permitted to editorialize that Burr was "not proved" guilty, then qualify that grudging statement with the phrases "under this indictment" and "by any evidence submitted to us." Marshall let the verdict stand, though he instructed the clerk to enter it as "not guilty."[23]

"Marshall has stepped in between Burr and death," wrote William Wirt. "He has pronounced an opinion that our evidence is all irrelevant, Burr not having been present at the island with the assemblage, and the act itself not amounting to levying war." Attorney General Caesar Rodney agreed. "C[hief] Justice Marshall has," he wrote, "acquitted Burr."

George Hay's report to the president was bitter. The chief justice's opinion, he wrote, was "too obscure and perplexed to be understood." Marshall's discussion of *Ex Parte Bollman*, Hay continued, "renders it very difficult to comprehend what was before perfectly clear." Jefferson was no less bitter. He wrote to General Wilkinson that Marshall's ruling was "equivalent to a proclamation of impunity to every traitorous combination which may be formed to destroy the Union."

Physically and emotionally, Hay was a beaten man. Following the death of his wife in March, he had been running uphill for months, wrangling witnesses to Richmond, contesting the meaning of the Constitution with two men (Luther Martin and Edmund Randolph) who had helped write it, facing relentless opposition from a talented defense team, trying to make sense of his own poorly written indictment, all in front of a whip-smart judge who never accepted the prosecution's theory of Burr's treason. "My strength and flesh are declining," Hay told Jefferson. "I believe that the judge by cutting off all the trials here, saved my life."[24]

Marshall had saved Aaron Burr's life too.

25

A Drawn Battle

Richmond
September–November 1807

Despite the failure of the treason case against Burr, Jefferson was in no mood to give up. "It is now more indispensable than ever," he wrote to Hay, "that not a single witness be paid or permitted to depart until his testimony has been committed to writing either as delivered in court, or as taken by yourself." The president wanted to lay the fullest possible record before Congress so it could decide for itself whether "the defect has been in the evidence of guilt, or in the law, or in the application of the law." If he could not convict Burr in a court of law, Jefferson meant to convict him in the eyes of history.

Jefferson still feared Burr, complaining that the acquittal might make him the "rallying point of all the disaffected and the worthless." And the president still hoped to convict Burr of violating the Neutrality Act, where-upon the chief justice "must in decency give us some respite by some short confinement of him [Burr]." Jefferson exhorted Hay to soldier on. If the Neutrality Act prosecution failed, the president insisted, it "will heap coals of fire on the heads of the judges"; if successful, it would allow the government to mount a new treason prosecution against Burr, perhaps in Kentucky.[1]

First, however, the prosecutors had to sort through the rubble of their case to determine what remained. Within a few days, they dropped the treason charges against the other defendants. Hay resolved to try the Neutrality Act charges against Burr in Richmond and agreed that the others could post bail on that accusation.[2]

The Neutrality Act charge had its own defects. It accused Burr of violating the statute in seven minutely different ways: by beginning a military expedition against Spanish possessions, by "setting on foot" the expedition, by providing the means for it, and by doing so against Mexico (specifically), or against a "foreign territory unknown." The charges tracked the treason indictment in too many ways: the same massive run-on sentences bristling with formalistic language, and the same obsessive focus on events on Blennerhassett Island on December 10, 1806, when Burr was somewhere else.[3]

Chief Justice Marshall began the Neutrality Act trial on Wednesday, September 9. A new jury was chosen in only two days. Burr no longer worried about the biased jurors of Virginia, not with John Marshall presiding. In a brief opening statement, Hay argued that Burr's military expedition did not have to succeed to be illegal; the statute made it illegal simply to begin a military expedition.

Hay's first three witnesses stumbled through unremarkable testimony about events on the island in December.[4] When Hay called as a witness the printer who published Blennerhassett's "Querist" articles, the defense table roared to life. Burr argued that the printer could testify only about a military expedition, not about conversations with Blennerhassett when Burr was not present.

For three and a half days, the lawyers raged over this evidentiary question. The prosecutors demanded the right to present the evidence in the order they thought best. The defense lawyers objected to any testimony that did not demonstrate that Burr had provided "military means" on Blennerhassett Island. Chief Justice Marshall complained that the prosecutors were proceeding as though they had brought a conspiracy case, where testimony involving one conspirator could be heard against all conspirators. This indictment alleged no conspiracy.[5]

The crowds at the Hall of Delegates were thinning. Even the court stenographers were losing interest. One condensed the entire Neutrality Act trial into a few pages, while another omitted big chunks of the lawyers' arguments as "desultory" or "uninteresting."

On the morning of Monday, September 14, the chief justice ruled that the government's evidence had to "go directly to prove the charges laid in the indictment," which did not include conspiracy. He would accept evidence demonstrating that Burr's expedition was military, or was directed at Spanish territory. He would not accept statements by people who were not part of the expedition, made outside of Burr's presence. Acknowledging that Burr probably initiated the expedition, Marshall still insisted that the evidence must prove that he provided the "means" for it, as the indictment charged.[6]

The prosecutors persevered for a few more witnesses. With Burr demanding that only evidence of events on the island could be presented, William Wirt protested that each event was "one link in the great chain." Finally showing a trace of temper after enduring many weeks of the Burr case, Marshall suggested that the prosecutors should "consider whether they are not wasting the time and money of the United States, and of all those persons who are forced to attend here, whilst they are producing such a mass of testimony which does not bear upon the cause."[7]

Even Hay got the message. He tried to dismiss the Neutrality Act charges, but Burr insisted he was entitled to a jury verdict. Marshall agreed. After twenty minutes of deliberation, the jury declared Burr not guilty.

Hay dismissed the Neutrality Act charges against the other defendants, but he announced that the government wished to press a new treason case against Burr in another jurisdiction. He read through a much simpler treason indictment: that Burr and others had committed treason by levying war against the United States "at the mouth of the Cumberland River, in the state of Kentucky," and by other overt acts of levying war "at Bayou Pierre, in the Mississippi Territory, and on the Mississippi River, between the places above named." Hay asked the court to determine where Burr could be tried on this new charge.[8]

Even with Hay's new charges, things were looking distinctly up for Burr; his liberty secure for at least the immediate future, Theodosia and her husband returned to South Carolina. The former vice president began to entertain. Blennerhassett reported that Burr was "gay as usual, and as busy in speculations of reorganizing his projects for action, as if he had never suffered the least interruption." Burr again huddled with Jonathan Dayton. Incredibly, he urged Blennerhassett and Israel Smith to "remount" their western expedition, now "having a clearer view of the ground, and a more perfect knowledge of our men." Scarcely believing Burr's suggestion, the two men sat silent. Had the man forgotten what a disaster the first expedition had been? Did he really think any of the adventurers would be willing to try again?[9]

Burr attended to the ladies of Richmond. Receiving a perfumed note during a dinner party, he ostentatiously inhaled its scent and passed the envelope, still sealed, among his guests. He launched into an anecdote concerning a lady and perfume, the telling of which, according to Blennerhassett, "sunk full 15 years off his age." (Burr was fifty-one.) The Irishman marveled at Burr's "temperament and address which . . . seems to uphold his ascendancy over the sex."[10]

In court, the prosecutors asked the chief justice to arraign Burr, Blennerhassett, and Israel Smith for trial on the new treason charges. The case would be prosecuted, Hay said, in a western jurisdiction. Hay's request raised only the preliminary question whether there was probable cause for believing that Burr had committed that crime, which meant that Marshall was presiding over a preliminary hearing without a jury. The judge's attitude shifted dramatically. Now, he emphasized, he was acting on his own as an examining magistrate. No longer did he have a duty to screen improper evidence from a jury. After five weeks of helping the defense tie the prosecution in knots, Marshall began to rule in favor of the government.

Burr and his lawyers tried to short-circuit the proceeding by arguing that he had just been acquitted on treason charges. Surely that acquittal, under double jeopardy principles, foreclosed a new treason prosecution. "This is the sixth trial which I have had to encounter," Burr complained, "and it seems really desirous that I should know how many trials a man may undergo for the same thing."[11]

Burr's arithmetic was superficially flawless, though not every court proceeding had been a full-fledged trial: He had survived two attempted grand jury investigations in Kentucky, one in Mississippi, and had won two full trials in Virginia. But the chief justice was not sympathetic. Hay had finally framed a coherent accusation.

The government now charged that Burr's overt act of treason had occurred when he joined the adventurers at the mouth of the Cumberland River. That overt act actually involved Burr. Moreover, by the time the expedition reached the mouth of the Cumberland, it had more than doubled in size. Eight witnesses would testify that it had acquired military weapons, including muskets, bayonets, and tomahawks.[12] The first treason prosecution had to concentrate on Blennerhassett Island in order to keep the case in a Virginia court. A case in a western court would be free of that constraint. On the other hand, Burr was correct that new treason charges raised the risk that Burr would be tried a second time for the same crime, in violation of the double jeopardy clause of the Fifth Amendment. The new charges resembled those on which Burr had already been acquitted. But Burr could not press his double jeopardy objection until a grand jury actually indicted him. The current proceeding before the chief justice was merely a preliminary arraignment. Marshall let the government go forward.

Another factor in Marshall's decision may have been the public reaction to the two acquittals so far. Republican newspapers sharply criticized him. "Burr acquitted, though guilty," ran the headline in the *Philadelphia Aurora*. Burr's acquittal, one Virginian wrote, "has excited the wonder of many, and numbers there are who accuse the chief justice of undue exertions to screen the traitor from the pains of the crime." Jefferson's views in a private letter were more extreme:

> The scenes which have been acting at Richmond are sufficient to fill us with alarm. We had supposed we possessed fixed laws to guard us equally against treason and oppression. But it now appears we have no law but the will of the judge.[13]

Marshall was particularly irritated by the contention that he had reversed his earlier decision in *Ex Parte Bollman*, and he said so in open court.[14]

Nevertheless, the change in the judge's attitude was dramatic. Defense objections were now brushed aside or ignored.[15] A dozen adventurers, who had been loitering in Richmond for weeks, finally testified. They described an expedition with a decidedly military flavor, featuring drill, weapons, and a chain of command. Yet many of the adventurers, out of self-preservation, professed to be uncertain what the expedition's purpose was.

By Monday, September 21, Burr recognized he was losing ground. "There may be need of apology," he said meekly while explaining an objection to Marshall, "for such apparent opposition to what appears to be the mind of the court."[16]

Burr and his colleagues closely questioned the government witnesses. Burr sometimes contradicted witnesses about facts that he knew firsthand—in effect, giving his own unsworn testimony.[17] He continued to demand originals of the letters sent by Wilkinson to Jefferson on October 21 and November 12 of the previous year, but Marshall made clear that the defense would have to make do with edited copies Hay had provided.[18]

With the judicial floodgates open, the prosecutors paraded three dozen witnesses through the courtroom. "It is impossible to predict when this business may terminate," Burr wrote to Theodosia on September 28, "as the chief justice has gradually relaxed from former rules of evidence, and will now hear anything."[19] Public interest in the trial sank to new lows.

One moment of high drama remained: General Wilkinson, at long last, would testify in public.

On Saturday, September 26, Wilkinson took the stand. After his drubbing at the hands of the grand jury and after Burr's two acquittals, the general had lost his strut. According to Blennerhassett, he "exhibited the manner of a sergeant under court martial rather than the demeanor of an accusing officer confronted with his culprit."[20]

Wilkinson began with Sam Swartwout's arrival in Natchitoches the previous October, when he delivered the cipher letter. This led to the awkward but unavoidable fact of the general's alterations of the cipher letter. The defense lawyers queued up to cross-examine in their customary tag-team format. When Wilkinson began his second day of testimony, he asked Marshall for permission to clarify earlier remarks, as he feared misunderstandings could have resulted from "the rapidity with which the interrogatories were put, and the promptitude of my answers." The prosecutors tried to

protect the general; they presented affidavits from other witnesses to justify
his alterations of the cipher letter, or to explain the cipher itself. But he was
a difficult witness to protect.[21]

On Tuesday, September 29, John Wickham grilled Wilkinson for hours,
several times making him squirm, particularly over his extralegal efforts to
kidnap Burr and the orders he had received from his superiors:

> MR. WICKHAM. Did you receive any orders to attack Col. Burr and
>   his party?
> [WILKINSON.]   That question may require some qualification.
> MR. WICKHAM. Did you send any officer in disguise to take Col.
>   Burr?
> [WILKINSON.]   I sent three.
> MR. WICKHAM. Their names?
> [Objection by Mr. Hay]
> [WILKINSON.]   If the question goes to criminate myself, I presume
>   that I am not bound to answer. . . .
> MR. WICKHAM. Did you direct them to go without uniform?
> [WILKINSON.]   I feel real delicacy in revealing my orders.

Wilkinson's already slight credibility suffered from his refusals to
answer. When Wickham asked whether the general seized private letters
directly from the post office, he declined to answer. Did he have orders to
arrest Swartwout and Bollman? Wilkinson was not sure he should answer
that, either. At day's end, Blennerhassett exulted that Wickham had been
"masterly and ingenious."[22]

Then there was the correspondence between the general and Burr.
Wilkinson said he could not recall much about the letter he wrote to Burr
from Natchitoches the previous October, then had intercepted himself and
destroyed in Natchez. As to the letters that he and Burr still possessed from
each other, the two adversaries maintained their positions of mutual deter-
rence: Neither would violate the trust of the other gentleman by disclosing a
confidential letter. So much for the search for truth.[23]

The general fell back on his performance skills, but they were wearing
thin. On Wilkinson's third day of testimony, a stenographer recorded that

the general protested his truthfulness "before God (turning up his eyes to heaven, and placing his hands on his heart)."[24]

By the time Wilkinson was done, even George Hay did not believe him. Hay urged Jefferson to investigate the general. "My confidence in him," Hay wrote to the president, "is shaken if not destroyed. I am sorry for it, on my own account, in the public account, and because you have expressed opinions in his favor. But you did not know then what you will soon know."[25]

After the evidence was in, the lawyers stepped up for closing arguments. For seven days, the hall again echoed with learned speeches. Luther Martin consumed three days with an address that Blennerhassett deplored for "want of arrangement, verbosity, and eternal repetitions."[26]

Not until October 30 did the chief justice end the struggle. After nearly three months, he cast the barest glimmer of light toward the prosecution. Having listened closely to the adventurers, Marshall was particularly struck by Burr's reticence when he addressed them at the mouth of the Cumberland. Burr said then that he could not disclose his plans to them. The key point, Marshall emphasized, was that Burr did *not* say he intended to settle the Ouachita: "He did not wish those to whom he addressed himself to consider the Ouachita as his real ultimate object." But the chief justice had heard little evidence that Burr was aiming his force at the United States. As he first ruled in *Ex Parte Bollman* more than eight months before, Marshall held that "the enterprise was really designed against Mexico." Burr's use of New Orleans as a staging area could have subverted the American government there, but the charge was that Burr had committed his overt act of treason at the mouth of the Cumberland, not in New Orleans. In any event, Burr's expedition never reached New Orleans. Consequently, Marshall refused to sustain the treason charges, though he did find probable cause that Burr had violated the Neutrality Act at the mouth of the Cumberland by setting on foot an invasion of Mexico.[27]

Burr and Blennerhassett each posted $3,000 bail on the Neutrality Act charge, which was transferred to the federal court in Ohio. Steadfast Luther Martin posted half of Burr's bail.

"After all," Burr wrote to Theodosia, "this is a sort of drawn battle." He saw the chief justice's final opinion as "a sacrifice of principle to conciliate Jack Cade"—Burr's derogatory term for Jefferson, comparing him to a populist rebel in fifteenth-century England. Burr reported that George Hay would recommend against any further prosecution. Burr, it seemed, might just be a free man.[28]

The remarkable feature of the Richmond trials of Aaron Burr was how much evidence was not presented against him: not the Burr-Wilkinson letters that neither man would release, even as Burr simultaneously demanded copies of the president's correspondence; not the diplomatic reports of Burr's treasonous overtures to the Spanish and British ministers, which would lie buried in diplomatic archives for decades; not the testimony of any witnesses from his inner circle, such as Bollman or Dayton or Sam Swartwout. The mores of criminal prosecution were very different in the early nineteenth century. Neither the prosecutors nor the chief justice thought they should compel the production of confidential letters. After Erich Bollman refused to accept a pardon in return for giving his testimony, George Hay never offered any of Jefferson's blank pardons to the other Burr insiders: Sam Swartwout, John Adair, John Smith, Jonathan Dayton, Comfort Tyler, Israel Smith, Harman Blennerhassett, or Davis Floyd.

Moreover, two features of Hay's indictments cost the prosecutors the ability to present much of the evidence they had assembled. The heavy focus on events on Blennerhassett Island on December 10, 1806, driven by the decision to try Burr in Virginia, hamstrung the prosecutors terribly. Burr, after all, was not on the island then. To ensure a trial in Virginia, the prosecutors imposed this drastic limitation on their case. It proved a poor bargain.

The second defect was the absence of a conspiracy allegation, which the chief justice noted, and which made even more evidence inadmissible. This defect is puzzling, because the grand jury indicted seven individuals for both treason and violating the Neutrality Act. Charging those individuals with conspiring with one another, and with others known and unknown, would have been both simple and logical. The result might have been a more complicated trial with multiple defendants, but far more evidence could have been presented in such a proceeding.

Prosecutors in the twenty-first century would be appalled by Hay's delicacy about acquiring evidence and testimony, while the doctrines of criminal law have become considerably friendlier to the prosecution. Broad conspiracy allegations and a plethora of federal criminal statutes now can be applied to conduct like Burr's. Prosecutors today would instantly demand all documents from Burr and Wilkinson, seek papers from foreign governments through diplomatic channels, and begin offering immunity from prosecution to Burr's associates in return for their testimony. A witness who refused a grant of immunity, as Bollman did, now would likely be thrown in jail until he changed his mind. Without deploying such tools, Burr's prosecutors were left to pursue him through a darkened room where only he knew the location of the furniture.

In dissecting Marshall's decisions in the Burr case, some scholars have concluded that his narrow application of the law of treason erected an invaluable rampart against despotism. Others have seen his actions as politically motivated payback against his distant cousin in the executive mansion.[29] Both versions overlook the courtroom reality that Marshall confronted, beginning with the *Ex Parte Bollman* hearing in February: The government presented no evidence of overt acts of treason by Burr.

The case frames a central historical irony. Marshall, the last great figure of the aristocratic Federalist party, proponent of strong national power, shut down this national security prosecution and tenaciously protected Burr's rights. Jefferson, the supposed advocate of individual liberty, proclaimed Burr's guilt on the basis of fragmentary evidence, then avidly pursued Burr's conviction in flawed prosecutions. The Richmond trials underscored the wisdom of Jefferson's professed policy of avoiding legal conversations with John Marshall, since his cousin always seemed to get the better of him. Marshall did it again in 1807.

Though Marshall concluded the Burr trials with his reputation intact, even burnished in some quarters, he later called it "the most unpleasant case which has ever been brought before a Judge in this or perhaps in any other country." In an odd aside, he said he wished he could have treated the trial "as a jest . . . but it was most deplorably serious and I could not give the subject a different aspect by treating it in any manner which was in my power."[30]

During the trial and long after, Jefferson stood by the odious General Wilkinson. He never defended the general against the ample evidence that

Wilkinson had initially joined Burr's enterprise and that he was a paid agent of Spain. But the president stoutly championed Wilkinson's repressive regime in New Orleans. Here Jefferson the idealist took a backseat to Jefferson the practical politician. "A strict observance of the written laws is doubtless one of the high duties of a good citizen," he later wrote about the episode, "but it is not the highest." He continued:

> The laws of necessity, of self-preservation, of saving our country when in danger, are of higher obligation. To lose our country by a scrupulous adherence to written law, would be to lose the law itself, with life, liberty, property and all those who are enjoying them with us; thus absurdly sacrificing the end to the means.

In Jefferson's view, Wilkinson wisely established military rule in New Orleans and correctly arrested Burr's associates without legal process. Without those steps, Jefferson feared that the critical situation would have been controlled by "the tardiness and weakness of the law, apathy of the judges, active patronage of the whole tribe of lawyers, unknown disposition of the judges, [and] an hourly expectation of the enemy." The debate about means and ends is an eternal one, but when it came to Burr's expedition, Jefferson cared little about the means.[31]

Though Jefferson's legal strategy failed, his unorthodox response to Burr's political challenge was entirely successful. Through most of 1806, while reports piled up that Burr was fomenting secession and insurrection, Jefferson bided his time. When the president finally moved, prompted by Wilkinson's message from Orleans Territory, the timing proved to be perfect: late enough that there was mounting evidence of Burr's nefarious intentions, early enough to discourage many of Burr's supporters, and at a moment when Burr could not effectively counter Jefferson's accusations. When the dust settled, Jefferson had eliminated Burr as a political force in the United States.

By February 1808, Jefferson could happily write to George Hay of Burr's disappearance from the public scene: "Burr, who gave you so much trouble, has become absolutely invisible. There are conjectures of his being in Philadelphia, but nobody can say they have seen him."[32]

Although Jefferson declared victory, Aaron Burr would not admit defeat. While the trials were still grinding on in Richmond, he had been laying plans to travel to London, there to seek support for a military expedition to liberate Spain's American colonies. As the threat of war over the *Chesapeake/Leopard* affair receded, the Spanish possessions still called to him. Despite enduring six court proceedings and still facing a seventh, despite being hauled as a prisoner through a thousand miles of wilderness and being jailed in the Richmond penitentiary, despite the many creditors who circled wherever he happened to rest, and even though the lives of many of his friends had been blighted by their association with him, Aaron Burr would not relinquish his dream.[33]

26

To Britain

America to Great Britain
October 1807–May 1809

I n late October 1807, Burr headed north from Richmond. He caught up
with Blennerhassett and Luther Martin in Baltimore, but the city was
far from welcoming. In language mimicking the cipher letter, handbills
announced the hanging at three o'clock of "four 'choice spirits'": Burr,
Chief Justice Marshall, Blennerhassett, and "Lawyer Brandy-Bottle." Fifteen
hundred citizens, according to Blennerhassett, marched through the streets,
hauling four effigies in two carts, "in full huzza, with fife and drum—playing
the rogue's march." After breaking windows at Luther Martin's house,
which was guarded by armed men loyal to him, the mob strung up the effigies and burned them.[1]

The refugees from the Richmond trial found a more placid reception
in Philadelphia, where Blennerhassett confronted Burr over the money he
had lost on the expedition. Though lawsuits filed against Burr in Richmond
demanded $36,000 (over $1.4 million in today's money), the Irishman was
convinced that Burr had ample resources hidden away. Blennerhassett's belief proved to be wishful thinking. Burr was reduced to bartering with some

creditors by giving them family portraits. Turned away without a dime, Blennerhassett dismissed his former leader as "a heartless swindler in the last swoon of his disorder."[2]

Burr endured dark days in Philadelphia. The elation of his acquittal in Richmond dissipated when he faced the harsh realities of his situation. He was a political untouchable now, a rival to Benedict Arnold for the title of most despised American. He had neither money nor property and could not ply his profession, the law. No client would wish to be identified with him. At a dinner party, Blennerhassett thought Burr seemed dejected. When Charles Biddle visited in the evenings, he usually found Burr alone, "with little light in his room," looking pale and depressed. Biddle feared his friend would "end his sufferings with a pistol."[3]

In mid-November, good news came from New Jersey. The state's supreme court quashed the three-year-old indictment against him for murdering Hamilton. Burr resolved not to appear in Ohio for the federal prosecution on the Neutrality Act indictment. The case sputtered for many months more, but the government ultimately abandoned it.[4]

Only one man from Burr's expedition was convicted of a crime. An Indiana court convicted Davis Floyd of violating the Neutrality Act. He was jailed for three hours. Upon Floyd's release, the Indiana territorial assembly quickly appointed him its clerk.[5]

A special Senate committee investigated Senator John Smith of Ohio, who had conferred so often with Burr and followed him down the Mississippi rather than take his seat in Congress. A report composed by John Quincy Adams concluded that without the government's intervention, Burr would have caused "a war of the most horrible description . . . both foreign and domestic." Adams dismissed the acquittals in Richmond as the offspring of "artificial rules" which obscured "the daylight of evidence." The Senate voted to expel Smith by a margin of 19 to 10, one vote short of the two-thirds majority required. Smith resigned his seat anyway.[6]

Controversy continued to follow General Wilkinson. He challenged two of his adversaries to duels: defense lawyer John Wickham and Congressman John Randolph, foreman of the Richmond grand jury. Neither agreed to fight. Randolph's patronizing reply enraged the general. "In you, sir, I recognize no right to hold me accountable for my public or private opinion of your character," Randolph wrote. "I cannot descend to your level." When the general issued a second challenge, the congressman made no reply at all. Wilkinson retaliated by posting handbills in Washington City calling Randolph "a prevaricating, base, calumniating scoundrel, poltroon, and coward."[7]

Jefferson continued to protect the general. To forestall a congressional investigation into Wilkinson's involvement in Burr's expedition, the president arranged for Wilkinson to face a court-martial before three officers who were the general's creatures. They produced a whitewash.[8]

To dig himself out of his depression, Burr sought the remedy he had always prescribed to Theodosia for the "fiend ennui": activity. He needed a purpose that was worthy of his talents, and he found a familiar one. He resolved to pursue anew the dream of glory in a military expedition to liberate Spanish colonies. If he could not launch that expedition from the United States, perhaps he could find a sponsor in Europe. He had to know his chances for success were slight, but he once more set off to achieve the unlikely.

Turning his back on the many aftershocks of his expedition, Burr set his sights on London. When Theodosia came to see him off in June 1808, he fretted over her inconsistent health and lectured her about writing style and deportment. Burr, who would sail under the pseudonym "G.H. Edwards," using his mother's maiden name, instructed Theodosia to sign her letters as "Mary Ann Melville." His letters from Britain, he warned, would be disguised with various signatures and handwriting, "sometimes feminine."[9]

Although Burr's penchant for secrecy could seem exaggerated, his new venture involved considerable risk. He was ducking out on the still-pending Ohio prosecution to travel to a Europe that had known mostly revolution and war for the last twenty years. There, despite his own government's hostility toward him, he proposed to enter political intrigues at the highest level in order to tear away Spain's colonial empire. In any event, his efforts at secrecy were, as usual, unsuccessful. As early as December 1807, a British diplomat was informing his government that Burr would come to London and claim that with a moderate financial subsidy, he could gather forces to "subdue the Floridas, Cuba and revolutionize South America." Somehow, the fear of Burr survived his signal failures on the western rivers. The diplomat added:

His enterprising spirit can not easily be curbed. . . . He will be constantly exerting his great abilities in contriving schemes to vex and harass those whom he considers as the authors of his misfortunes, who have much to apprehend from the extraordinary faculties he possesses.

When Burr boarded his ship, *Clarissa Ann,* Theodosia indulged both "tears and reproaches" over his perilous course. Having failed to rally his own countrymen to his cause, what prospects could he have in a foreign land? Yet Burr's optimism returned with the invigorating bustle of departure. Calling his journey the "grand Hegira," he sailed east.[10]

The records of Burr's new quest bring a drastic change of perspective. The enigmatic man of secrets began to keep a journal. He intended, according to his own entries, to record his schedule and daily activities. When he was reunited with Theodosia, he meant to use those entries to jog his memory, helping him to regale her with fascinating and amusing tales.[11] As his trip dragged on for four years, such an aid to memory became essential. In number and length, his tales would come to rival Scheherazade's.

Unlike his correspondence, which often had a hasty, superficial quality, some of Burr's journal entries sparkled with economy and clarity. He wrote some passages in French, and he liked to adapt stray words from other languages and apply them in playful ways.

As the journey evolved, so did the journal. Burr rarely recorded political comments. He was under observation by several governments, and he knew that hostile eyes might read what he wrote. No such reserve applied to his observations about the people and customs he encountered, the landscapes he traveled through, or his own life. The journal became one side of an intimate conversation with Theodosia, the only person on the planet he cherished. On its pages Burr emerges in many dimensions: beguiling, sunny, cranky, rueful, ambitious, spoiled, empathetic, arrogant, and sentimental. And to his journal he even confided moments of stabbing loneliness.

One entry recorded a woman friend's criticism of his unkempt lodgings. "I am more than comfortable," he protested to her, admitting that "of the nine chairs in my room, eight were lumbered with clothes, &c.," as were two tables, a chest of drawers, and the mantelpiece. But, he continued whimsically, no more than fifty articles lay on the floor, an arrangement that "is my taste; it is order; everything is found without opening trunks or drawers." With a wry shudder, he added that English maids, "if they once get into your room, hide everything; and this they call neatness," leaving him "the work of some days to find the things most usually wanted."[12]

Burr often could not find what he wanted. After placing a letter, handkerchiefs, and other articles in the pockets of the coat he planned to wear, he set off in a different garment. "What a curse," he wrote, "to have two coats!" In a single day he misplaced his ticket for a stagecoach, then his gloves, and "lost or spent 28 shillings." "Truly," he observed, "I want a guardian more than at 15." A later entry was candid: "Lost watch. In rage all weekend." Door keys and umbrellas passed through his hands like water. He could lose track of the days, observing occasionally that the dates of his last several journal entries were probably wrong.[13]

On occasion, his carelessness had sad consequences. Theodosia was distraught to receive a letter encoded in a cipher for which he had not given her the key. "I have worked, and wept," she wrote, "and torn the paper, and thrown myself down in despair, and rose full of some new thought, and tried again to fail again, till my heart is worn out."[14]

Burr recorded his foolish moments. Sleepless one night (as he often was), he could not light his candle with matches or flint. Recalling his pistol, Burr filled its pan with gunpowder and was about to light the candle with its ignition. Remembering that there might be a ball in the pistol's chamber, he transferred the gunpowder to a piece of paper. After many attempts, he managed to ignite the powder, as well as his shirt and all the papers on his table, while singeing his fingers. When he had extinguished the fires, he noted with satisfaction, the candle glowed warmly. He spent the balance of the night reading an interesting historical work.[15]

Frequently short of funds, Burr triumphantly recorded small economies and ruefully admitted large outflows. "I save in sous [French pennies]," he wrote, "and waste in crowns." On one occasion, he borrowed 30 francs from a friend; after twenty-four hours, he had only 40 sous left. He rarely tried to economize on tobacco; his affection for "segars" was a constant.[16]

Burr could shop obsessively and was difficult to please. When *Clarissa*

Ann stopped in Nova Scotia, Burr wanted to acquire a Newfoundland dog. He examined thirty of the breed, "but not one suited." In London, he searched for days for the perfect chess table for a friend. He bought one, then concluded it "was not the thing" and visited twenty more cabinetmakers. In Paris he haunted booksellers for the best French dictionaries for Theodosia, often returning editions he had previously purchased. He constantly hunted for watches for himself and Theodosia and his grandson.[17]

Burr doted on every child he met. Almost all were, according to his journal, wonderful, beautiful, or handsome, and laden with talents that delighted. After meeting a three-year-old and a five-year-old, he wrote that it was "impossible to imagine anything more lovely than they are." Of two sisters, he recorded, "Hannah is handsome, Patty beautiful." The children certainly noticed Burr, who liberally distributed bon-bons and demanded that each sing him a song or dance him a dance. At social events, he sometimes abandoned the adult company in favor of his hosts' children.[18]

Burdened with much spare time while he waited for senior officials to grant him audiences, Burr played cards and chess constantly. He read voraciously. Some of his reading was serious, including tomes by Montesquieu. Burr could amuse himself for hours with a nation's criminal code or other statutory compilation. More often, though, he selected French dramas, using them as a window on the revolutionary changes in French society.[19]

Burr liked to visit graves associated with great men like Rousseau, Milton, Shakespeare, and King Hamlet of Denmark. He met luminaries who still lived, including the poet Goethe in Germany, the painter David in Paris, and the writer Sir Walter Scott in Edinburgh.[20]

Like all travelers in 1808, Burr bore discomfort reasonably well, though he despaired over the dirty sheets in English inns. Attacked by bedbugs in a Swedish hostelry, he recorded, "Fought hard till 4, slaying thousands, but the number of the enemy increasing, resolved in a retreat." He spent the balance of the night on the floor.[21]

Occasionally sick, Burr was tortured by dental woes. He spent so much time with a Parisian dentist that he became a regular at the family's dinner table. Though he self-medicated with laudanum, a form of opium that was then freely available, one toothache was so violent that he contemplated extraction. He delayed the operation, however, "as the tooth is the most important one of the few I have left." Ultimately, out it came, but the mouth pain did not end.[22]

He had a discerning eye for how people lived. On a day of heavy rain, he wrote, "How sorry I feel for the lower orders of people when it rains on a holiday. They have so few enjoyments, in Europe especially, nowhere so few as in England." Traveling through a snowy German landscape, Burr gave an old man a ride in his wagon. When they reached the man's home, three young women ran out "and seemed to strive for the first embrace," while an old woman watched from the window. "That man, thought I, has lived happy and will die happy."[23]

Burr's journal comprehensively recorded his fascination with every female he encountered. He defended the woman's point of view in conversation and sought out books about women. In England, he took pride in befriending the daughters of Mary Wollstonecraft, the women's rights advocate who had died some years before. In Sweden, Burr delighted to discover that his coachman was a woman, then that his boatman was a woman, and then that the fishermen he passed were women.[24]

Burr was most interested, though, in the pretty ones. His admiration spanned many categories, and he contrived a variety of flattering descriptions. One woman was the "best looking woman of 63" he had ever seen. Another was the "finest she animal" encountered. A third was "the handsomest and youngest woman I ever saw having a son 23 years of age." A fourth was simply "most beautiful, most seductive."[25]

Burr was by no means aloof with women. When possible, he pursued affairs with women of his station. In Germany, he was so infatuated with the Baroness Reizenstein—"a sorceress!"—that he fled from her. One more meeting with her, he wrote, "and I might have been lost, my hopes and projects blasted and abandoned."[26]

When romantic opportunities were not available, he patronized prostitutes. Using a code by which he referred to such events as a "folly" or "muse," an "accident" or a "rencontre," Burr recorded dozens of them. The entries usually included the money he spent and could feature commentary, such as "fat, not bad," or "bad," or "pretty good; voluptuous," or "tolerable," or the unmistakable "Bah!" Several entries described multiple episodes in a day, or encounters with two women at once. On occasion, Burr expressed regret for his "follies" with prostitutes, observing once, "how unnecessary and how silly." Yet in other passages he described sexual release as the only remedy for his restlessness and irritability.[27]

Rarely, Burr allowed himself a fuller description. A sequence of encounters in Stockholm was worthy of any romance novel. While shaving one morning, he wrote, "came into my room a tall, graceful, pretty woman." After establishing that neither could speak a language that the other also spoke, Burr "made her, however, understand that I . . . would be glad to see her again on Tuesday morning at the same hour." She arrived at the assigned day and hour. "Being unable to communicate anything by the ear," he wrote, "we tried, successfully, all the other senses. Passed an hour."[28]

Though this window into Burr's sexuality is fascinating, it has a disturbing element. He began the journal as an aid to memory for telling Theodosia about his trip. Why would he refer to these episodes, where she might see those references?

When Burr traveled, he carried a portrait of his daughter Theodosia, who was one of the most accomplished women of her time.

For all of Burr's focus on his daily routines, on women, and on sex, the strongest emotion in the journal is his loneliness for Theodosia. He traveled with her portrait in a trunk and revered it as an icon, hanging it on the wall of any lodging where he stayed for an extended period. When he warmed to new acquaintances, he often invited them to admire her picture, and proudly recorded the compliments offered to it. He found it painful to pack the portrait away. "I bid you *bon soir* a dozen times before I shut you up in that dark case," he wrote. "I can never do it without regret. It seems as if I were burying you *alive*."[29]

Again and again, the journal addressed Theodosia directly, chiding her, answering her imagined comments, fondly calling her "you hussy." His time writing to her, talking to her in his mind, was precious. "Wrote to you," he recorded one night, "and for you, and about you." He exulted to receive a note from her—"A letter, a letter, a letter!"—and specially described sights like castles that she would savor. In her turn, Theodosia was unstinting in her adoration of her father. "I witness your extraordinary fortitude with new wonder," she wrote in a letter. "You appear to me so superior, so elevated above all other men, I contemplate you with such a strange mixture of humility, admiration, reverence, love, and pride."[30]

The pain of separation hurt most on New Year's Eve. "Happy New Year!" he wrote on December 31, 1810. "Mother and Gampy [Burr's grandson]! Ah! I catched you both!" The following year he wrote again, "Happy New Year! Don't scream so Gampillo, you'll wake father!"[31]

Burr arrived in Britain on July 13, 1808, and was in London three days later. His timing was execrable. In February, just five months before, the future Duke of Wellington had developed plans for ten thousand British troops to join another invasion of South America by Francisco Miranda. But then Napoleon deposed King Carlos V of Spain and installed his own brother, Joseph Bonaparte, on the Spanish throne. Several Spanish cities formed "juntas" to resist the Bonapartes. The British promptly gave the juntas full diplomatic and military support. The juntas, now Britain's allies, insisted on retaining Spain's American colonies. Britain could no longer seriously entertain any proposal for an expedition to liberate South America.[32]

Burr's prospects grew even darker when he discovered that Charles Williamson, his intimate friend and agent, had left England on a mission to Jamaica. In a letter to Williamson, Burr admitted that "the new state of things defeats, for the present, the speculations we had proposed," but he insisted that "it opens new views, not less important." Burr resolved to press his case without Williamson, closing, "In whatever I may engage, I shall invite you to participate."[33] No invitation would ever be delivered. Within months, Williamson was dead of tropical fever.

Burr began to scale the British social and governmental world. Starting with the family connections of his long-dead wife, he secured interviews with high officials, brandishing a sheaf of maps of Florida, New Orleans, Mexico, and the United States. He conferred with South Americans who shared his goals, including the son of a Peruvian revolutionary. In a month, Burr knew it was going poorly. By October, American newspapers reported that his mission had failed. Burr began to feel desperate. "If there should remain even a remote hope of obtaining the countenance of this government," he wrote, "I will not quit the field."[34]

Burr chafed during long periods of waiting. "When one has nothing to do," he complained to Theodosia, "one finds no time to do anything." His daughter offered solace from afar. Calling the failure of his Spanish American project inevitable, she still mourned it as "so perfectly suitable to you, so complete a remuneration for all the past." Theodosia worried about him. "Tell me," she wrote, "that you are engaged in some pursuit worthy of you. This is the subject that interests me."[35]

Over the Christmas and New Year's holidays, Burr traveled to Scotland. The trip was partly social. "I lead a life of the utmost dissipation," he wrote in early January. "At some party almost every night. Wasting time, and doing many silly things." But he also was trying an end-run on British officialdom. Charles Williamson's family and best connections were in Scotland; Burr hoped to take advantage of those. In early February, he learned that the tactic might have worked. He hurried back to London for high-level meetings to retrieve his Mexican plan (which he referred to as "X"). By March, though, he knew the British would not help him.[36]

In one respect, Burr met complete success in Britain. He formed an intense attachment to the political philosopher Jeremy Bentham. Then sixty years old, Bentham had crusaded for social and legal reform for decades. He is best remembered for his articulation of the first principle of "utilitarianism"—that society should pursue whatever measures create the greatest possible happiness of the greatest possible number. Burr avidly subscribed to Bentham's theories and was delighted to know Bentham, while the Englishman found Burr an interesting specimen, an intelligent politician with a daring streak. "He was pregnant with interesting facts," Bentham recalled, and "meant really to make himself Emperor of Mexico."[37]

Burr lived in Bentham's London house for weeks at a time and also stayed at the philosopher's country home. He delighted in dinners and tête-à-têtes with Bentham, when conversation ranged over all the topics of the world. On one occasion they spoke of "tattooing, and how to be made useful; of infanticide; of crimes against Nature, &c., &c." Burr's feelings for Bentham sometimes resembled infatuation. "Every hour of every day I have conversed with you," he wrote from Scotland.

> In solitude, in company, at dinners, routes, balls—during the discussion of things the most remote from all association with you, you appear and look me in the face, but eminently in the midst of my follies. Why is it so? You are present; yet always with a look so benign and complacent that cheers; sometimes, perhaps, admonishes.

Bentham returned the respect, if not the passion. On one occasion he invited the American to review an essay he was laboring over. The task had sunk the shoulders of Bentham, he wrote, and now was "waiting for those of Hercules Burr, on which it will sit as lightly as little Jesus on those of great St. Christopher in the Cathedral of Notre Dame."[38]

Burr found validation, even a type of redemption, in forming a close friendship with a man he admired so much. He recruited Theodosia to the cause, proposing that she translate Bentham's works into French and come immediately to England to meet him. "In case of any accident to me," Burr wrote to his son-in-law, Theodosia "will find a father in the venerable sage and philosopher."

Theodosia could hardly mistake Bentham's importance to her father: Burr sent her a bust of the philosopher. Nevertheless, she adopted an impishly astringent tone when she wrote that she was "sorry Jeremy Bentham likes cats. I hate them; but henceforth I shall treat them with ultimate deference."[39]

Burr was sponsor and friend to the painter John Vanderlyn of the Hudson Valley. This painting, titled *Eye of Theodosia Burr,* reflects the playful relationship they enjoyed.

The correspondence between father and daughter often touched on their mutual maladies. Burr's were financial, and Theodosia worried constantly about him. Hers were physical. Barely in her midtwenties, she seemed to be developing symptoms of the cancer that had prematurely taken her mother. The treatments of the day, including poisonous mercury compounds, made her worse until she abandoned them.[40]

In March 1809, as Burr gave up hope of winning British support, he became apprehensive. He was being watched. "It is quite obvious," he wrote to a British friend, "that I am but an object of suspicion and alarm." American agents also had followed him, reporting where he was living and whom he was seeing. Although James Madison had succeeded Jefferson as president, there was no change in the American government's profound antagonism toward Burr. He resolved to leave Britain.[41]

On the afternoon of April 4, 1809, four "coarse-looking men" entered Burr's lodging without knocking, arrested him, and seized his papers. At the request of the Spanish ambassador, the British were expelling Burr from the country. Burr's captors hustled him to the Alien Office, where he was well known. When Burr landed in Britain nine months before, he had made a clever though unwise claim to British nationality, pointing out that he was born a British subject in 1756. The claim had snarled British officialdom but was ultimately rejected; it was derided in both British and American newspapers.[42]

Detention was nothing new for Burr. Held for two days in the home of his jailer, Burr played chess and whist. He rued the seizure of his papers. "Not plots or treasons, to be sure," he wrote, "but what is worse, all my ridiculous journal, and all my letters and copies." When Burr was released, the British ordered him to leave the country immediately.[43]

On April 26, he boarded a ship for Sweden, assuring Theodosia that he had long wished to visit there. He warned a British friend that letters might be delivered for him in the names of Edwards, Melville, Kirby, or Dunbar. "I have as many names as any thief or nobleman in England," he wrote. "While in Sweden I hope to have no occasion for any other name than . . . A. Burr."[44]

27

On the Continent

Sweden, Germany, France
May 1809–June 1812

Burr loved Sweden. The people were friendly and open. "Honesty is not a virtue here," he wrote to Theodosia, "it is a mere habit." After Britain, he added, "where no vigilance can secure you against fraud and theft, it is like passing to another planet." Burr admired Swedish law, concluding: "There is no country with whose jurisprudence I am acquainted in which personal liberty is so well secured." He praised the Swedes' demeanor at concerts, their "perfect attention, and the uncommon degree of feeling exhibited." Using introductions from a Swedish diplomat in New York and from friends in England, Burr entered the highest levels of society. After dressing for a royal audience, he wrote in his journal, "You would have laughed to see Gamp with his sword and immense three-cornered hat." [1]

Sweden was a haven, far from the corridors of global power that he had stormed without success. "How these French and English," he observed, "do torment the whole world." He viewed museums and puppet theaters, ancient ruins and the mint, explored the countryside in gentle midsummer days. His lone complaint was that Swedes entered rooms without knocking. Confronting a locked door, "they unlock the door and in they come. It is vain to desire them to knock; they do not comprehend you and if they do, pay no manner of attention to it."[2]

Burr hoped to return to America as soon as he could do so safely, but the signs were discouraging. As the Nordic summer ended, he mused in his journal, "Why stay here? To be sure I am unmolested and live at no great expense, but [time flies] and nothing done." He would leave Sweden, he concluded, "without knowing exactly why or where."[3]

When he wrote those words, he knew exactly why and where. There was only one remaining hope for his X project: Napoleon's France. If Britain no longer wanted independence for the Spanish colonies, then France, its bitter enemy, should. France could not rival the overwhelming sea power of the Royal Navy, but it did wield the moral force of its recent revolutionary past. So Burr would go to France. Burr did not care which European power supported him in achieving his dream. For that matter, he did not care which power won the generation-long struggle for supremacy in Europe. He cared only which of the European combatants would help him.

Deciding to go to France, however, was not the same as doing so. His own government would obstruct him. France, a totalitarian state, did not allow foreigners to enter and leave freely. Somehow, alone and with little money, Burr would have to make his way to Paris and to the ear of the emperor.

His path was indirect, through Denmark and a variety of German principalities, all occupied by France. Cheering news in late December steeled his resolve. Napoleon had issued a decree calling for the liberation of Spain's American colonies. "Now why the devil," Burr wrote in his journal, "didn't he tell me of this two years ago!" Burr began writing letters to influential Frenchmen.[4]

Winter storms slowed his progress. A January day in Eisenach was so frigid that Burr thought it "would be called cold in Albany." He endured more dental agonies, but his financial distress subsided briefly when a Swedish friend unexpectedly sent him money. Burr reached the French border in late January 1810, only to be denied a passport for Paris. He took up his pen and courted local French officials. "I can," he urged one, "better than any other man, perform a service greatly desired by the emperor." By February 16, he had reached Paris. He was, he wrote, "very bad company and unsocial, my head being so full of X matters."[5]

Napoleon's government quickly received Burr. Within three days of his arrival in Paris, Burr had a thirty-minute interview with Napoleon's foreign minister. In March, Burr had several more conferences with the minister's aide and submitted four memoranda detailing his proposal. For almost six years, since before the Hamilton duel, Burr had been considering versions of this expedition. Now, for the first time, he wrote down what he proposed to do. Then he had it translated into formal French.

The French Foreign Ministry organized his memoranda in a logical sequence.[6] The first one, titled "The United States," featured some of the outright puffery that appears in most sales pitches. Burr asserted that there was a third political party in the United States that was "superior to the two others in talents and energy." This third party, according to Burr, had a "recognized leader [Burr]" and had followers who "ask only to follow him and obey him." Any one of those statements was dubious in 1810, but surely the fate of Burr's expedition three years earlier had fatally undermined the last one.

Burr insisted that forty thousand unemployed Americans stood ready "to engage in any undertaking whatsoever, however foolish it may be, provided that it offers a remote prospect of honor and rewards." This force was available, he explained, because Jefferson had halted America's foreign trade in order to retaliate against British naval policies—in effect, choosing economic suicide in a vain effort to hurt Britain's mighty economy. In addition, Burr wrote, five hundred naval officers and students, "the choice of the nation," longed for war with Britain.

The second memorandum, "Louisiana," explained why Burr's plans had always featured an uprising in New Orleans. Burr described the Louisianans' unhappiness with the American government, then struck a personal note. While he was in New Orleans in 1805, the Creoles were preparing a petition imploring Napoleon to come to their protection. "I advised them to suppress this Memoir," he wrote, "and promised to come to their aid in another manner. They are still waiting for me to keep my promise."

In France, Burr wrote out for the Emperor Napoleon his proposal for an expedition to liberate Spain's colonies in America.

In the third memorandum, "The Spanish Colonies," Burr promised that the French could defeat Britain by extending their war to the Western Hemisphere. Among residents of Spanish America, he insisted, "the desire for independence is universal," and they soon would overthrow the vestiges of Spanish colonial government. If France did nothing, he warned, Great Britain would fill the resulting void, winning the region's trade and riches. But if France authorized Burr to act, Napoleon's name soon would become part of the prayers and songs of those lands, and "monuments will be erected to his glory in all the vast reaches of America from the Arctic regions to the mouths of the Missouri." When Burr began to execute his plan, he continued, the United States would naturally seize Canada and Nova Scotia from Britain, while its talented sailors would expel the Royal Navy from American waters. France would become "the depository of all the gold and products from America." Within a year, he predicted, Britain would have to beg France for peace.

Burr's final memorandum—"Removal of the Spanish Colonies from the English Sphere of Influence"—specified exactly what Burr proposed to do. With twelve hundred men, Burr would seize Pensacola, the best port on the northern shore of the Gulf of Mexico. Drawing on plans developed years earlier, Burr pledged that he could readily take St. Augustine, Mobile, and Baton Rouge. He would raise a corps of four thousand men from the Floridas and Mississippi Territory, men who were "robust, hardened to the climate, hunters all of them." He expected an equal contingent from New Orleans, and more from Kentucky and Tennessee, whose inhabitants "have for several years shown the strongest attachment to him [Burr]." He knew these men, he wrote, having visited those lands in trips that "were not for mere curiosity or pleasure." After an amphibious landing at Vera Cruz, Burr would take Mexico City and New Granada (today's Colombia).

Burr distinguished between conquest and liberation. "A. Burr does not propose to conquer the Spanish colonies," he wrote, "but only to shield them from Spanish domination." He did not write down what government might succeed Spanish domination and who would sit at the top of it, but that required little imagination.

Then there was the problem of ships, one that had preyed on Burr's mind from the beginning. Though he was straining to pay for his plain lodging in Paris, Burr insisted he could easily raise the money to purchase and arm twenty American ships that were then in European harbors, idled by the British blockade of the Continent and the reciprocal French embargo. Of course, he added, if Napoleon could spare "two or three frigates and a few little ships with the necessary money," then Burr could execute his plan more quickly.

The Foreign Ministry official assigned to work with Burr recorded supplemental information and alternative scenarios. The American adventurer had explained that his expedition could be limited to seizing the Bahamas or Jamaica, or expanded to include Canada. In either event, according to Burr, success would be easy. An entire memorandum described Burr's scheme for liberating Canada from British control.

Having unburdened himself formally and at length, Burr awaited the emperor's response. Days passed without a word, then weeks. The imperial silence was not surprising. Burr was retailing plans that might have seemed barely plausible in a smoky Kentucky tavern in 1805 or 1806. In a Parisian drawing room in early 1810, they were fantastic, even delusional. Many of Burr's assertions had been tested and disproved. The people of Tennessee and Kentucky had not rallied to his cause. The Creoles of New Orleans had never petitioned Napoleon to deliver them from American rule, nor had they risen in rebellion to welcome Burr. Five long years had passed since he was last in their city. Burr's ability to raise the funds for the expedition was plainly nonexistent. Indeed, by claiming he also could conquer Canada, Burr revealed a desperate eagerness that exposed him as a gambler playing with borrowed money, down to a last throw of the dice.

The objections to Burr's proposal were large and obvious. The Royal Navy still patrolled the Atlantic, ready to scoop up any expedition from a Continental port. If France supported Burr, it would antagonize the United States. And why would Spanish America welcome Burr, who had never been there? He could not even speak Spanish.

By the end of March, the American was gloomy, finding "no reason to believe that my business advances, or that I shall do anything here." He sought other avenues to reach the emperor. He arranged a meeting with the senior adviser to Jerome Bonaparte, another imperial brother who was king of Westphalia (part of Germany). On several occasions during the winter of 1804, Burr had met in America with Jerome and his then-wife, Elizabeth Patterson of Baltimore. Through Jerome, Burr submitted a letter directly to Napoleon. Another initiative went through the feared national police chief. From Napoleon, though, came only silence. He was not intrigued by the audacious plan from the refugee American who commanded neither men nor resources, but offered only his dream and his talents.[7]

For four months, Burr lingered in Paris in this twilight state, a would-be revolutionary hoping to make the connection that would make his dream come true. He toured sights, attended shows and a French treason trial, and shopped for watches. By the end of July 1810, he gave up. He asked for permission to return to the United States. He was refused. "Here I am a state's prisoner," he wrote in his journal, "and almost without a cent."[8]

Burr bent his efforts to winning a precious passport home. He schemed for an audience with the new police chief but mistakenly attended an official reception in which the chief heard petitions from all citizens. Burr counted forty-seven other petitioners in the room. When the doors were flung open, the petitioners formed a horseshoe, with the police chief in full dress at the open end. Burr quickly maneuvered to be the last to speak with the chief, but "some three or four others, with like design, got after me." Burr was received politely, but this was not the sort of treatment to which he was accustomed.[9]

It was, however, a foretaste of what lay ahead. For almost another year, Burr was marooned in the French empire, at the mercy of rancorous American diplomats who refused to issue the certifications required by the baffling French bureaucracy. On one occasion, a former political associate of Burr's, now an American consular official, said he would authorize Burr's return to the United States only for the purpose of standing trial. "The man who evades the offended laws of his country," the official wrote, "abandons for the time, the right to their protection." Worse yet, another American official in Paris was Alexander McRae, the Virginia lawyer who had helped prosecute Burr in Richmond. With such men barring his homeward path, Burr could only curse fortune.[10]

Burr's financial situation grew more dire, forcing him to cadge money from friends on a regular basis. "My affairs are quite stagnant," he wrote in October, "and I have no other prospect but that of starving in Paris." He tried to economize, in his own way. He resolved to give up sugar in his coffee and tea, often went without a fire in his room, and attempted—with limited success—to reduce his spending on prostitutes. Through the winter, he took a self-righteous pleasure in recording how cold his room was. During one spell of bitter weather, the inside temperature hovered in the 40s (Fahrenheit) and dropped to 25 in the adjoining room. When his room reached 52 degrees, he pronounced it "a very sufferable temperature."[11]

Burr attempted a speculation in shares of the Holland Company, a major landholder in western New York State and a former client of his, and he seems to have earned at least some funds for his trouble. Less successful was a scheme to develop a new use for a byproduct of vinegar. He agreed to translate an American book into French, even though the volume included "a quantity of abuse and libels on A.B. [Aaron Burr]." Through it all, he labored to remain cheerful. To Theodosia and his grandson, he wrote, "My stock of nonsense to amuse you both increases daily, and we shall have a deal to laugh at."[12]

His frustrations mounted. Burr the francophile developed a deep aversion to France. "I have not yet learnt," he wrote in November, "what is the season that denominates this a fine climate." In Paris, he complained, carts and carriages passed directly next to the houses, so a pedestrian must "save yourself by bracing flat against the wall, there being, in most places, stones set up against the houses to keep the carts from injuring them." But the street gutters also ran against the houses. "It is fine sport for the . . . drivers to run a wheel in one of these gutters, always full of filth, and bespatter fifty pedestrians who are braced against the wall." On rainy days, pedestrians lining the walls also would be splashed by water running from the roofs of the houses. Albany's streets used to have the same problems, he noted, "but Albany reformed the evil." When a traveling New Yorker praises Albany, he is well and truly homesick.[13]

Despite his economic hardship, Burr was flummoxed by the French love of bargaining. Uncomfortable with haggling, he enlisted his maid to buy his milk and coal, as she could get "double the quantity for the same price." In many stores, he insisted, "they keep boys to run after the customers, and bring them back to take the thing at their [previous] best offer."[14]

Inexplicably, Burr briefly took instruction in the Spanish language. To be sure, his ambition to reign in Mexico while unable to speak Spanish was itself inexplicable. But it approached perversity to begin to learn the language after his ambition had turned to dust. Burr evidently reached the same conclusion, giving up after only four lessons.[15]

In July 1811, seventeen months after Burr had arrived in France, a clever French official overcame the American refusal to issue the papers Burr needed. The deft stroke involved persuading an unnamed Frenchwoman to press Burr's request on a key American official, one with whom she presumably enjoyed a special relationship. In a day, the necessary papers were in hand.[16]

In mid-September, Burr bought passage on *Vigilant,* which would soon sail from Holland for the United States. "I feel as if I were already on the way to you," he wrote to Theodosia in his journal, "and my heart beats with joy." Burr admitted to "mingled emotions" over returning to America. "Yet, alas! that country which I am so anxious to re-visit will perhaps reject me with horror." He also was anxious about the Royal Navy, which was seizing merchant ships leaving Napoleon's Europe. *Vigilant,* he hoped, was sufficiently innocuous that the British would let her go. That night he watched the Great Comet of 1811 from shipboard, impatient to be under way, "lulled by the beating of the waves on the shore. . . . But what a long, long, night this will be!" [17]

His luck continued bad. On the day *Vigilant* sailed, British warships forced it to land in England.

For seven more months, Burr was stalled, this time in England. He struggled with hostile American officials and indifferent British ones. Unable to pay his fare to the United States, his financial gyrations became fanciful. He renewed his "vinegar project," adding to it a scheme to design a superior steamboat (Robert Fulton's steamboat had sailed in the Hudson River four years before). He also tried to peddle false teeth developed by his Parisian dentist. He sometimes made light of his money troubles. "Have left in cash 2 halfpence," he wrote on Leap Day, 1812, "which is much better than one penny, because they jingle, and thus one may refresh one's self with the music." [18]

The opportunity to renew his friendship with Bentham was a consolation, but a small one, and Burr carefully concealed his straitened circumstances from his friend. He feared the prospect of war between Britain and the United States, which could strand him in England even longer. As the months dragged on, Burr's declining spirits seeped into his journal. He had not recorded an earlier event, he wrote at Christmastime, "during some of those black weeks when I wrote you nothing." In mid-March, he observed, "I never go to bed but with regret." The journal came to embarrass him: "I am really ashamed to send you such a mass of dull repetition and inanity. When I go to bed and get up, and where I go and do nothing, and come home and do nothing." [19]

By late March, having pawned and repurchased his watches multiple times, with his thirteen trunks and portmanteaus packed, Burr, registered as "Adolphus Arnot," was on board *Aurora*, bound for Boston. His thoughts again turned to home. He hoped to bring his grandson to live with him and to oversee the boy's education. He expected "implacable malice" from his fellow citizens and would struggle with many debts, yet he expressed confidence "in my own industry and resources." His great concern was Theodosia. She admitted that her in-laws, weary of Burr's notoriety, made her life

difficult, "but my husband," she wrote, "is not to be swayed by their machi-
nations." Her health was the real source of concern. "My great and only real
anxiety," he wrote, "is for your health. If your constitution should be ruined,
and you become the victim of disease, I shall have no attachment to life." [20]

In early May, disguised with a wig and huge whiskers, Burr walked the
streets of Boston unrecognized. On June 8 he reached New York, which had
finally abandoned the murder prosecution against him. He sought out the
Swartwout brothers, who had remained true to him throughout. Now he
could begin to reestablish his life.

He promptly wrote the glad tidings to Theodosia in South Carolina. He
received a ghastly reply, dated July 12, 1812:

> A few miserable days past, my dear father, and your late letters
> would have gladdened my soul; and even now I rejoice at their
> contents as much as it is possible for me to rejoice at anything; but
> there is no more joy for me; the world is a blank. I have lost my boy.
> My child is gone forever. He expired on the 30th of June.

Aaron Burr Alston had died of a fever at age eleven. [21]

Burr and Joseph Alston, his son-in-law, agreed that Theodosia should
join her father in New York. Burr sent a friend to escort her from South Carolina. They boarded a small ship, *Patriot*, on New Year's Eve, 1812. The
ship was never heard from again, presumed lost in a gale, though a legend
developed that pirates seized it.

When he learned of the ship's disappearance, Burr wrote to Alston. He
felt, he wrote, "severed from the human race." [22]

28

The History of Thy Crimes

O n a cold day in January 1831, a young state senator from western New York, William H. Seward, climbed narrow stairs to the
upper story of the Merchants' Exchange in Albany, which he
described as "one of the fourth-rate houses of this city." Waiting for him was
the seventy-four-year-old Aaron Burr, huddled in an overcoat. Never a large
man, age had diminished him. Burr, according to Seward, was "shriveled
into the dimensions almost of a dwarf." Seward, who was beginning a brilliant career that would make him Abraham Lincoln's Secretary of State, saw
vanity in the arrangement of the old man's "few gray hairs, just filled with
powder, put on as thickly as paste, wet down and smoothed over his head."
Only one of Burr's features, his "keen, brilliant eye," still expressed "the
daring spirit of his youth." The historic figure seated before Seward fired
the younger man's imagination. "Is this the same proud spirit," he wrote to
his wife afterward:

> which, determined to rule, raised the standard of treason and at-
> tempted alone and almost single-handed to the conquest of Mexico
> and the establishment of empire? Do I actually grasp the hand

which directed only too successfully the fatal ball which laid low
Alexander Hamilton? Unhappy man, to drag out a dishonored
existence among a generation which knows thee only by the history
of thy crimes.

The two men were meeting on legal business. Though old and stoop-
ing, Burr's energy was still strong. He was seeking to revive a case that
Seward had already won against two earlier lawyers. Burr would have no
success with the lawsuit, but he bewitched Seward with reminiscences of
the Revolutionary War, of Washington and Lafayette and Hamilton. In a second session, held in Seward's rooms with the young man's family gathered
round, Burr frequently interrupted his recollections to direct a compliment
to Mrs. Seward, and he "all the while held one or two children on his knee."

In his stories, Burr did not portray the nation's Founders as brilliant or
inspired. George Washington, he said, was "entirely without independence
of character and without talent, and completely under the influence of

After his return to New York, Burr practiced law until he could work no longer and
raised several children in his household.

Alexander Hamilton." The first president, according to Burr, did not trust himself to write an invitation to a dinner. Hamilton, though talented, was "a parasite of Washington, unamiable and ungenerous toward all others." The old man snickered over Jefferson, the weakling, who would have fled from Monticello upon hearing that Burr had approached as near as Alexandria or Georgetown. He spoke warmly of Benjamin Franklin, who was "all suavity, courtesy, and kindness." Seward exulted that his children had sat on the knee of Aaron Burr, and he despaired that Burr's description of the Hamilton duel had been interrupted by the arrival of another visitor.[1]

It was a vintage performance by Burr, the inconvenient survivor of America's founding era, resolutely fouling the punch bowl during any celebration of those he had known well and disdained roundly. He would not, it seemed, go away. After all the failures and the excruciating personal losses, Burr had gone back to work in 1813 as a lawyer in New York City. He served as co-counsel with such leading lights as Daniel Webster of Boston and Martin Van Buren, the future president. He paid some of his debts and contested others, dabbled in South American affairs, and never stopped working.

Cruelly stripped of his own small family, Burr established an unconventional household, taking in several children as his wards. Two young girls were the children of a client who had, Burr believed, been meanly swindled. Burr oversaw their education and their marriages to men of distinction. Burr adopted two boys—Aaron Columbus Burr and Charles Burdett—who were widely believed to be his illegitimate sons. Asked once about his paternity of certain children born out of wedlock, Burr replied that if a woman "does me the honor to name me the father of her child, I trust I shall always be too gallant to show myself ungrateful for the favor." Aaron Columbus Burr established a jewelry business and developed a plan to resettle American blacks in Honduras. Burdett graduated from Princeton, served in the navy, and became a writer of novels.[2]

Burr remained loyal to his friends. For the last three years of Luther Martin's life, the Burr household included Burr's former defense lawyer, grown demented from a stroke and decades of inebriation. Aaron Ogden, his boyhood playmate and the man who persuaded the New Jersey courts to quash the murder indictment from the Hamilton duel, was jailed for debt.

Burr won Ogden's release by securing legislation that barred the imprisonment for debt of a Revolutionary War veteran.[3]

Burr nearly finished his years without more scandal, but in 1833 he
married Eliza Jumel. He was seventy-seven; she was fifty-eight and equally
unconventional. From humble beginnings in Providence, Rhode Island, the
future Eliza Jumel may well have entered prostitution. Blond and beautiful,
she became the mistress of a wealthy wine merchant, Stephen Jumel, then
married him in 1804. Her marriage to Burr came within a year of Stephen
Jumel's death.

The new couple separated after six months. Madame Jumel sued for divorce, charging Burr with adultery and plundering her assets. Burr returned
her charges of adultery, adding descriptions of her corrosive temper. As time
passed, he stopped resisting the divorce. After suffering a stroke in 1834, he
was cared for in a New York boardinghouse for two years. A relative then
moved him to a hotel in the Port Richmond neighborhood of Staten Island,
across the Kill Van Kull from Burr's childhood home in Elizabethtown. Burr
died on September 14, 1836, at the age of eighty. His divorce became final
on the same day.

For many years, Burr's friends puzzled over his western expedition and
bemoaned their involvement in it. His persistent air of secrets had attracted
them but often left them feeling ill used. Blennerhassett described Burr as a
man who "disguised his very hints," and one who "never puts pen to paper,
but under the influence of necessity." The architect Latrobe wrote in 1812
of such laments: "I have found myself sometimes in company with half a
dozen of Mr. Burr's friends, all cursing him for having duped them, and all
duped in different manner . . . always adapted to their peculiar characters."[4]

The fates of Burr's confederates principally turned on how close they
had been to him. Those who were most intimate—Jonathan Dayton, Harman Blennerhassett, and Senator John Smith—ended their days in disgrace
and penury.

Sam Swartwout, who had delivered the cipher letter to General Wilkinson on the Sabine border, evaded the initial fallout from the expedition. Enlisting early as a supporter of Andrew Jackson's presidential ambitions, in
1829 he received the plum appointment as customs collector for New York

City. Nine years later, Swartwout fled to England, leaving behind a shortfall in his office accounts of one million dollars (about $40 million in current value). As a precaution, he took one-fifth of the money with him, for leverage in negotiating over the shortfall. After three years, and an official determination that a subordinate had embezzled most of the money, Swartwout settled the matter and returned to America.[5]

The collapse of the Burr expedition reduced Erich Bollman to several years of manual labor, but the resourceful German built two new careers, first developing a technique for the commercial production of platinum and then making himself an economic theorist. Bollman wrote important essays on structuring a system of paper currency, a chronic challenge for governments in the early nineteenth century. After advising the Austrian empire on monetary issues, he settled in London.[6]

William Henry Harrison and Andrew Jackson got away clean, insisting that they had believed Burr's assurances that he had the secret support of the Jefferson administration, and that the expedition would proceed only in the event of war between the United States and Spain.[7] Both men reached the White House despite their connections to Burr. As president during the nullification crisis of 1833, Jackson faced down the threat of southern secession, distancing himself further from accusations that he plotted secession with Burr.

For three Kentucky politicians, Burr's expedition proved a hazard, but a survivable one. Henry Clay, Burr's defense lawyer in the Frankfort case, became Speaker of the U.S. House of Representatives in 1812 as leader of the "war hawks" who clamored for war with Britain. Clay also served as Secretary of State and morphed into the "Great Compromiser" of the United States Senate. Like Jackson, Clay entered history as a stalwart defender of the union, vigorously shedding the taint of involvement with Burr and secession.[8]

When Jefferson fired Joseph Hamilton Daveiss as Kentucky's United States attorney in 1807, Burr's prosecutor challenged two local Republicans to duels, but both declined. In 1811, Daveiss led a militia unit against Tecumseh's emerging confederation of Indians. Killed at the Battle of Tippecanoe that year, Daveiss left his name, misspelled, on counties in Kentucky, Illinois, and Indiana.[9]

In 1820 John Adair, Burr's military-minded compatriot, ran for governor of Kentucky. Accused of complicity with Burr's treason, Adair released a lengthy and entirely incredible refutation. The statement, however, did the job. Adair won the election and later won a seat in Congress. Adair also sued General Wilkinson for false imprisonment in New Orleans and won a judgment of $3,500, which the government paid.[10]

Of the lawyers from the treason trial, prosecutor William Wirt advanced the farthest. He went on to argue 174 cases in the United States Supreme Court and served for twelve years as Attorney General of the United States. Wirt, a Mason, mounted an incomprehensible bid for president in 1832 as the candidate of the Anti-Masonic party. He won the seven electoral votes of Vermont.[11] Burr's lead prosecutor, George Hay, married the only daughter of James Monroe and became a federal judge in 1825.[12]

While Burr's grand jury was gathering in Richmond in June 1807, William C.C. Claiborne, the governor of Orleans Territory, demanded a duel with his constant critic, the merchant-politician Daniel Clark. Claiborne survived a serious thigh wound to become the first elected governor of the state of Louisiana in 1812.[13]

And then there was James Wilkinson. He faced two more investigations into his conduct with Burr. During a court-martial in 1810, he was defended by Roger Taney, future chief justice of the Supreme Court, while a congressional committee investigated him in 1811. Wilkinson rode out both inquiries. The War of 1812 brought his military career to an end after he led an unsuccessful invasion of Canada. Of Wilkinson, the saying became current that he never won a battle or lost an investigation.[14]

More permanent, however, has been the judgment on Wilkinson offered by Theodore Roosevelt: "In all our history, there is no more despicable character."[15]

Reaching a final judgment on Burr is difficult, beginning with the chronic confusion over what he was really doing out West. The confusion has persisted because he had several alternative goals, and because he said so many different things to so many different people. Then he stood before his adventurers at the mouth of the Cumberland and declined to say what his goal was.

Some statements by Burr and his confidants are entitled to particular weight because they were delivered in circumstances in which the speaker had every reason to tell the truth, were reported by credible witnesses, and because they fit the objective facts. These include Burr's statements to British minister Anthony Merry; Erich Bollman's statements to Jefferson and Madison, which matched his statements to Wilkinson; the cipher letter, for all its weirdness; Blennerhassett's statements to his neighbors about Burr's intentions; and Burr's statements to Napoleon in 1810. From these sources and others, there can be no question that Burr meant to raise a private force that would invade and seize the Floridas and Mexico, and perhaps even New Granada. A war between Spain and the United States would have made the expedition far easier to mount, but Burr intended to proceed even if there were no war, inciting one himself if need be.

And Burr expected General Wilkinson to join his expedition. There is no other explanation for Burr's repeated consultations with the general, for their veiled correspondence (especially Wilkinson's message in the summer of 1806, "I am ready"), for their mutual suppression of letters they exchanged, or for Burr's angry reaction when his flotilla reached Mississippi and he found Wilkinson arrayed against him. That Wilkinson betrayed Burr is no more difficult to believe than that Wilkinson was an agent of the Spanish king while he commanded the United States army.

But the evidence demonstrates more. Burr expected an uprising in New Orleans upon his approach to the city, and he anticipated entering as a liberator. As he told Napoleon in 1810, he believed the city would revolt and he had promised to come to its aid. Had he arrived in New Orleans with two thousand men, with four thousand more on the way, he would have commanded the city and could have done as he pleased. Bollman insisted that Burr intended to pass through New Orleans without violence if possible, but a force that size surely would have unleashed the Creoles' separatist sentiment. Similarly, no evidence supports the suggestion that Burr intended to settle those six thousand adventurers on the Bastrop Tract. Such a massive influx of men—all without families—would have required extensive planning and preparation for food, tools, and division of land. Burr made no such preparations.

Burr's ultimate goal, if events had broken his way, was a new empire that ringed the Gulf of Mexico from Key West all the way around to Central America. Could the United States, led by Thomas Jefferson and then James Madison, have ousted Burr from such a position if he had achieved that dream? Probably not by direct attack, even though New Orleans was a critical prize for westerners. Neither president was warlike, and Burr's legions would have numbered mostly other Americans. Jefferson wrote in 1803 that westerners would remain "our sons" even if they seceded; an attack on Burr's new nation would have been a war against those sons. Moreover, Burr's quest for a British alliance and the protection of the Royal Navy might well have succeeded; the British would have welcomed Burr's creation because it weakened both the United States and Spain. Even without a direct American challenge, though, it seems doubtful that Burr could have established a stable government on the shores of the Gulf, integrating such disparate elements: Americans, Creoles, Spaniards, and all the Indian nations. Still, he never had the chance to try.

Burr always protested that he never intended to cause the secession of America's western lands. He told John Graham, Jefferson's bloodhound, that he anticipated western secession only from "moral, not physical causes." But that was a lawyer's dodge, constructed to deflect accusations of treason. Burr encouraged secession, repeatedly telling westerners they should leave the union, and he intended to benefit from secession without directly leading it. Once his empire was established, Burr expected the western states to fall into his hands. If his new empire had included New Orleans, controlling the only practical trade route between the West and the rest of the world, the pressure for western secession would have been overwhelming. By preaching that the union would inevitably break up as he invited westerners to join his expedition, Burr intended for those messages to merge in his listeners' minds, and they did.

For all of his overlapping and alternative goals—settling the Bastrop Tract, joining an American army invasion of Mexico, mounting his own private invasion, or leading a New Orleans insurrection—Burr incontestably achieved none of them. Though many admired his talents and feared his ambition, his failure was on a continental scale. His contemporaries rarely tired of trying to explain that failure.

Stewing in the Richmond penitentiary in the summer of 1807,

Blennerhassett concluded that Burr "had sometimes been too cautious; sometimes too little so." The Irishman could not understand why Burr placed any confidence in General Wilkinson. A Federalist senator struck a similar note, marveling that the "subtle, cunning Burr" had confided his plans to Wilkinson, William Eaton, and Thomas Truxtun: "Three vainer men I never saw—hasty, imprudent, unguarded men—incapable of retaining a secret."[16] Andrew Jackson also puzzled over Burr's contradictory qualities. "He is as far from a fool as I ever saw," Jackson said, "and yet as easily fooled as any man I ever knew." Daniel Clark of New Orleans faulted Burr for misreading the men he recruited. "Colonel Burr," he explained, "was apt to construe every civility into a declaration of service."[17]

The architect Benjamin Latrobe also reflected on Burr's character. "He combines within his own, the two most opposite characters," Latrobe wrote, "the most sanguine and the most suspicious; while he is careless of his interest, and even of public opinion, he is cautious to a degree of folly." Latrobe insisted that he would not trust Burr to conduct "an intrigue to elect a common councilman." Yet when Latrobe was sued in connection with his investment in Robert Fulton's steamboat, he retained Burr to represent him.[18]

The responsibility for Burr's failure was his own. He misjudged Wilkinson, an error that doomed all his other efforts. Moreover, as was true for Burr's entire political career, he formed no effective alliance with any figure of substance, anyone who might be considered his peer, who might lend heft and stature to his expedition. The closest he came to such a partnership was with Andrew Jackson, yet Burr ultimately was unable to keep the volatile Tennessean in his camp. The others in his expedition—Dayton and Smith, Blennerhassett and Bollman, De Pestre, Tyler, and Floyd—were acolytes and followers, not leaders in their own right.

In the end, Burr was resolved to stand or fall on his own. Daring an audacious expedition on borrowed funds, out of office, with a checkered reputation, he fell.

One last historical judgment remains for Burr. Was he, despite the dexterous reasoning of Chief Justice Marshall, and despite the sullen verdict of the Richmond jury, a traitor? It is the brand of traitor that has most disfigured him in the eyes of history.

In strictly legal terms, if Chief Justice Marshall was correct that Burr intended only to mount a private invasion of Spanish lands, then Burr did not levy war against the United States. Yet because Burr's expedition ended before he reached New Orleans, Marshall's analysis was incomplete. The chief justice did not have to consider how Burr would have mounted that invasion from New Orleans.

According to Bollman, and by any plausible interpretation of Burr's plans, the adventurers had to seize ships in that port city to transport themselves to Vera Cruz. To take those ships, Burr would have had to take control of the city, brushing aside the Orleans government and any federal forces in the area. Thus, even if the Creoles had not rebelled against the United States, he intended to take steps that constituted levying war against the United States. In short, had he reached New Orleans, he intended acts that constituted the crime of treason.

But characterizing Burr as a traitor is as much a moral judgment as a legal one. In the context of his time, the moral verdict is less clear.

Burr scoffed at the suggestion that he was a traitor. He wished to lead the liberation of Spanish territories. If that act were to cause the West to secede—and he hoped it would—secession was no more than the right of self-determination held by any liberty-loving American citizen. New Englanders had considered secession in 1804. Why not westerners in 1807? Indeed, on two occasions recited at the beginning of this book, President Jefferson insisted that westerners were free to secede from the United States if they concluded it was in their best interest to do so. Why should that right evaporate when it might redound to the glory of Aaron Burr?

By the standards of many Americans in his day, Burr's plans were not those of a traitor. In its early years, the United States was a republican experiment of uncertain longevity, with fluid physical dimensions. It plainly could grow, and parts might break off. It was the Civil War that fundamentally transformed the way Americans think about secession. Secession to preserve slavery is a far different moral proposition from secession in pursuit of personal liberty or economic advantage. That Jefferson was able to paint Burr as an irredeemable traitor—despite the Richmond jury's acquittal— reflects the mistrust that attached to an enterprise so shrouded in secrecy and misdirection, so rich in alternative and contingent plans.

•   •   •

Burr's expedition had great implications beyond the individual fates of its leader and his allies. As former president John Adams wrote during the treason trial, "Something must come out on the trial, which will strengthen or weaken our confidence in the general union."

The union proved to be stronger than Burr had hoped. Despite his two years of agitation, and despite the friction between the West and the Atlantic states, few westerners answered his call to arms. That lack of response showed a lack of enthusiasm for Burr's uniquely personal brand of leadership. When recruiting, Burr did not speak of ideals, of liberty or self-determination. He did not propose more freedom or more democratic government. He offered adventure, wealth, and personal glory, along with his own charismatic personality. Those inducements were not enough. Americans were not seeking a New World Napoleon.

Burr's secretive style undermined his leadership and, for many, marked his expedition as a conspiracy. Though Burr's expedition has borne the label of conspiracy for two hundred years, the label does not fit particularly well. Not only was the expedition openly discussed among thousands of Americans before a single boat entered the Ohio River, but it also was the subject of extensive newspaper speculation. And the act of leading thousands of men down the western rivers would have been no act of conspiracy but an open act of buccaneering.

The feeling of a conspiracy was reinforced by Burr's juggling of alternative and contingent goals, which made it difficult to grasp what he intended. Burr could not conceal that he was planning a major venture, but he succeeded in obscuring its goal. By combining the notion of secession with the trappings of conspiracy, Burr's expedition inadvertently reinforced the union and degraded the appeal of secession. To be sure, secessionist impulses remained alive in the United States, and they imperiled the nation more than fifty years after Burr's expedition. But in his efforts to realize his dream, Burr roused unionist sentiments in many Americans. Thomas Jefferson, for one, never again wrote so fecklessly that secession was a matter of indifference to him, that for any section of the nation, "Keep them in union, if it be for their good, but separate them, if it be better."

With justice, Jefferson boasted that his extraordinarily slow response allowed the people themselves to reject Burr's expedition, a rejection that was especially devastating. In Jefferson's place, Burr would have moved decisively to suppress any such challenge to his leadership. But suppression from above lacks the finality that Jefferson achieved by allowing Burr to drift down the western rivers with his few men, desperately scrabbling for recruits, to the anticlimactic showdown in Mississippi and the comic-opera arrest in the forest. Jefferson also was lucky. He was lucky that the *Western World* increased public suspicion of Burr. He was lucky that the prosecutions of Joseph Hamilton Daveiss slowed Burr down, and that William Eaton's revelations sapped public support for Burr, so Wilkinson had time to settle with Spain and take control of New Orleans. And he was lucky that Wilkinson double-crossed Burr.

Wilkinson's military takeover of New Orleans left a more ambiguous legacy. When Erich Bollman told the general in early December 1806 that Burr would arrive with two thousand men, Wilkinson had every reason to be apprehensive. He may previously have received similar predictions directly from Burr. Yet Burr was nowhere near New Orleans when Wilkinson, trampling legal processes, sent his troopers through the city to arrest Burr's friends, shipping five of them to the Atlantic coast. Wilkinson's heavy-handed actions were more reprehensible because they were designed to conceal his own connections to Burr and to extort more bribes from Spain. Patriotic action does not ordinarily include demanding a king's ransom from a foreign government. Jefferson, the advocate of liberty who disliked most things military, found himself trapped between Burr and a hard place. In the name of national security, he defended Wilkinson's repression and gave short shrift to individual rights.

Jefferson detested the acquittals of Burr, though there is no quarreling with the carefully worded verdict returned by the first jury: that Burr was "not proved to be guilty under this indictment by any evidence submitted to us." The evidence of Burr's guilt was not presented in court. Had such evidence been presented, it still might not have been sufficient in the republic of 1807, which had few criminal statutes and a pro-defendant culture. Yet in both his *Bollman* decision and his opinions during Burr's trials, Chief Justice Marshall established central principles of our legal and political system. The right of habeas corpus survives in national security cases; though Congress has repeatedly attempted to limit that right in "War on Terror" legislation in this century, the Supreme Court has resisted those attempts. Treason prosecutions must meet the exacting requirements of the Constitution's treason clause. And the president is not above the law when it comes to providing evidence for court cases. One final principle shines through the massive verbiage of the courtroom struggle over Burr: Even the most controversial defendants are entitled to a fair trial.

Equally striking, though, is Burr's geopolitical foresight. Studying his maps, judging the political winds from Europe and across the Western Hemisphere, Burr saw that the people of the United States would sweep into the Floridas and much of what was then Mexico. He saw, also, that the man who could make that happen would win glory in his generation and for many more. Despite his desperate efforts, it was not to be Burr's glory. "There," he is supposed to have exclaimed when he read of the Texas rebellion of 1835. "I was right! I was only thirty years too soon! What was treason in me is patriotism now!" [19]

The glory went to others, and there was plenty of it. West Florida fell to the Americans in 1811. Andrew Jackson took the rest of Florida from Spain in 1818, increasing his reputation as a champion of American expansion. Sam Houston emerged as the hero of the Texas rebellion in 1835 and father of that new nation. A decade later, General Winfield Scott and General Zachary Taylor shared the glory of conquering Mexico, winning lands from the Sabine River to the California coast; Taylor rode that triumph into the White House in 1848, while the victory made Scott a presidential candidate in 1852.

It took all those men, and the passage of forty years, to realize Aaron Burr's dream. None of them, though, tried to become emperor.

ACKNOWLEDGMENTS

My work on this book was supported by the Hodson Trust—John Carter Brown Library Fellowship, which included residential stays at the JCB Library in Providence, Rhode Island, and Washington College in Chestertown, Maryland. Adam Goodheart of the Starr Center at Washington College and Ted Widmer at the JCB have been warm colleagues and friends, and eased my stays at both locations.

The list of people who helped with this book seems even longer than for my first two, but it has to start with my editor, Alice Mayhew, who has provided great encouragement and incisive guidance. It has been a privilege to have had her assistance with all three of my books. Her colleagues at Simon & Schuster, including Roger Labrie, Karen Thompson, Gypsy da Silva, and Rachel Bergmann, are unfailingly helpful and knowledgeable. I have been fortunate to work with all of them.

Because Burr's story sprawled down the East Coast, and then the Ohio and Mississippi Rivers, so did I. I am grateful, first, to Jim Clifford and my son Colin, who accompanied me on rambles in the footsteps of Burr. Garrett Epps took me by the hand in Richmond, his hometown, and sponsored me through Burr's old haunts. My time in Natchez was enriched by several residents with extensive knowledge of their history, including Barbara and David Haigh, Joan McLemore, and Stanley Nelson. Holmes Sturgeon guided me on a relentless quest, in a persistent drizzle, for the remains of Fort Adams, an outing which inflicted only modest losses on my wardrobe.

A great many researchers and archivists assisted me in tracking down different parts of the story. The Library of Congress has been my unofficial home for all three of my books. Numerous professionals there have helped me, but I should note particularly Thomas Mann in the general reference section and Jeff Flannery of the document room. Extra credit also goes to Mike Klein in the map room, who helped me figure out what has happened with the "Burr maps," and Mary Ammen, who unearthed the value of General Wilkinson's extorted Mexican pesos in 1807.

Donald Ritchie, historian of the United States Senate, gave an insightful explanation and tour of the rooms where much of the story unfolded—including the old

Senate Chamber and the Supreme Court's first hearing room in Washington City. Mark Greenough provided comparable enlightenment at the Virginia State Capitol, as did Ray Swick at Blennerhassett Island Historical State Park, Steve Knowles of Falls of the Ohio State Park, and Katherine Craig at Boxwood Hall, the former home of Jonathan Dayton. I am grateful for the help provided by Anne Shepherd with the important collection at the Cincinnati Historical Society Library. Others who extended important assistance include Nancy McLemore of Copiah-Lincoln Community College, Minor Weisiger of the Library of Virginia, Frances Pollard of the Virginia Historical Society, Debbie Vaughan of the Chicago History Museum, Olga Tsapina of the Huntington Library, Tara Craig and Catherine Carson of the Butler Library at Columbia University, Jason Ford at the Louisiana State University Library, Kim Nusco at the John Carter Brown Library, Janet Bloom at the Clements Library at the University of Michigan, Emily Walhout at the Houghton Library at Harvard University, and D. J. Salmon of the North Yorkshire County Record Office. I also received help from the Western Reserve Historical Society and the American Antiquarian Society. Janet Seaton and B.K. Winetrobe assisted with research at the British Archive, and Lawrence Feldman provided translations of several Spanish diplomatic documents.

I have benefited from conversations with a number of people who have shared their special knowledge of Burr and those with whom he intersected. These include Gordon Wood, Brian Jay Jones, and Mary-Jo Kline. I offer special thanks to Walter Stahr, who brought to my attention the passages in Seward's memoirs relating to Burr, which begin the final chapter of this book. Then there are the writing friends who have been kind enough to slog through early drafts of the manuscript and point out some of its weaknesses, beginning with James McGrath Morris. This time around, the members of my writing group, which is sneaking up on ten years in operation, included Solveig Eggerz, Catherine Flanagan, Robert Gibson, Tom Glenn, Linda Morefield, Gerry Hogan, Leslie Rollins, Susan Clark, Phil Harvey, Alice Leaderman, Joye Sheppard, and Frank Joseph. Thank you. None of these fine people, sad to say, is responsible for any lingering barbarisms and wrongheaded statements within.

Like my first book, this volume is dedicated to my wife, Nancy, around whom my own history continues to revolve these many years later.

APPENDIX 1

The Cipher Letter

At his trial, Burr denied that he wrote the cipher letter, the single most powerful piece of evidence of the scope of his ambitions. The authorship of that letter has intrigued scholars for many years. James Wilkinson produced two versions of the letter; both are held in the Newberry Library in Chicago. Sam Swartwout handed Wilkinson one of the versions on an evening in October 1806 in Natchitoches. A messenger from Erich Bollman in New Orleans delivered the second copy to Wilkinson in early November. A respectable argument, though not a conclusive one, has developed that Jonathan Dayton played a central role in producing the two copies of the cipher letters that Wilkinson received.[1] Nevertheless, there seems little basis for doubting that the letter, its sentiments, and its instructions came from the mind of Aaron Burr.

According to Sam Swartwout, the cipher letter he delivered was the second version of a letter intended for Wilkinson. In Philadelphia in late July 1806, Burr gave Swartwout a letter for Wilkinson which the young man copied and converted into the three forms of cipher used by Burr and Wilkinson, a laborious task that must have taken many hours. Swartwout left Philadelphia with that letter but was overtaken in Pittsburgh by Peter Ogden, Dayton's nephew and another young messenger for Burr. Ogden gave Swartwout a new version of the cipher letter, which was sealed, and directed that Swartwout destroy the first version. This second version was largely identical to the copy that Erich Bollman carried when he sailed from Philadelphia to New Orleans that summer.

Two principal factors have caused some to question whether Burr actually approved the second version of the cipher letter. First, the overheated prose of the letter does not seem consistent with Burr's ordinarily crisp, even guarded style. Few passages in Burr's other correspondence bear much resemblance to a phrase like "The gods invite us to glory and fortune." Second, the handwriting for the letters, both copies of which appear to have been written by the same hand, is supposed to resemble Dayton's handwriting. Other expressed reasons for doubting Burr's authorship of the cipher letter have included its reference to him in the third person (as "Burr") and the statement that he would bring his daughter and grandson on the expedition with him. No sane father and grandfather, the argument proceeds, would risk his loved ones in such an enterprise.

Dayton's involvement in the preparation of the cipher letter seems undeniable. Indeed, Swartwout and Bollman each carried other letters signed by Dayton. In one addressed to Wilkinson and delivered by Swartwout, Dayton predicted that Congress soon would remove General Wilkinson from his position at the head of the United States army. "Are you ready?" Dayton's letter asked. "Are your numerous associates ready? Wealth and glory, Louisiana and Mexico."[2] In a separate note delivered by Bollman, Dayton wrote, "Everything, and even Heaven itself, appears to have conspired to prepare the train for a grand explosion; are you also ready?"[3]

Yet there is little reason to conclude that Dayton was solely, or even largely, responsible for the contents of the cipher letter. Burr referred to himself in the third person in a variety of other letters, both as "Burr" and as "AB."[4] The reference to his family coming west on the expedition is also not particularly notable; indeed, it is merely descriptive. While Burr traveled the West in the autumn of 1806 to organize the expedition, his daughter and grandson traveled as far as Lexington, Kentucky, to be with him. They may have planned to go farther if events had permitted it. Having them travel even so far as Lexington seems peculiar in some respects, particularly since both Theodosia and her son had endured recent illnesses, but they did it.

The supposed resemblance of the cipher letter to Dayton's handwriting is difficult to test reliably. Comparing the two versions of the cipher letter at the Newberry Library with a letter from Dayton in the same library (albeit one written twenty-five years earlier) demonstrates some similarity in penmanship, most strikingly a backward-leaning swirl when a word ends with the letter "D." Yet other writers of that day sometimes exhibited that characteristic. When the cipher letters are compared with later letters by Dayton from 1796, 1804, and 1807, the similarity seems less notable. Handwriting comparisons, alas, are inherently subjective.[5]

That the cipher letter was not in Burr's hand is hardly surprising. According to Swartwout, he created the first version of the cipher letter by enciphering a writing by Burr. In another instance, involving a letter from Burr to Bollman, Burr's secretary Charles Willie described the same practice: Burr wrote the letter out and Willie enciphered it.[6] Translating a long letter into cipher was a tedious, time-consuming chore, one that Burr would be glad to delegate to some reliable aide. Though Dayton was a relatively senior figure to undertake such a chore, the cipher letter was a particularly sensitive document, one that was not necessarily beneath his dignity to encipher for Burr.

Finally, there is the question of the florid language of the cipher letter, which was certainly not Burr's ordinary "voice" in correspondence or conversation. Those passages may have been clumsy efforts to mimic Wilkinson's penchant for hyperbole—to speak to the general in his own language. Nevertheless, despite the perfervid phrases, the content of the letter reflects Burr's customary caution with the written word. Though the letter announces the expedition in a martial tone and implies an attack on Mexico, it describes neither insurrection in New Orleans nor western secession. In his first review of the cipher letter, in the habeas corpus case of Swartwout and Bollman, Chief Justice Marshall immediately noted that the content of the letter was not treasonous.

That Peter Ogden brought to Pittsburgh a redraft of the cipher letter certainly demonstrates that Burr had second thoughts about his initial draft. Something in that draft, or omitted from it, bothered him. So the second version was created. Dayton could have participated in preparing both drafts of that message. He was Burr's closest confidant throughout the planning of the expedition, and he was the only other participant in the delicate overtures to the Spanish and British ministers.

But nothing said by Swartwout, Ogden, or Bollman reflected any doubt that the cipher letter derived from Burr. Indeed, Swartwout also carried a letter of introduction from Burr, while Bollman affirmed that the cipher letter came from Burr.[7] Even Commodore Thomas Truxtun reported that in the summer of 1807, Burr invited him to send a message to Wilkinson since Burr was sending *two* couriers to Wilkinson at that moment in time, plainly a reference to Swartwout and Bollman.[8] Finally, nothing in Dayton's history, or in his relationship with Burr through the months of expedition planning, provides a motive for him to insert anything into such a critical letter that was not exactly what his close friend and leader wanted. Burr was the alpha figure in their lifelong friendship; Dayton was the follower. Burr's denials of authorship of the cipher letter are most plausibly viewed as a reasonable attempt to save his skin, or a lawyerly insistence that another hand actually held the pen that formed the figures on the pages.

The full text of the cipher letter, dated July 22, 1806, is as follows:

Your letter postmarked 13th May is received. I have at length obtained funds, and have actually commenced. The Eastern detachments, from different points under different pretense, will rendezvous on Ohio on 1 November.

Everything internal and external favor our view. Naval protection of England is secured. T[ruxtun] is going to Jamaica to arrange with the admiral there and will meet us at Mississippi. England, a Navy of United States ready to join, and final orders are given to my friends and followers. It will be a host of choice spirits. Wilkinson shall be second to Burr only and Wilkinson shall dictate the rank and promotion of his officers.

Burr will proceed westward 1 August—never to return. With him go his daughter and grandson. The husband will follow in October with a corps of worthies.

Send forthwith an intelligent and confidential friend with whom Burr may confer. He shall return immediately with further interesting details. This is essential to concert and harmony of the movement. Send a list of all persons known to Wilkinson westward of the mountains, who could be useful, with a note delineating their characters. By your messenger send me four or five of the commissions of your officers, which you can borrow under any pretence you please. They shall be returned faithfully. Already are orders to the contractor given to forward six months' provisions to points you may name. This shall not be used until the last moment, and then under proper injunction.

Our project my dear friend is brought to the point so long desired: I guarantee the result with my life and honor, with the lives, the honor and fortunes of hundreds, the best blood of our country.

Burr's plan of operations is to move rapidly from the falls on fifteenth November, with the first five hundred or one thousand men, in light boats now constructing for that purpose—to be at Natchez between the 5 and 15 of December, there to meet you; then to determine whether it will be expedient in the first instance to seize on or pass by B.R. [Baton Rouge]. On receipt of this send me an answer. Draw on me for all expenses.

The people of the country to which we are going are prepare[d] to receive us—their agents now with me, say that if we will protect their religion and will not subject them to a foreign power, that in three weeks all will be settled.

The gods invite us to glory and fortune—it remains to be seen whether we deserve the boon.

The bearer of this goes express to you. He will hand a formal letter of introduction from me.

He is a man of inviolable honor and perfect discretion, formed to execute rather than project—yet capable of relating facts with fidelity, and incapable of relating them otherwise. He is thoroughly informed of the plans and intentions of [empty space in letter] and will disclose to you as far as you shall inquire and no further. He has imbibed a reverence for your character, and may be embarrassed in your presence—put him at ease and he will satisfy you.

Doctor Bollman equally confidential better informed on the subject & more enlightened will hand this duplicate.

APPENDIX 2

Indictment,
United States v. Aaron Burr
(District of Virginia, 1807)

The grand inquest of the United States of America, for the Virginia district, upon their oath, do present, that Aaron Burr, late of the city of New York, and state of New York, attorney at law, being an inhabitant of, and residing within the United States, and under the protection of the laws of the United States, and owing allegiance and fidelity to the same United States, not having the fear of God before his eyes, nor weighing the duty of his said allegiance, but being moved and seduced by the instigation of the devil, wickedly devising and intending the peace and tranquility of the same United States to disturb and to stir, move, and excite insurrection, rebellion and war against the said United States, on the tenth day of December, in the year of Christ, one thousand eight hundred and six, at a certain place called and known by the name of 'Blannerhassett's Island,' in the county of Wood, and district of Virginia aforesaid, and within the jurisdiction of this court, with force and arms, unlawfully, falsely, maliciously and traitorously did compass, imagine and intend to raise and levy war, insurrection and rebellion against the said United States, and in order to fulfill and bring to effect the said traitorous compassings, imaginations and intentions of him the said Aaron Burr, he, the said Aaron Burr, afterwards, to wit, on the said tenth day of December, in the year one thousand eight hundred and six, aforesaid, at the said island called 'Blannerhassett's Island' as aforesaid, in the county of Wood aforesaid, in the district of Virginia aforesaid, and within the jurisdiction of this court, with a great multitude of persons whose names at present are unknown to the grand inquest aforesaid, to a great number, to wit: to the number of thirty persons and upwards, armed and arrayed in a warlike manner, that is to say, with guns, swords and dirks, and other warlike weapons, as well offensive as defensive, being then and there unlawfully, maliciously and traitorously assembled and gathered together, did falsely and traitorously assemble and join themselves together against the said United States, and then and there with force and arms did falsely and traitorously, and in a warlike and hostile manner, array and dispose themselves against the said United States, and then and there, that is to say, on the day and in the year aforesaid, at the island aforesaid, commonly called 'Blannerhassett's Island,' in the county aforesaid of Wood, within the Virginia district and the jurisdiction of this court, in pursuance of such their traitorous intentions and purposes aforesaid, he, the said Aaron Burr, with the said persons so as aforesaid, traitorously assembled and armed and arrayed in manner aforesaid, most wickedly, maliciously and traitorously did ordain, prepare and levy war against the said United States, contrary to the duty of their said allegiance and fidelity, against the constitution, peace and dignity of the said United States, and against the form of the act of the congress of the said United States in such case made and provided[.] And the grand inquest of the United States of America, for the Virginia district, upon their oaths aforesaid, do further present that the said Aaron Burr, late of the city of New York, and state of New York, attorney at law, being an inhabitant of, and residing within the United States, and under the protection of the laws of the United States, and owing allegiance and fidelity to the same United States, not having the fear of God before his eyes, nor weighing the duty of his said allegiance, but being moved and seduced by the instigation of the devil, wickedly devising and intending the peace and tranquility of the said United States to disturb, and to stir, move and excite insurrection, rebellion and war against the said United States, on the eleventh day of December, in the year of our Lord one thousand eight hundred and six, at a certain place called and known by the name of 'Blannerhassett's Island,' in the county of Wood and district of Virginia aforesaid, and within the jurisdiction of this court, with force and arms unlawfully, falsely, maliciously and traitorously did compass, imagine and intend to raise and levy war, insurrection and rebellion against the said United States; and in order to fulfill and bring to effect the said traitorous compassings, imaginations and intentions of him, the said Aaron Burr, he, the said Aaron Burr, afterwards, to wit: on the said last mentioned day of December, in the year one thousand eight hundred and six aforesaid, at a certain place commonly called and known by the name of 'Blannerhassett's Island,' in the said county of Wood, in the district of Virginia aforesaid, and within the jurisdiction of this court, with one other great multitude of persons whose names at present are unknown to the grand inquest aforesaid, to a great number, to wit: to the number of thirty persons and upwards, armed and arrayed in a warlike manner, that is to say, with guns, swords and dirks, and other warlike weapons, as well offensive as defensive, being then and there unlawfully, maliciously and traitorously assembled and gathered together, did falsely and traitorously assemble and join themselves together against the said United States, and then and there with force and arms did falsely and traitorously, and in a warlike and hostile manner, array and dispose themselves against the said United States, and then and there, that is to say, on the day and in the year last mentioned, at the island aforesaid, in the county of Wood aforesaid, in the Virginia district, and within the jurisdiction of this court, in pursuance of such their traitorous intentions and purposes aforesaid, he, the said Aaron Burr, with the said persons so as aforesaid traitorously assembled, and armed and arrayed in manner aforesaid, most wickedly, maliciously and traitorously did ordain, prepare and levy war against the said United States, and further to fulfill and carry into effect the said traitorous compassings, imaginations and intentions of him the said Aaron Burr, against the said United States, and to carry on the war thus levied as aforesaid against the said United States, the said Aaron Burr, with the multitude last mentioned, at the island aforesaid, in the said county of Wood, within the Virginia district aforesaid, and within the jurisdiction of this court, did array themselves in a warlike manner, with guns and other weapons, offensive and defensive, and did proceed from the said island down the river Ohio in the county aforesaid, within the Virginia district and within the jurisdiction of this court, on the said eleventh day of December, in the year one thousand eight hundred and six aforesaid, with the wicked and traitorous intention to descend the said river and the river Mississippi, and by force and arms traitorously to take possession of a city commonly called New Orleans, in the Territory of Orleans, belonging to the United States, contrary to the duty of their said allegiance and fidelity, against the constitution, peace and dignity of the said United States, and against the form of the act of the congress of the United States in such case made and provided.

APPENDIX 3

United States Constitution, Article III, Section 3 (Treason Clause)

Treason against the United States, shall consist only in levying War against them, or in adhering to their Enemies, giving them Aid and Comfort. No Person shall be convicted of Treason unless on the Testimony of two Witnesses to the same overt Act, or on Confession in open Court. The Congress shall have Power to declare the Punishment of Treason, but no Attainder of Treason shall work Corruption of Blood, or Forfeiture except during the Life of the Person attainted.

NOTES

In some instances in the text, I have amended quotations to use modern spellings, to replace ampersands with "and," and also have eliminated the sometimes random capitalizations employed in the early nineteenth century.

The hodgepodge character of the papers left by Aaron Burr reflect both bad luck and his not-always-organized personality. He confided some of his papers to his daughter, Theodosia, when he traveled to Europe in 1808. Those papers disappeared with Theodosia when her ship was lost in early 1813. Upon Burr's death, his remaining papers were reviewed by his literary executor, Matthew Davis, who destroyed many of them out of concern for the reputations of those (male and female) whom Burr had known. Finally, Davis cut and slashed from Burr's most revealing document, his private journal from his years in hopeful European exile. The careless handling of Burr's documents has left five major sources for his own writings:

- Burr writings and Burr-related material gathered in the two-volume collection of Burr's papers. Mary-Jo Kline, ed., *Political Correspondence and Public Papers of Aaron Burr,* Princeton: Princeton University Press (1983) (cited as "Kline").
- The two-volume "Memoirs" produced by Davis after Burr's death, which includes many personal letters and excerpts from letters. Matthew L. Davis, ed., *Memoirs of Aaron Burr,* New York: Harper & Brothers (1838) (cited as "Davis, *Memoirs*").
- The two-volume "Private Journal of Aaron Burr" published by Davis, also shortly after Burr's death. This source is useful mostly for the correspondence that Davis inserted into the volumes, not for Burr's own journal entries, which Davis heavily altered. Matthew Davis, ed., *The Private Journal of Aaron Burr,* New York: Harper & Brothers (1838) (cited as "Davis, *PJAB*").
- The two-volume "Private Journal of Aaron Burr" published privately in 1903 by an industrialist, William Bixby, which is an unexpurgated version of Burr's journal. Although Bixby printed only 250 copies of his version, it

is now available on the Internet at http://www.archive.org/stream/private-journalof01burr2/privatejournalof01burr2_djvu.txt. William L. Bixby, *The Private Journal of Aaron Burr*, Rochester: The Genesee Press (1903) (cited as "Bixby, *PJAB*").

- Other papers relating to Burr that have been gathered by the Library of Congress and are available on microfilm as both the "Burr Papers" and the "Burr Conspiracy Papers."

The papers of Thomas Jefferson and James Madison are important to Burr's story, but unfortunately the official collections of their papers have not been completed for the central years covered by this book. This is a greater problem with the Jefferson papers, the published versions of which reach only to 1801. The Madison papers project is complete for his time as Secretary of State through 1805; I have cited those materials in Madison's Secretary of State series simply as "Madison Papers," with the volume and page number. For Jefferson, I have provided citations to earlier collections of Jefferson papers when they include relevant material. These include Andrew A. Lipscomb and Albert Ellery Bergh, eds., *The Writings of Thomas Jefferson*, Washington, D.C.: Thomas Jefferson Memorial Association (1903–04) (cited as "Lipscomb and Bergh"); and Paul Leicester Ford, *The Writings of Thomas Jefferson*, New York: G.P. Putnam's Sons (1892–99) (cited as "Ford"). When there is no published source for Madison or Jefferson documents, I have usually relied on the manuscript originals of their letters posted on the website of the Library of Congress as part of its "American Memory" program.

I have consulted many additional manuscript collections, including four collections of papers of General James Wilkinson: in the Chicago Historical Society, at the Regenstein Library of the University of Chicago, at the Newberry Library in Chicago, and at the Library of Congress. The Newberry Library also holds papers of Charles Williamson, Burr's British friend, and I have drawn from the online collection of the papers of John Adams maintained by the Massachusetts Historical Society. The Cincinnati Historical Society contains five very useful collections of papers that touch on the Burr conspiracy: records of the federal court for the Southern District of Ohio, the Jacob Burnet Papers, the John Stites Gano collection, the John Smith papers, and the William Prince papers. The Library of Congress holds numerous manuscript collections of interest, in addition to those already listed, including those of William Henry Harrison, Albert Gallatin, Joseph Nicholson, William Plumer, Edmond B. O'Calloghan, and George Bourne, as well as a microfilm version of the Albert Gallatin Papers housed in the Columbia University Library. I also drew on collections at the Princeton University Library, the William Clements Library at the University of Michigan (for Jonathan Dayton), the Gilder-Lehrman Collection, the William P. Van Ness Papers and other materials at the New-York Historical Society, the DeWitt Clinton Papers and materials at the New York Public Library, Louisiana State University, the Butler Library at Columbia University, the Virginia Historical Society, the Huntington Library, the John Carter Brown Library, and the Filson Historical Society in Louisville.

For those contemporaneous newspapers not yet digitized, I have drawn on the collections at the Library of Congress, the American Antiquarian Society, and the Western Reserve Historical Society.

Some important parts of Burr's story are revealed in Spanish diplomatic materials that were first explored by Henry Adams seventy years after the event. Versions of those materials are lodged in the Library of Congress, both in handwritten copies commissioned by Adams and as photostats made during the early part of the last century. With the assistance of translator Lawrence Feldman, I have drawn from those materials and have cited those Spanish records directly in those instances. Those items stored in the Archivo de los Indias in Seville are cited as "Papeles de Cuba," while those from the national archive in Madrid are cited as "Archivo Nacional Historico."

For records of the Burr trials in Richmond, I have relied on court records held by the Library of Virginia and two stenographic transcripts prepared at the time: David Robertson, *Reports of the Trials of Colonel Aaron Burr,* Philadelphia: Hopkins and Earle (1808) (cited as "David Robertson"); and T. Carpenter, *The Trial of Col. Aaron Burr on an Indictment for Treason,* Washington, D.C.: Westcott & Co. (1808) (cited as "T. Carpenter"). For the final phase of the Richmond proceedings, which involved evidence presented to justify charges to be pressed against Burr in Ohio federal court (in a trial that never occurred), I have relied solely on Carpenter's record. Some of the testimony from that final stage of the trial was published in *American State Papers, Miscellaneous,* volume 1, and I have cited those entries in some instances.

PART I

1. Richard Pevear and Larissa Volokhonsky, trans., Leo Tolstoy, *War and Peace,* New York: Vintage (2008), p. 41.

1. The Dark Star of the Founding

1. John Adams to Benjamin Rush, April 12, 1807, in John A. Schutz and Douglass Adair, eds., *The Spur of Fame: Dialogues of John Adams and Benjamin Rush, 1805–1813,* Indianapolis: Liberty Fund (1966), pp. 84–85.

2. Gordon Wood, *Revolutionary Characters: What Made the Founders Different,* New York: Penguin Press (2006), p. 225; Joseph Ellis, *Founding Brothers: The Revolutionary Generation,* New York: Alfred A. Knopf (2000), pp. 44–45.

3. Charles J. Nolan, *Aaron Burr and the American Literary Imagination,* Westport, CT: Greenwood Publishing Group (1980); Edward Everett Hale, *The Man Without a Country,* Boston: Little, Brown and Company (1921); James Thurber, "A Friend to Alexander," in *My World and Welcome to It,* New York: Harcourt (1969); Eudora Welty, "First Love," in *Selected Stories of Eudora Welty,* New York: The Modern Library (1992); Gore Vidal, *Burr: A Novel,* New York: Random House (1973).

4. *Philadelphia Aurora,* April 14, 1804; I.B. Hazleton, *Little Burr, the Warwick of America,* Boston: Robinson, Luce Co. (1905).

5. Davis, *Memoirs*, 1:91–92.

6. Charles Burr Todd, *A General History of the Burr Family in America*, New York: E. Wells Sackett & Bro. (1878), p. 124.

7. Theodore Sedgwick to Jonathan Dayton, November 19, 1796, in Harold C. Syrett, ed., *Papers of Alexander Hamilton*, New York: Columbia University Press (1979), 20:405, 407.

8. John Davis, *Travels of Four Years and a Half in the United States of America During 1798, 1799, 1800, 1801, and 1802*, London: R. Edwards (1803), p. 25.

9. Burr pronounced many of these views in conversation with the young William Henry Seward in the 1830s. William H. Seward, *An Autobiography*, New York: Derby and Miller (1891), p. 98. Burr expressed similar views to President John Adams, announcing that "he despised Washington as a Man of No Talents, and one who could not spell a sentence of common English." When Burr said this to Adams, the president scolded him, because to Adams's "certain knowledge, Washington was not so illiterate." John C. Miller, *Alexander Hamilton and the Growth of the New Nation*, New York: Harper and Brothers (1959), p. 480.

10. James Parton, *The Life and Times of Aaron Burr*, New York: Mason Brothers (1858), p. 635.

2. Do Not Play the Fool with His Name

1. James Nicholson to Albert Gallatin, May 6, 1800, in Albert Gallatin Papers, LOC, Reel 4.

2. Charles Biddle, *Autobiography*, Philadelphia: E. Claxton & Co. (1883), p. 309; Todd, p. 116 (quoting *New York Leader*); James Cheetham, *A View of the Political Conduct of Aaron Burr, Esq.*, New York: Denniston & Cheetham (1802), pp. 25, 42; Alice Elizabeth Trabue, *Corner in Celebrities*, Louisville: Geo. G. Fetter & Co. (1923), p. 13; R. W. Jones, "Some Facts Concerning the Settlement and Early History of Mississippi," in *Publications of The Mississippi Historical Society*, Franklin I. Riley, ed., Oxford, MS (1898), 1:85, 86; Erwin G. Gudde, "Aaron Burr in Weimar," *South Atlantic Quarterly* 40:361–63 (1941); *Frankfort Palladium*, September 7, 1805; Stuart O. Stumpf, ed., "The Arrest of Aaron Burr: A Documentary Record," *Alabama Historical Quarterly* (Fall & Winter 1980), p. 119; Nancy Isenberg, *Fallen Founder: The Life of Aaron Burr*, New York: Penguin Press (2007), p. 321.

3. James Nicholson to Albert Gallatin, May 7, 1800, in Albert Gallatin Papers, LOC, Reel 4; Deposition of James Nicholson, December 26, 1803, in DeWitt Clinton Papers, Butler Library, Columbia University; George Clinton to DeWitt Clinton, December 13, 1803, in *id.*

4. Kline, 1:432 (quoting letter of James Nicholson to Albert Gallatin, certified on December 26, 1803); Hannah Gallatin to Albert Gallatin, May 6, 1807, in Henry

Adams, *The Life of Albert Gallatin,* Philadelphia: J.B. Lippincott & Co. (1879), p. 243.

5. Albert Gallatin to Hannah Gallatin, May 12, 1800, in Adams, *Life of Gallatin,* p. 243.

6. Jefferson to Madison, December 19, 1800, in Barbara Oberg, ed., *Papers of Thomas Jefferson,* Princeton University Press (2005), 32:322. Two reasons are usually offered for the Republican failure to have one elector throw away his second vote. First, that the Adams-Jefferson contest was so tight that Republicans failed to concentrate on the need to have one vote cast for a noncandidate. Second, that Burr's complaints over his treatment in the 1796 election, which were communicated through James Nicholson and by other routes, deterred Jefferson and his top advisers from openly directing that even a single vote be diverted from Burr. Edward J. Larson, *A Magnificent Catastrophe: The Tumultuous Election of 1800, America's First Presidential Campaign,* New York: Free Press (2007), pp. 241–43; Isenberg, *Fallen Founder,* pp. 207–08.

7. Burr to Samuel Smith, December 16, 1800, in Kline, 1:471.

8. Burr to Samuel Smith, December 29, 1801, in Kline, 1:478; Burr to William Eustis, January 16, 1801, in *id.,* 1:490; Joanne B. Freeman, "Affairs of Honor: Political Combat and Political Character in the Early Republic," Ph.D. thesis, University of Virginia (1998), pp. 312–13.

9. Larson, *Magnificent Catastrophe,* pp. 244–46; Jefferson to James Monroe, December 20, 1800, in *Papers of Thomas Jefferson,* 32:330. The Congress that was elected in the autumn of 1800 would not take office until the following November, so the lame-duck Congress elected in 1798 chose the president.

10. When Hamilton faced a possible duel with future president James Monroe in 1797, Burr acted as Monroe's second and helped broker a peaceful resolution of the dispute. Kline, 1:306–14.

11. Hamilton to unnamed correspondent, September 21, 1792, *Papers of Alexander Hamilton,* 12:408; Hamilton to unnamed correspondent, September 26, 1792, in *id.,* 12:480; Hamilton to G. Morris, December 1800, in *id.,* 25:275; Hamilton to Oliver Wolcott Jr., December 16, 1800, in *id.,* 25:257.

12. Hamilton to Harrison Gray Otis, December 23, 1800, in *Papers of Alexander Hamilton,* 25:271; Hamilton to G. Morris, December 24, 1800, in *id.,* 25:272; Hamilton to James Bayard, December 27, 1800, in *id.,* 25:277.

13. Hamilton to James Ross, December 29, 1800, in *id.,* 25:280; Hamilton to Oliver Wolcott Jr., December 1800, in *id.,* 25:287; Hamilton to Theodore Sedgwick, January 10, 1801, in *id.,* 25:311.

14. Hamilton to James Bayard, January 16, 1801, in *id.,* 36:319, 321, 323.

15. Manasseh Cutler to Ephraim Cutler, March 21, 1801, in William Parker Cutler and Julia Perkins Cutler, eds., *The Life, Journals, and Correspondence of Rev. Manasseh Cutler, LL.D.,* Cincinnati: Robert Clarke & Co. (1888), 2:44; John

Marshall to Alexander Hamilton, January 1, 1801, in Charles F. Hobson, ed., *Papers of John Marshall,* Chapel Hill, NC: University of North Carolina Press (1990), 6:46–47.

16. Burr to Samuel Smith, February 4, 1801, in Kline, 1:497; Isenberg, *Fallen Founder,* pp. 159–60.

17. *Annals of Congress,* 6th Cong., 2d Sess., pp. 1022–27 (February 11–13, 1801).

18. Theodore Sedgwick to Theodore Sedgwick Jr., February 16, 1801, in Kline, 1:486; James Bayard to Richard Bassett, February 16, 1801, in Elizabeth Donnan, ed., *Papers of James A. Bayard, 1796–1815,* Washington: American Historical Association (1915), p. 126.

19. William Cooper to Thomas Morris, February 13, 1801, in Davis, *Memoirs,* 2:113; James Bayard to Hamilton, March 8, 1801, in *Papers of Alexander Hamilton,* 25:345.

3. The Duel

1. Biddle, *Autobiography,* p. 309; B. R. Brunson, *The Adventures of Samuel Swartwout in the Age of Jefferson and Jackson,* Lewiston: The Edwin Mellen Press (1989), p. 2.

2. Burr to Alston, August 2, 1802, in Kline, 1:734; *id.,* 1:735, n.3; Evan Cornog, *The Birth of Empire: DeWitt Clinton and the American Experience, 1769–1828,* New York, Oxford University Press (1998), pp. 43–44; DeAlva Stanwood Alexander, *A Political History of the State of New York,* Port Washington, NY: Ira J. Friedman, Inc. (1969) (original ed. 1909), 1:127.

3. Thomas Fleming, *Duel: Alexander Hamilton, Aaron Burr, and the Future of America,* New York: Basic Books (1999), pp. 50, 127; Cornog, *Birth of Empire,* p. 48; Roger G. Kennedy, *Burr, Hamilton, and Jefferson: A Study in Character,* New York: Oxford University Press (1999), p. 185; Joanne B. Freeman, "Dueling as Politics: Reinterpreting the Burr-Hamilton Duel," *William and Mary Quarterly* 53:289, 306 (1996); *New York Evening Post,* November 8, 1803, November 10, 1803.

4. Freeman, "Dueling as Politics," p. 294, n.16. In the winter of 1804, the editor of the newspaper owned by Hamilton, the *New York Evening Post,* killed a Republican rival in a duel on the New York side of the river. Allan Nevins, *The Evening Post: A Century of Journalism,* New York: Boni and Liveright (1922), p. 48.

5. Freeman, "Dueling as Politics," p. 294; Biddle, *Autobiography,* p. 303.

6. Burr to Theodosia, July 10, 1804, and Burr to Alston, July 10, 1804, in Davis, *Memoirs,* 2:275–78.

7. Fleming, *Duel,* p. 321; Statement of Mr. Evans, boatman, in *William P. Van Ness v. People,* in William P. Van Ness Papers, New-York Historical Society.

8. *New York American Citizen,* March 1, 1804.

9. Biddle, *Autobiography,* p. 305.

10. Burr to Eustis, May 13, 1801, in Kline, 1:579; Burr to Pierpont Edwards, July 15, 1802, in Kline, 2:728; Burr to Joseph Alston, July 19, 1802, in *id.*, 2:730; *New York American Citizen,* January 9, 1804.

11. Kline, 2:881–82; Biddle, *Autobiography,* p. 302; Dixon Ryan Fox, *The Decline of Aristocracy in the Politics of New York, 1801–1840,* New York: Harper & Row (1965) (original ed. 1919), p. 59.

12. *Albany Register,* April 24, 1804, reprinted in Harold C. Syrett & Jean G. Cooke, eds., *Interview in Weehawken,* Middletown, CT: Wesleyan University Press (1960), p. 48.

13. Hamilton to Burr, June 20, 1804, in *Interview,* pp. 52–53.

14. Burr to Hamilton, June 21, 1804, in *Interview,* pp. 56–58.

15. *Papers of Alexander Hamilton,* 26:278–80.

16. *Interview,* pp. 101–02.

17. *Interview,* pp. 154–55.

18. Burr to Alston, July 13, 1804, in Davis, *Memoirs,* 2:327; Burr to Van Ness, July 13, 1804, in Kline, 2:884.

19. Arnold A. Rogow, *A Fatal Friendship: Alexander Hamilton and Aaron Burr,* New York: Hill and Wang (1998), p. 253.

20. *New York Evening Post,* July 16, 1804; *New York American Citizen,* July 16, 1804. Gouverneur Morris, the eulogist for George Washington five years before, delivered Hamilton's funeral oration. He confided to his diary the most ambivalent feelings toward the chore. Hamilton was, Morris noted, "indiscreet, vain, and opinionated" and opposed to republican government. Morris thought he could not omit those points from his address but should tread lightly on them. Strikingly, Morris also did not wish to be unfair to Burr, who "ought to be considered in the same light with any man who had killed another in a duel." Accordingly, the orator took pains "not to excite any outrage" against Burr. Anne Cary Morris, ed., *The Diary and Letters of Gouverneur Morris,* New York: Charles Scribner's Sons (1888), 2:457; Oration, in *Papers of Alexander Hamilton,* 26: 324–28.

21. *New York American Citizen,* July 17, 18, 20, 21, 23, 30, 1804. The publication of the Hamilton-Burr correspondence confirmed that Pendleton and Van Ness were seconds for the duel, which was widely known anyway.

22. Hamilton to Elizabeth Hamilton, July 10, 1804, in *Interview,* p. 133; *id.,* p. 151 (Nathaniel Pendleton's Amended Version of his and William P. Van Ness's Statement of July 11, 1804); *id.,* pp. 101–02 (Alexander Hamilton's Remarks on his Impending Duel with Aaron Burr); Charles R. King, ed., *The Life and Correspondence of Rufus King,* New York: G. P. Putnam's Sons (1897), 4:396–97.

23. Ron Chernow, *Alexander Hamilton,* New York: Penguin Press (2004), p. 683; Ian W. Toll, *Six Frigates: The Epic History of the Founding of the U.S. Navy,* New York: W. W. Norton & Co. (2006), p. 218.

24. Kline, 2:882.

25. *Interview,* p. 141; Testimony of David Hosack, Evans, and David Wilson, in *William P. Van Ness v. People,* in William Van Ness Papers, New-York Historical Society.

26. *Interview*, p. 154.

27. Burr to Biddle, July 18, 1804, in Kline, 2:887.

28. Quoted in W. J. Rorabaugh, "The Political Duel in the Early Republic," *Journal of the Early Republic*, 15:1, 12 (1995); J.Q. Adams to Louisa Adams, July 19, 1804, in Worthington Chauncey Ford, ed., *Writings of John Quincy Adams*, New York: Macmillan Co. (1914), 3:41.

29. Burr to Joseph Alston, July 13 and July 18, 1804, in Davis, *Memoirs*, 2:327–28; Burr to Biddle, July 18, 1804, in Kline, 2:885.

30. Burr to Biddle, July 18, 1804, in Kline, 2:887.

31. When he reached safety in Philadelphia, Burr sent back to New York for additional clothes. His slave Peggy sent him two shirts, five waistcoats, a pair of drawers, one nankeen pantaloons, two cravats, a dressing gown, a pair of small clothes (short trousers), eight pairs of stockings, and one pair of socks. Peggy Gartin to Burr, July 31, 1804, in Burr Papers, Reel 5.

32. Truxtun to Burr, February 14, 1802, in Kline 1:677; Truxtun to Burr, March 22, 1802, in *id.*, 1:699–700; Truxtun to Burr, July 17, 1803, in *id.*, 1:778–79; Truxtun to Burr, March 19, 1804, in *id.*, 2:859; Toll, *Six Frigates*, pp. 92, 130, 169–72; Biddle, *Autobiography*, p. 316; Kline, 2:890.

33. Biddle, *Autobiography*, p. 303; Kline, 2:890.

34. Burr to Joseph Alston, July 29, 1804, in *Memoirs*, pp. 328–29; Coroner's Inquest, July 13–August 2, 1804, in *Papers of Alexander Hamilton*, 26:318–20.

35. *Papers of Alexander Hamilton*, 26:319 (August 2, 1804, Report of Coroner's Inquest); Swartwout to Burr, August 2, 1804, in Davis, *Memoirs*, 2:329; *New York American Citizen*, August 4, 1804.

36. Burr to Alston, July 29, August 3, 1804; Burr to Theodosia, August 3, 1804, in Davis, *Memoirs*, pp. 329, 330, 331.

37. Burr to Theodosia, July 20, August 2, 1804, in Davis, *Memoirs*, 2:328, 330.

38. Burr to Theodosia, August 2, 11, 1804, in Davis, *Memoirs*, 2:330, 332. His earlier references to "La G" appear in letters to Theodosia on June 11 and June 13. *Id.*, 2:247–48.

39. *Maryland Gazette*, November 8, 1804.

40. Burr to Major R. Alden, February 15, 1781, in Davis, *Memoirs*, 1:198; Burr to Theodosia, January 26, 1800, in Davis, *Memoirs*, 1:401.

4. On the Frontier

1. Burr to Lord Belgray, January 21, 1812, in Davis, *PJAB*, 2:286; Williamson to Burr, May 16, 1804, in Burr Papers, Reel 5. Williamson complained to Burr that his wife had the "temper of the devil."

2. Helen I. Cowan, *Charles Williamson, Genesee Promoter*, Clifton, NJ: Augustus M. Kelley Publishers (1973), pp. 270, 277; Thomas Robson Hay, "Charles Williamson and the Burr Conspiracy," *Journal of Southern History* 2:175 (May 1936).

3. Merry to Lord Harrowby, August 6, 1804, in Kline, 2:892.

4. William Plumer, Jr., *The Life of William Plumer*, Boston: Philips, Sampson and Co. (1856), pp. 298–99; Pickering to George Cabot, January 29, 1804, in Henry Cabot Lodge, *Life and Letters of George Cabot*, Boston: Little, Brown & Company (1877), p. *337*; Kline, 2:865 (remarks of Oliver Wolcott); Hamilton to Theodore Sedgwick, July 10, 1804, in *Papers of Alexander Hamilton*, 26:309.

5. Rufus King Memorandum of A Conversation between Burr and Roger Griswold, April 5, 1804, in Kline, 2:864; *Life of William Plumer*, p. 295.

6. Richard Cutts to Madison, June 9, 1804, in Madison Papers, 7:296.

7. Burr to Biddle, August 11, 1804, in Kline, 2:893; Kennedy, *Study in Character*, pp. 204–05.

8. Indictment, *Papers of Alexander Hamilton*, 26:341–43 (August 14, 1804).

9. Cowan, *Charles Williamson*, p. 279.

10. Burr to Theodosia, August 31, 1804, in Davis, *Memoirs*, 2:287; Burr to Theodosia, September 6, 1807, in *id.*, 2:288; Burr to Biddle, September 1, 1804, in Kline, 2:894.

11. Ramon Roberto Cabot, "Los ultimos anos de la soberania Espanola en la Florida, 1783–1821," Ph.D. thesis, Universidad de Sevilla (1983), cited in Paul E. Hoffman, *Florida's Frontiers*, Bloomington: Indiana University Press (2002), pp. 238–39.

12. Andrew McMichael, *Atlantic Loyalties: Americans in Spanish West Florida, 1785–1810*, Athens, GA: University of Georgia Press (2008), p. 1; Thomas D. Clark and John D.W. Guice, *The Old Southwest, 1795–1830, Frontiers in Conflict*, Norman, OK: University of Oklahoma Press (1996), p. 49; Isaac Cox, "The American Intervention in West Florida," *American Historical Review*, 17:290, 293 (1912); Amos Stoddard, *Sketches Historical and Narrative of Louisiana*, Philadelphia: Matthew Carey (1812), p. 114.

13. *New York American Citizen*, September 17, 1804; *New York Republican Watch-Tower*, September 19, 1804, cited in William C. Davis, *The Rogue Republic: How Would-Be Patriots Waged the Shortest Revolution in American History*, Boston: Houghton Mifflin Harcourt (2011), p. 63.

14. Burr to Theodosia, September 12, 1804, in Davis, *Memoirs*, 2:339.

15. Burr to Alston, August 11, 1804, in Davis, *Memoirs*, 2:332; Walter Flavius McCaleb, *The Aaron Burr Conspiracy*, New York: Wilson-Erickson (1936) (original ed. 1903), p. 28, quoting Yrujo to Cevallos, May 24, 1805; Stoddard, *Sketches*, p. 111; Burr to Theodosia, September 15, 1804, in Davis, *Memoirs*, 2:282.

16. Kennedy, *Study in Character*, p. 221, citing Burr to White, September 22, 1804; Burr to Theodosia, September 15, 1804, in Davis, *Memoirs*, 2:292; Burr to Theodosia, September 26, 1804, in *id.*, 2:294; October 1, 1804, in *id.*, 2:344; October 2, 1804, in *id.*, 2:345.

17. Burr to Theodosia, October 2, 1804, in *id.*, 2:345.

18. Burr to Biddle, October 14, 1804, in Kline, 2:895.

19. Burr to Theodosia, October 31, 1804, in Davis, *Memoirs*, 2:348.

20. Burr to Alston, November 4, 1804, in *id.,* p. 299; *Papers of Alexander Hamilton,* 26:348–49 (New Jersey indictment of October 23, 1804).

21. *New York Evening Post,* November 10, 1804, quoted in Kline, 2:896 n.2; Everett S. Brown, ed., *William Plumer's Memorandum of Proceedings in the United States Senate,* 1803–1807, New York: Da Capo Press (1969) (originally 1923), November 7, 1804, p. 185.

22. Kline, 1:lviii–lx.

23. William Priest, *Travels in the United States of America,* London (1802), p. 132; Isenberg, *Fallen Founder,* pp. 94–96; Burr to Jefferson, February 3, 1999, in Kline, 1:383; Burr to Samuel Latham Mitchill, February 4, 1803, in *id.,* 2:751–52; Burr to Theodosia Prevost Burr, August 7, 1788, in Davis, *Memoirs,* 1:281–83.

24. Kline, 1:189–96; Charles William Janson, *The Stranger in America, 1793–1806,* New York: Burt Franklin (1971) (original ed., 1807), pp. 269–71.

25. Kline, 1:257–62.

26. Burr to Williamson, November 1, 1799, in Kline, 1:411; Cowan, *Charles Williamson,* p. 167; Joshua V. H. Clark, *Onondaga or Reminiscences of Earlier and Later Times,* Syracuse: Stoddard and Babcock (1849), pp. 373–74; *Annals of Congress,* 10th Cong., 1st Sess. (April 8, 1808), p. 249 (Sen. J. Q. Adams).

27. Burr to Abraham R. Ellery, January 29, 1804, in Kline, 1:824; Dayton to Burr, May 18, 1804, in Kline, 1:867.

28. Wilkinson to Burr, May 23, 1804, in Burr Papers, Reel 5; Biddle to Burr, March 13, 1802, in *id.*

29. Davis, *Travels of Four Years and a Half,* p. 25; Pierre Clement de Laussat, *Memoirs of My Life,* Baton Rouge: Louisiana State University Press (1978), pp. 73–74; John F. Watson to Edmund B. O'Calloghan, September 12, 1800, in O'Calloghan Papers, Vol. 18, LOC.

30. Andro Linklater, *An Artist in Treason, The Extraordinary Double Life of General James Wilkinson,* New York: Walker & Co. (2009), p. 191; Jefferson to Nathaniel Macon, May 14, 1801, LOC; Kline, 2:683, n.4; Wilkinson to Burr, May 16, 1802, in Kline, 2:720–22.

31. Wilkinson to Burr, May 24, 26, 27, 1804, in Burr Papers, Reel 5.

32. Dayton to Burr, May 18, 1804, in Burr Papers, Reel 5.

33. Wilkinson to Gardoqui, January 1, 1789, in Alcee Fortier, *A History of Louisiana,* New York: Manzi, Joyant & Co. (1904), 2:141–42. On another occasion, Wilkinson took a similarly dark view of human nature. "Self-interest regulates the passions of nations, as well as of individuals," he wrote, "and he who imputes a different motive to human conduct either deceives himself or endeavors to deceive others." William R. Shepherd, "Wilkinson and the Beginnings of the Spanish Conspiracy," *American Historical Review* 9:490, 496 (1904).

5. The Restless West

1. J.F.P. Smyth, *A Tour in the United States of America*, Dublin: T. Kenshall (1784), 1:204; Jacob Burnet, *Notes on the Early Settlement of the North-Western Territory*, New York: D. Appleton & Co. (1847), p. 66; Clark and Guice, *Old Southwest*, p. 8.

2. Henry Adams, *History of the United States of America During the Administrations of Thomas Jefferson*, New York: The Library of America (1986) (original ed., 1889-1891), p. 14; Dumas Malone, *Jefferson and His Time*, Boston: Little, Brown (1948-1977), 4:333.

3. Josiah Espy, "A Tour in Ohio, Kentucky, and Indiana Territory, in 1805," *Ohio Valley Historical Series*, Cincinnati: Robert Clarke & Co. (1871), p. 24; Ephraim Kirby to Jefferson, May 1, 1804, in Clarence Edwin Carter, ed., *The Territorial Papers of the United States*, Washington: Government Printing Office (1940), 5:322-23; Frederick W. Thomas, *John Randolph of Roanoke and Other Sketches of Character*, Philadelphia: A. Hart (1853), p. 19; Daniel Drake, *A Pioneer Life in Kentucky: A Series of Reminiscential Letters*, Cincinnati: Charles D. Drake (1907), excerpted in Joyce Appleby, ed., *Recollections of the Early Republic, Selected Autobiographies*, Boston: Northeastern University Press (1997), p. 61.

4. Burnet, *Notes*, p. 37; Henry Adams, *History*, p. 35; Robert Sutcliff, *Travels in Some Parts of North America in the years 1804, 1805, & 1806*, York: W. Alexander (1815), p. 45; Clark and Guice, *Old Southwest*, pp. 197-98; Drake, *Pioneer Life*, in Appleby, *Recollections*, pp. 63-64; Affidavit of Peter Smith, John Manley, and Francis Woods, July 30, 1804, in Box 7, Regenstein Library, University of Chicago, Special Collection, Reuben T. Durrett Collection; Elliot J. Gorn, " 'Gouge and Bite, Pull Hair and Scratch': The Social Significance of Fighting in the Southern Backcountry," *American Historical Review* 90:18, 23-24 (1985).

5. Smyth, *Tour*, 2:217; Espy, "Tour," p. 24.

6. Janson, *Stranger in America*, p. 448; Jefferson to Joseph Priestley, January 29, 1804, LOC.

7. Jefferson to John Breckinridge, August 12, 1803, LOC.

8. Jefferson to Robert Livingston, April 18, 1802, in Lipscomb and Bergh, 10:311-16; Dwight L. Smith & Ray Swick, eds., *A Journey Through the West: Thomas Rodney's 1803 Journal From Delaware to the Mississippi Territory*, Athens: Ohio University Press (1997), pp. 61-62; Mary K. Bonsteel Tachau, "The Whiskey Rebellion in Kentucky: A Forgotten Episode of Civil Disobedience," *Journal of the Early Republic*, 2:239, 241 (1982).

9. Max Sevelle, *George Morgan, Colony Builder*, New York: Columbia University Press (1932), pp. 204-26.

10. James Ripley Jacobs, *Tarnished Warrior: Major General James Wilkinson*, New York: Macmillan Co. (1938), pp. 45-65; Linklater, *Artist in Treason*, pp. 44-59, 68.

11. Humphrey Marshall, *The History of Kentucky*, Frankfort: Geo. S. Robinson (1824), 1:165.

12. Andro Linklater, *The Fabric of America: How Our Borders and Boundaries Shaped the Country and Forged Our National Identity*, New York: Walker & Company (2008), p. 121; Linklater, *Artist in Treason*, p. 85; Jacobs, *Tarnished Warrior*, pp. 80–82.

13. Deposition of Daniel Clark, Document VI, in James Wilkinson, *Memoirs of My Own Times*, vol. II, Philadelphia: Abraham Small (1818); Wilkinson to Governor Miro, August 1, 1787, in Papeles de Cuba, LOC, Legajo 2373, Doc. 40; Wilkinson to Miro, September 16, 1787, in Papeles de Cuba, LOC, Legajo 2373, Doc. 46.

14. Jacobs, *Tarnished Warrior*, pp. 115–16, 152; Wilkinson to Carondelet, December 15, 1792, Papeles de Cuba, LOC, Legajo 2374; Affidavit of John Mercier, August 31, 1807, Court Records, Southern District of Ohio, Cincinnati Historical Society; Linklater, *Artist in Treason*, p. 87; Undated Memorandum, Papeles de Cuba, LOC, Legajo 2373, Doc. 25.

15. Arthur Preston Whitaker, *The Spanish-American Frontier, 1783–1795*, Lincoln: University of Nebraska Press (1969), p. 118 (original ed. 1927); John C. Symmes to Dayton, June 17, 1792, in Francis W. Miller, *Cincinnati's Beginnings*, Cincinnati: P.G. Thompson (1880), p. 196.

16. "Daniel Clark's Statement to Congress," January 11, 1808, in Daniel Clark, *Proofs of the Corruption of Gen. James Wilkinson*, New York: William Hall, Jr., & George W. Pirie (1809), Note No. 41, p. 105; Marshall, *History of Kentucky*, 1:283–84.

17. Ellicott to Pickering, November 14, 1797, quoted in Catherine van C. Mathews, *Andrew Ellicott: His Life and Letters*, New York: Grafton Press (1908), pp. 161–63; Andrew Ellicott Deposition, reprinted in Wilkinson, *Memoirs*, vol. II, app. XXVIII; Papeles de Cuba, Legajo 2373, part I (paper by Mark Rhoads, U.S. Signal Corps, explaining ciphers used in Wilkinson correspondence (1930)); John Adams to James Wilkinson, February 4, 1798, reprinted in Wilkinson, *Memoirs*, 2:155.

18. Buckner Melton, *The First Impeachment*, Macon, GA: Mercer University Press (1998), pp. 85–87; McCaleb, *Burr Conspiracy*, pp. 16–17; Reuben Gold Thwaites, *How George Rogers Clark Won the Northwest*, Chicago: A.C. McClurg & Co. (1903), pp. 69–70; *Richmond Enquirer*, January 10, 1807. Genêt commissioned Clark as "Chief of the Independent and Revolutionary Legion of the Mississippi." In newspaper notices calling for volunteers, Clark described his mission as "the reduction of the Spanish posts on the Mississippi, for opening the trade of said river, and giving freedom to its inhabitants."

19. Jon Kukla, *A Wilderness So Immense*, New York: Alfred A. Knopf (2003), pp. 164–77; Tachau, "Whiskey Rebellion in Kentucky," pp. 247–48; Melton, *First Impeachment*, pp. 94–96.

20. Timothy J. Henderson, *The Mexican Wars for Independence,* New York: Hill and Wang (2009), pp. 35–36; Malone, *Jefferson,* 1:239; Clark and Guice, *Old Southwest,* p. 83.

21. Malcolm Rohrbough, *The Land Office Business: The Settlement and Administration of American Public Lands, 1789–1837,* New York: Oxford University Press (1968), p. 48.

22. Thomas Rodney to Caesar Rodney, August 9, 1804, in Simon Gratz, "Thomas Rodney," *Pennsylvania Magazine of History and Biography,* 44:47, 55 (1920); Gordon Wood, *Empire of Liberty: A History of the Early Republic, 1789–1815,* New York: Oxford University Press (2009), p. 316.

23. Baron de Carondelet to Thomas Power, May 26, 1797, in Clark, *Proofs of Corruption,* n.38, p. 83; Power to Carondelet, December 5, 1797, pp. 97–98. Though the passion for secession ebbed in the West, the urge lingered to liberate or acquire Spanish lands. Some Americans became involved with the schemes of Francisco Miranda of Venezuela, a former Spanish soldier who ached to lead a South American revolution. Alexander Hamilton backed Miranda but wanted American forces to lead the venture. In that event, Hamilton observed hopefully in 1798, "the command . . . would very naturally fall upon me." Arthur Preston Whitaker, *The Mississippi Question, 1795–1803,* New York: D. Appleton-Century Co. (1934), pp. 176–84; Kukla, *Wilderness So Immense,* pp. 214–15; Madison to Charles Pinckney, June 9, 1801, in Madison Papers, 1:273–79; Madison to Robert Livingston, September 28, 1801, in *id.,* 2:142–47.

24. Whitaker, *Spanish-American Frontier,* pp. 210, 223; Jefferson to Livingston, April 18, 1802, in Ford, 8:144; Adams, *History,* pp. 276–77.

25. Kukla, *Wilderness So Immense,* pp. 259–61; Whitaker, *Spanish-American Frontier,* pp. 190–92; William Plumer to Jeremiah Smith, January 29, 1803, in William Plumer Papers, LOC; Jefferson to James Monroe, January 10, 1803, in Ford, 9:416–17.

26. Senate Exec. Journal, 7th Cong., 2d Sess., p. 436 (January 12, 1803); *Annals of Congress,* 7th Cong., 2d Sess., pp. 371–74 (January 12, 1803); Jefferson to Monroe, January 13, 1803, LOC.

27. Livingston to Madison, Midnight, April 13 [or 14], 1803, in Madison Papers, 4:512; Kukla, *Wilderness So Immense,* pp. 270–83.

28. William Harrison Smith to Margaret Bayard Smith, July 5, 1803, in Margaret Bayard Smith, *The First Forty Years of Washington Society* (Gaillard Hunt, ed.), New York: Frederick Ungar (1965) (original ed. 1906), p. 38; Jefferson to W.C. Nicholas, September 7, 1803, in Ford, 8:247.

29. Joseph T. Hatfield, *William Claiborne: Jeffersonian Centurion in the American Southwest,* Lafayette: University of Southwestern Louisiana Press (1976), pp. 39–40. During the vote in the House of Representatives to break the Jefferson-Burr deadlock in the election of 1800, Claiborne helped to hold Tennessee in Jefferson's column despite Burr's close connections to that state.

30. Pierre-Clement de Laussat, *Memoirs of My Life,* Baton Rouge: Louisiana State Univ. Press (2003), pp. 88–89; John F. Watson to Edmund B. O'Calloghan, September 12, 1800, in O'Calloghan Papers, vol. 18, LOC; Laussat to Decres, April 8, 1804, reprinted in Adams, *History,* pp. 807–8.

31. Laussat, *Memoirs,* pp. 92–93.

32. Wilkinson to Folch, January 1, 1804, Papeles de Cuba, LOC, Legajo 1573, Packet C, Letter No. 1; Affidavit of John McDonogh, in Court Records, Southern District of Ohio, Cincinnati Historical Society (reprinted in Clark, *Proofs of Corruption,* n. 24, pp. 51–52).

33. Thomas Perkins Abernethy, *The Burr Conspiracy,* New York: Oxford University Press (1954), p. 21.

34. Isaac Joslin Cox, "General Wilkinson and His Later Intrigues with the Spaniards," *American Historical Review* 19:794, 798–801; Jacobs, *Tarnished Warrior,* pp. 205–6; Linklater, *Artist in Treason,* pp. 207–8.

35. *E.g.,* Jefferson to Ephraim Kirby, July 15, 1803, in Ford, 8:16–19.

36. Livingston to Madison, May 20, 1803, in Madison Papers, 5:18; Monroe to Jefferson, June 7, 1803; Jefferson to Madison, August 25, 1803, in Ford, 8:245; Jefferson to John Dickinson, August 9, 1803, LOC. Livingston to Madison, September 21, 1804, in Madison Papers, 8:74. Henry Adams provides a balanced view of this argument. See Adams, *History,* pp. 348–51.

37. *Annals of Congress,* 8th Cong., 1st Sess., pp. 1253–58 (February 24, 1804); Stoddard, *Sketches,* pp. 116–17; Jared W. Bradley, "W.C.C. Claiborne and Spain: Foreign Affairs under Jefferson and Madison, 1801–1811," *Louisiana History* 12:297, 304–06 (1971); Davis, *Rogue Republic,* pp. 19, 56–57; Malone, *Jefferson,* 4:441–46. In 1804, Congress declared a revenue district that included Mobile, even though the town was still under Spanish control. The Jefferson administration prudently elected not to assert jurisdiction over Mobile.

38. Davis, *Rogue Republic,* pp. 38–45; McMichael, *Atlantic Loyalties,* pp. 1, 84–88; McMichael, "The Kemper 'Rebellion': Filibustering and Resident Anglo American Loyalty in Spanish West Florida," *Louisiana History* 43:133 (2002); Clark and Guice, *Old Southwest,* pp. 46–47; Joseph Briggs to Madison, August 24, 1804, in Madison Papers, 7:637; Marquis de Casa Yrujo to Madison, October 22, 1804, in *id.,* at 8:203; Claiborne to Madison, December 11, 1804, in *id.,* 8:370; *New York American Citizen,* September 17, 1804; *Kentucky Gazette,* January 7, 1805. William C.C. Claiborne, governor of Orleans Territory, feared increasing violence on the West Florida border, but the Kemper brothers were already back on United States soil when Claiborne warned Secretary of State Madison that the situation was getting worse. Claiborne to Madison, September 8, 1804, in Madison Papers, 8:32; Joseph Briggs to Madison, August 24, 1804, in *id.,* 7:637.

39. Jefferson to Madison, July 5, 1804, in Ford, 8:35–36; Abernethy, *Burr Conspiracy,* p. 47; Isaac Joslin Cox, "Louisiana-Texas Frontier, Part II," *Southwestern Historical Quarterly* 17:140, 185 (1914); Adams, *History,* p. 500.

40. Livingston to Madison, September 21, 1804, in Madison Papers, 8:74–75.

41. Claiborne to Madison, July 15, 1804, in Madison Papers, 7:457.

42. Abernethy, *Burr Conspiracy*, p. 17; Jeremiah Browne, *Short Letter to a Member of Congress concerning The Territory of Orleans*, Washington City (1806), pp. 6–9, 14–16; Hatfield, *William Claiborne*, p. 195; Clark and Guice, *Old Southwest*, pp. 47–48. Creole discontent was stirred by the presence of two Spanish officials who remained in New Orleans to negotiate the festering boundary issues, along with fifty Spanish soldiers to protect them. Governor Claiborne complained of seeing "daily, persons in Spanish uniform." Disaffected Louisianans were drawn toward the Spaniards. Claiborne to Madison, September 23, 1804, in Madison Papers, 8:88; Claiborne to Madison, October 3, 1804, in *id.*, at 8:122; Claiborne to Madison, October 20, 1804, in *id.*, 8:196; Jared W. Bradley, "W.C.C. Claiborne and Spain: Foreign Affairs under Jefferson and Madison, 1801–1811," *Louisiana History* 12:297, 300–301 (1971).

43. Claiborne to Jefferson, November 25, 1804, in Clarence Carter, ed., *The Territorial Papers of the United States*, Washington, D.C.: U.S. Government Printing Office (1940), 9:338, 341.

44. Wilkinson to Secretary of War Dearborn, January 11, 1804, in Carter, *Territorial Papers*, 9:159–60; Claiborne to Madison, September 21, 1804, in Madison Papers, 8:76; Claiborne to Madison, November 1, 1804, in *id.*, 8:260–61; Claiborne to Madison, November 8, 1804, in *id.*, 8:266 [also in Dunbar Rowland, ed., *Official Letter Books of W.C.C. Claiborne, 1801–1816*, Jackson, MS: State Dept. of Archives and History (1917), 3:1]; Claiborne to Madison, November 24, 1804, in Madison Papers, 8:319; Claiborne to Madison, December 31, 1804, in *id.*, 8:436.

45. John W. Gurley to Postmaster General, July 14, 1804, in Carter, *Territorial Papers*, 9:262–65; Hatch Dent to James H. McCulloch, July 14, 1804, in *id.*, 9:265–67; *New York American Citizen*, August 21, 1804; Abernethy, *Burr Conspiracy*, p. 17.

46. Clark and Guice, *Old Southwest*, pp. 17–18; Abernethy, *Burr Conspiracy*, pp. 17–18; *Richmond Enquirer*, August 30, 1805; William B. Hatcher, *Edward Livingston, Jeffersonian Republican and Jacksonian Democrat*, Gloucester (MA): Peter Smith (1970), pp. 110–13.

47. Claiborne to Madison, June 29, 1804, in Madison Papers, 7:395–96; Claiborne to Madison, July 13, 1804, in Madison Papers, 7:448–49; Claiborne to Madison, October 1, 1804, in Madison Papers, 8:120; Claiborne to Madison, October 13, 1804, in *id.*, 8:167.

48. Clark letter, October 10, 1804, in Clark and Guice, *Old Southwest*, pp. 17–19; Clark Deposition, January 11, 1808, reprinted in Wilkinson, *Memoirs*, App. V; Claiborne to Madison, October 1, 1804, in Madison Papers, 8:120; Claiborne to Madison, November 1, 1804, in Madison Papers, 8:260–61. According to Claiborne, Clark effectively spread the memorial's message through the territory. Claiborne to Madison, October 13, 1804, in *id.*, 8:167. Before the Louisiana

Purchase, Clark had urged that the United States seize New Orleans by force. Clark to Wilkinson, April 13, 1803, in Wilkinson, *Memoirs*, App. XVI; Deposition of Isaac Briggs, April 13, 1810, in *id.*, App. LVIII.

49. Jefferson to Gallatin, September 1, 1804, LOC.

50. Memorandum of Captain Sir Home Popham to Viscount Dundas, First Lord of the Admiralty, October 14, 1804, reprinted in "Miranda and the British Admiralty," *American Historical Review* 3:508, 513 (1901).

6. Vice President Burr

1. John Adams to Abigail Adams, January 21, 1794, in Adams Papers, Massachusetts Historical Society; Thomas Jefferson, *A Manual of Parliamentary Practice for the Use of the Senate of the United States,* Washington: Davis & Force (1820); John Adams to Abigail Adams, December 19, 1793, in Adams Papers.

2. Burr to Joseph Alston, March 8, 1802, in Davis, *Memoirs,* 2:185; Brown, *Plumer's Memorandum,* pp. 74–75.

3. Burr to Alston, March 8, 1802, in Davis, *Memoirs,* 2:185.

4. Joseph Wharton Deposition, in *Report of the Committee to Inquire Into the conduct of General Wilkinson, February 26, 1811,* Washington: A. and G. Way (1811), p. 203 ("Report of the Wilkinson Committee"); J.Q. Adams to John Adams, November 3, 1804, in Ford, *Writings of John Quincy Adams,* 3:78; Burr to Truxtun, January 6, 1805, in Burr Papers, Reel 6, LOC; Deposition of Captain George Peter, in Wilkinson, *Memoirs,* App. LXVII; Davis, *Memoirs,* 2:381.

5. Janson, *Stranger in America,* p. 210; James Sterling Young, *The Washington Community, 1800–1828,* New York: Columbia Univ. Press (1966), p. 20; Oliver Wolcott to Mrs. Wolcott, July 4, 1800, in Oliver Wolcott, *Memoirs of the Administrations of Washington and John Adams,* New York: George Gibbs (1846), 2:377–78; Constance McLaughlin Green, *Washington, Village and Capital, 1800–1878,* Princeton: Princeton Univ. Press (1962), 1:40–41; Davis, *Memoirs,* 2:172.

6. Richard Griswold to Mrs. Fanny Griswold, December 6, 1800, quoted in Green, *Washington,* 1:23; Oliver Wolcott to Mrs. Wolcott, July 4, 1800, in Wolcott, *Memoirs,* 2:377–78; Malcolm Lester, *Anthony Merry Redivivus, A Reappraisal of the British Minister to the United States, 1803–6,* Charlottesville: University of Virginia Press (1978), pp. 17–18.

7. Green, *Washington,* 1:20–21; John Melish, *Travels through the United States of America in the years 1806 & 1807 and 1809, 1810, & 1814,* Philadelphia: John Melish (1815), 1:208; *Plumer's Memorandum,* p. 337; Melish, *Travels,* 1:193.

8. Young, *Washington Community,* pp. 71–72, 99–101.

9. Janson, *Stranger in America,* p. 212; Smith, *First Forty Years,* pp. 13–14; Richard Beale Davis, ed., *Jeffersonian America: Notes on the United States of America Collected in the Years 1805–6–7 and 11–12 by Sir Augustus John Foster, Bart,* San Marino, CA: The Huntington Library (1954), pp. 8, 19.

10. Smith, *First Forty Years,* pp. 10–11.

11. Young, *Washington Community,* p. 75.

12. Toll, *Six Frigates,* pp. 223–26; Melish, *Travels,* p. 195; Green, *Washington,* p. 36.

13. John P. Kennedy, *Memoirs of the Life of William Wirt,* Philadelphia: J.B. Lippincott & Co. (1860), p. 26; Mary Lee Mann, ed., *A Yankee Jeffersonian,* Cambridge, MA: Belknap Press (1958), p. 207; Janson, *Stranger in America,* p. 215; Young, *Washington Community,* pp. 47, 49, 102; Davis, *Foster Notes,* pp. 8–9, 88.

14. Green, *Washington,* p. 45; William Lowndes to his wife, January 8, 1815, quoted in Young, *Washington Community,* p. 34.

15. *Plumer's Memorandum,* p. 185 (November 7, 1804); *id.,* p. 203 (November 23, 1804).

16. Giles to Governor Joseph Bloomfield, November 24, 1804, reprinted in Biddle, *Autobiography,* pp. 306–08; Bloomfield to Burr, September 17, 1802, in Kline, 2:737; Burr to Joseph Alston, December 15, 1804, in Davis, *Memoirs,* 2:353.

17. Jefferson to John Dickinson, December 19, 1801, in Lipscomb and Bergh, 10:301, 302; Jefferson to Joel Barlow, March 14, 1801, LOC.

18. *Extracts from the Journal of the United States Senate in All Cases of Impeachment, 1798–1904,* 62d Cong., 2d Sess., Washington: Government Printing Office (1912), pp. 32–33. The Pennsylvania state court judge was Alexander Addison.

19. Latrobe to Burr, December 17, 1804, in Burr Papers, Reel 5, LOC; Latrobe to Burr, January 6, 1805, in Burr Papers, Reel 6, LOC; Young, *Washington Community,* p. 45; George Bourne, *Cursory Remarks on the United States of America,* April 5, 1802, p. 2, in Bourne Papers, LOC; Davis, *Foster Notes,* p. 14.

20. Davis, *Memoirs,* 2:356–57; Uriah Tracy to James Gould, February 4, 1805, in Jane Shaffer Elsmere, *Justice Samuel Chase,* Muncie, IN: Janevar Publishing Co. (1980), pp. 225–26; *Annals of Congress,* 8th Cong., 2d Sess., pp. 92–100 (January 2, 1805); Plumer Diary, pp. 237–39 (January 2, 1805).

21. Burr asked Chief Justice John Marshall, who testified for the prosecution, whether Chase's conduct of the Callender trial was "tyrannical, overbearing, and oppressive," as alleged in the impeachment charges. Marshall evaded the question. *Annals of Congress,* 8th Cong., 2d Sess., pp. 168, 180, 215–16, 224–25, 236, 252, 266 (February 9–16, 1805).

22. Elsmere, *Chase,* pp. 244, 243, 246; *Plumer's Memorandum,* p. 278 (February 8, 1805), pp. 282–83 (February 11, 1805).

23. *Annals of Congress,* 8th Cong., 2d Sess., p. 502 (February 25, 1805); Samuel Taggart to John Taylor, February 25, 1805, quoted in Elsmere, *Chase,* p. 269; William Plumer to Jeremiah Smith, February 23, 1803, in *Life of William Plumer,* p. 257; John Quincy Adams to John Adams, March 14, 1805, in Ford, *Writings of John Quincy Adams,* pp. 114–17.

24. "Dr. Mitchill's Letters from Washington: 1801–1813," *Harper's New Monthly Magazine* 58:740, 749 (1879). The Chase trial served as an eerie precursor of Burr's treason trial, which lay only thirty months in the future. Many of the

significant figures in the Chase trial would also be central to that later contest. George Hay, a Virginia lawyer, testified at the Chase trial; he was Burr's lead prosecutor. Chief Justice John Marshall was a slippery defense witness for Chase; he presided over Burr's trial. Congressman John Randolph of Virginia led the Chase prosecution; he served as foreman of the grand jury that charged Burr with treason. Luther Martin of Maryland, a feared and notoriously alcoholic lawyer, defended both Chase and Burr. Burr's position in the later trial, of course, would be dramatically different. R.W. Carrington, "The Impeachment Trial of Samuel Chase," *Virginia Law Review* 9:485, 499 (1923).

25. Burr to Theodosia, November 17, 1804, in Davis, *Memoirs,* 2:350; Burr to Theodosia, December 31, 1804, in *id.,* 2:353.

26. Burr to Theodosia, December 4, 1804, in Davis, *Memoirs,* 2:352; Burr to Theodosia, January 28, 1805, in *id.,* 2:355.

27. *Plumer's Memorandum,* February 4, 1805, p. 245; Burr to William Van Ness, February 2, 1805, in Kline, 2:908. Burr was represented in New Jersey by his boyhood friend Aaron Ogden, a member of the Ogden clan, which was deeply intertwined with Burr. Burr to Charles Biddle, January 7, 1805, January 9, 1805, January 31, 1805, Burr Papers, Reel 6.

28. Burr to Theodosia, June 7, 1803, June 8, 1803, June 11, 1803, January 4, 1804, January 15, 1804, January 28, 1804, in Davis, *Memoirs,* 2:224–29, 267, 354–55. Burr's relations with women, including with Celeste, are explored at length in Isenberg, *Fallen Founder,* pp. 236–43.

29. Richard P. McCormick, "New Jersey's First Congressional Election, 1789: A Case Study in Political Skullduggery," *William and Mary Quarterly* 6:237, 241 (1949); Theodore Thayer, *As We Were: The Story of Old Elizabethtown,* Elizabeth: Grassman Publishing Co. (1964), p. 149; *Richmond Enquirer,* September 12, 1806 (reprinting item from the *Western World*). Rudolph J. Pasler and Margaret C. Pasler, *The New Jersey Federalists,* Rutherford, NJ: Fairleigh Dickinson University Press (1975), pp. 76, 84. The Paslers comment that Dayton "sometimes engaged in schemes that bordered on the illegal or treasonous." *Id.,* p. 208.

30. Norman K. Risjord, "House Committees and the Powers of the Speaker, 1789–1801," *William and Mary Quarterly* 49:628 (1992); Stuart Seely Sprague, "The Louisville Canal: Key to Aaron Burr's Western Trip of 1805," *Register of the Kentucky Historical Society* 71:69, 72, 84 (1973); Burnet, p. 413; Thayer, *As We Were,* p. 149; Davis, *Foster Notes,* p. 280; Dayton to Elias Dayton, April 4, 1798, in Dayton Family Papers, Princeton University; Dayton to Burr, May 12, 1804, in Burr Papers, Reel 5. Raymond Fitch, ed., *Breaking with Burr: Harman Blennerhassett's Journal, 1807,* Athens: Ohio University Press (1988), p. 135; Dayton to Wilkinson, April 15, 1796, December 29, 1797, March 23, 1798, April 27, 1798, in Wilkinson Papers, Newberry Library; Dayton to Burr, October 7, 1803, in John K. Porter Autograph Collection, Library of Congress. The scandalmonger

James Cheetham included a swipe at Dayton in his 1802 pamphlet attacking Burr, *A Narrative of the suppression by Colonel Burr of the History of the Administration of John Adams:* "Some crimes are so horrible in their nature as will not endure the lash of censure; and the actions of Dayton are of this class" (p. 62).

31. *National Intelligencer,* November 21, 1803; Cornog, *Birth of Empire,* p. 42; William Henry Harrison to Dayton, January 12, 1804, in Harrison Papers, Reel 1, LOC; Laussat, *Memoirs,* pp. 33–34; Daniel Clark to James Madison, January 24, 1804, in Clark, *Proofs,* Note 89, p. 175.

32. Melish, *Travels,* pp. 149–52; Zadok Cramer, *The Navigator,* Pittsburgh: Cramer & Spear (1808), p. 14.

33. Sprague, "The Louisville Canal," p. 69; Isaac J. Cox, "The Burr Conspiracy in Indiana," *Indiana Magazine of History* 25:257 (1929); Abernethy, *Burr Conspiracy,* pp. 22–23.

34. Affidavit of Peter Derbigny, in Clark, *Proofs,* n. 18, p. 39. While warming himself before one of the Senate's great hearths, Burr observed to a Federalist senator that although the Senate would confirm William Claiborne's permanent appointment as governor of Orleans Territory, "not a single Senator believed he was qualified for the office." *Plumer's Memorandum,* p. 221 (December 12, 1804).

35. "Act for the Government of the Louisiana Territory," in Carter, *Territorial Papers,* 9:405–07 (March 2, 1805). One western issue seems not to have engaged the interest of the vice president: the lengthy soap opera over the "Yazoo frauds," an epic land swindle in Mississippi Territory, named for the slow-moving Yazoo River. In 1795, land speculators bribed most of the Georgia legislature to win grants of huge chunks of the future states of Mississippi and Alabama. Public outrage forced the revocation of the grants, and in 1798 the federal government assumed ownership of the lands and created the Mississippi Territory. Many investors (mostly New Englanders) ended up with overlapping claims to millions of acres of land. Sorting through those competing claims roiled the federal government for more than a decade, until 1814. Although Yazoo claims were held by several of Burr's co-venturers, including General Wilkinson, Burr seems to have been a spectator on the issue. Magrath, *Yazoo, Law and Politics in the New Republic, The Case of Fletcher v. Peck,* Providence: Brown Univ. Press (1966); Abernethy, *Burr Conspiracy,* pp. 33, 75; Janson, *Stranger in America,* pp. 273–76, 269–71; Malone, *Jefferson and His Time,* 4:448–56, 5:232.

36. Burr to Theodosia, March 10, 1805, in Davis, *Memoirs,* 2:360; Burr to Jefferson, March 10, 1805, in Kline, 2:918.

37. Arthur Preston Whitaker, *The United States and the Independence of Latin America,* New York: Norton (1964), p. 96; Dayton to Jacob Burnet, July 10, 1807, in Jacob Burnet Papers, Cincinnati Historical Society; Wilkinson to Charles Biddle, March 18, 1805, in Cox, "Hispanic-American Phases of the 'Burr Conspiracy,'" *Hispanic American Historical Review* 12:145, 155 (1932); John Adair to Wilkinson, December 10, 1804, in Reuben T. Durrett Collection, Regenstein Library,

University of Chicago; Casa Yrujo to Cevallos, May 24, 1805, in McCaleb, *Burr Conspiracy,* p. 28; Henderson, *Mexican Wars,* p. 23.

38. Cox, "Later Intrigues," p. 801; Isenberg, *Fallen Founder,* p. 287; Jacobs, *Tarnished Warrior,* p. 212; Andrew Ellicott to Burr, June 11, 1804, in Burr Papers, Reel 5; Memorandum of General Henry Lee, 1807, in Wilkinson Papers, Box VII, Folder 577, Newberry Library; Isaac Joslin Cox, "Opening the Santa Fe Trail," *Missouri Historical Review* 25:36 (1930). Von Humboldt later published a report on his travels in Mexico. Alexander V. Humboldt, *Political Essay on the Kingdom of New Spain,* Lexington: University of Kentucky Library (1957) (translated by Hensley C. Woodbridge).

39. Burr to Theodosia, March 10, 1805 (postscript dated March 13), in Davis, *Memoirs,* 2:360; Samuel Latham Mitchill to Mrs. Mitchill, March 2, 1805, in "Dr. Mitchill's Letters," p. 749; Davis, *Memoirs,* 2:23.

40. Because there is no verbatim transcript of Burr's remarks, they must be patched together from several versions. I have relied heavily on the longest account, printed in the *New York Morning Chronicle,* March 19, 1805, reprinting from the *Washington Federalist*; Plumer, *Diary,* p. 312.

41. Mitchill to Mrs. Mitchill, March 2, 1805, in "Dr. Mitchill's Letters," p. 750; Kline, 2:914 (reprinting Adams's diary entry). Federalist senator Timothy Pickering of Massachusetts described Burr's address as "marked by the good sense which you know he possesses." Pickering to Rufus King, March 2, 1805, in *Life and Correspondence of Rufus King,* 4:443–44; Gordon L. Thomas, "Aaron Burr's Farewell Address," *Quarterly Journal of Speech,* October 1953, p. 278.

42. Mitchill to Mrs. Mitchill, March 2, 1805, in "Dr. Mitchill's Letters," p. 750.

7. *"I . . . Shall Seek Another Country"*

1. Deposition of Matthew Lyon, in Wilkinson, *Memoirs,* App. LXVIII.

2. Anthony Merry to Lord Harrowby, March 29, 1805, in Kline, 2:927–30; Williamson to Sir Evan Nepean, February 2, 1805, in Charles Williamson Papers, Newberry Library.

3. Anthony Merry to Lord Harrowby, March 29, 1805, in Kline, 2:927–30. In a later memoir, an aide to the British minister confirmed that Burr sought British help "in his attempt at forming a separate dominion in the western states." When General Wilkinson, too, called on the minister that spring, the British wondered if the general and the former vice president were working at cross-purposes. Wilkinson "affected to be a disappointed, dissatisfied man, and insinuated that he was in an understanding with Burr," the diplomat remembered, but "he over-acted his part." The Englishmen suspected that Wilkinson was trying to pump the British for information about Burr, which the general could then reveal to President Jefferson. Or Wilkinson could have been sent by Burr to gauge British interest in his proposal. Davis, *Foster Notes,* pp. 281–82.

4. Lester, *Anthony Merry*, p. 103; Burr to Theodosia, March 10, 180[5], in Davis, *Memoirs*, 2:359.

5. Burr to Joseph Alston, March 22, 1805, in Davis, *Memoirs*, 2:365.

6. Burr to Theodosia, March 29, 1805, in Davis, *Memoirs*, 2:366–67 (emphasis added).

7. *Kentucky Gazette*, April 9, 1805.

8. Jefferson to Thomas Cooper, November 29, 1802, in Ford, 8:178; Malone, *Jefferson and His Time*, 4:484; Adams, *Life of Gallatin*, p. 603.

9. Smith, *First Forty Years*, p. 6; Davis, *Foster Notes*, p. 10; George Bourne, *Cursory Remarks on the United States of America*, April 5, 1802, p. 52, in Bourne Papers, LOC.

10. Benjamin Latrobe to Mary Latrobe, November 30, 1802, in Talbot Hamlin, *Benjamin Henry Latrobe*, New York: Oxford University Press (1955), pp. 576–77.

11. Jefferson to W.S. Smith, November 18, 1787, in Lipscomb and Bergh, 6:371, 373; "Reply to Address" (1790), in Ford, 5:147.

12. *Plumer's Memorandum*, p. 470 (interview of April 2, 1806); Wood, *Empire of Liberty*, pp. 10–11, 172.

13. Jefferson to Philip Mazzei, July 18, 1804, in Ford, 9:41; Margaret Bayard Smith to Mrs. Fitzpatrick, May 4, 1806, in Smith, *First Forty Years*, p. 50.

14. Benjamin Henry Latrobe to Mary Latrobe, November 30, 1802, in Hamlin, *Latrobe*, App., pp. 556–57; Annette Gordon-Reed, *The Hemingses of Monticello*, New York: W.W. Norton (2008); Jon Kukla, *Mr. Jefferson's Women*, New York: Knopf (2007).

15. Lipscomb and Bergh, 1:448 (January 26, 1804, *Anas*); Chernow, *Hamilton*, pp. 395–97, 402–05; Kline, 1:532–40.

16. Claiborne to Madison, October 22, 1804, in Madison Papers, 8:199; Madison to Monroe, November 9, 1804, in *id.*, 8:269; Jefferson to Madison, March 23, 1805, LOC.

17. Davis, *Memoirs*, 2:24. One old friend recalled that Burr "was very fond of alluding to events in his military life. Indeed I think he chiefly prided himself on his military character." Charles Burr Todd, *The True Aaron Burr*, New York: A. S. Barnes & Co. (1902), p. 53.

18. A British diplomat wrote of the Turreaus' domestic scene:

> He often beat her and had a private secretary who played on the violincello while she was crying, to prevent her screams from being heard, till at last they became so loud and frequent that Dr. Thornton, the magistrate . . . thought himself called upon to violate the sacredness of diplomatic privilege, and, forcing open the door, obliged this Bluebeard to let out his wife.

Davis, *Foster Notes,* p. 58. Turreau's abuse of his wife was reported as far away as Kentucky, where a newspaper proclaimed that his wife sought refuge among her neighbors on a weekly basis. K.K. Van Rensselaer to Dayton, January 6, 1807, in Dayton Papers; *Richmond Enquirer,* October 10, 1806, reprinting article from the *Western World* of Kentucky. In December 1806, Turreau reportedly hired French sailors to force his wife onto a French ship in Annapolis to be returned to France. Madame Turreau's maid raised such a ruckus in the street, however, that neighbors intervened and prevented the abduction, ignoring the French minister's gun-wielding demands that they desist. *Plumer's Memorandum,* p. 521 (December 4, 1806).

19. Turreau to Talleyrand, March 9, 1805, Archives du Ministere des Affaires Estrangeres, Paris, Correspondence Politique, Etats Unis, LVIII, at 67, reprinted in Henry Adams, *History,* p. 578.

8. The Adventure Begins

1. Wilkinson found time to write a letter introducing Burr to the Marquis de Casa Calvo in New Orleans, one of the Spanish officials who paid the general's bribes. Burr to Wilkinson, April 5, 1805, in Kline, 2:930; Wilkinson to Casa Calvo, March 18, 1805, in Papeles de Cuba, LOC, Legajo 2375, Document 87.

2. Merry to Lord Mulgrave, April 29, 1805, in Kline, 2:932–33.

3. *New York American Citizen,* May 1, 1805, reprinting from *Philadelphia Aurora; Kentucky Gazette,* May 14, 1805, reprinting from *Philadelphia Gazette.*

4. Burr to Theodosia, April 30, 1805, in Davis, *Memoirs,* 2:368.

5. Leland R. Johnson, "Aaron Burr: Treason in Kentucky?," *Filson Historical Quarterly* 75:1, 8 (2001); Leland D. Baldwin, "Shipbuilding on the Western Waters, 1793–1817," *Mississippi Valley Historical Review* 20:29 (1933).

6. Smith and Swick, *Journey Through the West,* p. 67; Cramer, *Navigator,* p. 51; Gene A. Smith, *"For the Purposes of Defense": The Politics of the Jeffersonian Gunboat Program,* Newark: University of Delaware Press (1995), pp. 65–67.

7. Ray Swick, "Aaron Burr's Visit to Blennerhassett Island," *West Virginia History* 35:205 (1974); Smith and Swick, *Journey Through the West,* pp. 70–72; Therese Blennerhassett-Adams, "The True Story of Harman Blennerhassett," *Century Magazine* 62:351 (1901); Cramer, *Navigator,* p. 53; Fortescue Cuming, *Cuming's Tour of the Western Country, 1807–1809,* Pittsburgh: Cramer, Spear & Richbaum (1810), pp. 128–29; Davis, *Memoirs,* 2:368; *Ne-Ha-Sa-Ne Park Ass'n v. Lloyd,* 55 N.Y. Supp. 108, 111 (Herkimer County, 1808). Burr's companion for this part of the journey was Gabriel Shaw, a New York merchant.

8. Swick, "Burr's Visit," pp. 212–14; Smith and Swick, *Journey Through the West,* p. 72; David Robertson, *Reports of the Trial of Aaron Burr,* Philadelphia: Hopkins and Earle (1808), 1:523 (testimony of Dudley Woodbridge).

9. This account is based on Blennerhassett family records, beginning with Harman Blennerhassett's affidavit of 1807. Raymond E. Fitch, ed., *Breaking with*

Burr: Harman Blennerhassett's Journal, 1807, Athens: Ohio University Press (1988), p. 188. Other sources include an undated manuscript prepared by Harman Blennerhassett Jr. and reproduced in Swick, "Burr's Visit," p. 217, and the account of another family descendant, Blennerhassett-Adams, *supra.* One scholar has suggested that the Blennerhassetts were not at the island in May 1805, and thus they did not meet Burr at that time but met on another occasion shortly after. Kline, 2:951. As there is no documentation for that supposed later encounter, I credit the accounts of the Blennerhassetts. Milton Lomask, *Aaron Burr: The Conspiracy and Years of Exile, 1805–1836,* New York: Farrar Straus Giroux (1982), pp. 63–64. While in Marietta, Burr negotiated a note for $200 with David Wallace, the gentleman who had purchased the microscope for Blennerhassett. Burr to Biddle, May 4, 1805, Burr Papers, Reel 6.

Shortly after Burr left the island, the inimitable Wilkinson came floating down the river with a detachment of troops and a military band. The general, wearing a coat with Spanish doubloons in place of buttons, left an indelible impression. As his boats drew near, the band honored Blennerhassett by playing "Rule Britannia" (not a cherished tune for every Irishman) and Wilkinson came ashore for a visit. Lyon Deposition, in Wilkinson, *Memoirs,* App. LXVIII; Swick, "Burr's Visit," p. 218.

10. Richard C. Wade, *The Urban Frontier: Pioneer Life in Early Pittsburgh, Cincinnati, Lexington, Louisville, and St. Louis,* Chicago: University of Chicago Press (1959), p. 67; Smith and Swick, *Journey Through the West,* pp. 103–04; Espy, "Tour in Ohio," pp. 7–8; Melish, *Travels,* p. 126; Robert Wilhelmy, "Senator John Smith and the Aaron Burr Conspiracy," *Cincinnati Historical Bulletin* 28:39, 43 (1970); *Kentucky Gazette,* May 21, 1806; Wilkinson, *Memoirs,* p. 278 n.* and App. LXVII (George Peter Deposition); Sprague, "Louisville Canal," pp. 76–77.

11. Wilhelmy, "Senator John Smith," p. 44; Statement of R.J. Meigs Jr., in John Stites Gano Papers, Cincinnati Historical Society, Deposition of Reuben Kemper, *Carlisle Gazette,* May 31, 1811. Burr touched on the same themes when he stopped at Marietta earlier. "Affidavit of David C. Wallace," in the Burr-Blennerhassett Papers, *Quarterly Publication of the Historical and Philosophical Society of Ohio* 9:58 (1914) ("Burr-Blennerhassett Papers").

12. Affidavit of George Williamson and Affidavit of Samuel Hildreth, in John Smith Papers, Cincinnati Historical Society; Peter Deposition, in Wilkinson, *Memoirs,* App. LXVII. From Cincinnati, Burr and his intimates each set off for a different destination. Wilkinson continued to his new post in St. Louis as governor of Louisiana Territory. Senator Dayton was slated to return east as the "confidential person" who would brief the British minister. A serious illness, however, kept him in Ohio for several months. Senator Smith traveled down the Mississippi. He aimed to gauge the sentiments of the people in Orleans and West Florida about whether they wished to be part of the United States or not. While there, Smith

likely spent time with the obstreperous Kempers and their neighbors, learning about conditions on the West Florida side of the border. Burnet, *Notes*, p. 295. Years later, Smith claimed he had traveled to Mississippi at the request of President Jefferson, who supposedly wanted to know the citizens' attitudes there. Even if Smith had spoken with the president about such a downriver journey, his trip directly followed and plainly sprang from his conference with Dayton and Burr. Lester, *Anthony Merry Redivivus*, pp. 102–3.

13. Davis, *Rogue Republic*, pp. 2–10; McMichael, *Atlantic Loyalties*, pp. 60, 83–85; Wilhelmy, "Senator John Smith," pp. 39, 45; Clark and Guice, *Old Southwest*, p. 44; Smith, *Gunboat Program*, pp. 81–82; Johnson, "Treason in Kentucky," pp. 1, 8.

14. Cox, "Burr Conspiracy in Indiana," pp. 263–64, 269; Floyd to William Henry Harrison, May 22, 1805, in Harrison Papers, Reel 2, LOC; "Appointment of Davis Floyd and John Owens" (as river pilots), December 24, 1803, in Harrison Papers, Reel 1, LOC.

15. Lyon Deposition, in Wilkinson, *Memoirs*, App. LXVIII; Sprague, "Louisville Canal," p. 77; John R. Bedford, "A Tour in 1807 Down the Cumberland, Ohio, and Mississippi Rivers from Nashville to New Orleans," *Tennessee Historical Magazine* 5:40, 48 (1919); Johnson, "Treason in Kentucky," pp. 8, 11; Stuart Seely Sprague, "Senator John Brown of Kentucky, 1757–1837: A Political Biography," Ph.D. dissertation (New York University, 1972), p. 257; *Kentucky Gazette*, May 28, 1805; Wade, "Urban Frontier," pp. 18, 21, 69; Tom L. Walker, *History of the Lexington Post Office from 1794 to 1901*, Lexington: E.D. Veach (1901), pp. 17–18; *Kentucky Gazette*, June 4, 1805; Melish, *Travels*, pp. 185–87; *Kentucky Gazette*, April 2, 1805; Smith, *Gunboat Program*, pp. 81–82.

16. Lyon Deposition, in Wilkinson, *Memoirs*, App. LXVIII; Burr to Theodosia, May 23, 1805, in Davis, *Memoirs*, 2:369; Joe Gray Taylor, "Andrew Jackson and the Aaron Burr Conspiracy," *West Tennessee History Society Papers* (1947–48), p. 81; H. W. Brands, *Andrew Jackson, His Life and Times*, New York: Doubleday (2005), pp. 118–19; Andrew Burstein, *The Passions of Andrew Jackson*, New York: Alfred A. Knopf (2003), p. 72.

17. Peter Deposition, in Wilkinson, *Memoirs*, App. LXVII; Davis, *Memoirs*, 2:370; Bedford, "Tour in 1807," pp. 54–55.

18. Wilkinson to Gilberto Leonard, June 9, 1805, in Papeles de Cuba, LOC, Legajo 2375, Document 88. The general later claimed that they talked about Burr's wish to become a congressman from Orleans Territory (Wilkinson, *Memoirs*, p. 281), but Burr demonstrably had no interest in a congressional seat from any jurisdiction.

19. Wilkinson to Clark, June 9, 1805, in Wilkinson, *Memoirs*, App. LXXI; Clark, *Proofs*, pp. 120–21. Wilkinson wrote another letter that year to Colonel John McKee, federal agent to the Choctaw tribe in Mississippi, asking if he could raise a corps of cavalry for an expedition to Mexico. McKee Deposition, in Wilkinson, *Memoirs*, App. LXXX.

20. Wilkinson to Adair, May 28, 1805, in Clark, *Proofs*, n. 78, p. 158.

21. Davis, *Memoirs*, 2:370; Smith and Swick, *Journey Through the West*, p. 170.

22. Bedford, "Tour in 1807," 5:119; Cramer, *Navigator*, p. 119; William C. Davis, *A Way Through the Wilderness: The Natchez Trace and the Civilization of the Southern Frontier*, New York: HarperCollins (1995), p. 110.

23. Cramer, *Navigator*, p. 149; Davis, *Memoirs*, 2:370.

24. Ten years before, Burr opened his New York home for use as a French school run by a teacher who had fled the revolutionary Terror. The school linked Burr to many French expatriates, while the teacher's young ward became the companion of Theodosia and a foster daughter to Burr. Thomas Tisdale, *A Lady of the High Hills, Natalie Delage Sumter*, Columbia, SC: University of South Carolina Press (2001), pp. 18–23. A Frenchman reported that the residents of New Orleans had a passion for reading and, with an enthusiasm that is not entirely credible, that "social and cultural life is as developed here as it is in Paris." De Laussat, *Memoirs*, p. 119.

25. "A letter from Dr. John Sibley," *National Intelligencer*, January 13, 1804; Burr to Theodosia, in Davis, *Memoirs*, 2:370–71; de Laussat, *Memoirs*, p. 50.

26. Burr to Theodosia, in Davis, *Memoirs*, 2:371.

27. Adam Szaszdi, "Governor Folch and the Burr Conspiracy," *Florida Historical Quarterly* 38:239, 246 (1960); Merry to Lord Mulgrave, November 25, 1805, in Kline 2:943; Fitch, *Breaking with Burr*, pp. 192–93.

28. Wilkinson, *Memoirs*, pp. 283–84; Clark, *Proofs*, p. 94; Abernethy, *Burr Conspiracy*, pp. 25, 29–30; Clark to James Wilkinson, February 6, 1806, attached to Daniel Coxe Testimony, in Clark, *Proofs*, No. 55; McMichael, *Atlantic Loyalties*, p. 60; Davis, *Memoirs*, 2:381.

29. Stoddard, *Sketches*, p. 154; Davis, *Memoirs*, 2:371, 382; Adam Rothman, *Slave Country: American Expansion and the Origins of the Deep South*, Cambridge: Harvard Univ. Press (2005), p. 217; Malcolm J. Rohrbaugh, *Trans-Appalachian Frontier: People, Societies, and Institutions, 1775–1850*, Bloomington: Indiana Univ. Press (2008), p. 178.

30. Abernethy, *Burr Conspiracy*, p. 29; Claiborne to Madison, August 6, 1805, in Carter, *Territorial Papers*, 9:489; Jacobs, *Tarnished Warrior*, p. 221; Cox, "Later Intrigues," p. 801; Wilkinson to Casa Calvo, September 14, 1805, Burr Papers, Reel 6.

31. Clark, *Proofs*, p. 94.

9. Early Doubts

1. Sprague, "Louisville Canal," p. 79; Abernethy, *Burr Conspiracy*, p. 36; Burr to Major Isaac Guion, July 15, 1805, and Burr to Winthrop Sargent, July 1805, in Burr Papers, Reel 6. Burr hinted to Theodosia that romance flickered in Natchez, writing that he "saw some tears of regret when I left." Davis, *Memoirs*, 2:373.

2. Rothman, *Slave Country*, pp. 37, 41; Rohrbaugh, *Trans-Appalachian Frontier*, pp. 80, 126. Burr's traveling companion was army captain Daniel Bissell, who was on

his way to St. Louis, another serendipitous connection. Bissell would soon command Fort Massac in Indiana Territory, a key point on the lower Ohio. Davis, *Memoirs*, 2:373; Davis, *A Way Through the Wilderness*, p. 27; John McKee to Wilkinson, August 1, 1805, in Court Records, Southern District of Ohio, Cincinnati Historical Society; Kline, 2:938 n.1; Burr to Wilkinson, July 30, 1806, in *id.*, 2:937.

3. Adams, *History*, pp. 758–59; Lester, *Anthony Merry Redivivus*, p. 104; Abernethy, *Burr Conspiracy*, p. 33; McCaleb, p. 38; Isaac Joslin Cox, "Western Reaction to the Burr Conspiracy," *Transactions of the Illinois State Historical Society* 35:74, 78–79 (1928); Sprague, "Louisville Canal," pp. 82–83; Malone, *Jefferson and His Time*, 5:231.

4. Davis, *Memoirs*, 2:372; *Orleans Gazette*, September 18, 1805.

5. "Gen. Adair's Defence," *Lexington Reporter*, July 26, 1820; William Garrard Leger, "The Public Life of John Adair," Ph.D. dissertation, University of Kentucky (1953), pp. 98–99; *Frankfort Palladium*, September 7, 1805. While in Kentucky, Burr learned that the Indiana legislature had chartered his canal company, though rumors insisted that the company would become a vehicle for land speculation. Burr certainly knew how to manipulate a corporate charter. He wrote the law chartering the Manhattan Company to deliver fresh water to New York City, then used that charter to create the bank that grew into Chase Manhattan. *Kentucky Gazette*, March 3, 1805; Isenberg, *Fallen Founder*, pp. 183–88; Cox, "Burr Conspiracy in Indiana," pp. 263–67; Sprague, "Louisville Canal," pp. 85–86.

6. Davis, *Memoirs*, 2:373; *Kentucky Gazette*, September 3, 1805.

7. Burr to Wilkinson, July 30, 1805, in Kline, 2:937; Burr to Biddle, August 27, 1805, Burr Papers, Reel 6, LOC.

8. Wilkinson to John Smith, August 11, 1805, in Smith Papers, Cincinnati Historical Society; Swick, "Burr's Visit," p. 218; *Kentucky Gazette*, August 13, 1805; *Mississippi Messenger*, September 13, 1805.

9. Testimony of Major James Bruff, in *Report of the Wilkinson Committee*, pp. 208–13, 223.

10. Timothy Kibby Affidavit, in Carter, *Territorial Papers*, 14:133; McCaleb, *Burr Conspiracy*, p. 31.

11. Wilkinson, *Memoirs*, pp. 292–93.

12. Wilkinson to Dearborn, September 8, 1805, in Wilkinson Papers, Regenstein Library, University of Chicago.

13. Wilkinson to Casa Calvo, September 14, 1805, in Burr Papers, Reel 6, LOC; Kline, 2:941.

14. Bruff to Joseph Nicholson, October 22, 1805, in *id.*, p. 233; Linklater, *Artist in Treason*, p. 231. Another sign of tension between Burr and the general is that Burr asked a local official to recommend a leader for an expedition to Santa Fe, a question more properly directed to Wilkinson. T. Carpenter, 3:343.

15. Dearborn to Wilkinson, August 24, 1805, in Wilkinson Papers, Chicago Historical Society; Clark to Wilkinson, September 7, 1805, in *Report of the Wilkinson*

Committee, pp. 475–76. Wilkinson later claimed that it was during Burr's visit to St. Louis that he first learned of Burr's plans for insurrection and invasion of Spanish lands. Wilkinson, *Memoirs,* p. 292; Deposition of Captain Daniel Hughes, in *id.,* App. LXX. That claim was contradicted by much of the general's conduct before the St. Louis visit, including his statements that summer to Major James Bruff, Timothy Kibby (a militia officer), and Major Seth Hunt, noted in the text. Wilkinson also insisted that he wrote a letter to the Secretary of the Navy after Burr left St. Louis, reporting that "Burr is about something, but whether internal or external, I cannot discover." Though this supposed letter was never received by the Navy Secretary or found in any government files, one of Wilkinson's subordinates swore that it was sent. If such a letter was sent, it reflected Wilkinson's penchant for betrayal—something about Burr was making him nervous—rather than any patriotic sentiment.

16. Dan L. Flores, *Jefferson and Southwestern Exploration,* Norman, OK: University of Oklahoma Press (1984), pp. 75–76, 84.

17. Burr to Wilkinson, September 26, 1805, in Kline, 2:940; Robert M. Owens, *Mr. Jefferson's Hammer: William Henry Harrison and the Origins of American Indian Policy,* Norman: University of Oklahoma Press (2007), pp. 129–30.

18. Deed from Jonathan Dayton, August 23, 1802, in Harrison Papers, Reel 1; Harrison to Dayton, January 12, 1803, Harrison to Dayton, May 29, 1804, and Harrison to Auguste Chouteau, April 7, 1805, *id.;* Owens, *Mr. Jefferson's Hammer,* p. 128. Symmes engaged in the lucrative practice of selling parcels of land that he did not actually own. Dayton helped Symmes survive one scrape with the law by inducing Congress to sell Symmes certain lands that the developer had already resold. Andrew R.L. Cayton, *The Frontier Republic: Ideology and Politics in the Ohio Country, 1780–1825,* Kent, OH: Kent State University Press (1986), p. 61.

19. Burr to unknown Kentucky correspondent, October 7, 1805, in Kline, 2:942–43; Kline, 2:1003; *Scioto Gazette,* October 24, 1805; Johnson, "Treason in Kentucky," p. 12; Burr to Joseph Alston, November 29, 1805, in Davis, *Memoirs,* 2:374–75.

20. Cuming, *Cuming's Tour,* p. 350 n.218.

21. "Unsigned deposition [Elias Glover]," *Burr-Blennerhassett* Papers, p. 61.

22. J.P. Beresford Memorandum, December 13, 1806, in Beresford-Peirce Archive, North Riding Record Office, County Office, Northallerton, UK; *New York Daily Advertiser,* September 11, 1807.

23. An Ohio newspaper published a report from New Orleans in late October that observed: "Nothing new has transpired since our last, to throw any light on the state of our affairs with Spain—and we cannot venture to say what will be the event of the misunderstanding." *Scioto Gazette,* October 31, 1805. Yet a week later the same newspaper was reporting that five thousand Spanish soldiers were marching from Mexico to the Louisiana border. *Scioto Gazette,* November 7, 1805.

10. On the World Stage

1. Williamson to Lord Justice Richard Clark, January 6, 1806, in Charles Williamson Papers, Box VI, Newberry Library; Isaac Joslin Cox, "Hispanic-American Phases of the 'Burr Conspiracy,'" *The Hispanic-American Historical Review* 12:145, 166 (1932).

2. Merry to Lord Mulgrave, November 29, 1805, in Kline, 2:943–46.

3. *Mississippi Messenger,* September 2, 1805; *National Intelligencer,* December 18, 1805; William Baskerville Hamilton, *Anglo-American Law on the Frontier: Thomas Rodney & His Territorial Cases,* Durham, NC: Duke University Press (1953) p. 76; McMichael, *Atlantic Loyalties,* pp. 91–93; Davis, *Rogue Republic,* pp. 70–76.

4. *Mississippi Messenger,* September 27, 1805; *Orleans Gazette,* September 18, 1805; *Kentucky Gazette,* August 27, 1805, November 7, 1805, November 21, 1805. In September 1805, the Spaniards in Mobile harbor seized an American merchant ship and charged that it had failed to pay required duties, ratcheting up tensions among American settlers on the West Florida border who sent their products to market through Mobile. Edmund Gaines to Isaac Briggs, September 10, 1805, in Isaac Briggs Papers, LOC; Cabinet Memorandum, in Ford, 1:308 (November 12, 1805).

5. Eric Beerman, "Spanish Envoy to the United States (1796–1809): Marques de Casa Irujo and his Philadelphia Wife Sally McKean," *The Americas* 37:445, 448 (1981); Adams, *History,* p.480.

6. Adams, *History,* pp. 764–66.

7. Yrujo to Cevallos, December 5, 1805, Archivo Historico Nacional, LOC, No. 590 (Adams transcription). This letter is also reproduced in part in Adams, *History,* pp. 764–65, and McCaleb, *Burr Conspiracy,* pp. 53–55.

8. Yrujo to Cevallos, January 1, 1806, Archivo Historico Nacional, LOC, Estado 5545, expediente 15, Number 605 (partially reprinted in Adams, *History,* pp. 766–68, and McCaleb, *Burr Conspiracy,* pp. 56–58).

9. Pinckney and Monroe to Madison, May 25, 1805, LOC; Adams, *History,* pp. 625–29.

10. The Royal Navy's domination of the Atlantic shipping lanes forced the major combatants in the Napoleonic Wars into a remarkable series of accommodations that permitted Spain to receive some benefit from its Mexican silver wealth. The arrangements, which were made with the tacit support of Britain, France, and the United States, involved two separate trading patterns through the Mexican port of Vera Cruz. Both involved trade goods brought to Vera Cruz by neutral ships (many of them American), which then departed with Mexican goods and silver. Much of the silver was delivered to American ports and used to create commercial credits that ultimately redounded to the benefit of the Spanish government, or to buy goods that could be resold for Spanish profits, so Spain could then pay levies imposed upon it by Napoleon. The American and British

governments also received a cut of the trade. As one historian has observed, when Napoleon's army confronted the Austrians at the Battle of Wagram in 1809, both sides were subsidized by Mexican silver. Roger G. Kennedy, *Orders from France: The Americans and the French in a Revolutionary World, 1780–1820*, New York: Alfred A. Knopf (1989), pp. 246–64; Carlos Marichal, *Bankruptcy of Empire: Mexican Silver and the Wars between Spain, Britain, and France, 1760–1810*, Cambridge University Press (2007), pp. 193–204; Vincent Nolte, *Fifty Years in Both Hemispheres, or Reminiscences of the Life of a Former Merchant*, Freeport, NY: Books for Libraries Press (1972). It is difficult to imagine that Burr, with his many friends among America's merchant and political elite, was not aware of— and partly inspired by—this unique trading arrangement, which underscored the importance of Mexican silver to the world economy.

11. Annual Message, December 3, 1805, *Annals of Congress*, 9th Cong., 1st Sess., p. 13; Jefferson to Judge Cooper, February 16, 1806; Adams, *History*, pp. 679–80; Jefferson to Madison, August 4, 1805, in Ford, 9:168; Jefferson to Madison, August 27, 1805, in *id.*, 9:172; Jefferson to Madison, September 16, 1805, in *id.*, 9:174; Jefferson to Gallatin, October 23, 1805, in *id.*, 9:178; Jefferson, Cabinet Memorandum, in *id.*, 1:308; Adams, *History*, pp. 652–56.

12. *Annals of Congress*, 9th Cong., 1st Sess., pp. 1117–44, 1226–27; *Mississippi Messenger*, May 6, 1806 (printing letter dated March 31, the first public disclosure of the Two Million Dollar Act) and May 20, 1806; Timothy Pickering to Rufus King, February 13, 1806, in *Life and Correspondence of Rufus King*, 4:489–94; Malone, *Jefferson and His Time*, 5:71–76, 91; Burr to Jackson, March 24, 1806, in Jackson Papers, 2:92. The purchase price was to be offset by the value of losses inflicted by Spanish seizures of American merchant ships.

13. Turreau to Talleyrand, July 9, 1805, quoted in Adams, *History*, p. 661; McMichael, *Atlantic Loyalties*, p. 97.

14. Burr to Alston, November 29, 1805, in Davis, *Memoirs*, 2:375; Burr to Wilkinson, December 12, 1805, in Kline, 2:948; Burr to Wilkinson, January 6, 1806, in *id.*, 2:953.

15. William Ogden Wheeler, *The Ogden Family in America, Elizabethtown Branch, and Their English Ancestry*, Philadelphia: J.P. Lippincott Co. (1907), pp. 154–55. As one chronicler of New York commerce wrote in the nineteenth century, "There are many honored mercantile names among the citizens of different periods, but none stand higher than that of 'Ogden.'" Walter Barrett [a/k/a, Joseph A. Servile], *Old Merchants of New York City*, New York: Carleton (1864), p. 200. He added that Samuel G. Ogden "was one of the New Jersey Ogdens. His father was a clergyman at Newark. Samuel G. Ogden was one of several sons; one went to China."

16. In his memoirs, Wilkinson acknowledged that in a letter to Burr he had described Miranda as taking the bread out of Burr's mouth. Wilkinson, *Memoirs*, p. 305. Casa Yrujo to Cevallos, January 1, in Archivo Historico Nacional, LOC, Estado

5545, expediente 15, No. 605; T. Carpenter, 3:292 (testimony of grand juror, Tazewell, relating grand jury testimony of Sam Swartwout); David Robertson, 1:546 (Eaton); Biddle, *Autobiography,* p. 314.

17. *The History of Don Francisco de Miranda's attempt to effect a Revolution in South America,* Boston: Oliver & Munroe (1808), pp. 7–8.

18. Jefferson to William Duane, March 22, 1806, in Ford, 9:94, 96; Miranda to Madison, January 22, 1806, LOC; Rufus King to C. Gore, March 9, 1806, in King, *Life and Correspondence,* 4:529–30; *The Trials of William S. Smith and Samuel G. Ogden for Misdemeanors,* July 1806 (Thomas Lloyd, stenographer), New York: I. Riley & Co. (1807), pp. xxi, 105, 135–37, 148.

19. "Miranda and the British Admiralty," *American Historical Review* 6:508, 517 (1901) (William Armstrong to Capt. Edward Moore, from *Leander,* February 12, 1806); *Smith and Ogden Trials,* pp. vi, xviii, 113.

20. *National Intelligencer,* February 26, 1806 (reprinting from *Philadelphia Gazette,* February 19, 1806). The Republican *National Intelligencer* published a long defense of the Jefferson administration's conduct toward Miranda in its June 18, 1806 edition. The *Philadelphia Gazette* responded with a denunciation of the government's performance on July 14.

21. *Smith and Ogden Trials,* pp. xxi, 114–19, 81, 187, 242, 245; *National Intelligencer,* August 20, 1806; Malone, *Jefferson and His Time,* 5:88. Burr had ready access to news about the Smith and Ogden trials. His uncle, Pierpont Edwards, helped prosecute both cases, while Burr's friend John Swartwout testified for both defendants. Indeed, William Smith had been Swartwout's second during his 1803 duel with DeWitt Clinton. As the federal marshal of New York City, Swartwout also selected the pool of citizens from which the jury was chosen. Jeffersonians accused Swartwout of packing the jury pool with Federalists sympathetic to the defense. A few days after separate juries acquitted both defendants, Jefferson fired Swartwout.

22. *E.g., National Intelligencer,* July 21, 1806, and August 20, 1806; *Richmond Enquirer,* September 5, 1806; *Orleans Gazette,* October 16, 1806. Miranda's expedition was not the only British intrusion in South America that year. A Royal Navy squadron attacked Buenos Aires in July, leading to a year-long struggle for control of that trade center. By striking at South America, Britain hoped to injure Spain's ally Napoleon, and also to develop markets for English goods. With the French excluding English trade from Europe, export goods were crowding British warehouses. *An Authentic Narrative of the Proceedings of the Expedition under the command of Brigadier-Gen. Crawford, with an account of the operations against Buenos Ayres under the command of Lieut.-Gen. Whitelocke,* London (1808), pp. 2, 93–96; *Notes on the Viceroyalty of La Plata in South America,* London: J.J. Stockdale (1808), pp. 111–28.

23. *American Historical Review* 6:522–24; *National Intelligencer,* May 9, 1806, and *Kentucky Gazette,* May 24, 1806, and June 14, 1806 (wrongly reporting that Miranda had landed on the Spanish Main); *National Intelligencer,* June 11, 1806,

June 23, 1806, and June 27, 1806 (Miranda lost two schooners to Spanish ships); *Richmond Enquirer*, October 14, 1806 (Miranda landed at Coro); *Scioto Gazette*, April 24, 1806, July 3, 1806, October 9, 1806, and November 27, 1806.

24. Burr to Jackson, March 24, 1806, in Kline, 2:956. Burr made the same point in a letter to an Ohio militia general. Burr to Edward Tupper, March 30, 1806, in Kline, 2:960 n.7.

11. Burr's Threats

1. Louis B. Wright & Julia H. Macleod, "William Eaton's Relations with Aaron Burr," *Mississippi Valley Historical Review* 31:523 (1945); Toll, *Six Frigates*, pp. 260–62.

2. *National Intelligencer*, December 2, 1805, and December 6, 1805 (recounting public dinner honoring Eaton); *id.*, January 23, 1807 (Eaton's deposition describing Burr's overtures); *Annals of Congress*, 9th Cong., 1st Sess., pp. 48–50 (January 13, 1806), p. 233 (April 10, 1806); David Robertson, 1:474–80; T. Carpenter, 3:233–34; *The Life of the Late General William Eaton*, Brookfield, MA: E. Merriam & Co. (1813), pp. 396–402.

3. David Robertson, 1:480; Letter from Stephen Pynchon to Eaton, September 22, 1807, reprinted in *New York American Citizen*, November 11, 1807.

4. *Kentucky Gazette*, February 13, 1806; Benjamin Latrobe to Albert Gallatin, November 19, 1806, in John C. Van Horne, ed., *The Correspondence and Miscellaneous Papers of Benjamin Henry Latrobe*, New Haven, CT: Yale University Press (1986), 2:290, 292, 444–45 n.1; T. Carpenter, 3:381; Wright & McLeod, "Eaton's Relations with Burr," pp. 527–28; David Robertson, 1:485–89, 550; Johnson, "Treason in Kentucky," pp. 13–14; Kline, 2:1003.

5. Blennerhassett to Burr, December 21, 1805, in Kline, 2:949. The former vice president also sponsored E.I. Dupont, the munitions manufacturer, in exploring the use of nitre deposits in Kentucky to make gunpowder. Burr shortly would have an acute need for Dupont's product. Burr to Samuel Brown, January 19, 1806, in *id.*, 2:955. Burr wrote on behalf of Dupont to the brother of former senator John Brown, one of the Kentuckians Burr solicited during his western journey. Burr recommended that Brown introduce Dupont to John Jordan Jr., Burr's host in Lexington, who was a director of the Indiana Canal Company and the Kentucky Insurance Company.

6. Wilkinson ordered that all soldiers must have short hair, but Colonel Thomas Butler, a veteran of the Revolution and the Indian wars, refused to cut off his long, braided queue. Wilkinson had Butler court-martialed for tonsorial insubordination. After two trials, which sharply divided the army's officer corps, Wilkinson was greatly relieved when Butler died of a fever in the fall of 1805. Linklater, *Artist in Treason*, p. 230; *Mississippi Messenger*, September 27, 1805; Theodore J. Crackel, *Mr. Jefferson's Army: Political and Social Reform of the Military Establishment, 1801–1809*, New York University Press (1987), pp. 116–20.

7. *Kentucky Gazette,* March 15, 1806, February 26, 1806, January 30, 1806; William E. Foley, "James A. Wilkinson: Territorial Governor," *Missouri Historical Society Bulletin* 25:3 (1968).

8. Burr to Wilkinson, December 12, 1805, in Kline, 2:948; Burr to Wilkinson, January 6, 1806, in *id.,* 2:953.

9. George Morgan of Pennsylvania also reported that Burr spoke eagerly of attacking the United States government in Washington City. The credibility of Morgan and Eaton has been questioned. Morgan is said to have been old and somewhat senile, and Eaton too emotional to be believed. The accuracy of Casa Yrujo's report to his government has not been challenged, since his job was to provide an accurate account of such conversations, but some historians have claimed that Burr did not seriously propose to attack Washington City but only made the threat to deceive the Spaniards. Strikingly, however, none of these three witnesses had any connection to the other nor any opportunity to contrive together to create such a false story. Rather, three witnesses from very different parts of the American world reported that—over a ten-month period—Burr and Dayton talked openly of the possibility of staging a coup in Washington City. Those who wish to disregard those reports have provided no persuasive reason to do so.

10. Anonymous to Jefferson, December 1, 1805, LOC; Anonymous to Jefferson, December 5, 1805, LOC. Secretary of State Madison actually received a warning more than a year before these unsigned letters arrived for the president. William Cooke wrote to him that "there is brewing a most formidable and treasonable conspiracy against Louisiana." Cooke to Madison, October 6, 1804, in Carter, *Territorial Papers,* pp. 309–10. Cooke's warning, however, did not mention Burr.

11. Daveiss to Jefferson, January 10, 1806, in Clark, *Proofs,* No. 92; Jefferson to Daveiss, February 15, 1806, in Ford, 9:231.

12. Hatfield, *William Claiborne,* pp. 134, 147–49; *Mississippi Messenger,* January 8, 1806; Claiborne to Jefferson, April 10, 1806, in Dunbar Rowland, ed., *Letter Books of W.C.C. Claiborne,* 2:289.

13. *Annals of Congress,* 9th Cong., 1st Sess., p. 570 (March 5, 1806); Hatfield, *William Claiborne,* pp. 157–59; Claiborne to Jefferson, November 13, 1805.

14. *Report of the Wilkinson Committee,* pp. 330–32; Clark, *Proofs,* pp. 94–95, 102; McCaleb, *Burr Conspiracy,* p. 34;

15. Claiborne to Madison, January 24 and January 29, 1806, in Rowland, *Letter Books of W.C.C. Claiborne,* 2:248, 252–53.

16. Claiborne to Madison, October 24, 1805; J.C.A. Stagg, *Borderlines in Borderlands: James Madison and the Spanish-American Frontier, 1776–1821,* New Haven, CT: Yale University Press (2009), pp. 54–56; Edmund Gaines to Isaac Briggs, September 10, 1805, in Papers of Isaac Briggs, LOC; *Mississippi Messenger,* April 8, 1806; *Kentucky Gazette,* April 16, 1806; *Scioto Gazette,* April 24, 1806, and May 8, 1806; *National Intelligencer,* April 28, 1806; Edward

Livingston, *A Faithful Picture of the Political Situation in New Orleans,* Boston (1808), pp. 6–7; Claiborne to James Madison, August 26, 1805, January 29, 1806, March 25, 1806; Claiborne to Jefferson, March 3, 1806, LOC.

17. Francis Paul Prucha, *The Sword of the Republic: The United States Army on the Frontier, 1783–1846,* New York: The Macmillan Co. (1969), p. 73; Claiborne to Madison, October 24, 1805, in Rowland, *Letter Books of W.C.C. Claiborne,* p. 213; Claiborne to Madison, March 27, 1806, LOC.

18. Claiborne to Jefferson, March 3, 1806; *Report of the Wilkinson Committee,* pp. 318–28; Burr Papers, LOC, Oversize (statements of Lt. Luckett and Lt. Murray); Davis, *Rogue Republic,* pp. 86–91, 97; Reuben Kemper Deposition, *Carlisle Gazette,* May 31, 1811.

19. *Scioto Gazette,* February 20, 1806.

20. Hatfield, *William Claiborne,* pp. 216–17; McMichael, *Atlantic Loyalties,* p. 92; Major Moses Porter to Dearborn, February 8, 1806, in *Report of the Wilkinson Committee,* p. 357; "Special Message on Spanish Boundaries," March 20, 1806, in Ford, 9:238; Flores, *Jefferson and Southwestern Exploration,* pp. 86–87.

21. *National Intelligencer,* February 19, 1806; "Special Message," in Ford, 9:240; Dearborn to Wilkinson, March 14, 1806, in *Report of the Wilkinson Committee,* p. 357; Dearborn to Wilkinson, May 6, 1806, in Wilkinson Papers, Newberry Library. There were certainly voices for war at the time. *Kentucky Gazette,* February 13, 1806; Claiborne to Jefferson, April 10, 1806, in Rowland, *Letter Books of W.C.C. Claiborne,* 2:288.

22. Burr to Jackson, March 24, 1806, in Kline, 2:956; *id.,* 2:960 n.7.

23. Only weeks before, Jefferson had confided to the French minister, "We do not want war." Turreau to Talleyrand, January 20, 1806, quoted in Adams, *History,* p. 688; Jefferson to Caesar A. Rodney, March 24, 1806, in Ford, 9:245.

24. Daveiss to Jefferson, February 10, 1806, LOC. Daveiss also listed two Kentucky judges long on the payroll of Spain, plus William Henry Harrison and the rising young politician Henry Clay.

25. Jefferson, "Memorandum of a Conversation with Burr," April 15, 1806, in Kline, 2:962–64.

26. Burr to Wilkinson, April 16, 1806, in Kline, 2:968. Burr used pseudonyms to refer to the American officers on the Sabine border.

12. The Baron of the Ouachita Valley

1. Jennie O'Kelly Mitchell & Robert Dabney Calhoun, "The Marquis de Maison Rouge, the Baron de Bastrop, and Colonel Abraham Morhouse—Three Ouachita Valley Soldiers of Fortune: The Maison Rouge and Bastrop Spanish Land 'Grants,'" *Louisiana Historical Quarterly* 20:289, 398 (1937) (quoting C.C. Robin, *Voyages dan L'Interieur de Louisiane, de le Floride Occidentale, et dans les Isle de la Martinique et de Saint-Dominique, pendant les annees 1802, 1803, 1804, 1805 et 1806,* Paris (1807), 2:344). The Mitchell and Calhoun article is an

impressive piece of scholarship. The discussion of Baron Bastrop's tract relies on that article and the summary presented in Kline, 2:992–93.

2. Abernethy, *Burr Conspiracy,* pp. 73–74; Flores, *Jefferson and Southwestern Exploration,* p. 84. Livingston acted as the baron's lawyer for a short time. Livingston to Madison, September 15, 1804, in Madison Papers, 8:55.

3. *American State Papers: Indian Affairs,* Washington: Gales and Seaton, 1:705, 733–34 (February 19, 1806). The lands were described in the February report to Congress from the Lewis and Clark expedition, even though the famed explorers had never been in the Ouachita Valley. Their report incorporated the findings of other explorers, George Hunter and Dr. William Dunbar, who ascended the Red and Ouachita Rivers in 1804.

4. At least one writer has speculated that Burr, who espoused abolitionist beliefs, wished to create a haven for freed slaves on the Bastrop lands. Kennedy, *Study in Character,* pp. 243–47, 252. Although the speculation is an interesting one, there is no evidence that Burr, while in Mississippi and New Orleans, questioned the slave practices there. No one associated with Burr ever suggested that abolition was a purpose of his venture. Indeed, Burr himself sometimes owned slaves.

5. T. Carpenter, 3:238.

6. Hamlin, *Benjamin Henry Latrobe,* pp. 138–40, 171–76; Burr to Theodosia, June 1806, Burr Papers, Reel 6, LOC; Burr to Robert Goodloe Harper, May 29, 1804, in Kline, 2:870 n.2. Bollman undertook the waterworks and the metal-rolling plant with Nicholas Roosevelt of New York, the ancestor of two presidents.

7. *Correspondence of Latrobe,* 2:445 n.1; Casa Yrujo to Cevallos, May 14, 1806, No. 676 (Adams transcript); Justus Erich Bollman to Thomas Jefferson, January 23, 1807, "Notes on Report about Burr," LOC; Michael Stephen Wohl, "A Man in Shadow: The Life of Daniel Clark," Ph.D. thesis, Tulane University (1984), pp. 143–44 (citing Casa Yrujo to Cevallos, December 10, 1806, Gilpin Family Papers, Historical Society of Pennsylvania, File 3).

8. Casa Yrujo to Cevallos, June 9, 1806, Archivo Historico Nacional, LOC, Estado 5545, expediente 15; Casa Yrujo to Cevallos, July 12, 1806, in *id.,* Legajo 5542, expediente 22.

9. Merry to C.J. Fox [Prime Minister], June 1, 1806, reprinted in Adams, *History,* p. 776.

10. Davis, *Foster Notes,* p. 63; Biddle, *Autobiography,* p. 313; Cox, "The Burr Conspiracy in Indiana," p. 269 (1929); Kline, 2:1003; Cowan, *Charles Williamson,* pp. 282, 286. To a visitor, Burr explained that he was speculating on lands near the Spanish border because westerners were eager for a Spanish war, "some to secure their prop[er]ty, and some on the expectation of a chance to signalize themselves and advance their fortunes." Statement of Paul Henri Mallet-Prevost, in Kline, 2:970–71.

11. Biddle, *Autobiography,* p. 314; David Robertson, 1:485–89; Johnson, "Treason in Kentucky," pp. 13–14.

12. Latrobe to Gallatin, November 19, 1806, in *Correspondence of Latrobe,* 2:18; Note, *id.,* 2:49. In a more sensible move, Burr secured from Latrobe a design the architect had developed for boats to be used on the western rivers.

13. Latrobe to Christian Ignatius Latrobe, January 5, 1807, in *Correspondence of Latrobe,* 2:349.

14. Burr to Blennerhassett, July 24, 1806, in Kline, 2:991.

15. *Orleans Gazette,* July 5, 1806.

16. Peter Ogden's father was Matthias Ogden, the boyhood friend with whom Burr first enlisted in the Continental Army in 1775. Peter's mother was Hannah Dayton, sister to Jonathan Dayton.

13. The Western World *Ignites*

1. *Frankfort Palladium,* July 17, 1806, reprinting from the *Western World;* Abernethy, *Burr Conspiracy,* p. 93.

2. Latrobe to Gallatin, November 19, 1806, in *Correspondence of Latrobe,* 2:291; *National Intelligencer,* September 19, 1806 (claiming the Marshall family was behind the *Western World*).

3. *Frankfort Palladium,* September 11, 1806; *Richmond Enquirer,* September 5, 1806, September 12, 1806; *Kentucky Gazette,* May 31, 1808 (column of "Regulus," a pseudonym for Henry Clay), reprinted in James F. Hopkins, ed., *The Papers of Henry Clay: The Rising Statesman, 1797-1814,* Lexington: University of Kentucky Press (1959), 1:329. One of the editors of the *Western World,* John Wood, wrote in October 1806 that his life was afflicted by "certain individuals of a certain family as remarkable for their coldness towards each other as to strangers interposed." One of those family members, he continued, was Joseph Hamilton Daveiss, a brother-in-law of Chief Justice John Marshall and the United States attorney in Kentucky. Wood's letter also complained that his editor-partner, Joseph Street, was being courted by the Marshalls who kept their "utmost distance" from Wood, and specifically named two brothers of the chief justice, Alexander K. Marshall and Dr. Louis Marshall. Wood to Henry Clay, October 9, 1806, in *id.,* 1:244–46.

   A recent writer has suggested that Jonathan Dayton bankrolled the *Western World* but recites no source for the speculation. Linklater, *Artist in Treason,* p. 234. As a Federalist with western interests, Dayton might conceivably have had an interest in supporting a Federalist voice on the other side of the Appalachians. Yet the *Western World*'s crusade against western conspiracies plainly was directed at upending the plans of Burr and Dayton. Dayton would not have set up a newspaper to destroy his own project.

4. Anderson Chenault Quisenberry, *The Life and Times of Hon. Humphrey Marshall,* Winchester, KY: Sun Publishing Co. (1892), p. 23; Jean Edward Smith, *John Marshall, Definer of a Nation,* New York: Henry Holt & Co. (1996), pp. 30–31, 74–75.

5. Marshall, *History of Kentucky*, p. 375; Ronald Rayman, "Frontier Journalism in Kentucky: Joseph Montfort Street and the *Western World*, 1806–1809," *Register of the Kentucky Historical Society* 76:98, 105–07 (1978); *Frankfort Palladium*, August 7, 1806 (calling Wood a "hermaphrodical author"). Wood wrote with some candor of his feelings for Street in a letter to Henry Clay (Wood to Clay, October 9, 1806, in Hopkins, *Papers of Henry Clay*, 1:244–47):

> Perhaps such an ardent friendship is unfortunate, as it frequently entails misery on those who are the slaves of such a strong passion; but be that as it may, it has always been my lot and probably ever shall, to confine my regard exclusively to one person. This species of solitary regard constitutes my only happiness, and when deprived of the object of my affections, I feel the most miserable of mortals. This enthusiasm was likewise a principal motive which induced us to travel from Richmond together, and had it not been for some interference . . . I trust we should not have had a day's separation.

6. Fitch, *Breaking with Burr*, p. 29. Other British expatriate editors of the era included William Cobbett of *The Porcupine*, James Cheetham of the *New York American Citizen*, James Duane of the *Philadelphia Aurora*, and James Callender of the *Richmond Recorder*.

7. James Cheetham, the newspaperman who served as a mouthpiece for the faction of DeWitt and George Clinton, denounced Burr's action as an attempt to defend Federalists, a charge that helped drag down Burr's reputation in New York. James Cheetham, *A Narrative of the Suppression by Col. Burr, of the History of the Administration of John Adams, Late President of the United States*, New York (1802); Isenberg, *Fallen Founder*, pp. 244–45.

8. Thomas C. Leonard, *News for All: America's Coming-of-Age with the Press*, New York: Oxford University Press (1995), pp. 4, 6, 18; Alfred McClung Lee, *The Newspaper in America: The Evolution of a Social Instrument*, New York: The Macmillan Company (1947), pp. 258–59; Charles G. Steffen, "Newspapers for Free: The Economies of Newspaper Circulation in the Early Republic," *Journal of the Early Republic* 23:381, 384, 387, 408 (2003); Wade, *Urban Frontier*, p. 141.

9. *Kentucky Gazette*, August 5, 1806; *Frankfort Palladium*, August 7, 1806; *Frankfort Palladium*, October 2, 1806; Marshall, *History of Kentucky*, p. 577; Quisenberry, *Humphrey Marshall*, pp. 174–76.

10. An altercation in the newspaper offices between Preston Brown and Joseph Street is described at numbing length in the July 24, 1806, issue of the *Frankfort Palladium*. An early installment of the Spanish conspiracy series wrote of the secession movement (*Kentucky Gazette*, July 22, 1806):

> Sincere would be the pleasure, could we declare that Kentucky, the State of Ohio, Tennessee, the Indiana, and the Mississippi Territories, were free

of traitors; but unhappily, many, very many, in whom the citizens place the highest confidence, are, at this moment, organized, for the express purpose of effecting a separation of these States from the Union.

11. Rayman, "Frontier Journalism," pp. 103–04; Marshall, *History of Kentucky*, 2:378. The assailant, George Adams, was defended by Henry Clay, then a rising young lawyer-politician in Kentucky. Abernethy, *Burr Conspiracy*, p. 95.

12. Abernethy, *Burr Conspiracy*, p. 95; Senator John Brown to Jefferson, July 25, 1806; Wilkinson, *Memoirs,* App. LIX (deposition of Isaac Briggs); Thomas Rodney to Caesar Rodney, September 6, 1806, in Gratz, "Thomas Rodney," p. 291.

13. Isaac Joslin Cox and Helen A. Swinford, "Introduction," in *Quarterly Publication of the Historical and Philosophical Society of Ohio* 12:53 (1917); Clay to Richard Pindell, October 15, 1828, in Robert Seager II, ed., *The Papers of Henry Clay, Secretary of State,* Lexington: University of Kentucky Press (1982), 7:501.

14. W.E. Beard, "Colonel Burr's First Brush with the Law," *Tennessee Historical Magazine* 1:3 (1915); Hugh O. Potter, *History of Owensboro and Daveiss County, Kentucky,* Owensboro: Daveiss County Historical Society (1974), pp. 6–7.

15. Daveiss to Jefferson, March 28, 1806, in Joseph Hamilton Daveiss, *View of the President's Conduct Concerning the Conspiracy of 1806,* Cincinnati: Abingdon Press (1917, original in 1807), pp. 78–79.

16. Daveiss to Jefferson, April 21, 1806, in *id.,* pp. 85–87.

17. *Id.,* pp. 89–90.

18. Daveiss to Jefferson, July 14, 1806, in *id.,* p. 91.

19. Dearborn to Wilkinson, May 6, 1806, in Wilkinson Papers, Newberry Library.

20. McCaleb, *Aaron Burr Conspiracy,* pp. 60–61.

21. Abernethy, *Burr Conspiracy,* pp. 49–50; Jacobs, *Tarnished Warrior,* p. 226; Wilkinson to Cushing, May 8, 1806, in *American State Papers, Miscellaneous,* 1:562; Wilkinson to Dearborn, May 27, 1806, in Wilkinson Papers, Newberry Library; Prucha, *Sword of the Republic,* pp. 91–93; McCaleb, *Aaron Burr Conspiracy,* pp. 106–07; Wilkinson to Dearborn, August 2, 1806, in *Report of the Wilkinson Committee,* p. 378; Wilkinson, *Memoirs,* pp. 308–10.

22. *Richmond Enquirer,* October 10, 1806; Edward Turner to Claiborne, August 8, 1806, Claiborne to Herrera, August 26, 1806, Claiborne to Dearborn, August 28, 1806, in Rowland, *Letter Books of W.C.C. Claiborne,* 3:382–88; Crackel, *Jefferson's Army,* pp. 126–28; Flores, *Jefferson and Southwestern Exploration,* pp. 88, 173, 282; *Frankfort Palladium,* September 17, 1806 (nine hundred Spaniards crossed the Sabine); *Kentucky Gazette,* October 23, 1806 (a correspondent in New Orleans wrote that "war between us and Spain appears inevitable"); *id.,* November 3, 1806 (militias dispatched); Hatfield, pp. 217–18; Prucha, *Sword of the Republic,* pp. 94–96; Isaac Joslin Cox, "The Freeman Red River Expedition," *Proceedings of the American Philosophical Society* 92:115 (1948).

23. Malone, *Jefferson and His Time,* 5:124; *Kentucky Gazette,* July 26, 1806; *Scioto Gazette,* May 29, 1806 (Virginia drought), and August 28, 1806 (western drought and forest fire in Maine). On October 3, the *Richmond Enquirer* reported that the year's crop was so bad many demanded that courts not enforce judgments for debt against farmers.

24. Jefferson to John Sanderson, August 31, 1820, LOC; Malone, *Jefferson and His Time,* 5:124, 135.

14. High Water Mark

1. Clark, *Onondaga,* pp. 371–76; Abernethy, *Burr Conspiracy,* pp. 62, 101; *Richmond Enquirer,* November 18, 1806; *National Intelligencer,* November 12, 1806. Abernethy describes Tyler's payments as drafts on the firm of Samuel G. Ogden and William S. Smith, who had just been acquitted of illegally supporting Miranda's expedition to Caracas. Abernethy and his sources likely were confusing George Ogden's firm with Ogden and Smith, as Burr's drafts otherwise were all drawn on the George Ogden firm. Major Israel Smith was brother-in-law to Burr loyalist John Swartwout, who had been U.S. marshal in New York City. Elias Willard Smith, "Details of the Life of Israel Smith," September 1857, in William L. Clements Library, University of Michigan.

2. *New York American Citizen,* September 23, 1806, *Richmond Enquirer,* October 7, 1806, and *Mississippi Messenger,* November 4, 1806 (all reprinting from the *Herkimer Farmer's Monitor*).

3. Sevelle, *George Morgan,* pp. 204–28; John W. Reps, "New Madrid on the Mississippi," *Journal of the Society of Architectural Historians* 18:21 (1959).

4. David Robertson, 1:566–71.

5. Deposition of Colonel J. Barker, in Burr-Blennerhassett Papers, p. 62; W. H. Harrison to David Robb, June 19, 1822, in William Prince Papers, Cincinnati Historical Society. Harman Blennerhassett predicted that autumn that more than two thousand men would ultimately join Burr. James Wilson to Madison (undated, but before December 10, 1806), Burr Conspiracy Papers, LOC.

6. Depositions of Elias Glover (signed and unsigned), in Burr-Blennerhassett Papers, pp. 58–61.

7. Fitch, *Breaking with Burr,* pp. 191–93.

8. Evidence of Alexander Henderson, in Walter Lowrie, ed., *American State Papers, Miscellaneous,* Washington: Gales and Seaton (1934), 1:526 ["*ASP, Misc.*"].

9. *Ohio Gazette,* September 18, 1806; Fitch, *Breaking with Burr,* p. 195; Thomas Perkins Abernethy, "Aaron Burr at Blennerhassett Island and in Ohio," *Bulletin of the Historical and Philosophical Society of Ohio,* 12:2, 6 (1954); *Richmond Enquirer,* November 4, 1806 (reprinting from the *Kentucky Gazette*); Burr to Blennerhassett, August 4, 1806, Burr Papers, Reel 6.

10. *Scioto Gazette,* October 9, 1806, October 23, 1806, November 6, 1806; *Richmond Enquirer,* November 11, 1806, and November 25, 1806 (reprinting from

the *Scioto Gazette*). Thomas Hinds wrote the articles under the name "The Fredonian." William Thomas Utter, "Ohio Politics and Politicians, 1802–1815," Ph.D. dissertation, University of Chicago (1929), p. 49. "Fredonia" was coined by Senator Samuel Latham Mitchill in about 1800 to stand for "land of freedom." It was applied to a town in western New York and also was adopted by Texans who rebelled unsuccessfully against Spanish control in 1826. Joseph Jones, "Hail, Fredonia," *American Speech*, 9:12 (1934). In the 1933 movie *Duck Soup*, the Marx Brothers seized control of a mythical Fredonia.

11. Jefferson to John Nicholson, September 19, 1806 (acknowledging warning letter); Jefferson to George Morgan, September 19, 1806 (same); Jefferson to Granger, March 9, 1814; Minutes of Cabinet meeting, October 22, 1806, Lipscomb and Bergh, 1:458–61; Kline 2:978.

12. Abernethy, *Burr Conspiracy*, p. 69; Davis, *Rogue Republic*, pp. 96–97; Reuben Kemper Deposition, *Carlisle Gazette*, May 31, 1811; *Richmond Enquirer*, November 25, 1806; John Taylor to James Madison, October 13, 1806, LOC.

13. Glover Depositions, Burr-Blennerhassett Papers, pp. 58–61.

14. De Pestre to Lewis de Mun, September 10, 1806, in *Report of the Wilkinson Committee*, p. 352; Abernethy, *Burr Conspiracy*, p. 70. Burr passed through Chillicothe, Ohio, then the state capital, before turning south to Cincinnati, Kentucky, and Tennessee. *Scioto Gazette*, September 4, 1806.

15. *Richmond Enquirer*, October 7, 1806 (reprinting from the *Western World*, September 13, 1806); Diary of Judge William Fleming, September 16–18, 1806, Filson Historical Society; T. Carpenter, 3:238 (Wilkinson testimony).

16. Abernethy, *Burr Conspiracy*, p. 71; Jackson to William Preston Anderson, September 25, 1806, in Harold D. Moser & Sharon Macpherson, eds., *The Papers of Andrew Jackson*, 1805–1813, Knoxville: University of Tennessee Press (1984), 2:110; Jackson to James Winchester, October 4, 1806, in *id.*, 2:110; Burstein, *Passions of Andrew Jackson*, p. 73; Joe Gray Taylor, "Andrew Jackson and the Aaron Burr Conspiracy," *West Tennessee History Society Papers* (1947–48), pp. 81, 85. As an act of friendship, Burr left his slave Sam at the Hermitage, assuring Jackson that Sam "understands as well as any man living how to drive a carriage and manage horses." Burr to Jackson, October 1806, Burr Papers, Reel 6.

17. *Richmond Enquirer*, November 11, 1806; Mitchell and Calhoun, "Ouachita Valley Soldiers of Fortune," p. 412; McCaleb, *Aaron Burr Conspiracy*, pp. 74–77; Abernethy, *Burr Conspiracy*, p. 72.

18. T. Carpenter, 3:312 (Charles Fenton Mercier); Theodosia to Augustine Prevost, August 18, 1806, in Burr Papers, Reel 6, LOC.

19. Abernethy, *Burr Conspiracy*, p. 50; Hatfield, *William Claiborne*, pp. 217–19; Herrera to Claiborne, August 28, 1806, in Wilkinson, *Memoirs*, App. XCIII; Crackel, *Jefferson's Army*, p. 128; Abernethy, *Burr Conspiracy*, p. 51.

20. *Scioto Gazette*, October 9, 1806; Hatfield, *William Claiborne*, p. 221.

21. Wilkinson to Dearborn, September 8, 1806, in Wilkinson, *Memoirs,* App. LX.

22. Thomas Perkins Abernethy, *The South in the New Nation, 1789–1819,* Baton Rouge: Louisiana State University Press (1961), p. 257.

23. Just three months before, the general again showed his interest in seizing Mexico when he sent an expedition to explore the headwaters of the Red River, where Colonel Freeman had been turned away by the Spaniards. Under the command of Lieutenant Zebulon Pike, and with the general's son James as a junior officer, the exploration party passed a frigid winter in the mountains of today's Colorado, then was arrested by Spanish troops and returned to American soil. Prucha, *Sword of the Republic,* pp. 91–93. Several researchers, including the indefatigable Professor Abernethy of the University of Virginia, have explored the Pike expedition in great detail, believing but never demonstrating that it was part of the overall plan developed by Burr and Wilkinson for attacking Mexico. Without better proof of such a connection, I have not included that expedition as part of the central narrative. Abernethy, *Burr Conspiracy,* pp. 119–37.

24. Wilkinson to Smith, September 26, 1806, in Abernethy, *Burr Conspiracy,* p. 143 (from *Louisiana Gazette,* March 11, 1808); Wilkinson to Adair, September 28, 1806, in McCaleb, *Aaron Burr Conspiracy,* p. 112 (from *Frankfort Palladium,* July 16, 1806).

25. *Report of the Wilkinson Committee,* pp. 311–14 (Robert Spence testimony); Brunson, *Adventures of Samuel Swartwout,* p. 8.

15. Dancing on the Sabine

1. Wilkinson to Salcedo, October 4, 1806, in *Report of the Wilkinson Committee,* p. 389; Flores, *Jefferson and Southwestern Exploration,* p. 285.

2. Wilkinson described this episode in trial testimony. T. Carpenter, 3:237–38. Colonel Cushing also provided generally corroborating testimony in a written statement. Cushing Deposition, in Wilkinson, *Memoirs,* App. XCII.

3. Ralph E. Weber, *Masked Dispatches: Cryptograms and Cryptology in American History, 1775–1900,* Washington: National Security Agency (1993), p. 94; Robert Taylor Deposition, in *Report of the Wilkinson Committee,* pp. 293–96. The letter was deciphered by Wilkinson and printed in the *Annals of Congress,* 9th Cong., 2d Sess., 1011–14. The editors of Burr's papers deciphered the letter on their own and produced a slightly different version, Kline, 2:986–87. I follow the later decipherment.

4. The text of the cipher letter is reproduced in Appendix 1. The Dayton letter appears at Kline, 2:988.

5. In retrospect, the Spanish minister, Casa Yrujo, stressed that King Carlos had purchased Wilkinson's loyalty. If he had stuck with Burr, the Spaniard pointed out, Wilkinson would have ended up like the dog in Aesop's fable who crossed a river with a piece of meat in his mouth. The dog, seeing his reflection in the water, dropped the meat in his mouth to try to snatch up both pieces at once, and

so ended with nothing. By backing Burr, Wilkinson "would lose the honorable employment he holds [in the American army] and the generous pension he enjoys from the King." Casa Yrujo to Cevallos, January 28, 1807, quoted in Adams, *History,* pp. 838–39.

6. Cushing Deposition, in Wilkinson, *Memoirs,* App. XCII; T. Carpenter, 2:237–38.

7. Wilkinson Testimony, in Burr-Blennerhassett Papers, p. 47; T. Carpenter, 3:406–07.

8. T. Carpenter, 3:268.

9. Kline, 2:976.

10. Wilkinson to Dearborn, October 21, 1806, in *American State Papers, Foreign Relations,* 2:304.

11. Deposition of Lt. Col. Thomas A. Smith, in Wilkinson, *Memoirs,* App. XCIV.

12. Abernethy, *Burr Conspiracy,* p. 154; *Frankfort Palladium,* November 20, 1806.

13. Order of November 5, 1806, in "General Wilkinson's Orderly Book, 1797–1807," in Wilkinson Papers, LOC; Wilkinson to Cordero, November 4, 1806, and Herrera to Wilkinson, November 5, 1806, in *Report of the Wilkinson Committee,* pp. 402–03; Deposition of Colonel Walter Burling, App. XCVII, in Wilkinson, *Memoirs.* Abernethy speculates that the viceroy of Mexico was engaged in a revolutionary plot with the king's prime minister, Manuel de Godoy, and hoped that a war with the United States could provide a spur to that insurrection. By this account, the local commander, Colonel Herrera, won approval of his "Neutral Ground" agreement because he had the power to reveal the viceroy's plot and ruin his superiors. Abernethy, *Burr Conspiracy,* pp. 145, 156–57.

14. Kline, 2:989; Abernethy, *Burr Conspiracy,* p. 158.

15. T. Carpenter 3:268.

16. Truxtun to Jefferson, August 10, 1806; Biddle, *Autobiography,* pp. 316–17; Latrobe to Benjamin Stoddert, April 16, 1808, in *Correspondence of Latrobe,* 2:598.

17. Presley Neville and Samuel Roberts to Madison, October 7, 1806, in Burr Conspiracy Papers, LOC; James Taylor to Madison, October 13, 1806, LOC. Professor William C. Davis has unearthed evidence that a special effort to warn Jefferson about Burr's plans ran awry, based on a deposition given by Reuben Kemper of Mississippi Territory, who had caused so much disruption along the Mississippi-Florida border. In July 1806, according to his deposition, Kemper traveled to Washington City and arranged a meeting with the president. Though he intended to warn Jefferson about Burr's designs on West Florida and Mexico, the frontiersman claimed that he lost his nerve and did not deliver the message. Davis, *Rogue Republic,* pp. 95–96; Reuben Kemper Deposition, *Carlisle Gazette,* May 31, 1811.

18. Jefferson to Granger, March 9, 1814; Belknap to Danielson, October 11, 1806, in Burr Papers, Reel 6; *The Life of the Late General William Eaton,* p. 402; Wright and MacLeod, "William Eaton's Relations," p. 528. The resolution of the citizens of Wood County to oppose the "disorganizing views of Aaron Burr and his

partisans in this Western Country" was adopted on October 6, 1806. *National Intelligencer*, November 7, 1806.

19. Lipscomb and Bergh, 1:459–62.

20. Dearborn to Wilkinson, January 21, 1807, in *Report of the Wilkinson Committee*, p. 418; Lipscomb and Bergh, 1:462 (October 25, 1806).

21. Graham to James Madison, March 23, 1804, Madison Papers, 6:615; Madison to Claiborne, January 7, 1805, *id.*, 8:460–61; *Report of the Wilkinson Committee*, pp. 331–33.

16. The Daveiss Factor

1. Burr to Harrison, October 24, 1806, in Kline, 2:996.

2. Cox, "The Burr Conspiracy in Indiana," p. 270; Fitch, *Breaking with Burr*, p. 194; James Ross to Dayton, January 7, 1807, in Dayton Papers; Deposition of Judge Walter Taylor, April 26, 1809, in William Prince Papers, Cincinnati Historical Society; W.H. Harrison to David Robb, June 19, 1822, in William Prince Papers, Cincinnati Historical Society.

3. Fitch, *Breaking with Burr*, p. 197.

4. Burr to William Wilkins, October 21, 1806, in Kline, 2:994; Burr to Latrobe, October 26, 1806, Burr Papers, Reel 6; Latrobe to Christian Latrobe, in *Correspondence of Latrobe*, 2:352 (January 5, 1807); Peter Taylor testimony, *ASP, Misc.*, 1:499–500.

5. Charles Duval Testimony, *ASP, Misc.*, 1:534; David C. Wallace Testimony, *id.*, 1:534; *New Jersey Journal*, January 27, 1807; Dudley Woodbridge Testimony, in Coombs, *The Trial of Aaron Burr*, W.H. & O.H. Morrison: Washington, D.C. (1864), p. 200; Deposition of Robert Wallace Jr., in John Stites Gano Papers, Cincinnati Historical Society. To Hiram Jones, Blennerhassett also said that the purpose of the expedition was to divide the union. Deposition of Hiram Jones, in John Stites Gano Papers, Cincinnati Historical Society.

6. *Kentucky Gazette*, October 30, 1806.

7. Peter Taylor testimony, *id.*; John Henderson testimony, in *ASP, Misc.*, 1:533; Fitch, *Breaking with Burr*, p. 197; *Mississippi Messenger*, January 6, 1807.

8. *Kentucky Gazette*, November 10, 1806; Samuel M. Wilson, "The Court Proceedings of 1806 in Kentucky against Aaron Burr and John Adair," *Filson Historical Quarterly* 10:31, 33 (1936); Daveiss, *View of the President's Conduct*, p. 96.

9. *Richmond Enquirer*, January 6, 1807; "The Report of the Special Committee . . . charging Benjamin Sebastian . . . with having received a Pension from the Spanish Government," Frankfort: Joseph M. Street (1806); *New York Commercial Advertiser*, December 27, 1807; *Philadelphia Aurora*, December 24, 1806; *United States Gazette* (Philadelphia), December 20, 1806; *Kentucky Gazette*, December 1, 1806; *Frankfort Palladium*, November 27, 1806. The committee concluded that Judge Sebastian had received a pension of $2,000 a year from Spain; the judge resigned his office. Judge Innes managed to keep his office even though he

was closely identified with Sebastian, Wilkinson, Senator John Brown, and others who supported Kentucky's independence in the 1780s and flirted with the Spaniards in the 1790s.

10. *Kentucky Gazette,* November 17, 1806; Burr to Blennerhassett, November 6, 1806, in Kline, 2:998.

11. Burr to Clay, November 7, 1806, in Hopkins, *Papers of Henry Clay,* 1:253; *Frankfort Palladium,* November 13, 1806.

12. Wilson, "Court Proceedings of 1806," p. 35; *Frankfort Palladium,* November 13, 1806.

13. *Frankfort Palladium,* November 13, 1806.

14. *Id.; Kentucky Gazette,* November 17, 1806; Wilson, "Court Proceedings of 1806," p. 36.

15. Burr to Charles Biddle, November 18, 1806, in Kline, 2:1001; Burr to Tupper, November 18, 1806, in Kline, 2:1002.

16. Daveiss, *View of the President's Conduct,* p. 102; *Kentucky Gazette,* November 27, 1806; Wilson, "Court Proceedings of 1806," p. 36; *Kentucky Gazette,* December 1, 1806.

17. Burr to Harrison, November 27, 1806, in Kline, 2:1005.

18. Burr to Clay, November 27, 1806, and Burr to Clay, December 1, 1806, in Hopkins, *Clay Papers,* 1:256–57; *National Intelligencer,* December 12, 1806 (results of Kentucky election); *Plumer's Memorandum,* pp. 606–08. Burr wrote a similar letter on October 26 to Senator John Smith, who had asked Burr to provide him with such a written denial. Wilhelmy, "Senator John Smith and the Aaron Burr Conspiracy," pp. 46–47; McCaleb, *Aaron Burr Conspiracy,* p. 84 (quoting letter from Casa Yrujo to Pedro Cevallos, December 4, 1806).

19. *Richmond Enquirer,* January 6, 1807, reprinting from *Frankfort Palladium,* December 11, 1806.

20. *Id.; Lexington Reporter,* July 26, 1820; Abernethy, *Burr Conspiracy,* p. 99.

21. Wilson, "Court Proceedings of 1806," p. 40.

22. Marshall, *History of Kentucky,* pp. 397, 411; Rayman, "Frontier Journalism," p. 108; Beard, "Colonel Burr's First Brush with the Law," p. 15; Alice Elizabeth Trabue, *Corner in Celebrities,* Louisville: Geo. G. Fetter & Co. (1923), p. 13.

23. Elijah Jones Testimony, *ASP, Misc.,* 1:598; Charles Duval Testimony, *id.,* 1:534; Deposition of Colonel J. Barker, Burr-Blennerhassett Papers, 9:62; Deposition of Henry Cushing, Court Records, Southern District of Ohio, in Cincinnati Historical Society.

24. *Report of the Wilkinson Committee,* pp. 311–12 (testimony of Robert Spence).

25. *Philadelphia Aurora,* January 8, 1807. A witness reported that Adair and Burr shared a room at the inn. Leger, "Public Life of John Adair," pp. 111–14. One of the least reliable accounts of Burr's actions in the fall of 1806 is an article that John Adair wrote thirteen years later during his election campaign for governor of Kentucky. *Lexington Reporter,* July 26, 1820. Attacked politically for his

association with Burr, Adair produced a lengthy and entirely vanilla account of his dealings with Burr. According to Adair, the court proceedings in Frankfort depressed the former vice president and caused him to abandon any military goal for his expedition. Adair described Burr despondently burning his correspondence at a Frankfort tavern while proclaiming, "I will go and settle my lands on the Washita, and gather my friends around me, and I will show you before many years that I am not afraid to fight the Spaniards, if Wilkinson is." A threshold problem with Adair's account is that news of Wilkinson's agreement with the Spaniards had not reached Kentucky at the time of this melodramatic scene, so Burr had no reason to question Wilkinson's spirit for battle. Indeed, at that moment, Burr thought the general was trying to provoke a war with Spain; Burr did not learn to the contrary for another five weeks. Adair also claimed in 1820 that he happened upon Burr in Nashville by chance and had fortuitously stayed at the same inn. Yet Adair traveled on to New Orleans—also Burr's destination—where he was greeted by Burr's friends as a senior officer for Burr. Adair's essay should be viewed as an electioneering document, not a reliable source.

26. Jackson to Claiborne, November 12, 1806, in Harold D. Moser and Sharon Macpherson, eds., *The Papers of Andrew Jackson,* Knoxville: University of Tennessee Press (1984), 2:115–16; Jackson to Daniel Smith, November 12, 1806, *id.,* 2:117–18; Jackson to George Washington Campbell, January 15, 1807, in *id.,* 2:148–49.

27. Abernethy, *Burr Conspiracy,* p. 112.

28. Second Deposition of Isaac Briggs, in Wilkinson, *Memoirs,* App. LIX; Wilkinson to Cushing, November 7, 1806, in Wilkinson, *Memoirs,* App. XCIX; Wilkinson to Claiborne, November 12, 1806, in Rowland, *Letter Books of W.C.C. Claiborne,* 4:55–56.

29. Second Deposition of Isaac Briggs, in Wilkinson, *Memoirs,* App. LIX; Wilkinson to Jefferson, November 12, 1806, in Wilkinson, *Memoirs,* App. C.

30. Abernethy, *Burr Conspiracy,* p. 161; Iturrigaray to Cevallos, January 20, 1807, Archivo Historico Nacional, LOC, Estado 5545, expediente 15, Number 531, reproduced as "A Letter of General James Wilkinson," *American Historical Review* 9:533 (1904). The viceroy, Jose de Iturrigaray, had no difficulty in rejecting Wilkinson's demand for payment.

31. Deposition of James Wilkinson, in *ASP, Misc.,* 1:473; Affidavit of Lt. George Peter, *id.,* 1:566.

32. Deposition of Thomas A. Smith, in Wilkinson, *Memoirs,* App. XCIV.

33. *Annals of Congress,* 9th Cong., 2d Sess., pp. 686–87 (November 27, 1806).

17. Escape from Blennerhassett Island

1. Jacob Allbright Testimony, *ASP, Misc.,* 1:504; Peter Taylor Testimony, *id.,* 1:500; Charles Duval Testimony, *id.,* 1:533; Evidence of General Joseph Buell, Burr-Blennerhassett Papers, p. 67; Testimony of Dudley Woodbridge Jr., in Coombs,

Trial of Aaron Burr, p. 201; Statement of Dudley Woodbridge Jr., in Court Records, Southern District of Ohio, in Cincinnati Historical Society.

2. Welch Testimony, *ASP, Misc.,* 1:519 (no agricultural tools). Heavy crates were packed on the island for the trip, but witnesses disagreed on their contents. Some said they were Harman Blennerhassett's books; others said muskets. James McDowell Testimony, *id.,* 1:513 (no agricultural tools, and few guns with bayonets visible; heavy boxes boarded at Blennerhassett Island); John Graham Testimony, *id.,* 1:530 (expedition consisted of men without families or "implements of husbandry"); Israel Miller Testimony, *id.,* 1:513 (adventurers did not have much gunpowder); Charles Fenton Mercier Testimony, *id.,* 1:597 (Blennerhassett's crates filled with books and other items); Jacob Allbright Testimony, *id.,* 1:505 (four or five "rough" trunks loaded from the island); Testimony of Dudley Woodbridge Jr., in David Robertson, 3:108–09; *Richmond Enquirer,* December 27, 1806; *Connecticut Courant,* December 31, 1806; *Philadelphia Aurora,* January 3, 1807.

3. Edward Tupper Deposition, in Burr-Blennerhassett Papers, p. 19; Statement of Moses Hewitt, in John Stites Gano Papers, Cincinnati Historical Society.

4. John Graham Testimony, *ASP, Misc.,* 1:529–32; Charles Duval Testimony, *id.,* 1:533–34; Fitch, *Breaking with Burr,* pp. 203–05.

5. James Wilson to Madison (undated, but before December 10, 1806), in Burr Conspiracy Papers, LOC; Alexander Henderson Testimony, *ASP, Misc.,* 1:527; John Henderson Testimony, *id.,* 1:533; John Munhollan Testimony, *id.,* 1:521; William Love Testimony, *id.,* 1:507.

6. Charles Duval Testimony, *ASP, Misc.,* 1:534; Maurice Belknap Testimony, *id.,* 1:509–10; Peter Taylor Testimony, *id.,* 1:500. Eaton's account of his conversations with Burr began to circulate in early November. *E.g., Richmond Enquirer,* November 7, 1806.

7. *Richmond Enquirer,* December 30, 1806 (printing legislation); Lewis Cass to his wife, December 6, 1806, in Cass Canfield, ed., *Gen. Lewis Cass, 1782–1866,* Norwood, MA: Plimpton Press (1916), p. 8; McCaleb, *Aaron Burr Conspiracy,* p. 204; Abernethy, *Burr Conspiracy,* p. 106. The sponsor of the Ohio legislation, Lewis Cass, was a future candidate for president of the Democratic party and a close friend of Harman Blennerhassett. Frank B. Woodford, *Lewis Cass: The Last Jeffersonian,* New York, Octagon Books (1973), pp. 39–40; draft of Lewis Cass Resolution concerning Burr conspiracy, Ohio General Assembly, December 26, 1806, in William L. Clements Library, University of Michigan.

8. John Munhollan Testimony, *ASP, Misc.,* 1:522; Edmund Dana Testimony, *id.,* 1:511; Jacob Allbright Testimony, *id.,* 1:504; Edward Tupper Deposition, in Burr-Blennerhassett Papers, p. 19.

9. Edward Tupper Deposition, in Burr-Blennerhassett Papers, pp. 24–26; Testimony of Return J. Meigs, in *id.,* p. 67; *History of Washington County, Ohio,* Knightstown, IN: The Bookmark (1976) (originally published in 1881), p. 467.

In responding to the legislation ordering the interception of Burr's expedition, the Marietta militia bypassed its local commander, General Tupper, who was compromised by his connections to both Burr and Blennerhassett, and who also had publicly denied the government's power to stop the expedition.

10. *History of Washington County, Ohio,* pp. 467–68; Joseph Buell Testimony, in Burr-Blennerhassett Papers, p. 67; James Barker Deposition, in *id.,* p. 62; Charles Duval Testimony, in *ASP, Misc.,* 1:534.

11. Simeon Poole Testimony, in *ASP, Misc.,* 1:509; Maurice Belknap Testimony, *id.,* 1:510; Edward Tupper Deposition, Burr-Blennerhassett Papers, p. 21.

12. The description of the last night on the island is assembled from several eyewitness accounts. Woodbridge Testimony, in David Robertson, 3:108; Edward Tupper Deposition, Burr-Blennerhassett Papers, pp. 20–23; Peter Taylor Testimony, in *ASP, Misc.,* 1:500–501; Edmund Dana Testimony, *id.,* 1:511; Jacob Allbright Testimony, *id.,* 1:504; John Munhollan Testimony, *id.,* 1:521; Robert Wallace Testimony, *id.,* 1:536. Before that night, Blennerhassett had always brushed aside the risk that hostile forces might challenge the expedition, insisting that the adventurers would make short work of any attack by landing and burning down any settlement that opposed them.

13. Abernethy, *Burr Conspiracy,* pp. 102, 109; *Philadelphia Aurora,* January 3, 1807, and January 22, 1807; *Pittsburgh Gazette,* January 13, 1807, in Burr Conspiracy Papers, LOC.

14. William Love Testimony, *ASP, Misc.,* 1:506–7; Abernethy, *Burr Conspiracy,* p. 109.

15. Daveiss, *View of the President's Conduct,* pp. 103–4; John Rowan to J. H. Daveiss, April 18, 1807, Filson Historical Society; John Pope to J. H. Daveiss, June 15, 1807, Filson Historical Society; *National Intelligencer,* February 2, 1807. At least one of the adventurers confirmed that Davis Floyd loaded a crate filled with muskets at Louisville. David Fisk affidavit, in *ASP, Misc.,* 1:524; John Murrell to Andrew Jackson, January 8, 1807, in *Annals of Congress,* 9th Cong., 2d Sess., App. 1017.

16. No copy has been found of the Shawneetown articles of agreement. John Munhollan Testimony, *ASP, Misc.,* 1:522; James Knox Testimony, *id.,* 1:491. The governor of Ohio issued a proclamation that the state militia had completely destroyed the Burr expedition, a considerably overstated claim that was carried in several newspapers, including the *National Intelligencer* of December 29, 1806, and the *Philadelphia Aurora* of January 6, 1807.

17. Cox, "Burr Conspiracy in Indiana," p. 272 (testimony of Robert Pryor); David Fisk Testimony, *ASP, Misc.,* 1:524; William Love Testimony, *id.,* 1:507; James McDowell Testimony, *id.,* 1:513; George Poindexter Testimony, *id.,* 1:570.

18. Chandler Lindsley Testimony, *id.,* 1:519; Israel Miller Testimony, *id.,* 1:513; Jacob Dunbaugh Testimony, *id.,* 1:514; Hugh Allen Testimony, *id.,* 1:523; Edmund Dana Testimony, *id.,* 1:512; Charles Duval Testimony, *id.,* 1:533; Jacob Allbright Testimony, *id.,* 1:504; Brian D. Hardison and Ray Swick, "A Recruit for Aaron Burr:

Lewis Wetzel and the Burr 'Conspiracy,'" *West Virginia History* 3:75, 80 (2009); T. Carpenter 3:222 (Duval), 3:223 (David Wallace), 3:317 (Elijah Jones).

19. Fitch, *Breaking with Burr*, pp. 176–77; James McDowell Testimony, *ASP, Misc.*, 1:514.

20. K.K. Van Rensselaer to Dayton, January 6, 1807, in Dayton Papers; Samuel White to Dayton, January 17, 1807, in *id.;* Jonathan Rhea to Dayton, January 20, 1807, in *id.*

21. *Richmond Enquirer*, December 5, December 9, and December 16, 1806; *National Intelligencer*, December 24, 1806; *Kentucky Gazette*, December 29, 1806; *Newark Sentinel of Freedom*, December 23, 1806; *Philadelphia Aurora*, November 20, 1806; *Walpole* (N.H.) *Political Observatory*, December 12, 1806.

22. *Richmond Enquirer*, November 7, 1806; *New York American Citizen*, December 5, 1806 (reprinting from the *Boston Repertory*); *Richmond Enquirer*, December 11, 1806 (reprinting from the *Philadelphia Aurora*); *id.*, December 27, 1806; *National Intelligencer*, December 22, 1806; *id.*, December 24, 1806; *Frankfort Palladium*, December 4, 1806.

23. *Richmond Enquirer*, December 30, 1806, and January 3, 1807.

24. T. Carpenter, 3:303–04 (Daniel Bissell); Jacob Dunbaugh Testimony, *ASP, Misc.*, 1:514–16; John R. Bedford, "A Tour in 1807 Down the Cumberland, Ohio, and Mississippi Ohio Rivers from Nashville to New Orleans," *Tennessee Historical Magazine* 5:40, 53 (1919). Burr sent to the fort a barrel of apples for Mrs. Bissell, whom he had known when she was a girl. Sergeant Dunbaugh's furlough was for only twenty days; Captain Bissell expected Burr to link up with General Wilkinson downriver so Dunbaugh could resume active army duty before the furlough expired.

25. Cayton, *Frontier Republic*, p. 92; John Ross to Jonathan Dayton, January 6, 1807, in Dayton Papers. Blennerhassett's predictions were reported by several witnesses. David Wallace Testimony, *ASP, Misc.*, 1:535; David Gillmore Testimony, *id.*, 1:537; John Graham Testimony, *id.*, 1:528; T. Carpenter, 3:348 (Major Bruff).

26. David Gillmore Testimony, *ASP, Misc.*, 1:537.

27. Jacob Dunbaugh Testimony, *ASP, Misc.*, 1:514–15; Israel Miller Testimony, *id.*, 1:512; Chandler Lindsley Testimony, *id.*, 1:521; T. Carpenter, 3:113 (James McDowell), 3:195 (John Munhollan); *Richmond Enquirer*, February 10, 1807 (reprinting from *Kentucky Gazette*, January 17, 1807).

28. T. Carpenter, 3:193 (Samuel Moxley); Fitch, *Breaking with Burr*, pp. 179–81.

29. T. Carpenter, 3:155 (Thomas Hartley); Samuel Moxley Testimony, *ASP, Misc.*, 1:520; Jacob Dunbaugh Testimony, *id.*, 1:516; Fitch, *Breaking with Burr*, p. 179.

30. Governor Edward Tiffin to Senator John Smith, December 23, 1806, in John Smith Papers, Cincinnati Historical Society (enclosing copy of resolution calling for Smith's resignation); Evidence of Lt. Jacob Jackson, *Annals of Congress*, 10th Cong., 1st Sess., pp. 683–86; Wilhelmy, "Senator John Smith and the Aaron Burr Conspiracy," p. 50; Davis, *Rogue Republic*, p. 100. Smith appears to have been

trying to remain on good terms with both Burr and the United States government. He spent more than a week in Kentucky while Burr was facing legal proceedings there, though Smith insisted he was not there to support Burr. Rather, he claimed, he was attempting to find a Kentucky bank that would honor two bills of exchange he had received from Burr. Evidence of Thomas Hart Jr., president of the Bank of Lexington, Kentucky, March 7, 1808, in Smith Papers, Cincinnati Historical Society; Evidence of Craven P. Luckett, March 17, 1808, *id.*; Evidence of John Jordan, March 7, 1808, in *id.* Suspected of providing supplies to Burr, Smith later asked that his business records be reviewed by Ohio militia officials, who declared themselves satisfied that he had not done so. Deposition of John Stites Gano, September 5, 1807, in *id.* Suspicions of Smith, however, lingered. Indeed, the cipher letter reports giving orders to "the contractor" to "forward six months' provisions to points you may name." Appendix 1. In view of Smith's close ties to Burr and Wilkinson, the reference appears to be to Smith. In early January, the Ohio legislature adopted a resolution asking Smith to resign his seat in the Senate because of his absence from the session of Congress then convened in Washington City. *Plumer's Memorandum,* p. 564 (January 9, 1807).

18. Wilkinson Unchained

1. Deposition of Colonel J. Bellechasse, Orleans Militia, in Clark, *Proofs,* Note 68.
2. Wilkinson to Jefferson, November 12, 1806, in *Report of the Wilkinson Committee,* p. 426.
3. McCaleb, *Aaron Burr Conspiracy,* p. 170; Dearborn to Wilkinson, November 27, 1806, in *Report of the Wilkinson Committee,* p. 408; Livingston, *A Faithful Picture,* pp. 11–13; Jacobs, *Tarnished Warrior,* p. 234.
4. Wilkinson to Jefferson, November 28, 1806, in Isaac Briggs Papers, LOC.
5. Wilkinson to Claiborne, December 6, 1806, and December 7, 1806, in Rowland, *Letter Books of W.C.C. Claiborne,* 4:46–49; Wilkinson to Dinsmore, December 4, 1806, in Wilkinson Papers, Newberry Library; T. Carpenter, 3:264 (Wilkinson). The American naval squadron consisted of four gunboats and two bomb ketches (sailing ships armed with mortars rather than cannon). The gunboats were a pet project of Jefferson's, who saw them as a low-cost alternative to expensive seagoing ships. He thought that gunboats, which could not venture far from America's coasts, would provide defensive firepower without encouraging the nation to engage in foreign wars. The gunboats, with a single heavy cannon on either end, were often ridiculed as ineffective craft. Upon seeing gunboats rising in Kentucky boatyards, an Englishman scoffed, "Though the inutility of these mockeries of men-of-war has been manifested on many occasions, yet the president persists in riding his naval hobbyhorse." Janson, *Stranger in America,* p. 217.
6. Wilkinson to Jefferson, November 27, 1806, in *Report of the Wilkinson Committee,* p. 430; Wilkinson Testimony, in *ASP, Misc.,* 1:469–70; *Richmond Enquirer,*

April 4, 1807 (reprinting from *National Intelligencer*); Abernethy, *Burr Conspiracy*, pp. 175–76.

7. Wilkinson to Folch, December 6, 1806, Wilkinson Papers, Newberry Library; Wilkinson to British Commander, Jamaica Station, December 7, 1806, in *Report of the Wilkinson Committee*, p. 416; Admiral Davies to Wilkinson, January 17, 1807, in *id.*, p. 418; Cox, "Wilkinson and His Later Intrigues," pp. 794, 803–04 (1914); Brunson, *Adventures of Samuel Swartwout*, p. 13; *Richmond Enquirer*, February 3, 1807.

8. Kline, 2:973–90. The editors of Burr's papers performed a painstaking analysis of these changes by comparing the version released by Wilkinson with both the altered version provided by Wilkinson and the duplicate that he had received from Bollman. Also, Wilkinson testified openly about some of his alterations to the letter. T. Carpenter, 3:245–46. The testimony of his New Orleans lawyer, A. L. Duncan, confirmed some of Wilkinson's changes. *Id.*, 3:243–45.

9. Claiborne to Wilkinson, December 8, 1806, Wilkinson Papers, Newberry Library; Wilkinson to Jefferson, December 9, 1807, in *Report of the Wilkinson Committee*, p. 435; T. Carpenter, 3:285 (Captain John Shaw); *National Intelligencer*, January 15, 1807; *Richmond Enquirer*, January 22, 1807; Livingston, *A Faithful Picture*, pp. 15–17.

10. Livingston, *A Faithful Picture*, pp. 19–20; *Frankfort Palladium*, January 22, 1807; *New York American Citizen*, January 24, 1807.

11. Swartwout to Nathaniel Evans, March 28, 1807, in Evans Family Papers, LSU Library; *Plumer's Memorandum*, p. 618 (February 21, 1807); Brunson, *Adventures of Samuel Swartwout*, p. 13.

12. Many of the affidavits and court papers for these events were printed in a contemporary magazine, *The Balance and Columbian Repository* 6:68–69, 82–86 (1807); Abernethy, *Burr Conspiracy*, pp. 178–80. Both Lewis Kerr and Judge Workman were tried on misdemeanor charges of aiding an invasion of a foreign nation; both won acquittals. "The Trials of Judge Workman and Colonel Kerr, etc.," *American Law Journal* 6:138–52 (1817).

13. *The Balance and Columbian Repository* 6:85 (1807) (affidavit of James Workman); Claiborne to Madison, December 9, 1806, Wilkinson to Claiborne, December 6, 1806, and December 15, 1806, in Rowland, *Letter Books of W.C.C. Claiborne*, 4:46–47, 50–52, 59–61; Wilkinson to Jefferson, January 3, 1807, in Burr Conspiracy Papers, LOC; Workman to Claiborne, January 5, 1807, February 11, 1807, and Affidavit of James Workman, January 13, 1807, in James Workman, *Essays and Letters on Various Political Subjects*, New York: I. Riley (1809), pp. 120, 122–24, 144.

14. Livingston, *A Faithful Picture*, p. 32; William R. Teebo, "General Wilkinson's Strategy to Thwart the Burr Conspiracy in New Orleans," Ph.D. thesis, California State University, Dominguez Hills (2003).

15. McCaleb, *Aaron Burr Conspiracy*, p. 201; Abernethy, *Burr Conspiracy*, p. 201; Livingston, *A Faithful Picture*, p. 29. Livingston published a denunciation of Wilkinson's methods in the *Louisiana Gazette* of December 30, 1806, but his words did not deflect the general from his course. The *Richmond Enquirer* reprinted Livingston's essay in its February 17, 1807, issue.

16. The territorial assembly's statement was printed in the *Orleans Gazette* of March 20, 1807, and is excerpted in McCaleb, *Aaron Burr Conspiracy*, pp. 197–98; Wilkinson to Jefferson, January 18, 1807, in *Report of the Wilkinson Committee*, pp. 446–47; Livingston, *A Faithful Picture*, p. 38; *Mississippi Messenger*, February 4, 1807. In April, when the territorial assembly was considering a petition to Congress attacking Wilkinson, the general turned for political help to the Spanish governor of West Florida, who wielded considerable influence with the "ancient Louisianans" in the assembly. The Spaniard, content that Wilkinson was defending Spain's interests in the crisis, not only produced enough votes in the assembly to defeat the draft petition but also to win approval of a resolution approving the conduct of Wilkinson and Governor Claiborne. "An Interview of Governor Folch with General Wilkinson," *American Historical Review* 10:832, 839–40; Wilkinson to Folch, January 25, 1807, Papeles de Cuba, LOC, Legajo 2375, Document 102.

17. "John Adair's Defence," *Lexington Reporter*, July 26, 1820; Deposition of Commodore Shaw and William Tharp, Esq., in *Report of the Wilkinson Committee*, p. 346; T. Carpenter, 3:283 (George Poindexter); *Philadelphia Aurora*, February 25, 1807; Livingston, *A Faithful Picture*, pp. 32, 44; Abernethy, *Burr Conspiracy*, p. 181.

18. Jefferson to Wilkinson, February 3, 1807, in Lipscomb and Bergh, 11:149–50; Wilkinson to Clark, December 10, 1806, in Clark, *Proofs*, p. 150.

19. Burr in Chains

1. Livingston, *A Faithful Picture*, p. 44; Hamilton, *Anglo-American Law on the Frontier*, p. 79; J.F.H. Claiborne, *Mississippi as a Province, Territory, and State*, Jackson, MS: Power & Barksdale (1880), 1:278; R.W. Jones, "Some Facts Concerning the Settlement and Early History of Mississippi," *Publications of the Mississippi Historical Society* 1:86 (1898).

2. Abernethy, *Burr Conspiracy*, p. 202; Kline, 2:1007–08; Jacob Dunbaugh Testimony, in *ASP, Misc.*, 1:517; Mead Declaration, December 23, 1806, in *Third Annual Report of the Director of the Department of Archives and History of the State of Mississippi*, October 1, 1903–October 1, 1904 (Nashville, 1905), pp. 42–43 ["Third Annual Report"]; *Mississippi Messenger*, January 20, 1807.

3. Testimony of David Fisk, *ASP, Misc.*, 1:525; Testimony of John Mulhollan, *id.*, 1:523; Testimony of Samuel Moxley, *id.*, 1:519; Testimony of Stephen Welch, *id.*, 1:519; Fitch, *Breaking with Burr*, p. 181; Abernethy, *Burr Conspiracy*, p. 205.

4. Fitch, *Breaking with Burr,* p. 181; Testimony of John Mulhollan, *ASP, Misc.,* 1:523; *Mississippi Messenger,* January 20, 1807; Abernethy, *Burr Conspiracy,* pp. 205–09; "Agreement with Cowles Mead," January 16, 1807, in Kline, 2:1014; Testimony of George Poindexter, *ASP, Misc.,* 1:568; W.H. Woldridge to Lt. Col. Cordridge, January 14, 1807, in Third Annual Report, pp. 54–55. The Mississippi state report published in 1905 includes much of the correspondence between Burr and Mead, and between Mead and his militia officers, during the negotiations. *Id.,* pp. 49–63.

5. *Mississippi Messenger,* January 20, 1807; Abernethy, *Burr Conspiracy,* pp. 204–05; Testimony of Jacob Dunbaugh, *ASP, Misc.,* 1:515; Burr to Mead, January 12, 1807, in Kline, 2:1008–09; Mead to Claiborne, December 14, 1806, in Rowland, *Letter Books of W.C.C. Claiborne,* 4:66; Claiborne to Colonel Fitzpatrick, January 13, 1807, in Third Annual Report, pp. 52–53.

6. John Carmichael Deposition, in *Report of the Wilkinson Committee,* pp. 347–49; Davis, *Rogue Republic,* pp. 98–100; Reuben Kemper Deposition, *Carlisle Gazette,* May 31, 1811; *Richmond Enquirer,* March 17, 1807. According to Sergeant Dunbaugh, Burr described to him the same plan: that the adventurers would seize Baton Rouge and wait for additional volunteers there. Jacob Dunbaugh Testimony, *ASP, Misc.,* 1:518.

7. Kline, 1:1016; *Frankfort Palladium,* February 19, 1807; *Orleans Gazette,* February 5, 1807.

8. George Poindexter Testimony, in *ASP, Misc.,* p. 569; Samuel Moxley Testimony, *id.,* p. 523; Jacob Dunbaugh Testimony, *id.,* p. 514; Stephen Welch Testimony, *id.,* 1:519; Lemuel Henry Testimony, *id.,* 1:602; Fitch, *Breaking with Burr,* pp. 115, 181–82.

9. *Mississippi Messenger,* January 20, 1807; Kline, 2:1017–18; Affidavit of Lt. Col. Thomas A. Smith, in Wilkinson, *Memoirs,* App. XCIV; *Mississippi Messenger,* January 27, 1807. Williams's return to duty evidently freed Cowles Mead, who was the territorial secretary, to fight a duel on the west side of the river against Army captain Robert Sample. Mead was wounded in the thigh. *Id.,* February 10, 1807.

10. Claiborne, *Mississippi,* p. 287, n.*; Harnett T. Kane, *Natchez on the Mississippi,* New York: William T. Morrow & Co. (1947), pp. 30–31.

11. Fitch, *Breaking with Burr,* pp. 182–87.

12. Lemuel Henry Testimony, in *ASP, Misc.,* 1:601–02; James F. Doster, "Early Settlements on the Tombigbee and Tensaw Rivers," *The Alabama Review* 12:83, 86 (1959).

13. John Graham Testimony, in *ASP, Misc.,* 1:529–30.

14. Wilkinson to Jefferson, January 23, 1807, in *Report of the Wilkinson Committee,* p. 449.

15. *Supplement to the Mississippi Messenger,* May 5, 1807, in Burr Conspiracy Papers, LOC. Of Bruin, Judge Rodney wrote that he had "acquire[d] such a strong habit of drinking spirituous liquors, that he cannot restrain himself." Hamilton,

Anglo-American Law on the Frontier, p. 74. A Mississippi resident complained that Bruin "is always drunk when he can get anything to drink" and was "drunk every day of the Court and sometimes took a nap on the bench." John Smith to Jefferson, February 2, 1807, in Carter, *Territorial Papers,* 5:510.

16. Smith and Swick, *Journey Through the West,* pp. 4–5.

17. Rodney to Jefferson, November 21, 1806, *Pennsylvania Magazine of History* 44:294–97 (1920), quoted in Hamilton, *Anglo-American Law on the Frontier,* pp. 78–81.

18. *National Intelligencer,* March 11, 1807; grand jury presentment, February 1807, in Burr Conspiracy Papers, LOC; George Poindexter Testimony, *ASP, Misc.,* 1:569; Hamilton, *Anglo-American Law on the Frontier,* pp. 260–63; Kline, 2:1019–20.

19. David Fisk Testimony, *ASP, Misc.,* 1:525; James McDowell Testimony, *id.,* 1:514; Stephen Welch Testimony, *id.,* 1:519; George Poindexter Testimony, *id.,* 1:569; Kline, 2:1020; Hamilton, *Anglo-American Law on the Frontier,* pp. 262–64; *Frankfort Palladium,* March 12, 1807; Thomas Rodney to Caesar A. Rodney, February 1807, in Gratz, "Thomas Rodney," pp. 289, 299.

20. James Wilkinson Testimony, *ASP, Misc.,* pp. 545–46; George Poindexter Testimony, *id.,* p. 569; John Graham Testimony, *id.,* p. 530; John McKee Testimony, *id.,* p. 593; Robert Williams to Jefferson, May 1, 1807, in Burr Conspiracy Papers, LOC.

21. Note (undated), in Burr Conspiracy Papers, LOC; *Mississippi Messenger,* February 17, 1807; Burr to Robert Williams, undated, and February 12, 1807, in Kline, 2:1022–23; *Frankfort Palladium,* March 12, 1807, March 19, 1807; *Richmond Enquirer,* April 7, 1807; *Mississippi Herald & Natchez Gazette,* March 18, 1807; Lemuel Henry Testimony, *ASP, Misc.,* 1:602; George Poindexter Testimony, *id.,* 1:570; John Graham Testimony, *id.,* 1:531; Robert Williams to Col. F.L. Claiborne, February 10, 1807, in Third Annual Report, p. 741; Thomas Rodney to Caesar A. Rodney, February, 1807, in Gratz, "Thomas Rodney," p. 301; T. Carpenter, 3:188 (Dunbaugh testimony).

22. Claiborne to Madison, undated, Burr Conspiracy Papers, LOC; Wilkinson to Jefferson, February 17, 1807, *id.*

23. Claiborne, *Mississippi,* p. 287, n.*; Kane, *Natchez on the Mississippi,* p. 33.

24. Stuart O. Stumpf, ed., "The Arrest of Aaron Burr: A Documentary Record," *Alabama Historical Quarterly* 42:113 (1980); Thomas Perkins Abernethy, "Aaron Burr in Mississippi," *Journal of Southern History* 15:9, 16 (1949); *Richmond Enquirer,* March 30, 1807; Abernethy, *Burr Conspiracy,* p. 224; Harry Toulmin to Jefferson, April 7, 1807, in Burr Conspiracy Papers, LOC; Abernethy, *Burr Conspiracy,* p. 222. Burr's German secretary turned up shortly after in nearby woods, looking for his employer. Thomas Maury to Wilkinson, March 29, 1807, in Burr Conspiracy Papers, LOC. Burr's initial companion when he passed through Wakefield was Robert Ashley, a veteran of previous intrusions

on Spanish territory, including a notorious expedition in 1801 that resulted in
the death of Philip Nolan, one of General Wilkinson's frontier protégés. Ashley
also had been connected to George Rogers Clark's effort in 1794 to organize a
French-sponsored expedition to open the Mississippi River to American trade.
Flores, *Jefferson and Southwestern Exploration*, pp. 34–35 and n.46. In a letter
to the press, Ashley disputed Perkins's account of the arrest in two respects. He
insisted that Burr was wearing a pair of overalls but was otherwise attired nor-
mally, and that Burr was on his way to Washington City. The first assertion is not
material, while the second is implausible but not impossible. *Richmond Enquirer*,
April 21, 1807. Wilkinson specifically urged Lieutenant Gaines at Fort Stoddert
to "procure [Ashley's] confession if possible," but Ashley's sworn testimony was
never preserved. Wilkinson to Jefferson, March 3, 1807, in Burr Conspiracy Papers, LOC.

25. Stumpf, "Arrest of Aaron Burr," pp. 121–22; Kline, 2:1026–27; Abernethy, *Burr
    Conspiracy*, p. 225; *Frankfort Palladium*, March 12, 1807.

26. Kline, 2:1028–29; Abernethy, *Burr Conspiracy*, pp. 225–26; Stumpf, "Arrest of
    Aaron Burr," p. 123; *Richmond Enquirer*, March 30, 1807.

27. John Randolph to Joseph Nicholson, March 25, 1807, in Joseph Nicholson Pa-
    pers, LOC.

28. Jefferson to Charles Clay, January 11, 1807, LOC; Thomas Rodney to Caesar A.
    Rodney, February 11–12, 1807, in Hamilton, *Anglo-American Law on the Fron-
    tier*, p. 82; Adams to Benjamin Rush, February 2, 1807, in Schultz and Adair, *The
    Spur of Fame*, p. 82.

29. Caesar Rodney to Jefferson, March 27, 1807, LOC.

30. Note of Egbert Benson, March 25, 1807, and Benson letter, recipient not listed,
    March 25, 1807, in Burr Conspiracy Papers, LOC; Burr to Theodosia, March 27,
    1807, in Davis, *Memoirs*, 2:405.

31. Burr to Biddle, April 9, 1807, in Kline, 2:1028; Caesar Rodney to Jefferson,
    March 27, 1807, LOC.

PART II

1. Adams to Benjamin Rush, September 1, 1807, in Schultz and Adair, *Spur of
   Fame*, p. 100.

20. When Cousins Collide

1. Samuel Smith to W.C. Nicholas, January 9, 1807, recited in Adams, *History*, p.
   833.

2. Dearborn to Wilkinson, November 27, 1806, in *Report of the Wilkinson Committee*, p. 448; Isaac Briggs Deposition, in Wilkinson, *Memoirs*, App. LIX.

3. Jefferson to Claiborne, December 20, 1806, in Ford, 9:329; Jefferson to Robert
   Smith, December 23, 1806, in *id.*, 9:330–31 (describing alternative plan of calling up twenty thousand militia and sending a naval squadron to New Orleans);

Jefferson to James Bowdoin, April 2, 1807, in *id.*, 9:382; Jefferson to Edward Tiffin, February 2, 1807, in *id.*, 9:21–22.

4. S. Taggart to Rev. John Taylor, January 13, 1804, in Malone, *Jefferson and His Time,* 5:444; Frederick W. Thomas, *John Randolph of Roanoke and Other Sketches of Character,* Philadelphia: A. Hart (1853), pp. 22, 24.

5. *Annals of Congress,* 9th Cong., 2d Sess., pp. 335–57 (January 16, 1807).

6. John Adams to Benjamin Rush, February 2, 1807, in Schultz and Adair, *Spur of Fame,* p. 83.

7. Presidential Message, *Annals of Congress,* 9th Cong., 2d Sess., pp. 39–43 (January 22, 1807).

8. *Mississippi Messenger,* February 17, 1807; Samuel White to Dayton, January 25, 1807, in Dayton Papers; *Plumer's Memorandum,* p. 596 (January 30, 1807).

9. Jefferson to Charles Clay, January 11, 1807, in Lipscomb and Bergh, 9:132; Jefferson to John Langdon, December 22, 1806, LOC; Samuel White to Dayton, January 25, 1807, in Dayton Papers; Fritz Redlich, "Erich Bollman and Studies in Banking," in *Essays in American Economic History,* New York: G. E. Stechert & Co. (1944), pp. 25, 29; Jefferson to Bollman, October 17, 1804, LOC; Jefferson to Bollman, October 6, 1805, LOC.

10. Madison's notes of the Bollman interview are available online at http://memory .loc.gov/cgi-bin/query/D?mjm:4:./temp/~ammem_RiwD. They also are printed in *Letters and Other Writings of James Madison,* Congressional Edition: Washington, D.C. (1865), 2:393–401.

11. Bollman's memorandum is reprinted in Redlich, "Erich Bollman and Studies in Banking," pp. 69–77.

12. Jefferson to Bollman, January 25, 1807, LOC; Bollman to Jefferson, January 26, 1807, LOC; Malone, *Jefferson and His Time,* 5:271.

13. *Annals of Congress,* 9th Cong., 2d Sess., p. 402 (January 26, 1807).

14. J. Q. Adams to John Adams, January 27, 1807, in *Writings of John Quincy Adams,* 3:158; *Plumer's Memorandum,* p. 590 (January 26, 1807).

15. *Annals of Congress,* 9th Cong., 2d Sess., pp. 402–25 (January 26, 1807).

16. J. Q. Adams to Louisa Adams, January 30, 1807, in *Writings of John Quincy Adams,* 3:159; Allen C. Clark, *Greenleaf and the Law in the Federal City,* W. P. Roberts: Washington (1901), p. 53 (letter from Judge Cranch to his father, February 7, 1807); Albert J. Beveridge, *The Life of John Marshall,* Boston: Houghton Mifflin Co. (1919), 3:344–45; *Richmond Enquirer,* February 6, 1806.

17. Nancy Ambler Brent to sister, 1810, reprinted in "An Old Virginia Correspondence," *Atlantic Monthly* 84:535, 547 (1899); William Wirt, *The British Spy, or, Letters to a Member of the British Parliament Written During a Tour Through the United States,* Newburyport (1804), pp. 99–100.

18. Jean Edward Smith, *John Marshall, Definer of a Nation,* New York: Henry Holt & Co. (1996), p. 4; Story's eulogy at Suffolk, MA bar, October 15, 1835, reprinted in John F. Dillon, ed., *John Marshall: Life, Character and Judicial*

Services, Chicago: Callaghan (1903), 3:327, 363–64; Joseph Story to Samuel P.P. Fay, February 25, 1808, in William W. Story, ed., *Life & Letters of Joseph Story,* Boston: Charles C. Little and James Brown (1851), 1:166–67.

19. Smith, *John Marshall,* pp. 159–61.

20. Rufus King to C.C. Pinckney, October 17, 1797, in *Life of King,* 2:234–35; Theodore Sedgwick to King, May 11, 1800, in *id.,* 3:237.

21. Smith, *John Marshall,* pp. 283–91; Young, *Washington Community,* pp. 76–77.

22. *Marbury v. Madison,* 5 U.S. 137 (1803).

23. Joseph Story to Samuel P.P. Fay, February 25, 1808, in *Life & Letters of Joseph Story,* 1:166–67; Charles Richard Williams, *Life of Rutherford Birchard Hayes,* Boston: Houghton Mifflin Co. (1914), p. 33 (Hayes's notes recording a lecture by Justice Story at Harvard Law School, in which he told the Jefferson anecdote). Jefferson's description of Marshall's reasoning abilities is strikingly similar to one by William Wirt, one of the prosecutors at Burr's trial who became a distinguished Supreme Court advocate and Attorney General of the United States:

> His art consists in laying his premises so remotely from the point directly in debate, or else in terms so general and so specious that the hearer, seeing no consequence which can be drawn from them, is just as willing to admit them, as not; but, his premises once admitted, the demonstration, however distant, follows as certainly, as cogently, as inevitably, as any demonstration in Euclid.

Wirt, *The British Spy,* p. 101.

24. Jefferson to Madison, November 26, 1795; Marshall to Henry Lee, October 25, 1830, quoted in Smith, *John Marshall,* p. 12.

21. What Is Treason?

1. The Supreme Court's published report of the case, printed at *Ex Parte Bollman,* 8 U.S. 75 (1807), includes a summary of arguments of counsel as well as a narrative of the two weeks during which the Court considered the case. Marshall and Justices Bushrod Washington, William Johnson, and Brockholst Livingston heard oral arguments. Justices Samuel Chase and William Cushing were ill and did not attend. The press followed the arguments closely. *E.g., Richmond Enquirer,* February 20, 1807 (reprinting from *National Intelligencer*). The case began when a lawyer sought habeas corpus relief on behalf of James Alexander, a New York lawyer who had sailed to New Orleans with Bollman and then was arrested by General Wilkinson and shipped east. Alexander dropped from the case when a lower-court judge ordered his release from jail. Lawyers for Bollman and Swartwout then pursued the petition for their clients.

2. Affidavits from James Donaldson, an aide to Wilkinson, and Lieutenant William Wilson and Ensign W.C. Mead offered no evidence against Bollman or Swartwout.

3. Thomas P. Slaughter, " 'The King of Crimes,' Early American Treason Law, 1787–1860," in Ronald Hoffman and Peter J. Albert, eds., *Launching the "Extended Republic,"* Charlottesville: University Press of Virginia (1996); Peter Charles Hoffer, *The Treason Trials of Aaron Burr,* Lawrence: University Press of Kansas (2008). James Wilson, a leading delegate to the Constitutional Convention from Pennsylvania, explained after the Convention that the Constitution defined treason narrowly because "a very great part of [government] tyranny over the people has arisen from the extension of the definition of treason." Wilson's remarks in the Pennsylvania ratifying convention are reprinted in Max Farrand, ed., *The Records of the Constitutional Convention,* New Haven: Yale University Press (1911), 3:163 (December 7, 1787).

4. Marshall acknowledged that two of his colleagues did not think that written affidavits—unsupported by live testimony and not subject to cross-examination— could ever be sufficient to jail Bollman and Swartwout. Because two other justices thought the affidavits were admissible, Marshall evaluated their legal significance.

5. *Plumer's Memorandum,* p. 619 (February 21, 1807).

6. Wilkinson to Jefferson, March 12, 1807, in McCaleb, *Aaron Burr Conspiracy,* p. 254; Jefferson to James Bowdoin, April 2, 1807, Lipscomb and Bergh, 9:185.

7. "Habeas Corpus in the Case of Emanuel Roberts," *American Law Journal* 2:192, 196 (1809); *Frankfort Palladium,* February 19, 1807; *Plumer's Memorandum,* p. 562 (January 8, 1807); *id.,* p. 614 (February 20, 1807); *id.,* p. 619 (February 21, 1807); *id.,* pp. 624–26 (February 24, 1807); Samuel White to Dayton, February 15, 1807, in Dayton Papers; Clark to Wilkinson, February 22, 1807, in Wilkinson, *Memoirs,* App. LXXVI; *Gettysburg Centinel,* March 25, 1807 (reprinting Adair letter from *National Intelligencer*).

8. *Richmond Enquirer,* March 24, 1807; *National Intelligencer,* March 18, 1807; *Bartgis's Republican Gazette* (Fredericktown, MD), March 20, 1807; *Providence Phenix,* April 4, 1807 (reprinting from the *Baltimore American*); *Philadelphia Democratic Press,* August 3, 1807; *Northampton* (MA) *Republican Spy,* December 9, 1807; *New York Public Advertiser,* November 23, 1807; Fitch, *Breaking with Burr,* p. 39 (August 19, 1807); William Stedman to Major Hays, February 20, 1807, Virginia Historical Society.

9. Notes of Cabinet meeting of February 27, 1807, in Jefferson's *Anas,* Lipscomb and Bergh, 1:466–67; Jefferson to James Bowdoin, April 2, 1807, in Ford, 9:382; Memorandum from C. A. Rodney, Attorney General of the United States, to John Clark, postmarked May 2, 1807, attaching three printed sheets of interrogatories, Filson Historical Society.

10. *Richmond Enquirer,* April 10, 1807; Jefferson to Dearborn, March 29, 1807, in Ford, 9:378; Crackel, *Jefferson's Army,* pp. 158–59. The army officer arrested in St. Louis was the son-in-law of territorial secretary Joseph Browne, who was Burr's brother-in-law.

11. Jefferson to William Branch Giles, April 10, 1807, in Ford, 9:383–85.
12. *Plumer's Memorandum,* p. 641 (March 4, 1807); Wirt, *The British Spy,* p. 101.

22. Sympathy for Villainy

1. Burr to Theodosia, June 3, 1807, and April 26, 1807, in Davis, *Memoirs,* 2:405, 408.
2. Melish, *Travels* pp. 218–19; Smyth, *A Tour,* 1:19–20; Douglas R. Egerton, *Gabriel's Rebellion: The Virginia Slave Conspiracies of 1800 & 1802,* Chapel Hill: University of North Carolina Press (1993), p. 18.
3. Egerton, *Gabriel's Rebellion;* Marianne Buroff Sheldon, "Black-White Relations in Richmond, Virginia, 1782–1820," *Journal of Southern History* 45:27 (1979); W. Asbury Christian, *Richmond, Her Past and Present,* Richmond: L.H. Jenkins (1912), p. 52.
4. Abernethy, *Burr Conspiracy,* p. 230; John P. Little, *History of Richmond,* Richmond: Dietz (1933) (original edition, 1851), pp. 103–04; T. Carpenter, 1:2–3.
5. Christian, *Richmond Past and Present,* p. 72; Samuel Mordecai, *Richmond in By-Gone Days,* New York: Arno Press (1975) (original edition, 1856), p. 57; *Richmond Enquirer,* April 28, 1807.
6. Attorney General Caesar Rodney wrote to Richmond for the United States attorney to retain John Wickham to help with the prosecution, "unless Burr has retained Wickham immediately on his arrival." Rodney to Jefferson, March 27, 1807, LOC. Burr had indeed snapped up Wickham before the government could retain him.
7. David Robertson, 1:6–8.
8. Caesar Rodney to Jefferson, March 30, 1807, LOC; David Robertson, 1:11–20.
9. Kline, 2:1032–33; Alston to Charles Pinckney, February 6, 1807, in William H. Safford, *The Blennerhassett Papers,* Cincinnati: Moore, Wilstach & Baldwin (1864), pp. 227–30; Isenberg, *Fallen Founder,* p. 329.
10. Mary Newton Stanard, *Richmond, Its People and Its Story,* Philadelphia: J. P. Lippincott Co. (1923), p. 94; Francis F. Beirne, *Shout Treason, The Trial of Aaron Burr,* New York: Hastings House (1959), p. 34; Winfield Scott, *Memoirs of Lieut.-General Scott, LL.D.,* New York: Sheldon & Co. (1864), p. 13.
11. Paul S. Clarkson and R. Samuel Jett, *Luther Martin of Maryland,* Baltimore: Johns Hopkins Press (1970), p. 311 (reprinting from *Memoirs of Roger Brooke Taney, L.L.D.*); William Pierce, "Character Sketches of Delegates to the Federal Convention," in Max Farrand, ed., *The Records of the Federal Convention of 1787,* New Haven: Yale University Press (1966), 3:93.
12. Jefferson to George Hay, June 19, 1807, LOC; Malone, *Jefferson and His Time,* 5:314. Martin still resented slanderous reports about Martin's father-in-law, a famous frontiersman, which appeared in Jefferson's *Notes on the State of Virginia,* published in 1781.
13. Burr to Theodosia, May 15, 1807, in Davis, *Memoirs,* 2:406.

14. Jefferson to Madison, April 14, 1807, in Ford, 9:42; Jefferson to Gallatin, April 18, 1807, LOC; Caesar Rodney to Jefferson, May 6, 1807, LOC. After the trial, Jefferson reported spending more than $11,000 from the contingency fund on legal expenses related to prosecuting Burr, though the government's total expenses were ten times that amount. *Annals of Congress,* 10th Cong., 1st Sess., p. 78 (January 8, 1808); *id.,* 10th Cong., 2d Sess., p. 321 (January 31, 1809).

15. *Virginia Magazine of History and Biography* 20:290 (1912) (obituaries in Richmond newspapers included "Mrs. Rebecca Hay, wife of George Hay," in the March 24, 1807, edition); Caesar Rodney to Jefferson, April 10, 1807, April 21, 1807, May 6, 1807, June 16, 1807, LOC; Jefferson's *Anas,* in Lipscomb and Bergh, 1:468 (March 17, 1807, Cabinet meeting); Cuming, *Cuming's Tour,* p. 237 (dining in Ohio with Mr. Smith of Cincinnati in July 1807, who was gathering evidence for the Burr trial).

16. Wood, *Empire of Liberty,* pp. 309–10 (citing Hay's "An Essay on the Liberty of the Press"); Michael Durey, *"With the Hammer of Truth": James Thomson Callender and America's Early National Heroes,* Charlottesville: University Press of Virginia (1990), pp. 131–33, 135, 164–65.

17. Hay to Jefferson, May 25, 1807, May 31, 1807, LOC.

18. *Virginia Argus,* April 7, 1807; *Richmond Enquirer,* April 10, 1807, April 28, 1807; C. Slaughter to Thomas Towles, May 16, 1807, Filson Historical Society; Joseph Wheelan, *Jefferson's Vendetta: The Pursuit of Aaron Burr and the Judiciary,* New York: Carroll & Graf (2004), pp. 100–02.

19. Scott, *Memoirs,* p. 14; Thomas, *John Randolph of Roanoke,* p. 37.

20. Jefferson to Joseph Hopper Nicholson, February 20, 1807, in Ford, 9:370; Jefferson to William Branch Giles, April 20, 1807, *id.,* 9:387.

21. Jefferson to G. Morgan, March 27, 1807, in Lipscomb and Bergh, 11:175; Jefferson to James Bowdoin, April 2, 1807, in *id.,* 11:183; Jefferson to William B. Giles, April 20, 1807, in *id.,* 11:187; Caesar Rodney to Jefferson, May 6, 1807, LOC.

22. Jefferson to Hay, May 20, 1807, in Ford, 9:394–401.

23. Jefferson to Caesar Rodney, May 7, 1807, and June 19, 1807; Jefferson to Hay, June 2, 1807, in Ford, 9:396; Jefferson to Hay, June 19, 1807, in *id.,* 9:402–03 n.

24. *Danville* (VT) *North Star,* June 16, 1807.

25. Scott, *Memoirs,* p. 13.

26. Hay to Jefferson, June 5, 1807, LOC.

27. David Robertson, 1:39–41 (May 22, 1807). John Ambler was cousin to the wife of the chief justice, Polly Marshall. Other grand jurors included Joseph Cabell, brother to Governor William Cabell, and three men who would be both governors and United States senators: James Pleasants, James Barbour, and Littleton Tazewell; The first two were Republicans.

28. *Id.,* p. 46.

29. Jacobs, *Tarnished Warrior,* p. 235; Linklater, *Artist in Treason,* pp. 259–60; Hay to Jefferson, June 14, 1807. Jackson gave evidence to the grand jury but did

not testify at Burr's trials. Scott, *Memoirs*, p. 15; Burstein, *Passions of Andrew Jackson*, pp. 79–82; *Jackson Papers*, 2:168–69 (grand jury testimony, June 25, 1807).

30. Hay to Jefferson, May 25, 1807, LOC; Burr to Theodosia, June 3, 1807, in Davis, *Memoirs*, 2:406.

31. *Newark Centinel of Freedom*, June 16, 1807 (reprinting from Norfolk newspaper).

32. Thomas, *John Randolph of Roanoke*, p. 39.

33. David Robertson, 1:66.

34. *Id.*, 1:29–106.

35. *Id.*, 1:128.

36. *Id.*, 1:179–84; Hay to Jefferson, June 9, 1807, LOC; Jefferson to Hay, June 12, 1807, in Ford, 9:399; Jefferson to Caesar Rodney, June 12, 1807, LOC; Jefferson to Hay, June 17, 1807, in Ford, 9:400–01; Jefferson to Hay, June 20, 1807, in *id.*, 9:403–05. Jefferson's observation about the "battle of giants" was made in a draft letter that was found in his papers. *Id.*, 9:407 n. The defense barraged Hay and the court with objections and motions on very minor points. For example, on Thursday, May 28, defense lawyers persuaded Chief Justice Marshall to exclude from evidence a deposition from Sergeant Jacob Dunbaugh, who joined Burr's expedition on a furlough from Fort Massac. The defense argued that the Dunbaugh deposition was certified by a "B. Cenas" of New Orleans, who purported to be a magistrate, yet there was no proof before the court that the signatory was the *real* Magistrate Cenas. This objection was the emptiest form of pettifoggery, since B. Cenas also certified Wilkinson's deposition, which was accepted into evidence without drawing objection from the defense. Because Dunbaugh was in Richmond and available to testify in person, however, Marshall's ruling on this point had no impact on the case. David Robertson, 1:98–101.

37. Washington Irving to Mrs. Josiah Ogden Hoffman, June 4, 1807, in Ralph M. Aderman, et al., eds., *Washington Irving, Letters, 1802–1803*, Boston: Twayne Publishers (1978), 1: 238.

38. Jefferson to Hay, May 20, 1807, and May 28, 1807, in Ford, 9:394–401.

39. David Robertson, 1:190–96. Through the summer of 1807, Bollman complained vociferously about his treatment at Jefferson's hands, particularly that Jefferson shared with Hay his written description of Burr's plans, as well as the offer of a pardon. Bollman insisted he did not need a pardon, but he also refused to testify based on his Fifth Amendment right against self-incrimination. *Philadelphia Aurora*, July 16, 1807.

40. Hay to Jefferson, May 31, 1807, LOC.

23. A Mammoth of Iniquity

1. Irving to James K. Paulding, June 22, 1807, in *Irving Letters*, 1:239–40; Wilkinson to Jefferson, June 17, 1807, in Burr Conspiracy letters, LOC; David Robertson, 1:197, n*.

2. Joseph Alston Cabell, "The Trial of Aaron Burr," in *Proceedings of the New York State Bar Association,* Albany, NY: The Argus Company (1900), 23:56, 77; T. Carpenter, 3:356; Richard Taylor Deposition, in *Report of the Wilkinson Committee,* pp. 293–300.

3. *Annals of Congress,* 10th Cong., 1st Sess., pp. 631–32 (testimony of Littleton Tazewell); *id.,* 10th Cong., 1st Sess., pp. 1397–98 (John Randolph remarks, January 11, 1808).

4. Randolph to Joseph Nicholson, June 28, 1807, and June 25, 1807, in Nicholson Papers, LOC.

5. David Robertson, 1:236–37, 1:257–62, 1:283–303.

6. *Id.,* 1:268–77.

7. *Id.,* 1:204–09, 1:212–29, 1:248; Burr to Theodosia, June 18, 1807, in Davis, *Memoirs,* 2:406–07.

8. *Id.,* 1:328–29; Hay to Jefferson, June 25, 1807, LOC.

9. Affidavit of A.L. Duncan, in Wilkinson, *Memoirs,* p. 334.

10. Once Burr was acquitted of all criminal charges then pending against him, Wilkinson made the empty offer to reveal the letters he had suppressed if Burr would reveal the letter dated May 13, 1806, which he received from Wilkinson. Burr declined the trade, concealing these most intriguing documents, evidently for all time. T. Carpenter, 3:295.

11. David Robertson, 1:305, 1:330, 1:350.

12. *Id.,* 1:354–56.

13. *Id.,* 1:350–51; 357–58.

14. Washington Irving to [Mary Fairlie?], July 7, 1807, in *Irving Letters,* 1:243; Burr to Theodosia, July 3, 1807, July 6, 1807, July 24, 1807, in Davis, *Memoirs,* 2:409–10; Fitch, *Breaking with Burr,* pp. 22, 24.

15. Irving to Gouverneur Kemble, July 1, 1807, and Irving to [Mary Fairlie?], July 7, 1807, in *Irving Letters,* 1:241–42; 2:244.

16. Fitch, *Breaking with Burr,* p. 13; Burr to Charles Biddle, April 21, 1807, in Kline, 2:1032; Burr to Jonathan Rhea, July 25, 1807, in *id.,* 2:1037; Robertson, 2:261; *New Jersey Journal,* July 7, 1807; Dayton to C. A. Rodney, July 16, 1807, John Wickham to Dayton, July 24, 1807, and Dayton to Hay, August 1807, in Dayton Papers; Wilkinson to Dayton, February 17, 1807, in *Report of the Wilkinson Committee,* p. 302; Wilkinson to Jefferson, March 1, 1807, in *id.,* p. 452; *Philadelphia Aurora,* August 11, 1807; Hamilton, *Anglo-American Law on the Frontier,* pp. 82, 96; letter of Gabriel Tichenor to Joseph C. Hornblower, June 14, 1807, in Harold A. Tichenor, *Tichenor Families in America,* Napton, MO: Harold Tichenor (1988), p. 52; Fitch, *Breaking with Burr,* pp. 1–8; *id.,* pp. 52, 69. Dayton, still suffering from compromised health, had never left his home in Elizabethtown, New Jersey, during the expedition. Wilkinson to Jefferson, June 17, 1807, in Burr Conspiracy Papers, LOC; Jefferson to Wilkinson, June 21, 1807, in *Report of the Wilkinson Committee,* p. 464. When Dayton learned he had been indicted, he set

off for Richmond, assuring his friends that he was blameless. Blennerhassett, Tyler, and Floyd had been arrested in Mississippi in February, but by late May the Mississippi court had decided it lacked jurisdiction to try them. After the Richmond indictments, Blennerhassett was rearrested in Kentucky and brought to Richmond in a taxing two-week journey. Burr's lawyers offered their services to both Dayton and Blennerhassett, even though Blennerhassett—grown resentful of Burr—insisted he would not pay them a dime. Major Israel Smith of New York arrived in Richmond in the third week of August and was confined in the penitentiary, where the defense lawyers greeted him, too. Davis Floyd, who had never set foot on Blennerhassett Island, was returned to Indiana for trial there.

Senator John Smith was in Baton Rouge, in Spanish West Florida, when he learned of the Richmond indictments. General Wilkinson expressed bafflement over Smith's indictment, assuring Smith that the grand jury had never previously mentioned his name. Not until September did the Mississippi governor organize an escort to take the senator to Richmond. Wilkinson to John Smith, June 28, 1807, Smith to Governor Robert Williams, August 15, 1807, and Smith to George Hay, September 2, 1807, in Smith Papers, Cincinnati Historical Society.

17. David Robertson, 1:430–32.
18. Marshall to William Cushing, June 27, 1807, Marshall Papers, 7:60.
19. Burr to Theodosia, June 24, 1807, in Davis, *Memoirs,* 2:408.
20. David Robertson, 1:434.
21. Toll, *Six Frigates,* pp. 294–308.
22. Christian, *Richmond Past and Present,* p. 69; *Frankfort Palladium,* August 13, 1807; Jefferson to Lafayette, July 14, 1807, LOC; Wirt to Carr, July 19, 1807, in Kennedy, *Memoirs of Wirt,* pp. 197–99; Scott, *Memoirs,* pp. 18–19.

24. Searching for an Overt Act

1. Burr to Theodosia, July 30, 1807, in Davis, *Memoirs,* 2:410–11; Fitch, *Breaking with Burr,* pp. 4–5.
2. David Robertson, 1:369–426.
3. *Id.,* 1:450. Hay's opening speech appears at *id.,* 1:433–451.
4. *Id.,* pp. 1:352–59.
5. *Id.,* 1:470, 473.
6. *Plumer's Memorandum,* p. 583 (January 21, 1807); Fitch, *Breaking with Burr,* p. 13; Benjamin Rush to John Adams, January 23, 1807, in Schultz and Adair, *Spur of Fame,* p. 81.
7. David Robertson, 1:475–77.
8. *Id.,* 1:484.
9. *Plumer's Memorandum,* pp. 541–42 (December 26, 1806).
10. David Robertson, 1:485–90.
11. *Id.,* 1:508, 510; Tupper Deposition, in Burr-Blennerhassett Papers, p. 23. Tupper told Blennerhassett that he "repelled with that disgust and contempt

suggested by his honor" the laborer's testimony. Fitch, *Breaking with Burr,* p. 30.

12. Fitch, *Breaking with Burr,* p. 16.

13. David Robertson, 1:555, 565, 582, 594.

14. Hay to Jefferson, September 1, 1807, LOC; David Robertson, 2:322.

15. Fitch, *Breaking with Burr,* p. 116. Martin's first visit to Harman Blennerhassett in prison left the Irishman bedazzled. The lawyer put away a tumbler of brandy in thirty-five minutes, while describing a week of trial, "with extracts from memory of several speeches on both sides, including long ones from his own," reciting newspaper columns Martin had written recently, denouncing Jefferson, explaining his history with Burr, and "interspers[ing] the whole with sententious reprobations and praises of several other characters."

16. *Id.,* pp. 67–69.

17. David Robertson, 2:337, 378.

18. *Id.,* 2:63, 81. Confined in his penitentiary apartment, Blennerhassett heard that "Wirt raised his reputation yesterday." Fitch, *Breaking with Burr,* p. 58.

19. David Robertson, 2:96–97.

20. *Id.,* 2:237–39; Fitch, *Breaking with Burr,* p. 61.

21. David Robertson, 2:193–94, 259, 279–80.

22. *Id.,* 2:404–08, 413–20, 428–29, 445.

23. *Id.,* 2:446 (emphasis added); *Boston Columbian Centinel,* September 8, 1807.

24. Wirt to Carr, September 1, 1807, in Kennedy, *Memoirs of Wirt,* p. 202; Jefferson to Wilkinson, September 10, 1807, in Ford, 9:142; Rodney to Madison, Sept. 18, 1807, in Malone, *Jefferson and His Time,* 5:338; Hay to Jefferson, September 1, 1807, LOC.

25. A Drawn Battle

1. Jefferson to Hay, September 4, 1807, September 7, 1807, LOC.

2. David Robertson, 2:448, T. Carpenter, 3:39, 3:42.

3. T. Carpenter, 3:43–45.

4. *Id.,* 3:40–43.

5. *Id.,* 3:48–92.

6. *Id.,* 3:93–102.

7. *Id.,* 3:107.

8. *Id.,* 3:108–11, 113.

9. Fitch, *Breaking with Burr,* pp. 87–88.

10. *Id.,* p. 91.

11. T. Carpenter, 3:139.

12. *Id.,* 3:154, 191 (William Love), 3:160 (Jacob Dunbaugh); 3:187–88 (David Fisk), 3:193 (Samuel Moxley), 3:196 (John Munhollan), 3:220 (Stephen Welch), 3:270 (Gabriel Van Horne), 3:401 (Jacob Jackson). A ninth witness, Blennerhassett, wrote in his diary about the expedition's muskets and "the solicitude with which

he [Burr] had afterwards had them all hid and sunk in the river." Fitch, *Breaking with Burr*, p. 113.

13. Smith, *John Marshall*, p. 373; *Philadelphia Aurora*, September 23, 1807; *National Intelligencer*, September 8, 1807, September 30, 1807; Richard Bates to Frederick Bates, September 17, 1807, in Virginia Historical Society; Jefferson to William Thomson, September 26, 1807, in Ford, 9:143.

14. T. Carpenter, 3:151.

15. *Id.*, 3:153–54, 162, 172, 202, 229.

16. *Id.*, 3:174.

17. *Id.*, 3:199, 214, 287.

18. David Robertson, 2:533–37; T. Carpenter, 3:46.

19. Burr to Theodosia, September 28, 1807, in Davis, *Memoirs*, 2:411.

20. Fitch, *Breaking with Burr*, p. 105.

21. T. Carpenter, 3:250–51 (Walbeck statement), 243–45 (Duncan statement), 259.

22. T. Carpenter, 3:255–56; Fitch, *Breaking with Burr*, p. 111.

23. T. Carpenter, 3:258, 261, 268.

24. *Id.*, 3:365.

25. Hay to Jefferson, October 15, 1807, LOC.

26. Fitch, *Breaking with Burr*, p. 132.

27. T. Carpenter, 3:415; Wirt to Carr, September 14, 1807, in Kennedy, *Memoirs of Wirt*, p. 203.

28. Burr to Theodosia, October 23, 1807, in Davis, *Memoirs*, 2:411–12.

29. Robert K. Faulkner, "John Marshall and the Burr Trial," *The Journal of American History* 53:247 (1966); James F. Simon, *What Kind of Nation: Thomas Jefferson, John Marshall, and the Epic Struggle to Create a United States,* New York: Simon & Schuster (2002), pp. 257–58; Slaughter, "The King of Crimes," *supra.*

30. Marshall to Richard Peters, November 23, 1807, Marshall Papers 7:164.

31. Jefferson to John B. Colvin, September 20, 1810, LOC.

32. Jefferson to Hay, February 16, 1808, in Lipscomb and Bergh, 19:164.

33. Fitch, *Breaking with Burr*, p. 98, 120; William Coburn to Madison, August 15, 1807, in James A. Robertson, ed., *Louisiana Under the Rule of Spain, France, and the United States, 1785–1807,* Freeport, NY: Books for Libraries Press (1969) (original ed., 1910–11), 2:359.

26. To Britain

1. Fitch, *Breaking with Burr*, pp. 139, 141–42, 149–53; *New York Advertiser*, November 11 and December 17, 1807; Clarkson and Jett, *Luther Martin of Maryland*, p. 274. The Baltimore handbill was reprinted in the November 9, 1807, issue of the *New York American Citizen*.

2. Fitch, *Breaking with Burr*, pp. 141–42, 172; Lomask, *Aaron Burr*, 2:296; John E. Stillwell, *The Burr Portraits*, private printing (1928), p. 3.

3. Fitch, *Breaking with Burr*, p. 168; Biddle, *Autobiography*, p. 322.

4. Kline, 2:902, n.1, 1042, 1045; *Northampton* (MA) *Republican Spy*, December 12, 1807; *New York American Citizen*, January 19, 1808; *National Intelligencer*, January 27 and February 5, 1808; *New York Gazette*, October 3, 1808. Burr's lawyer in the New Jersey case was Aaron Ogden, another lifelong friend from Elizabethtown. Aaron Ogden, the younger brother of Matthias Ogden, with whom Burr had volunteered for the Continental Army in 1775, also served as a Federalist United States senator from New Jersey.

5. J. P. Dunn, Jr., *Indiana: A Redemption from Slavery*, Boston: Houghton, Mifflin and Co. (1905), p. 327; Owens, *Mr. Jefferson's Hammer*, pp. 133–34; Thomas Davis to unnamed recipient, August 15, 1807, Burr Conspiracy Papers, LOC; *Rutland* (VT) *Herald*, October 31, 1807; *New York American Citizen*, November 2, 1807; *New York Evening Post*, October 23, 1807; *Boston Gazette*, November 9, 1807.

6. *Annals of Congress*, 10th Cong., 1st Sess., 61–62 (December 31, 1807); Wilhelmy, "Senator John Smith," pp. 53–57.

7. Jacobs, *Tarnished Warrior*, pp. 242–44; Wheelan, *Jefferson's Vendetta*, p. 260; Wilkinson to John Wickham, October 20, October 24, and October 29, 1807, Virginia Historical Society; *New York Daily Advertiser*, November 6, 1807; *Connecticut Courant*, January 13, 1808; John Quincy Adams to John Adams, December 27, 1807, in *Writings of John Quincy Adams*, 3:173.

8. Jacobs, *Tarnished Warrior*, pp. 243–44; Abernethy, *Burr Conspiracy*, p. 274; *New York American Citizen*, January 13, 1808; Linklater, *Artist in Treason*, pp. 278–80.

9. Burr to Theodosia, 1808, in Davis, *PJAB*, 1:13.

10. Lomask, *Aaron Burr*, 2:294 (quoting report of diplomat Phineas Bond); Davis, *PJAB*, 2:13–20 (undated notes from Burr to Theodosia, relating to his imminent departure on *Clarissa Ann*); *Maryland Gazette*, June 16, 1808. By one contemporary account, all of the passengers on *Clarissa Ann* knew that "Mr. Edwards" was Aaron Burr. *New York Evening Post*, July 7, 1808. As explained in the beginning of these endnotes, this book draws information from two different publications titled *Private Journal of Aaron Burr*. The Davis edition, published shortly after Burr's death in 1836, was dramatically expurgated and changed by the editor. I do not rely on that edition for Burr's journal entries but rather on the scholarly publication of the journal that was sponsored by William Bixby in 1903. The Davis edition, however, includes letters to and from Burr during his travels, and I rely on the Davis edition for those letters.

11. Bixby, *PJAB*, 1:27, 2:195.

12. Bixby, *PJAB*, 2:276–77.

13. *Id.*, 1:26, 1:45, 2:79, 2:266, 2:332, 1:169, 1:265, 2:219.

14. Davis, *PJAB*, 2:118 (Theodosia to Burr, January 8, 1811).

15. Bixby, *PJAB*, 1:220.

16. *Id.,* 1:463, 1:488, 2:4, 2:130.

17. Davis, *PJAB,* 1:101; Bixby, *PJAB,* 1:22, 1:24, 1:81 (chess table); *id.,* 1:426, 1:428, 2:209, 2:214 (dictionaries); 2:6, 2:191, 2:197 (watches); 2:366 (coins and medals).

18. Bixby, *PJAB,* 1:69, 1:117; 1:282, 1:310, 1:339; 2:345, 2:346; Burr to Jeremy Bentham, September 7, 1808, in Kline, 2:1058.

19. Bixby, *PJAB,* 1:25, 1:28; 1:120; 1:122; 1:323; 1:360; 1:227; 2:61; 1:169; 1:183; 1:158; 1:163; 1:170; 1:172.

20. *Id.,* 1:443; 1:247; 1:44; 1:47; 2:60; 2:64; 1:207.

21. *Id.,* 1:36; 1:188.

22. *Id.,* 1:288.

23. *Id.,* 1:344, 1:332.

24. *Id.,* 1:220–21; 1:85, 1:22; 1:151; 1:322; Burr to Theodosia, November 21, 1808, in Davis, *PJAB,* 1:98.

25. Bixby, *PJAB,* 2:51; 1:122; 1:237.

26. *Id.,* 1:358.

27. *Id.,* 1:253; 1:407, 2:73.

28. *Id.,* 1:138.

29. *Id.,* 1:5; 1:182; 1:239; 1:309; 1:362; 1:367–68; 2:267.

30. *Id.,* 1:14; 1:243; 1:329; Theodosia to Burr, August 1, 1809, in Davis, *Memoirs,* 1:285.

31. Bixby, *PJAB,* 2:79, 2:277.

32. William W. Kaufmann, *British Policy and the Independence of Latin America, 1804–1828,* New Haven: Yale University Press (1951), pp. 39–44; *London Morning Chronicle,* July 26, 1808; William Pinkney to James Madison, August 2, 1808, in Madison Papers, LOC. Some British officials had always been wary of revolutionary movements in South America, fearing that they would end up hostile to British interests. McCaleb, *Aaron Burr Conspiracy,* pp. 43, 46.

33. Burr to Williamson, July 19, 1808, in Davis, *PJAB,* p. 23.

34. Davis, *PJAB,* 1:225–26 (notes exchanged with British officials, July 1808); Burr to Sam Swartwout, August 19, 1808, in *id.,* 1:31; *National Intelligencer,* October 12, 1808; Burr to Jeremy Bentham, October 1, 1808, in Davis, *PJAB,* 1:61; Bixby, *PJAB,* 1:11–12, 1:15, 1:21, 1:32, 1:39–40; Kline, 2:1072 n.3.

35. Burr to Theodosia, September 9, 1808, in Davis, *PJAB,* 1:46; Bixby, *PJAB,* p. 21; Theodosia to Burr, October 31, 1808, in Davis, *PJAB,* 1:72.

36. Burr to Bentham, January 13, 1809, in Davis, *PJAB,* 1:135; Bixby, *PJAB,* 1:69–70, 77; J.H. Koe to Burr, January 17, 1809, in Davis, *PJAB,* 1:136–37; Burr to Koe, January 31, 1809, in *id.,* 1:143; David Williamson to Burr, February 1, 1809, in *id.,* 1:157; Burr to Lord Justice Clerk, March 1, 1809, in *id.,* 1:177.

37. Charles Milner Atkinson, *Jeremy Bentham, His Life and Work,* Westport (CT): Greenwood Press (1970) (original printing, 1905), p. 36; John Bowring, ed., *The Works of Jeremy Bentham,* Edinburgh: William Tait (1843), 10:432–33.

38. Bixby, *PJAB*, 1:12; Burr to Mrs. Prevost, August 27, 1808, in Davis, *PJAB*, 1:35; Burr to Bentham, January 23, 1809, in Bixby, *PJAB*, 1:166; Bentham to Burr, March 6, 1809, in *id.*, 1:185.

39. Bentham to Burr, March 6, 1809, in Davis, *PJAB*, 1:180; Burr to Theodosia, November 9, 1808, in *id.*, 1:80; Burr to Theodosia, February 15, 1809, in *id.*, 1:174; Theodosia to Burr, February 1, 1809, in *id.*, 1:160.

40. Theodosia to Burr, January 3, 1809, in Davis, *PJAB*, 1:129; Theodosia to Burr, February 1, 1809, in *id.*, 1:158–60; Burr to Theodosia, February 15, 1809, in *id.*, 1:175.

41. Burr to David Williamson, March 1, 1809, in Kline, 2:1079; William Pinkney to James Madison, August 2, 1808, in Madison Papers, LOC.

42. Isaac Joslin Cox, "Hispanic-American Phases of the 'Burr Conspiracy,'" *The Hispanic American Historical Review* 12:145, 171–72 (1932); *National Intelligencer,* June 19, 1809 (reprinting from *Bell's Messenger* of London); *Raleigh* (NC) *Register,* July 20, 1809.

43. Bixby, *PJAB*, 1:93–99; Kline, 2:1083–90; Burr to Reeves, April 5, 1809, in Davis, *PJAB*, 1:193.

44. Burr to James Achaud, April 25, 1809, in Davis, *PJAB*, 1:214.

27. On the Continent

1. Burr to Theodosia, October 13, 1809, in Davis, *PJAB*, 1:316; Burr to Henry Gahn, October 12, 1809, in *id.*, 1:312; Bixby, *PJAB*, 1:139, 128.

2. Burr to Madame _____, September 26, 1809, in Davis, *PJAB*, 1:310; Bixby, *PJAB*, 1:200.

3. Bixby, *PJAB*, 1:131, 1:226.

4. William Spence Robertson, *France and Latin American Independence,* New York: Octagon Books (1967), p. 73 (original ed., 1939); Kline, 2:1098 n.2; Bixby, *PJAB*, 1:338.

5. Burr to Comte de Volney, January 29, 1810, in Kline, 2:1097; Diedrich Lunning to Burr, October 21, 1810, in Bixby, *PJAB*, 1:255 n*; *id.*, 1:410.

6. Kline, 2:1103–1116.

7. Bixby, *PJAB*, 1:430–31; Burr to His Majesty, King of Westphalia, March 17, 1810, in Davis, *PJAB*, 1:441; Burr to the Duc d'Otrante, March 21, 1810, in Kline, 2:1122. Burr described his encounters with Jerome Bonaparte and Madame Bonaparte in several letters to Theodosia. Burr to Theodosia, December 3, 1803, in Davis, *Memoirs,* 2:247; December 9, 1803, in *id.*, 2:250; January 3, 1804, in *id.*, 2:266; January 17, 1804, in *id.*, 2:268; January 30, 1804, in *id.*, 2:275; May 8, 1804, in *id.*, 2:287.

8. Bixby, *PJAB*, 1:447–48, 1:457–59, 1:453.

9. Bixby, *PJAB*, 1:471–72.

10. Bixby, *PJAB*, 2:15, 2:22, 2:25, 2:28, 2:225; Jonathan Russell to Burr, October 26, 1810, and November 4, 1810; Burr to McRae, October 29, 1810; McRae

to Burr, October 29, 1818; Burr to Russell, November 1, 1810, in Kline, 2:1128–30.

11. Bixby, *PJAB*, 2:6, 1:456, 1:483, 2:4, 2:6, 2:101–6, 1:120.

12. Kline, 1:272, 2:322, 1:407–10, 1:338–44; Bixby, *PJAB*, 2:28, 2:95, 2:114–15, 2:131, 2:152, 1:497, 1:499, 2:27, 2:87, 2:74; Burr to Theodosia, September 26, 1810, in Davis, *PJAB*, 2:69.

13. Bixby, *PJAB*, 2:44, 2:138.

14. *Id.*, 1:466, 2:99.

15. *Id.*, 1:498, 2:2, 2:4.

16. Davis, *PJAB*, 2:216–19.

17. Bixby, *PJAB*, 244–45.

18. *Id.*, 2:279, 2:285, 2:289, 2:306–07, 2:334–35 (vinegar project); 2:269–70, 2:275 (steamboat); 2:260, 341–42 (false teeth); 2:347. Although Burr never sold any of the false teeth produced by Monsieur Fonzi, his dentist, evidently Fonzi produced the first "single mineral teeth" generally fabricated. The false teeth in Burr's mouth, however, were "blocks baked upon a patina plate." "Porcelain Teeth," *The Dental News Letter*, 7:4 (July 1, 1854).

19. Bixby, 2:271, 2:276, 2:286, 2:295–96, 2:301, 2:328 (Bentham); 2:275, 2:376, 2:380.

20. Burr to Theodosia, May [probably March] 12, 1812, in Davis, *Memoirs*, 2:396; Bixby, *PJAB*, 2:393–97; Theodosia to Burr, May 10, 1811, in Davis, *Memoirs*, 2:160.

21. Theodosia to Burr, July 12, 1812, and August 12, 1812, in Davis, *Memoirs*, 2:439–40.

22. Lomask, *Aaron Burr*, 2:361–63.

28. *The History of Thy Crimes*

1. Frederick Seward, *William H. Seward: An Autobiography from 1801 to 1834*, New York: Derby and Miller (1891), pp. 169, 97–98.

2. Isenberg, *Fallen Founder*, pp. 396–97; Kline, 2:1147; Lomask, *Aaron Burr*, 2:386–93.

3. Thayer, *As We Were*, p. 252.

4. Latrobe to Bollman, August 14, 1812, in Hamlin, *Latrobe*, p. 224; Fitch, *Breaking with Burr*, pp. 47, 120; *Report of the Wilkinson Committee*, p. 315 (testimony of Robert Spence); Latrobe to Erich Bollman, August 23, 1812, in *Correspondence of Latrobe*, 3:367.

5. Brunson, *Adventures of Samuel Swartwout, passim; Chicago Inter-Ocean*, June 30, 1876.

6. Redlich, "Eric Bollman and Studies in Banking," pp. 37, 39–43, 53–60.

7. Jackson to George Washington Campbell, January 15, 1807, in *Jackson Papers*, 2:148; Jackson grand jury testimony, in *id.*, 2:168–69 (June 25, 1807).

8. Before those achievements, however, Clay had to survive an 1809 duel with Humphrey Marshall, who underwrote the attacks on Burr in the *Western World*.

Their duel, ostensibly prompted by a dispute over the wearing of homespun versus imported fabrics, was a bloody affair. Clay grazed Marshall's belly in the first exchange. Both missed their second shots. Clay missed his third after receiving a thigh wound. Clay demanded a fourth round, but Marshall declined to shoot again. Quisenberry, *Humphrey Marshall,* pp. 100–02. In 1826, Clay fought another duel, this time while Secretary of State. When the election of 1824 had to be decided by the House of Representatives, Clay threw his support to John Quincy Adams and was rewarded with the leading position in the Cabinet. Randolph, then a senator from Virginia, joined the chorus of voices denouncing the sequence as a "corrupt bargain." Clay challenged him to a duel, so the Secretary of State squared off against the prominent senator in northern Virginia. They both missed their first shots and Clay missed his second. Randolph then fired into the air, and both men concluded that their honor had been suitably vindicated.

9. Daveiss, *View of the President's Conduct,* pp. 53, 55. Jo Daviess County in Illinois, Daviess County in Kentucky, and Daviess County in Indiana do not follow the spelling used by their namesake.

10. "Gen. Adair's Defense," *Lexington Reporter,* July 26, 1820; John S. Gillig, "In Pursuit of Truth and Honor: The Controversy Between Andrew Jackson and John Adair in 1817," *Filson Club History Quarterly,* 58:177, 199–200 (1984); McCaleb, *Aaron Burr's Conspiracy,* p. 250.

11. Wheelan, *Jefferson's Vendetta,* p. 214; Kennedy, *Memoirs of Wirt,* pp. 303–09, 331.

12. Malone, *Jefferson and His Time,* 5:310; Wheelan, *Jefferson's Vendetta,* p. 272.

13. John D. Winters, "William C.C. Claiborne, Profile of a Democrat," *Louisiana History* 10:189, 197–98 (1969).

14. Jacobs, *Tarnished Warrior,* pp. 263–74; Thomas Robson Hay, "Some Reflections on the Career of General James Wilkinson," *Mississippi Valley Historical Review* 21:471, 485–86 (1935).

15. Theodore Roosevelt, *The Winning of the West,* New York: G.P. Putnam's Sons (1917) (original ed., 1889), 3:124.

16. Fitch, *Breaking with Burr,* pp. 8, 9, 64; *Plumer's Memorandum,* pp. 541–542 (December 26, 1806); Latrobe to Bollman, August 14, 1812, in Hamlin, *Latrobe,* p. 224. As Latrobe put it in a letter to Erich Bollman, Wilkinson "was the last man in the world whom Burr would have trusted." Latrobe to Bollman, August 14, 1812, in Hamlin, *Latrobe,* p. 224.

17. Marquis James, *The Life of Andrew Jackson,* Indianapolis: Bobbs-Merrill (1938), p. 117; Wheelan, *Jefferson's Vendetta,* p. 200.

18. Latrobe to Bollman, August 14, 1812, in Hamlin, *Latrobe,* p. 224.

19. Parton, *Life and Times of Burr,* p. 670.

Appendix 1: The Cipher Letter

1. This theory was first explained by the editors of Burr's papers in the early 1980s, and also in a work by an independent scholar that was published at that time. Kline, 2:984–86; Milton Lomask, *Aaron Burr, The Conspiracy and Years of Exile, 1805–1836,* New York: Farrar Straus Giroux (1982), pp. 115–22.

2. Wilkinson, *Memoirs,* p. 316; Dayton to Wilkinson, July 25, 1806, in *American State Papers, Miscellaneous,* 2:558.

3. Kline, 9:989.

4. *E.g.,* Burr to Wilkinson, April 16, 1806, in Kline, 2:968.

5. Dayton to Henry Van Schaack, May 24, 1782, in Van Schaack Papers, Newberry Library; Dayton to Wilkinson, April 15, 1798, December 29, 1798, March 23, 1798, and April 27, 1798, in Wilkinson Papers, Newberry Library; Dayton to Burr, May 12, 1804, in Burr Papers, Reel 5; Dayton to C.A. Rodney, July 16, 1807, in Dayton Papers, University of Michigan. I have reviewed more than two dozen other letters from Dayton, all business correspondence. Each of those letters was meticulously written, not at all in the characteristic handwriting of a busy man of affairs, and often in different hands. I infer that most were produced by professional clerks or copyists, though initially drafted by Dayton.

6. David Robertson, 1:246.

7. Kline, 2:988; Annals of Congress, 9th Cong., 2d Sess., App. pp. 1009, 1011; Dayton to Wilkinson, July 16, 180[6], in *American State Papers, Miscellaneous,* 2:559.

8. David Robertson, 1:487.

ILLUSTRATION CREDITS

All illustrations are courtesy of the Library of Congress except for the following: Blennerhassett Island State Historical Park: 99, 153 (left); Collection of the New-York Historical Society: 22, 278, 287; Filson Historical Society, Louisville, KY: 148; Independence National Historical Park: 187; Kentucky Historical Society: 191; Joan McLemore: 196; Missouri Historical Society: 153 (right); National Portrait Gallery, Smithsonian Institution/Art Resource, NY: 60, 217, 230, 255; Newberry Library: 160; Senate House State Historic Site, Kingston, NY, New York State Office of Parks, Recreation and Historic Preservation: 282.

INDEX

Page numbers in *italics* refer to illustrations. Page numbers beginning with 319 refer to notes.

ABOUT THE AUTHOR

David O. Stewart is the author of the highly acclaimed *The Summer of 1787* and *Impeached*. He has practiced law in Washington, D.C., for more than a quarter century. He defended the impeachment trial of a Mississippi judge in the U.S. Senate in 1989 and has argued appeals all the way to the U.S. Supreme Court. He was law clerk to Justice Lewis Powell of that Court. He lives in Garrett Park, Maryland, with his wife.